P9-CFW-744

INDUSTRIAL RELATIONS RESEARCH
ASSOCIATION SERIES

New Approaches to Disability in the Workplace

EDITED BY

Terry Thomason, John F. Burton, Jr.,
and Douglas E. Hyatt

NEW APPROACHES TO DISABILITY IN THE WORKPLACE.
Copyright © 1998 by Industrial Relations Research Association. Printed in the
United States of America. No part of this book may be used without written permis-
sion, except in the case of brief quotations embodied in critical articles or reviews.

First Edition

Library of Congress Catalog Card Number: 50-13564

ISBN 0-913447-74-9

INDUSTRIAL RELATIONS RESEARCH ASSOCIATION SERIES (1998):
Proceedings of the Annual Meeting, Volume 1 and 2
Annual Research Volume
Membership Directory (published every fourth year)
IRRA Newsletter (published quarterly)
Perspectives on Work (published periodically)

Inquiries and other communications regarding membership, meetings, publications,
and general affairs of the Association, as well as notice of address changes should be
addressed to the IRRA national office.

INDUSTRIAL RELATIONS RESEARCH ASSOCIATION
University of Wisconsin–Madison
4233 Social Science Building, 1180 Observatory Drive,
Madison, WI 53706-1393 U.S.A.
Telephone: 608/262-2762   Fax 608/265-4591
irra@macc.wisc.edu

ii

CONTENTS

CHAPTER 1—Disability and the Workplace. 1
Terry Thomason, John F. Burton, Jr., and Douglas E. Hyatt

CHAPTER 2—Dispelling the Myths about Work Disability. 39
Marjorie L. Baldwin and William G. Johnson

CHAPTER 3—Prevention of Disability from Work-related Sources:
The Roles of Risk Management, Government
Intervention, and Insurance. 63
David Durbin and Richard J. Butler

CHAPTER 4—The Prevention of Behavioral Disabilities from
Nonwork Sources: Employee Assistance
Programs and Related Strategies. 87
Paul M. Roman and Terry C. Blum

CHAPTER 5—The Role of Unions and Collective Bargaining
in Preventing Work-related Disability. 121
Susan J. Schurman, David Weil, Paul Landsbergis, and
Barbara A. Israel

CHAPTER 6—Reducing the Consequences of Disability: Policies
to Reduce Discrimination against Disabled Workers. 155
Barbara A. Lee and Roger J. Thompson

CHAPTER 7—Facilitating Employment through Vocational
Rehabilitation 183
Monroe Berkowitz and David Dean

CHAPTER 8—Compensation for Disabled Workers:
Workers' Compensation. 205
Emily A. Spieler and John F. Burton, Jr.

CHAPTER 9—Social Security Disability Insurance:
A Policy Review 245
Jerry L. Mashaw and Virginia Reno

CHAPTER 10—Disputes and Dispute Resolution 269
Terry Thomason, Douglas E. Hyatt, and Karen Roberts

iii

CHAPTER 11—Convergence: A Comparison of European
         and United States Disability Policy   299
     Leo J.M. Aarts, Richard V. Burkhauser, and Philip R. de Jong

CHAPTER 1

Disability and the Workplace

TERRY THOMASON
McGill University

JOHN F. BURTON, JR.
Rutgers University

DOUGLAS E. HYATT
University of Toronto

In recent years, significant public attention has been focused on the problem of work and disability. One of the more visible manifestations of this concern is the passage in 1990 of the Americans with Disabilities Act (ADA), which *inter alia* represents a significant increase in federal regulation of the problem of disability as it relates to work. The ADA also brought to the fore a recognition that disability has at least as much to do with the attitudes of employers and other workers and the design of workplaces as it does with the functional limitations of the injured workers. Indeed, some individuals with a physical or emotional impairment may not be work-disabled given appropriate workplace accommodations.

Before proceeding, it is useful to define what we mean by "disability," as this term is often used to mean different things. Disability is one possible consequence of an injury or disease. Most immediately a person afflicted by injury or disease suffers an *impairment*, which is an anatomic or functional abnormality or loss, such as the amputation of a limb, blindness, or lower back sprain. Impairments can result in *functional limitations*, or limitations in physical or mental performance such as walking or climbing. In turn, functional limitations may lead to *disabilities*, which refers to the inability to perform various social roles. A distinction can be made between *work disability*, which represents the loss of earning capacity or the actual loss of earnings, and *nonwork disability*, which represents the effects of functional limitations on other aspects of life such as recreation and the performance of household

1

tasks. While the origin of a disability is an injury or disease, other factors such as educational attainment or the state of the labor market also affect the extent of disability.

Figure 1 illustrates the relationships among these various concepts of disability and the causes thereof.

FIGURE 1
Stages of the Disability Process

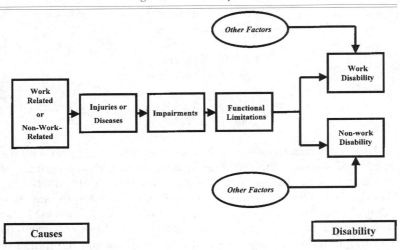

This volume adopts a broad definition of disability, including work disability and nonwork disability among workers. Moreover, the scope of the volume includes all disability regardless of origin, that is, disability whether or not caused by work. Thus while we refer to "work disability," this term is not limited to disabilities that are in some sense caused by work. We are also concerned with problems of work disability that results from non-work-related causes, such as auto accidents and diseases associated with the aging process. To this end we introduce the concept of the workers' disability system.

The Workers' Disability System

Issues of disability are complex, as are the responses generated to address these issues. There is a myriad of programs, both private and public, intended to resolve problems related to disability among workers. Taken as a whole, these programs are best conceptualized as a system with many constituent parts that are related to one another. A change in one part impacts the others. In this section we will examine this system, using a schema similar to that used by John Dunlop (1958) to examine union-management relations.

The workers' disability system is defined by the goals that it seeks to accomplish. Three goals may be identified: the prevention, accommodation, and compensation of disability. The actors in this system—which include workers and their representatives, employers, insurers, the medical community, and various agencies of government—establish policies and programs designed to achieve these goals. Performance of the system relative to these goals can be evaluated using several, sometimes conflicting, criteria. The particular set of programs and policies addressing disability problems as well as the criteria used to evaluate them are largely determined by the current ideology or shared beliefs of the actors. This ideology encompasses beliefs about the nature of disease and disability, the characteristics of the disabled population, and the responsibilities of the various actors involved in the workers' disability system. Ideology is, in turn, largely a product of the complex technological, economic, and political environment in which these programs exist.

Components of the Workers' Disability System

There are at least five sets of actors in the workers' disability system: workers (including potential workers) and their representatives, employers, insurers, the medical community, and government.

Workers and Their Representatives

This group, which includes persons who may not be currently employed or even in the labor force, can be further divided into two subgroups: disabled and nondisabled persons.

Nondisabled workers, while sympathetic to the problems of the disabled and their needs, are often oblivious to these problems and needs. They care about workplace health and safety but more typically are focused on other issues: wages and job security and, in recent years, health care costs. By and large, nondisabled workers are not interested in accommodation or rehabilitation issues. Of course, there are wide variations among workers within this subgroup; older workers are usually more interested in health and safety issues and in health insurance than younger workers.

The disabled population is also by no means homogeneous and includes many different groups with distinct and identifiable interests.

Baldwin and Johnson in Chapter 2 identify two such groups. There is a smaller group affected by mental or emotional problems or sensory or mobility limitations that occurred at birth or early in life. A much larger group experienced the onset of disability in middle age, typically as the result of musculoskeletal or cardiovascular problems. As the authors suggest, the former group is more likely to suffer employment discrimination and is therefore more likely to be interested in improving access to education and entry-level jobs. The latter group is more likely to be interested in rehabilitation and accommodation programs that aid the return to work as well as in compensation for lost wages.

Various persons or organizations represent the disabled, and they have interests that sometimes differ from those of their clientele. For example, workers seeking compensation for disability sometimes hire attorneys to represent them. However, attorneys who are paid on a contingency fee basis—so that their compensation is based on the size of the judgment—are frequently reluctant to represent disabled claimants seeking compensation from social insurance programs, such as workers' compensation or Social Security Disability Insurance, because of the paucity of potential fees. Other evidence suggests that contingent fees sometimes induce attorneys to settle workers' compensation claims for amounts that are substantially less than the claimants would receive if the claims were adjudicated.

They negotiate contract provisions designed to either enhance workplace health and safety or to compensate workers for unsafe jobs. They also assist injured workers in obtaining workers' compensation benefits, and they are active in political arenas in the promotion of social legislation, including legislation designed to prevent, accommodate, or compensate work disability.

However, unions are democratic political institutions that by and large reflect the interest of their members. As previously indicated, nondisabled workers (including union members) are often not interested in disability issues or even workplace health and safety but are more concerned about issues like wages and job security. Disabled persons are not likely to be well represented in the union since they are few in number to begin with and since their disability often forces them out of the labor force and, consequently, off union membership rolls.

In addition, there are a number of advocacy groups specifically interested in disability issues. These include both disability-specific organizations (for example, the Arthritis Foundation, the National Multiple Sclerosis Foundation, and the American Foundation for the Blind) as well as more general advocacy organizations (such as The Disabled People's International, The American Association of Disabled Persons, and the National Organization on Disability). Disability-specific organizations are primarily involved in funding research designed to find a cure. However, they also provide support and assistance to victims, including disabled workers. As the name implies, advocacy organizations are more involved in lobbying efforts to gain legislation favorable to disabled persons, in securing rights through litigation, and in influencing attitudes through public information campaigns.

Employers and Their Representatives

Employers play several roles in the workers' disability system. First, working conditions established by employers directly affect the incidence of work-related injuries and diseases. In addition, firm policies and practices also determine the employment prospects of the disabled as well as their compensation once employed. Employers also provide compensation to disabled workers in the form of disability or health insurance.

Table 1 provides data on the proportion of employees participating in various programs relevant to the workers' disability system that are voluntarily provided in whole or in part by employers. These programs range from compensation for non-work-related disability (i.e., paid sick leave, sickness and accident insurance, or long-term disability insurance) to health care insurance to wellness programs and EAPs. Of course, this table does not report participation in mandatory programs such as workers' compensation that compensate employees for lost income due to work-related disability.

Firm decisions about these issues are motivated, in large part, by profit considerations. For example, employers invest in workplace safety as a means of reducing accident costs. Also, as Roman and Blum (Chapter 4) suggest, the introduction of EAPs into the workplace was due to the recognition of the hidden costs of alcoholism for employers. Obviously, the firm's cost-benefit calculus is also affected by public policy. Widespread adoption of health insurance as part of the compensation package was partially motivated by income tax considerations. However, employer decisions pertaining to disabled workers may not be solely determined by economic considerations. As Baldwin and Johnson (Chapter 2) demonstrate, there is a wage gap between disabled and nondisabled workers that is not explained by productivity differences. It is difficult to reconcile this gap with employer profit maximization.

TABLE 1

Percent of Employees Participating in Private Employer Benefit Programs
Related to the Workers' Disability System

Benefit	All	Professional, Technical and Related	Clerical and Sales	Production and Service
Medium and Large Private Establishments, 1993				
Disability benefits:				
Short-term disability:				
Paid Sick Leave	65	85	80	45
Sickness and accident insurance	44	28	37	57
Long-term disability	41	64	50	23
Health care benefits:				
Medical care	82	84	79	82
Mental health care:				
Inpatient care	80	83	77	80
Outpatient care	80	82	77	79
Alcohol abuse treatment:				
Inpatient detoxification	80	82	77	80
Inpatient rehabilitation	66	66	63	58
Outpatient	67	69	65	68
Drug abuse treatment:				
Inpatient detoxification	80	82	77	80
Inpatient rehabilitation	64	65	60	66
Outpatient	66	68	64	65
Wellness programs	37	51	38	29
Employee assistance programs	62	74	64	53
Recreation facilities	26	34	25	23
Small Private Employers, 1994				
Disability benefits:				
Short-term disability	61	75	69	50
Paid sick leave	50	69	61	36
Sickness and accident insurance	26	27	27	25
Long-term disability	20	36	27	10
Health care benefits:				
Medical care insurance	66	80	70	57
Wellness programs	6	8	8	3
Employee assistance	15	19	18	11
Recreation facilities	5	7	5	4

Source: U.S. Bureau of Labor Statistics, Employee Benefits in Medium and Large
Private Establishments, 1993, Bulletin 2456; and Employee Benefits in Small Private
Establishments, 1994, Bulletin 2475.

Insurers

In the United States private insurance carriers play a critical role with respect to several aspects of the workers' disability system. Insurers are the primary financial intermediaries between employers and workers in the workers' compensation program as well as in employer-sponsored health insurance and, to a lesser extent, disability insurance. Like employers, insurance carriers are motivated by profit, and profit depends on their ability to accurately forecast costs associated with the cost of benefits paid by policyholders. Unexpected cost increases due, for example, to an unanticipated shift in the injury distribution can result in insurer losses.

Medical Community

While the medical community is involved in the pursuit of all goals of the workers' disability system, its primary role is to act as system "gatekeeper." Physicians legitimize patient complaints, determining who is disabled and who is not as well as the nature and cause of disability. Physicians determine eligibility for medical treatment as well as compensation and are also significantly involved in establishing the amount of compensation due. To a large extent, assumption of these roles has depended on social values that esteem scientific knowledge.

The medical community has several interests in the workers' disability system. In part, these interests are economic, since the system provides health care workers with income. However, medical providers also have an allegiance to professional values, and these economic and professional interests often conflict. As Spieler and Burton (Chapter 8) point out, increased emphasis on disability management by employers in recent years has increased the flow of communication between employers and physicians. They argue that this has led to the erosion of patient-provider confidentiality and perhaps to inappropriate job placements as employers seek to limit workers' compensation costs by encouraging physicians to authorize early returns to work.

Government

Prior to the industrial age, the problems of work disability were considered the responsibility of the family, the church, or the community. However, the breakdown of these institutions during the industrial revolution as well as the increased incidence of occupationally related injury and disease caused government to assume a greater role. Successive legislative initiatives in the United States since the turn of the century have produced a vast array of government agencies associated with every aspect of the workers' disability system. The resulting patchwork includes state workers' compensation agencies, the Social Security Administration, the Occupational Safety and Health Administration, various state-level OSHAs, the federal-state Vocational Rehabilitation program, the Veterans Administration, the National Institute for Occupational Safety and Health, the Equal Employment Opportunity Commission, and state insurance commissions.

Ultimately, the particular configuration of agencies and their missions—in a democratic society—are the product of the legislative and executive branches of government and the dominant political philosophy of the day. However, in the short run these agencies and their associated bureaucracies have an existence that it is somewhat insulated from the political branches of government. Some agencies can influence legislative and executive initiatives. Importantly, these agencies are typically staffed by people who identify with and believe in the agency's mission and who are likely to have close connections with other actors in the workers' disability system. As such, these agencies are subject to a natural inertia, making it difficult for subsequent political leadership to change the direction of the agency.

Goals of the Workers' Disability System

The goals of the workers' disability system are the prevention, accommodation, and compensation of disability. These goals are obviously intertwined. For example, to the extent that the system performs well with respect to the prevention or accommodation goals, then performance on the compensation goal becomes less critical. The priority given to each of these goals varies across systems and may shift over time. For example, Aarts, Burkhauser, and de Jong (Chapter 11) point out that in Germany, accommodation in the form of mandatory rehabilitation and a quota system that requires employers to hire disabled workers are combined with levels of disability compensation that are lower than those found in Sweden or the Netherlands.

Evaluation Criteria

Goals imply criteria by which system performance may be evaluated. Two criteria that are often used by economists to evaluate public policy are efficiency and equity. *Efficiency* refers to "social" welfare, which may be defined as the combined welfare (in terms of utility) of all individuals in society. An efficient system is one that maximizes social welfare. Similarly, to the extent that social welfare is enhanced by the adoption of a particular policy, that policy is said to be efficient. *Equity* refers to the distribution of welfare among individuals. Horizontal equity requires that individuals who are similarly situated should be treated similarly, while vertical equity requires individuals who are different in some important way should be treated differently. For example, in the context of disability, horizontal equity would require that individuals who suffer the same degree of loss should receive the same level of compensation, *ceteris paribus*, while vertical equity would require that individuals who experience greater losses should receive additional compensation, *ceteris paribus*.

While the economists' efficiency criterion is useful in the abstract analysis of public policy problems, it offers limited practical guidance to policymakers and program administrators. However, several additional criteria have been used in the social insurance field that are easier to operationalize and that are frequently used as benchmarks in policy debates. First, the resources devoted to a program should be *adequate*, that is, sufficient to accomplish the program's objectives. Second, the program's *delivery system*—the means by which the program's objectives are accomplished—should be *efficient*; that is, the administrative costs associated with a given level of services should be minimized. Third, the program should be *affordable*; that is, the program should not result in expenditures that result in serious adverse social consequences such as increased unemployment. Fourth, as previously suggested, benefits and services provided by the program should be equitable, both in terms of horizontal and vertical equity.

There is a fifth criterion that should also be used in evaluating social insurance programs which we term *system design efficiency*. Each disability program has multiple goals: prevention, compensation, and accommodation. Ideally, a program change should improve performance on at least one goal without undermining the other goals. To the extent that higher benefits help meet the compensation goal (by increasing adequacy) and also help meet the prevention goal (by providing greater safety incentives to employers via experience rating), the policy change is system design efficient. To the extent that higher benefits help meet the compensation goal (by increasing adequacy) but interfere with the prevention goal (e.g., by encouraging workers to take risks) or interfere with the accommodation goal (e.g., by discouraging workers from returning to work), the policy change is system design inefficient.

Finally, each of the five criteria can be applied to a single program (such as workers' compensation) in the workers' disability system or to all of the programs in the system. Thus if you look only at the benefits provided to injured workers by the workers' compensation program, you might conclude that the benefits were inadequate, while if you considered all benefits received by the workers, including sickness and accident insurance and long-term disability insurance, the benefits may be adequate. Or the cash benefits provided by a temporary disability insurance plan evaluated in isolation might be equitable, but if all benefits are considered (including sick leave plans), the workers' disability system may be inequitable. Thus there is program adequacy versus system adequacy, program equity versus system equity, etc. Most studies only evaluate specific programs in terms of adequacy, etc., but ideally should evaluate system adequacy, etc.

Prevention

The programs in the workers' disability income system often distinguish between disabilities that are in some sense caused by the individual's employment and disabilities that are not. This latter category includes disabilities arising from congenital defects, from degenerative processes associated with aging, and from leisure or other nonwork activities. Until recently, these non-work-related disabilities have largely fallen outside the scope of the prevention goal of the workers' disability system. However, researchers have come to recognize that working conditions influence the development of or recovery from disability among workers, even though the precipitating event may not be work-related. In addition, in the United States the combination of a health care system for workers that is largely financed through employer-sponsored health insurance and sky-rocketing health care costs have led to increased employer interest in the prevention of non-work-related disability. This increased interest is manifest in a variety of "wellness" programs, including employee assistance programs, which are examined in Chapter 4 by Roman and Blum.

Figure 2 depicts the recent history of the incidence of severity of occupational injuries and illnesses in the United States. Each of the three measures reported in the figure are expressed as a rate per 100 workers. These data series tell contradictory tales about workplace safety trends. As measured by the total number of injuries and illnesses, which fell by over 32% from 1973 to 1996, safety appears to have improved over this period. This is similar to trends for workplace fatalities reported by Durbin and Butler (Chapter 3). However, this reduction was primarily, or even solely, due to a drop in the number of non-lost-time cases—that

FIGURE 2
Work Injury and Illness Experience, 1973-1996

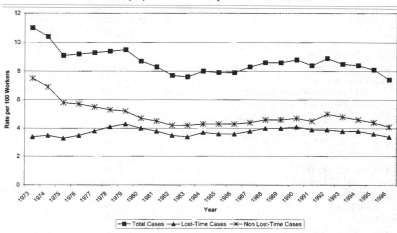

is, cases in which the worker suffered no work disability; the incidence of work-related disability has remained relatively stable.

Table 2 reports the distribution of fatal occupational injuries in 1995. The interesting aspect of these data is that 21% of these fatalities involve highway accidents, while another 20% involve an assault or some other violent act. This picture of industrial injuries is substantially at odds with the common perception of the typical work injury or illness.

Disability due to work-related injuries and diseases is an undesirable byproduct of the production process. Workers and employers both influence the likelihood of an industrial injury or disease. Employers can invest in capital or personal protective equipment or implement policies and practices designed to reduce the number of work injuries or diseases. Workers can take greater care on the job. Both actors engage in accident prevention to the extent that it reduces injury and disease costs, which include the costs of lost productivity, damage to equipment, lost wages, medical expenses, and worker pain and suffering. Optimal accident prevention occurs at the point where marginal accident costs are exactly balanced by the marginal cost of accident prevention.

Some economists argue that employers make optimal decisions about accident prevention in the absence of public policy regulating occupational health and safety. Specifically, if workers have good information about the risks of injury and disease associated with particular jobs and

TABLE 2

Distribution of 1995 Fatal Work Accidents, by Cause

Cause	Number of fatalities	Percent distribution
Total	6,210	100
Transportation accidents[1]	2,560	41
Highway accidents[1]	1,329	21
Collision between vehicles, mobile equipment	634	10
Noncollision accidents	350	6
Nonhighway accident (farm, industrial premises)	388	6
Aircraft accidents	278	4
Workers struck by a vehicle	385	6
Water vehicle accidents	84	1
Railway accidents	82	1
Assaults and violent acts[1]	1,262	20
Homicides[1]	1,024	16
Shooting	754	12
Stabbing	67	1
Self-inflicted injury	215	3
Contacts with objects and equipment[1]	915	15
Struck by object[1]	546	9
Struck by falling objects	340	5
Struck by flying object	63	1
Caught in or compressed by—equipment or objects	255	4
Collapsing materials	99	2
Falls	643	10
Exposure to harmful substances or environments[1]	598	10
Contact with electric current	347	6
Exposure to caustic, noxious or allergenic substances	101	2
Oxygen deficiency	94	2
Drowning, submersion	74	1
Fires and explosions	208	3
Other events and exposures	24	°

Source: U.S. Bureau of Labor Statistics, USDL News, Bulletins 95-288, August 3, 1995; 96-315, August 8, 1996, and unpublished data.

[1] Includes other causes, not shown separately.

° Less than 0.5 %.

sufficient mobility between jobs, they will receive higher wages as compensation for increased risk in the absence of mandatory workers' compensation insurance. In this theory the risk premium associated with a particular job will exactly equal the expected costs of accidents. Through the mechanism of this compensating risk differential, workers will shift part of the cost of accidents back to employers. If employers are aware of the relationship between expenditures and improved safety and utilize this knowledge, they will make efficient decisions about safety.

However, if workers do not possess good information about safety, a risk differential may not develop, or if it does, it may not be fully compensating (or may be more than fully compensating), so that employers will underinvest (or overinvest) in safety, and the accident and disease rate will be inefficiently high (or low). Under these conditions, government regulation may be appropriate and necessary.

Four public policy options may be identified: tort-based negligence rules, direct regulation, internal responsibility, and general financial incentives. All use sanctions to change the employer's cost-benefit calculus to encourage investment in workplace health and safety. They vary with respect to the size of the sanction and whether the sanction is imposed using outcome-based standards (i.e., actual manifestation of work-related injuries or diseases) or process-based standards (i.e., behaviors that are thought to result in injury or disease). All have advantages and disadvantages.

Tort-based negligence rules. Prior to the advent of workers' compensation legislation, a worker who suffered disability due to an occupational injury or disease had to demonstrate that the cause was employer negligence.[1] That is, the injured worker was required to bring suit in a court of law and prove that the injury was the direct result of the employer's failure to take "reasonable" precautions to protect the worker's health and safety. In this context, precautions are deemed "reasonable" if the cost of the precaution that would prevent the injury is less than the expected cost of injury. To the extent that the court adheres to this definition of "reasonable," these individual decisions of the negligence system are by definition efficient.

Unfortunately, as a prevention option, the tort system is problematic for at least two reasons. First, judges and juries may not apply an efficient negligence standard. Second, the transaction costs associated with tort suits in the form of the legal process required to establish fault are substantial. These costs may deter workers except those with the most serious injuries from initiating a lawsuit, since legal expenses could exceed the monetary award that the worker could hope to gain through a judgment. This means that absent punitive damages, firms will not consider all of the costs of workplace accidents and, specifically, will fail to consider the costs of relatively minor accidents that are not pursued by workers. It also suggests that the tort system will be inequitable, since workers with substantial losses are more likely to be compensated than workers with minor injuries.

Direct regulation. Under direct regulation, a government agency promulgates rules regarding specific employer behaviors, policies, or practices. For example, firms may be required to provide workers with certain personal protective equipment in specific work situations. Rules are enforced by a government inspectorate that imposes fines for deviations from the standard, which are typically small compared to the cost of workplace injuries. (However, while the fines are small, the costs of compliance with some standards may be high relative to the benefits.) In the United States this approach is embodied by the Occupational Safety and Health Act of 1970.

The primary disadvantage with this option is that it does not recognize firm heterogeneity with respect to the provision of workplace safety—practices and policies that are efficient in one firm may be inefficient for another. Assuming that the government can develop standards that are appropriate for the modal firm, these standards (to the extent that they are observed) will impose costs leading to a reduction in social welfare in the form of higher unemployment and lower productivity. In addition, since the government agency responsible for promulgating rules is removed from the shopfloor, the system will be slow to respond to technological change, so that agency standards, even if initially efficient, will become obsolete and inefficient over time. Finally, the system is administratively expensive, requiring a large professional bureaucracy to promulgate and enforce standards.

On the other hand, to the extent that economic incentives fail—because information or mobility problems prevent a compensating risk premium from developing or because workers' compensation is not fully experience-rated (see below)—a system of direct regulation can help fill the gap. Similarly, unequal bargaining power between workers and employers can result in an inefficient level of health and safety in the workplace. In addition, if there are externalities to workplace safety, such as medical costs that are not borne by employers and workers, then direct regulation may increase social welfare. Finally, to the extent that it redistributes resources from employers to workers, direct regulation may increase system equity.

Internal responsibility. This is the name given to a Canadian system that seeks to regulate workplace health and safety through worker empowerment.[2] (While we use the Canadian name, elements of this system are found in other industrialized nations and several U.S. jurisdictions.) As it exists in Canada, the internal responsibility system (IRS) has three elements: (1) the right of refusal to do unsafe work, (2) the right to information about workplace hazards, and (3) a requirement that employers form joint labor-management health and safety committees. The rationale is to increase the bargaining power of workers, who are intimately familiar with the hazards of the workplace and who presumably have incentives to improve workplace safety without seriously damaging firm profitability, so that they can successfully negotiate an efficient level of safety and health.

While IRS can provide a "customized" approach that recognizes interfirm variability and can easily adapt to address problems presented by technological change, it has some disadvantages. First, the effectiveness of IRS is critically dependent on employee bargaining power, so that it is likely to be more effective in unionized workplaces than in nonunion sites, raising equity concerns. Second, since unions are democratic political institutions that reflect the interests of their members, unions may trade off health and safety for gains in areas that are of more immediate concern to the rank and file, like wages and job security. Third, unions may use IRS as a vehicle to increase bargaining power in collective negotiations or as the basis for organizing nonunion firms. Finally, unions may lack the expertise to effectively set standards or police employer compliance, particularly with respect to health areas such as exposure to environmental toxins.

On the other hand, as Schurman, Weil, Landsbergis, and Israel (Chapter 5) indicate, workplace safety has many of the characteristics of a public good for workers, i.e., consumption is nonrival and is subject to excludability problems.[3] As such, the free-rider problem may prevent individual workers from "purchasing" safety when it is in their collective interest to do so. A joint health and safety committee can provide a mechanism for organizing workers to overcome the free-rider problem.

General Financial Incentives (GFI). Unlike the IRS or direct regulation, a system of general financial incentives attempts to regulate workplace health and safety by imposing outcomes-based sanctions. One form of this type of system is an "injury tax," whereby levies are imposed on employers based on the number (and possibly severity) of work injuries and diseases experienced by employers (Smith 1974). A more prosaic form is the firm-level experience rating of workers' compensation premiums. "Firm-level experience rating" refers to the practice of basing the firm's compensation premium, in whole or in part, on the compensation benefits paid to the firm's employees for work accidents and diseases experienced in prior years. A firm is said to be perfectly experience-rated if its compensation premiums bear a one-to-one relationship with its benefit payments. To the extent that wages do not reflect a fully compensating risk differential, the employer's investment in workplace safety is expected to approach optimality as the degree of experience rating increases.

Since under a GFI system, the employer is free to choose its own particular mix of health and safety policies, GFI does not suffer the inefficiencies due to firm heterogeneity and technological change associated with direct regulation. In addition, GFI is relatively inexpensive to administer and thus satisfies the delivery system efficiency criterion. However, since employer incentives under GFI are tied to reported injuries (or workers' compensation claims), firms are not only motivated to enhance workplace health and safety but to suppress injury or claims reporting. For example, firms may threaten or discharge workers who report injuries, dispute compensation for legitimate claims, or require workers to return to work at an earlier point than is desirable for their long-term recovery. In addition, for actuarial reasons, experience-rating systems are not generally feasible for small employers. Finally, due to the long latency between exposure and the manifestation of disability, it may be difficult to assign liability for occupational disease to one particular employer.

Accommodation

Accommodation of disability in the workplace can take two forms. The traditional approach, rehabilitation, attempts to accommodate injured workers to the demands of the job and the workplace (Berkowitz and Dean, Chapter 7). This approach includes the provision of medical services, such as prosthetic devices or physiotherapy, designed to allow disabled workers to restore lost functional capacity. It also includes vocational rehabilitation, which encompasses a wide range of services including educational and training programs, where the worker learns either to perform new duties for a new job or to perform the old job in a new way. It also includes job referral and placement services that assist workers in finding and holding new jobs.

Recently, increasing emphasis has been placed on the second approach— changing the work environment to accommodate the worker's disability—which involves modifying capital equipment used by the disabled worker, the physical layout of buildings where work is performed, or providing the disabled employee with special equipment or tools. In part, the increasing emphasis on this second approach is due to recent policy developments—in particular, the Americans with Disabilities Act of 1990, which requires employers to provide disabled workers with "reasonable accommodations."

The efficiency criterion suggests that accommodations should be provided when their marginal cost is less than or equal to their marginal benefit. In this context, the benefits of accommodation are increased productivity of the disabled person. Since the cost of accommodations are typically paid immediately while the benefits accrue over the disabled person's working life, this is fundamentally a human capital decision, and arguments for government involvement are essentially identical to those for other human capital decisions. If there is a fully functioning, competitive capital market and if there are no externalities associated with the accommodation, then government involvement is unnecessary. Since workers and employers share the benefits of accommodations, they share the costs.[4]

Problems arise when capital markets fail because disabled persons who lack access to capital will be unable to pay for efficient accommodations. If so, government intervention may increase social welfare. There are two broad policy options. The first is the subsidization of rehabilitation or accommodation measures. Subsidies can take the form of tax credits or direct monetary or in-kind payments made to disabled workers directly or to employers who provide accommodation, or loan guarantees. Examples are the federal-state vocational rehabilitation program or the sheltered workshops found in Sweden and the Netherlands. The second option involves mandates requiring employers to either provide accommodation or rehabilitation. Examples include the antidiscrimination provisions of the ADA, the requirement found in a few Canadian provinces that employers reemploy workers with work-related disability, and quotas that require employees to hire a certain proportion of disabled workers found in Germany.

Compensation

In general, compensation is provided to disabled workers when efforts at prevention and accommodation fail. A vast array of programs is in place to accomplish this goal. These include private programs, such as short- and long-term disability insurance and health care insurance, which are provided by employers as a part of an employment compensation package or purchased by individuals directly, as well as public programs such as workers' compensation or social security disability insurance. In general, programs fall into two categories: those designed to compensate persons disabled as the result of a work-related injury or disease (e.g., workers' compensation) and those that compensate persons regardless of cause for disability (e.g., social security disability insurance, Medicaid, and supplemental security income). Finally, programs may provide workers with cash benefits (SSI), in-kind benefits (Medicaid), or both (workers' compensation).

The specific goals of compensation programs vary substantially, but all are designed to provide injured workers with some sort of protection against income loss due to disability. For some programs, benefits replace a significant proportion of past earnings (SSDI or workers' compensation), while for others—such as SSI, where eligibility is means tested—compensation is tied to a minimal living standard.

Private as well as public programs pay compensation benefits. Private programs include sickness and accident insurance plans designed to compensate workers for short-term (less than six months) disability, which are purchased by individuals or employers; employer-paid sick leave; long-term disability insurance; and health care insurance, which pays medical expenses for non-work-related disability. There are a variety of public programs. These include but are not limited to workers' compensation; Social Security Disability Insurance; Supplemental Security Income; Medicare; Medicaid; and temporary disability insurance programs in California, Hawaii, New Jersey, New York, and Rhode Island, which pay short-term cash benefits for non-work-related disability.[5]

Table 3 presents data on the costs of selected cash benefits paid to the disabled. Panel A reports the cost of private and the principal public programs in nominal dollars, while Panel B reports real dollar expenditures. As can be seen, the private programs account for about one-third of total cash benefit expenditures. Both types of programs have experienced real growth over the period reported, although the public-sector programs grew by about 55% in real terms, compared to a more modest 33% for the private programs. There is substantial variation in growth across programs within the public and private sectors. For example, SSDI benefit payments were relatively static from 1980 to 1990, while workers' compensation benefits, which were less than SSDI at the beginning of the period, had surpassed SSDI by 1990. Since 1990, however, cash benefit expenditures by workers' compensation programs declined, while SSDI expenditures grew by nearly 35%.

Efficiency concerns about disability compensation—specifically concerns about system design efficiency—arise from its incentive effects on

TABLE 3

Cash Benefit Compensation Paid to the Disabled, Selected Years, by Type

Type	Year			
	1980	1985	1990	1994
Panel A: Current Dollars (Billions)				
Public Programs				
Social Security Disability Insurance[1]	14.8	18.3	24.3	37.1
Supplemental Security Income[2]	5.2	8.0	12.9	21.5
Temporary Disability Insurance	0.8	1.2	2.3	2.4
Workers' Compensation	10.6	16.0	25.3	26.7
Total Public	31.4	43.5	64.7	87.7
Private Programs				
Short-term disability:[3]				
Individual Insurance	10.0	12.4	16.8	19.0
Group benefits to workers in private employment	3.3	2.6	2.7	2.6
Private cash insurance	0.8	1.2	2.3	2.4
Sick leave	5.9	8.7	11.9	14.1
Sick leave for government employees	6.0	8.5	11.9	14.2
Long-term disability	1.3	1.9	2.9	2.9
Total Private	14.0	20.3	28.9	33.5
Total	45.4	63.7	93.6	121.2
Panel B: 1994 Constant Dollars (Billions)				
Public Programs				
Social Security Disability Insurance[1]	26.6	25.2	27.5	37.1
Supplemental Security Income[2]	9.4	11.0	14.6	21.5
Temporary Disability Insurance	1.4	1.6	2.6	2.4
Workers' Compensation	19.1	22.0	28.7	26.7
Total Public	56.5	59.9	73.4	87.7
Private Programs				
Short-term disability:[3]				
Individual Insurance	18.0	17.1	19.1	19.0
Group benefits to workers in private employment	5.9	3.6	3.1	2.6
Private cash insurance	1.4	1.6	2.6	2.4
Sick leave	10.7	11.9	13.4	14.1
Sick leave for government employees	10.9	11.7	13.5	14.2
Long-term disability	2.3	2.7	3.3	2.9
Total Private	25.2	27.9	32.8	33.5
Total	81.7	87.8	106.2	121.2

Sources: U.S. Social Security Administration, *Social Security Bulletin* and *Annual Statistical Supplement.*
[1] Includes payments to the children of disabled beneficiaries.
[2] Includes payments to the blind.
[3] Includes the first six months of long-term disability.

the behavior of compensation recipients and potential recipients. As Durbin and Butler (Chapter 3) note, workers' compensation benefits may induce workers either to take less care on the job—an effect they term "risk-bearing moral hazard"—or to report workers' compensation claims—an effect they term "reporting moral hazard." Some have speculated that these incentives sometimes lead workers to report nonwork injuries as work-related or to extend the time on compensation. Thomason, Hyatt, and Roberts (Chapter 10) indicate that to the extent that insurance premiums are experience-rated, compensation also affects employer behavior, leading firms to challenge and litigate compensation claims.

Ideology

As indicated, the parameters of workers' disability systems—that is, the particular array of programs, objectives, and criteria that constitute the system—are based on a shared set of beliefs among the various actors.[6] These shared beliefs include ideas about the nature of disability, its causes, the characteristics of the disabled population, the proper role of each of the actors in the system itself, and the criteria that should be used to evaluate system performance. In this section, we will illustrate how ideology animates the system and how changing ideology can affect system parameters.

While ultimately rooted in a biological or psychological abnormality, disability is fundamentally a social construction. That is, the labeling of an individual as disabled is a social process, which depends upon a shared belief about what constitutes a work disability and what does not. As Dembe (1996:3) notes,

> During the past several decades, there has been a growing realization that social forces shape the medical community's recognition of disease. . . . [S]tudies suggest that doctors' judgements are not merely impersonal deductions based on immutable empirical "facts," rendered independently from social considerations. They imply a more complex view of medical epistemology in which medical concepts and discoveries depend, in part, on social circumstances affecting physicians and the broader community in which they function.

These beliefs have changed dramatically over time. At the dawn of the industrial age, a work-related occupational disability was conceived to be solely an organic problem—traceable to an identifiable pathology. This belief was reflected in the original workers' compensation statutes that limited compensation to injuries resulting from accidents, except for a handful of specific diseases that were linked to particular occupations. On this basis, workers' compensation programs failed to compensate mental or emotional disabilities, particularly psychogenic ones. Nor would they compensate disabilities that developed over a long period (i.e., repetitive stress injuries or cumulative trauma disorders). In recent years, the disability concept has expanded to include mental or behavioral problems that may have their origins in nonphysical events. For example, alcoholism and drug addiction have become "medicalized," or as Roman and Blum indicate, "defined as illnesses, rather than sins, immoralities, or crimes" (Chapter 4).

The increasing incidence of workers' compensation claims involving soft tissue injuries, in general, and cumulative trauma disorders (CTDs), in particular, may be traced in part to changing social norms about the nature of disability. Dembe (1996) examines the history of three controversial occupational conditions: CTDs of the hand and wrist, back pain, and noise-induced hearing loss. He notes that CTDs of the hand and wrist were identified as occupationally related as early as 1713, although the disorder did not gain substantial attention from the medical community until the mid-nineteenth century. At this point, the greatly increased employment of clerks by newly established industrial firms in Britain led to an epidemic of writers' cramp. Initially, this problem was attributed to organic causes. However, by the end of the 19th century, medical science began to consider these problems as having a psychological rather than a biological origin, due to the inability to identify a pathological lesion associated with the disease. In addition, Dembe suggests that the transformation of these disorders from organic to psychological was in part due to the struggle between labor and management and the feminization of clerical labor force.

The conception of CTDs of the hand and wrist as psychogenic began to evolve once again as medical science identified pathological lesions associated with certain disorders. Nonetheless, there was a continued reluctance to accept these problems as occupationally related until the 1980s, when epidemiological studies began to detect a relationship between working conditions and disease incidence. Dembe also notes that labor activism, particularly in the meatpacking industry, played an important role in the recognition of the occupational connection. Nevertheless, as Dembe reports, the alleged occupational nature of these disorders is still controversial, and there are some within the medical community who consider CTDs to be "iatrogenic," that is, induced or caused by physicians. As Spieler and Burton (Chapter 8) report, this view would appear to be gaining ground in some states, as workers' compensation programs have limited compensability for conditions such as chronic stress and cumulative trauma disorders.

Environment and Technology

The workers' disability system is not static. It is the product of a complex environment. Changes in this environment can change the ideological foundation of the system and can ultimately change system parameters. Following Dunlop, we identify and discuss three dimensions of this environment. Two aspects of the technological environment are significant: the technology of the workplace (i.e., the technology used to produce goods and services) and the technology of medicine (i.e., the technology used to detect and treat injury and disease).

Production Technology

Changes in production technology affect the nature of the workplace hazards and, consequently, both the probability and severity of workplace injury. As Durbin and Butler (Chapter 3) report, there has been a long-term improvement in occupational health and safety as measured by the fatal injury rate. In part, this improvement is the result of a secular shift in employment from manufacturing to the service sector. However, in part, it is due to the increasing mechanization of the most arduous, tedious, and hazardous tasks performed in all workplaces.

Mechanization may have also increased the employment prospects of the disabled by reducing the proportion of physically demanding jobs. Indeed, the reduction in the extent of physically demanding employment may have laid the groundwork for antidiscrimination legislation by changing beliefs about the nature of work. In addition, mechanization more generally offers the possibility that technology may be further modified to accommodate disabled workers.

The workplace continues to change. Until recently, mass production technologies dominated manufacturing industries; due to their economic success, they provided a model for other sectors as well. These technologies relied on economies of scale achieved through the standardization and mechanization of work. The initial costs required to set up this production process were substantial, so that the product was also standardized. The logic of this technology implied narrowly defined and highly articulated jobs as well as an elaborate command and control hierarchy that minimizes individual worker judgment.

The introduction of computer technology into the manufacturing process has put a premium on flexibility. Unlike the older automated production process, computers controlling multipurpose machines substantially reduce set-up costs, so manufacturers can quickly respond to changes in market demand. In addition, computer technology allows firms to quickly access and process market data, further reducing response time.

Machine flexibility has created pressures for flexibility in work organization and human resource practices. The scope of jobs has broadened at the same time that the hierarchy has become flatter. Workers are required to perform a greater variety of tasks, including those formerly assigned to supervisors. The workforce is organized into teams of individual workers with interchangeable jobs. At the same time, compensation systems have changed to reflect the new work organization. There is a greater reliance on contingent compensation that is based on the performance of the team or the firm. Workers are paid for the skills that they possess rather than the particular position that they occupy. In addition to greater functional and compensation flexibility, firms are also requiring more staffing flexibility, increasing the utilization of short-term contractual relationships in place of lifetime employment.

It is difficult to predict the impact of these changes on the workers' disability system. Computers may be expected to lead to a continued mechanization of production processes, which will undoubtedly further enhance workplace health and safety and increase employment prospects for disabled persons. Certain human resource practice innovations could also have an impact, although the nature of this impact is uncertain. Work teams may be reluctant to include disabled persons since their compensation may be affected. Disabled workers may find it more difficult to handle broadly defined jobs. Both innovations could cause increased stress resulting in a greater incidence of work-related disability, as could lean production systems. Finally, disabled persons may have more difficulty adapting to an economy dominated by short-term contract employment relationships.

Medical Technology

Recent years have seen an explosion in medical technology. Treatment innovations have reduced the severity of many disabilities. Diagnostic innovations, like MRIs and CAT scans, improve the accuracy of diagnoses; and epidemiological advances, once again aided by high-speed computers, have become increasingly successful in identifying the occupational origin of disability. Among other things, these innovations have increased the likelihood of a diagnosis of cumulative trauma disorders and other soft-tissue injuries. They have also led to the increased diagnosis of certain diseases caused by environmental toxins like asbestosis as occupationally related. To the extent that this has occurred, it has placed an increased burden on workers' compensation programs. However, the opposite has also occurred. Advances in medical science have led to the recognition that many back disorders are traceable to a degenerative process rather than to a workplace accident. This recognition has caused these disabilities to be excluded from workers' compensation programs in some jurisdictions.

It is also clear that both treatment and diagnostic innovations, for which there is seemingly an unlimited demand by persons who are sick or injured or by insurance carriers and employers who have conflicting views on causation and treatment, have led to substantially increased health care costs, particularly in the United States.

Market

Changes in economic conditions have also had substantial impacts on the workers' disability system. As industrialization produced substantial growth in real per capita income, the demand for health care and disability insurance likewise grew, which at least partially accounts for the proliferation of these programs.

More recently, rising health care costs, coupled with anemic growth in real income since the 1970s, have created a health care crisis and a fundamental change in the way that health care is delivered in the United States. In particular, the adoption of various forms of "managed care" has reduced patient discretion with respect to the selection of a health care provider and even decisions about treatment. Similarly, substantial growth in deficits for social insurance programs, especially OASDHI (see Mashaw and Reno, Chapter 9), have created pressures to rationalize these programs in some way. In addition, since the Reagan administration, neoconservative politicians have successfully argued that in part these programs create incentives for program utilization, with adverse effects on productivity and even the national moral climate. These developments—higher costs and government budget deficits—have put increased emphasis on the affordability criterion, leading to pressures for a reduction in spending on all transfer programs, including those targeted for the disabled.

Finally, the gradual elimination of trade barriers and improvements in communication and transportation technologies have led to a globalization of markets. As a result, there is a fear that competition from low-wage nations—or even among developed countries, as in the European Community—will put pressure on all jurisdictions to compromise social insurance programs and lower employment standards. In particular, OSHA has come under fire as a productivity killer. It is possible that a reduction in standards could result in an increased incidence of disability due to work-related causes.

Power

One of the more profound changes in the American polity during the last fifty years was the rise of the Civil Rights movement and its articulation of the notion that discrimination based on innate characteristics unrelated to merit was wrong and that private parties, such as employers, were culpable and had a moral (and eventually legal) duty to end this type of discrimination. While this movement had its roots in the struggles of African Americans in the Jim Crow South, the core values of the original movement became entrenched in the political culture. Ultimately, programs initially launched by this movement—such as, laws prohibiting racial discrimination in employment—were extended to other groups claiming to suffer as the result of unjust discrimination.

One such group is the disabled. For them, the tangible result of this shift in political culture is the Americans with Disabilities Act. While the initial evidence is discouraging for disability advocates (see Lee and Thompson, Chapter 6), it remains to be seen what effect this legislation will eventually have on the lives of persons with disabilities. However, it is interesting to note that there are signs that the consensus concerning government intervention to correct problems of discrimination may be eroding as affirmative action comes under increasing political fire.

Another recent development in the political environment is the long-term decline of organized labor in the United States. The labor movement has long been one of the principal voices advocating for government intervention in workplace health and safety. The decline of their political influence has undoubtedly changed the political calculus of support for programs designed to aid the disabled. This is particularly evident in some states where significant curtailment in eligibility rules for workers' compensation benefits have been enacted in the 1990s, despite efforts by unions to resist these "reforms."

Chapter Summaries

The volume is organized as follows. The next chapter examines evidence concerning the scope of the problem of work disability in the

United States. Nine chapters that address issues relevant to the three goals of the compensation system follow this initial chapter: three chapters explore prevention, two address accommodation issues, while three chapters examine compensation. The volume concludes with an examination of the three goals of the workers' disability system in the international context.

Dispelling the Myths about Work Disability

In this chapter Marjorie Baldwin and William Johnson provide a portrait of the disabled population in the United States, including information about the incidence of work disability in the population as a whole as well as the distribution of disability by cause and by demographic and socioeconomic categories.

In addition, this chapter reviews the large and growing body of empirical research investigating labor market outcomes experienced by disabled workers. In particular, they examine research on the extent to which employment discrimination is responsible for lower wages and higher unemployment for the disabled relative to the nondisabled population. Baldwin and Johnson also summarize research examining the labor market experience of injured workers, including the stability of postinjury employment and the impact of workers' compensation (i.e., medical and vocational rehabilitation and indemnity benefits) on the return to work following an injury, the duration of work absence, and wages.

Baldwin and Johnson argue that there are a number of misconceptions about the nature of work disability and the disabled population. Contrary to the stereotype of the disabled person as someone forced into a wheelchair due to a traumatic accident or birth defect, they find that most disabled persons suffer from musculoskeletal or cardiovascular conditions caused by chronic, degenerative processes. As such, the onset of disability typically occurs in middle age, so that most disabled persons were not subject to discrimination upon their initial entry into the labor market. Baldwin and Johnson also find that labor market success of disabled persons depends not only on their medical condition but also on the condition of the labor market, the availability of workplace accommodations, the attitudes of the employer, and the characteristics of the worker and the job. Finally, they find that after controlling for differences in productivity, there are large wage differentials between disabled and nondisabled persons, which may constitute evidence of labor market discrimination. Baldwin and Johnson conclude by emphasizing the need for public policy to consider the diversity of the disabled population.

Prevention of Disability from Work-related Sources: The Roles of Risk Management, Government Intervention, and Insurance

As indicated, a variety of public policy options have been utilized to enhance workplace safety. These include worker empowerment, tort-based negligence rules, direct regulation, and general financial incentives such as experience-rated workers' compensation insurance premiums. In this chapter David Durbin and Richard Butler review evidence concerning recent trends in workplace health and safety as measured by the fatal and lost-time injury rates as well as the relative effectiveness of direct regulation and market-based general financial incentives.

Their analysis begins with an examination of the validity of work injury rates as measures of workplace health and safety. They argue that recent data on workers' compensation costs and the fatal and lost-time injury rate show that there is an "incentive disconnect" between compensation costs and the intrinsic level of workplace health and safety. They base this conclusion on the fact that compensation claims rates—and fatal injury claim rates, in particular—have been declining at the same time that costs have risen markedly. According to Durbin and Butler, these data suggest that while the average U.S. workplace has become safer, more generous compensation benefits since the 1970s have increased claim reporting.

Durbin and Butler also review the relevant empirical research relating to the safety effects of general financial incentives inherent in workers' compensation insurance prices. They argue that the results of this research suggest that experience rating is effective in improving workplace safety. They buttress these existing studies with an examination of fatal injury rates using two data sets and new measures of general financial incentives; their analyses confirm the salutary effects of these incentives for occupational health and safety. On the other hand, they conclude that direct regulation—specifically, the Occupational Health and Safety Act—has had, at best, modest effects on workplace safety while exacting a heavy price in terms of reduced productivity and wages and increased unemployment.

The Prevention of Behavioral Disability from Nonwork Sources: Employee Assistance Programs and Related Strategies

Employers have long engaged in a wide range of activities designed to reduce the frequency and severity of workplace injuries, including accident prevention programs and the management of workers' compensation claims. More recently, however, the rising cost of health insurance has led to programs to control costs associated with nonwork disability. These efforts run the gamut from marriage and family counseling to campaigns to assist employees to stop smoking to on-site physical fitness programs.

In this chapter Paul Roman and Terry Blum examine employer interventions designed to prevent the occurrence of work disability associated with behavioral disorders. In particular, the chapter focuses on Employee Assistance Programs (EAP) as a means of preventing disability associated with drug abuse and alcoholism.

They begin with an historical examination of the changing ideology related to alcoholism and drug abuse as well as the evolution of employer responses to workplace problems caused by these disorders. They note that in recent years these problems have become medicalized—defined as illnesses as opposed to sins or moral weaknesses—and increasingly linked to workplace factors. As these concepts changed, the activities of organizations concerned with these problems—and, in particular, the National Institute on Alcohol Abuse and Alcoholism, a federal agency established in 1970—began to focus on the costs for firms of "hidden" alcoholic employees. These efforts eventually led to EAPs as a means of curbing these costs.

Roman and Blum devote considerable attention to an examination of current employer practice with respect to EAPs. Specifically, they provide evidence of the extent and distribution of EAPs in American workplaces as well as the extent to which these programs are utilized by workers. In addition, Roman and Blum provide a detailed description of the core functions and technology utilized by EAPs. They also review empirical research examining the efficacy of EAPs as well as the methodological problems associated with this research. Finally, they examine alternative employer interventions that address alcohol and drug abuse problems in the workplace. These alternatives include the prohibition of psychoactive substances in the workplace, testing job applicants and current employees to determine whether a problem exists, health promotion and stress management programs designed to prevent the development of these disorders, and programs directed toward peer and occupational groups. The last alternative represents a joint labor-management approach to these problems.

The Role of Unions and Collective Bargaining in Preventing Work-related Disability

Unions arguably have the potential to increase the effectiveness of all of the mechanisms for promoting safety. Unions may use their bargaining power to secure larger risk premiums. They also may use their expertise and comparative advantage in collecting and interpreting information on workplace hazards to negotiate and enforce health and safety provisions in collective agreements and to obtain contractual guarantees against unjust dismissal, which allow workers to exercise their rights under the law. They also act as a political force in shaping the legal environment, lobbying Congress and state legislatures in the pursuit of social insurance and legislation to enhance workplace safety and the lives of disabled workers.

In this chapter Susan J. Schurman, David Weil, Paul Landsbergis, and Barbara Israel examine the empirical evidence on the impact of unions using a general framework of the disability development and prevention process that emphasizes its multicausal nature. This framework portrays work-related disability as the outcome of the intersection of two sets of determinants linked by the work process. One set of determinants, labeled *macro-level* factors, collectively determine the nature and design of work and a set of human resource practices affecting the likelihood and severity of workplace disabilities. The other, labeled *micro-level* factors, influence the path of disability of development following the onset of symptoms. In turn, the work process is determined by individual factors, workplace factors (human resource practices, job accommodations) and social systems (in particular, health care and workers' compensation systems) that influence the probability that a worker will return to work. The framework posits that every "stage" of the process is modified by factors related to individuals' biological, behavioral, and socioeconomic characteristics.

This analysis has several implications for future labor initiatives with respect to workplace health and safety. First, the authors argue for a more systematic approach to prevention than found in the de facto policies pursued in many parts of the labor movement. Second, they suggest that since the macro- and micro-determinants of workplace health and safety problems are different in different work contexts, the appropriate union response to these problems will vary across industries and occupations. Finally, they claim that unions (as well as employers and government regulators) need to consider a wider variety of tools to address health and safety, including technology choice, broader human resource policies, and the network of social service agencies available to the ill or injured.

Reducing the Consequences of Disability: Policies to Reduce Discrimination against Disabled Workers

The passage of the Americans with Disabilities Act (ADA) offered a new hope of access to the labor market for those with physical and emotional disabilities that had previously been denied by perceived systemic barriers. To some employers, the ADA was daunting in scope and raised fears of litigation, enormous costs of accommodating disabled workers, and ultimately the threat of becoming uncompetitive. It has probably been the case that the most optimistic expectations of disabled persons and the most pessimistic fears of employers have failed to materialize, yet the ADA has had important implications for both workers and employers.

Barbara Lee and Roger Thompson examine the scope and effectiveness of public policies that encourage the employment of workers with disabilities. Specifically, the chapter reviews the history, rationale, and recent experience with Second Injury Funds in workers' compensation as well as law prohibiting discrimination against disabled or handicapped persons and, in particular, the Americans with Disabilities Act.

Prior to the advent of Second Injury Funds, disabled workers were disadvantaged under workers' compensation statutes relative to the nondisabled population. If a previously disabled worker suffered additional disability due to a work injury, either the worker was penalized—compensation was limited to the additional disability associated with the second injury—or the employer was penalized—the employer assumed liability for the combined disability. In either event, this policy discouraged the employment of the disabled. Second Injury Funds remove these disincentives by limiting the employer's financial exposure, while providing compensation for the worker's combined disability.

Lee and Thompson note that Second Injury Funds have had a rocky history. The initial funds were criticized for their narrow coverage, which was limited to the loss of a member and to workers who were permanently and totally disabled as the result of the second injury. Many states responded to this criticism by broadening coverage, but they failed to provide sufficient reserves for future liability, leading to substantial deficits in fund accounts. In some states this has led to restrictions on fund utilization. For example, some states have begun to require certification of the preexisting condition. Other states have completely abandoned these funds, questioning whether the original rationale continues to be compelling in light of recent enactment of antidiscrimination legislation.

This chapter also examines evidence on the effects of the Americans with Disabilities Act and other antidiscrimination legislation. Specifically, the authors review recent court decisions interpreting the key provisions of the act as well as statistical data and empirical research on utilization, enforcement, and outcomes such as employer policies and attitudes toward the disabled. They conclude that few individuals have successfully challenged employer decisions under the ADA and that "it is unlikely that employers have increased their recruitment and hiring of individuals with disabilities." They note that federal courts have interpreted the definition of "disability" narrowly so that many persons with impairments are excluded. Interpretations of other key provisions have similarly limited the application of the ADA.

Facilitating Employment through Vocational Rehabilitation

Vocational rehabilitation (VR) services are the primary tool used to facilitate the disabled person's entry or reentry into the labor market. A variety of services are provided under a number of auspices, including workers' compensation and state and federal training programs. Monroe Berkowitz and David Dean examine the complex institutional framework of vocational rehabilitation in North America as well as the economic and social rationale for these programs. Their examination is organized around four issues: who administers the services, what services are provided, who pays for the services, and who receives these services.

VR programs are administered by both public and private organizations, although both types of organizations typically purchase services from the same set of vendors. The principal public sector agencies are the federal-state partnership referred to as the VR program, Veterans' Administration (VA) services, and the state workers' compensation programs. Services may include both medical restoration and vocational rehabilitation, including job referral and placement services, training, and education, although the basis by which these services are provided varies substantially between the public and private sectors. Berkowitz and Dean indicate that public agencies often provide services in order to maximize the potential of the individual client, while in the private sector the decision to provide services is more likely to be based on a cost-benefit analysis.

VR clientele vary substantially among programs. Berkowitz and Dean note private programs have much greater flexibility with respect to their choice of clientele. On the other hand, they note that legislation and political considerations largely determine the clientele of the public sector agencies. For example, the authors indicate that the clientele for the federal-state VR program has changed markedly as congressional priorities shifted. Initially designed to provide services to persons disabled as the result of a work injury, in recent years Congress has shifted the emphasis to persons with severe disabilities with little attachment to the labor market.

Berkowitz and Dean also review research examining the effectiveness of VR programs. However, they note there is little credible evidence on this issue for either public or private sector programs. The public VR program is the most well investigated, but early research suffered from significant methodological problems. More sophisticated analyses have found only "modest" earnings gains for program participants. Similarly, a recent GAO study concluded that the VA program was able to place only a small proportion of participants in jobs.

Workers' compensation programs do not routinely collect data on VR outcomes. Berkowitz and Dean note that while many compensation programs mandate referral to VR, an evaluation by rehabilitation personnel, or a plan of rehabilitative services, there is little follow-up to determine the results of this process. Similarly, evaluation of private sector programs is essentially limited to case studies that are difficult to generalize.

Compensation for Disabled Workers: Workers' Compensation

Workers' compensation is the oldest form of social insurance in North America and is the primary source of compensation benefits for work-related disability. Nevertheless, rapidly increasing costs of workers' compensation in the late 1980s led to significant pressures for systemic reform.

In this chapter Emily Spieler and John F. Burton Jr. provide an overview of the fundamentals of workers' compensation, including benefit structure, financing, and administration. They review recent developments in these programs, particularly as they affect the compensation goal. They examine these developments in light of two criteria used to evaluate performance relative to this goal: (1) benefits should be adequate and (2) costs should be affordable.

Their historical examination reveals wide fluctuations in benefit generosity in U.S. workers' compensation programs over the past forty years. Prior to the 1970s, benefits had fallen to levels approaching the poverty threshold. The deterioration in real benefits, in part, prompted the establishment of a National Commission on State Workmen's Compensation Laws that in its 1972 report recommended federal legislation if states did not substantially improve benefit levels. The threat of a federal takeover prompted the states into action, and benefits improved in subsequent years. Initially, the cost impact of these reforms was masked by high interest rates, which allowed insurers to keep rates low despite increasing benefit payments. However, when interest rates fell in the mid- and late 1980s, escalating costs and insurance industry losses led to a period that Spieler and Burton term "the Neo-Reform Era."

Spieler and Burton examine five developments that characterize this period, which roughly corresponds to the decade of the 1990s. First, many state legislatures significantly reduced statutory benefit levels, particularly with respect to permanent partial disabilities. Second, eligibility rules were substantially changed in several states, leading to contractions in the availability of benefits. These rule changes include limiting the compensability of conditions like chronic stress and cumulative trauma injuries, narrowing the definition of permanent total disability, and raising the standard of proof for compensation claims. Third, the health care delivery system has been transformed as compensation programs have sought to contain skyrocketing health care costs. These transformations include the (re-) introduction of medical payment limits, fee schedules, limits on claimant choice of physician, and managed care organizations. Fourth, there is an increased emphasis on disability management and encouragement of the reemployment of injured workers. Finally, limitations on the availability of compensation has led to a number of challenges to the exclusive remedy doctrine, so that increasingly workers are winning tort judgments for disabilities that were once covered by workers' compensation.

One of their conclusions is that there is an inevitable conflict between adequacy and affordability, whereby "reforms" are characterized as gains for workers at the expense of employers and vice versa. However, they argue that studies showing that workers pay for increased benefits in the form of lower wages suggest that the conflict is largely an illusion. They also conclude that the decentralized nature of the workers' compensation program is substantially responsible for concerns about affordability, as states compete with one another to reduce compensation costs for employers, adversely affecting benefit adequacy.

Social Security Disability Insurance: A Policy Review

With the possible exception of the several state workers' compensation programs considered collectively, Social Security Disability Insurance (SSDI) is the largest and most important government program addressing the needs of the long-term disabled. However, unlike workers' compensation, it provides income support to all totally disabled workers, irrespective of whether their injuries have a work-related origin. SSDI has undergone substantial change since the 1970s when benefit rolls and costs reached an historic high. These trends led to legislation that severely tightened eligibility criteria in the 1980s. More recently, the Congress enacted legislation intended to encourage the beneficiaries' return to the labor market. However, beneficiary rolls began to rise once again, prompting renewed legislative interest in SSDI. In 1991 the chairman of the House Ways and Means Committee asked the National Academy of Social Insurance to undertake a comprehensive review of SSDI and its companion program Supplemental Security Income (SSI).

In this chapter, Jerry Mashaw and Virginia Reno review the findings of a panel of experts convened by the National Academy to investigate issues raised by the Ways and Means Committee Chairman. Specifically, the chapter examines the answers the academy found with respect to three specific questions: (1) Do benefits provided by SSDI and SSI provide disincentives for workers to remain in or reenter the workforce? (2) Can rehabilitation be built into these programs without (a) greatly increasing costs or (b) undermining benefit security? and (3) Can changes in income support policy be made that will better promote work?

With respect to the first question, the panel found that due in part to the strict eligibility requirements and the modest level of cash benefits of both programs, cash benefits under SSDI and SSI create only small disincentives for work. However, they also find that health care coverage gaps offer incentives for disabled workers who fear losing Medicare or Medicaid eligibility to remain on SSDI and SSI rolls. These workers have relatively high medical expenses and will generally have difficulty obtaining affordable coverage elsewhere.

The panel made several recommendations in response to questions (2) and (3) examined by Reno and Mashaw. These include tax credits given to disabled workers to delay or prevent their entry onto disability benefit rolls and "return-to-work" vouchers given to current beneficiaries, which could be used to obtain vocational rehabilitation services. Payment to VR providers would be tied to successful rehabilitation, i.e., the provider receives one-half of the value of benefits that would have been paid to the beneficiary had he or she remained on the rolls. To eliminate disincentives associated with the loss of health care coverage, the panel also recommended that DI recipients be permitted to buy continued Medicare coverage if they return to work. Finally, the panel also recommended a number of changes to program administration to promote a return to work, including "fair and effective" continuing disability reviews.

The panel rejected a number of alternative policy initiatives. These include time-limited, long-term disability benefits, short-term disability insurance, partial disability benefits, and linking benefit eligibility to the Americans with Disabilities Act. Reno and Mashaw examine why each of these policies was rejected.

Disputes and Dispute Resolution

Workers' compensation arose out of the inadequacies of the tort system, which had previously resolved disputes over workplace injuries. In return for benefits paid with certainty and financed by the employer, workers forfeited the right to sue employers. In return, employers got a no-fault collective liability system and protection from judgments in favor of a worker injured in their place of employment. It was envisioned that such a system would reduce the litigation associated with workplace injuries.

Nevertheless, disputes seem to be an unavoidable byproduct of disability insurance programs. Significantly more than other social insurance programs, benefit eligibility is based on criteria that are often vague and equivocal. There are reasons to believe that the design of dispute resolution procedures has significant social welfare implications. In recent years policy makers have grown increasingly concerned over the costs of more and more extensive litigation involving disability; yet litigation may lower systemic costs by reducing judicial error. Despite its centrality to the effective functioning of disability insurance programs, the issue of disputes and dispute resolution procedures in disability insurance remains a relatively underresearched topic. Very little is known about the optimal design of dispute procedures.

In this chapter Terry Thomason, Doug Hyatt, and Karen Roberts examine theory and empirical research relevant to the problems of disputes and dispute resolution in disability insurance programs but particularly workers' compensation. Specifically, they examine two approaches to these problems. The first approach suggests that parties will respond to economic incentives presented by the institutional framework of dispute resolution. To the extent that those incentives are at odds with social objectives, utilization of dispute resolution procedures will result in suboptimal social welfare. This approach also suggests that the design of dispute resolution procedures can also have important equity implications. The second approach recognizes that the parties—and, in particular, claimants—are concerned with and therefore affected by the process as well as the outcomes of dispute resolution. In addition, procedural concerns also have important implications for social welfare.

Convergence: A Comparison of European and U.S. Disability Policy

Countries outside of North America have implemented a set of public policy responses to the problems of disabled workers which provide interesting contrasts with those found in the United States and Canada. In Germany, for example, employers face specific quotas for hiring disabled workers. Some nations have questioned the potential adverse social consequences of having the costs of disability fall entirely on the worker and/or the employer and have instituted policies which share the costs of accommodating the workplace needs of disabled workers with others in society.

Leo Aarts, Richard Burkhauser, and Philip de Jong compare disability policies in three European countries—the Netherlands, Sweden, and Germany—with U.S. policy. They find dramatic differences in the prevalence of disability transfer recipients per worker across these countries and argue that these differences are explained by differences in the institutions of the workers' disability system in these nations. The authors also argue that due to social, economic, fiscal, and demographic pressures, these European systems are converging toward the U.S. system, which they describe as "more actuarially fair but potentially more adversarial."

Aarts, Burkhauser, and de Jong examine the institutional framework of the workers' disability systems in these four countries in the context of the countries' overall social welfare systems. Using a taxonomy that classifies programs as involving temporary income transfers, longer-term transfers, or work enhancement (i.e., programs providing rehabilitation or jobs), they provide a detailed description of existing programs.

Based on an examination of disability transfer rates and payment data, among other things, they claim that employers and workers have strong incentives to use the disability transfer system as an alternative to rehabilitation or unemployment insurance. As a result, the number of disability benefit recipients will be "unnecessarily large" where administrative regulations fail to offer counter incentives. They argue that disability rolls in the Netherlands, in part, were particularly large because administrative decisions concerning benefit eligibility were made by a bipartite organization that lacked government control and that did not have to bear the fiscal consequences of its actions.

In part due to need to bring government spending under control in order to achieve Single Currency Union goals, the authors report that the Dutch system is being dismantled in favor of a more privatized one.

Benefit eligibility has been tightened, benefit levels have been reduced, experience-rating of disability insurance has been introduced, and administrative structures have been substantially altered. While they suggest that it is too early to know whether these reforms will be successful in bringing the system under fiscal control, they conclude that "Dutch disability policy, which has been used as an example of what not to do in cross-national comparisons over the last two decades, may now be seen as the trendsetter among European countries."

Endnotes

[1] See Spieler and Burton (Chapter 8) for a more detailed description of the pre-workers' compensation tort system.

[2] Canadian provinces also have a system of direct regulation that is viewed as a complement rather than as a substitute for internal responsibility.

[3] A good is nonrival if its consumption by A does not affect B's ability to also consume the good. A good is excludable if it is possible for the producer to limit consumption. Goods may be rival and excludable (e.g., hamburgers), rival and nonexcludable (e.g., space on a crowded city sidewalk), nonrival and excludable (e.g., concert music), and nonrival and nonexcludable (e.g., sunshine). Public goods have the properties of nonrival consumption and nonexcludability. As such they are subject to free-rider problems, since potential consumers will wait for some other consumer to purchase the good, at which point they can enjoy it without cost to themselves.

[4] Which party should pay depends on whether the accommodation results in increased specific or increased general human capital. If the accommodation increases the worker's general human capital, the costs may be paid directly out of pocket, while the parties may share the costs of specific human capital accommodations.

[5] Most of the benefits in workers' compensation and in some of the temporary disability insurance programs are paid by private carriers and self-insurers. The plans are "public" in the sense that benefits are mandated by statute.

[6] This does not imply unanimity of opinion with respect to these issues. The basic framework of the system does require consensus, although specific programs or policies may, in fact, be controversial.

References

Dembe, Allard. 1996. *Occupation and Disease: How Social Factors Affect the Conception of Work-related Disorders*. New Haven, CT: Yale University Press.

Dunlop, John T. 1958. *Industrial Relations Systems*. New York: Holt.

Smith, Robert S. 1974. "The Feasibility of an 'Injury Tax' Approach to Occupational Safety." *Law and Contemporary Problems*, Vol. 38, pp. 730-44.

CHAPTER 2

Dispelling the Myths about Work Disability

MARJORIE L. BALDWIN
East Carolina University

WILLIAM G. JOHNSON
Arizona State University

Work disability is a costly problem in the U.S. In 1988, for example, the costs of work disability included $22 billion in SSDI payments, $11 billion in SSI payments to the blind and disabled, $19 billion in Medicaid expenditures, and $27 billion (1987) in workers' compensation payments (Piacentini and Cerino 1990).

Passage of the Americans with Disabilities Act of 1990 (ADA) heightened public awareness of the problems encountered by persons with disabilities and their desire to participate more fully in society. Yet the stereotypes that have evolved in the years since the act was passed have perpetuated misconceptions of the disabled population and their ability to work. The stylized drawing of a person in a wheelchair that has come to symbolize the ADA does not, for example, represent the typical disabled person. A woman with chronic low back pain or a man with cardiovascular disease are more typical examples.

At the same time, the current trend toward retrenchment in all public assistance programs has generated concerns about rapidly rising expenditures for health care and income supplements for disabled persons. There is increasing pressure to move less severely disabled recipients off the disability rolls and into paid employment. Yet closer examination shows that these efforts may also be based on misconceptions. Most recipients whose benefits are canceled remain unemployed and rely on other sources of income for support (Yelin 1992).

This chapter describes what we know about disability and the workplace. The chapter is organized around four principles that contradict common misconceptions of disability and work. Those principles are:

• The most frequent types of disabilities are not those that are caused by birth defects or traumatic accidents. Instead they are musculoskeletal conditions, such as arthritis or cardiovascular conditions, typically caused by chronic degenerative processes that increase as persons age. Among younger age groups, mental illness is the most prevalent disabling condition.

• Most workers with disabilities were not disabled as children and were not, therefore, subject to discrimination in education or to labor market discrimination at the time of entry into the labor market.

• The ability of a disabled person to work does not depend solely on the nature of his impairment and the quality of medical care received. Many other factors, including characteristics of the worker and his usual job, attitudes of employers, labor market conditions, and the availability of workplace accommodations, are important determinants of employment outcomes for disabled workers.

• There are large wage differentials between disabled and nondisabled workers that are not entirely explained by health-related differences in productivity. Although productivity differentials are one important factor explaining the wage differentials, employer discrimination also contributes to the low wage rates of workers with disabilities.

The chapter begins by defining key terms. In the four sections that follow we present evidence in support of each of the principles above. A concluding section discusses policy implications from this new view of disability and work.

Definitions

Disability is a measure of limitations in activities, such as working or keeping house, rather than an attribute, such as gender or race. To understand the meaning of the term "disability" it is important to distinguish it from "impairments" and "functional limitations," terms that are often used synonymously but have different meanings.

An impairment is a "physiological or anatomical loss or other abnormality." An impairment may or may not cause a *functional limitation*, that is, a restriction of sensory, mental, or physical capacities. A disability occurs when a functional limitation restricts the ability to perform normal daily activities such as working or attending school.[1]

Consider, for example, a worker with an impairment, such as epilepsy. The impairment causes a functional limitation, namely, the inability to walk and perform physical tasks during severe seizures. If seizures are not controlled through medication and restrict the worker's ability to perform his usual job, he has a work disability (Chirikos and Nestel 1984). If seizures are almost completely controlled, which is fairly typical, the functional limitation need not create a work disability, but the worker may still be subject to discrimination.

According to the economists' definition, economic discrimination occurs when two groups of workers with equal average productivity have different average wages or opportunities for employment. Discrimination in employment can be expressed as refusals to hire, job terminations in response to reductions in the demand for labor, or refusals to rehire workers after they are absent because of an illness or injury. Wage discrimination is expressed as differences in the average wages of two groups of workers that are unrelated to differences in average productivity or to characteristics of the jobs in which they are employed.

We are concerned with persons whose impairments limit their ability to perform some kinds of work. Although they are work disabled, most persons with disabilities are able to perform some types of work and may, in fact, be as productive as nondisabled persons in certain types of jobs. Their productivity is determined by the usual human capital variables and by interactions between the functional limitations imposed by impairments and the physical and mental demands of their jobs. If, for example, the limitation applies to a function that is not required by the jobs for which he or she is otherwise qualified, the individual is not work disabled.

The next section provides evidence on the distribution of impairments among the disabled population, showing that the most common disabling health conditions impose few, if any, limitations in most jobs.

Distribution of Impairments

Contrary to the stereotypes promulgated by the ADA, the most common disabling health conditions are not paralysis or blindness but chronic degenerative conditions such as arthritis, back problems, and heart disease. Such conditions often develop after a person reaches middle age and has completed his education and job training and accumulated a number of years of work experience. Evidence that the most common causes of work disability are health conditions associated with aging comes from such diverse sources of national survey data, discrimination complaints filed with the Equal Employment Opportunity Commission (EEOC), and statistics on work-related injuries.

National Survey Data

Information on the distribution of disabling health conditions among the general population comes from two national surveys: the 1983-85 National Health Interview Survey (NHIS) and the 1984 panel of the Survey of Income and Program Participation (SIPP).[2] Other national surveys, such as the CPS, include information on disability, but the NHIS and SIPP are the only surveys with sufficient information to compute prevalence rates for different health conditions. Both surveys collect data from samples representative of the noninstitutionalized civilian population of the U.S.[3]

In both surveys, persons are defined as "work-disabled" if they respond that a health condition or impairment limits the amount or kind of work they can do.[4] The information on disability is self-reported and subject to the biases and misinterpretations inherent in such questions. Nevertheless, Stern (1989) has shown that self-reports yield reasonably accurate estimates of work disability.

Figure 1 shows the distribution of conditions reported to be the main cause of work limitation among those persons who report a work

FIGURE 1

Distribution of Impairments among the Disabled Population

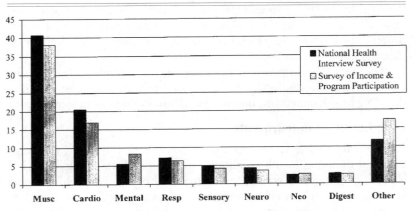

Musc = Musculoskeletal
Cardio = Cardiovascular/Circulatory
Mental = Mental illness, mental retardation,
    substance abuse
Resp = Respiratory
Source: GAO (1993), Table 2.2, p. 29.

Sensory = Visual & Hearing
Neuro = Neurological
Neo = Neoplastic
Digest = Digestive
Other

disability (GAO 1993). Musculoskeletal conditions are the most common causes of work disability, followed by cardiovascular and circulatory conditions.[5] Musculoskeletal conditions include arthritis, back or spine problems, amputation, or missing extremities. Cardiovascular and circulatory conditions include heart disease, hypertension, and stroke. Together these conditions account for 57% to 62% of the total population with work disabilities.

The single most common disabling health condition is back pain. It also represents the largest injury category of workers' compensation cases and the bulk of employment discrimination complaints to the EEOC since the ADA was passed.

Work-related Injuries

In 1992, 3.3 million disabling injuries occurred at the workplace; of these 8,500 were fatalities (NSC 1993). Work-related injuries represented 19% of all disabling injuries and 10% of accidental deaths in 1992 (NSC 1993). The total costs of work-related injuries, including medical care costs, indemnity payments, and lost work time, were $116 billion, or 2% of GDP (NSC 1993).[6]

Back injuries occur more often than any other single type of injury or illness.[7] In 1992, back pain represented 24% of work-related injuries and 31% of workers' compensation costs, because the average cost of a back injury was 38% higher than the average cost of other work-related injuries (NSC 1993).

While soft tissue injuries consistently represent the largest single type of work-related injury, the greatest percentage increase in workers' compensation claims in recent years has been for mental impairments. Between 1982 and 1993, mental disorders increased from 10% to 25% of claims (Welch 1996). The increase is especially large among younger workers (Kaye et al. 1996).

Complaints Filed with the EEOC

Responsibility for enforcement of the employment provisions of the ADA rests with the Equal Employment Opportunity Commission. Between July 1992 and June 1997, the agency received approximately 82,000 disability-related complaints that resulted in monetary settlements exceeding $150 million (EEOC 1997). Figure 2 summarizes the distribution of complaints, through May 1994, across impairment categories (West 1994). Approximately one-fifth of the complaints are filed by persons with back pain. Neurological and mental impairments each

FIGURE 2

Distribution of Impairments among Persons Filing
Discrimination Complaints with EEOC

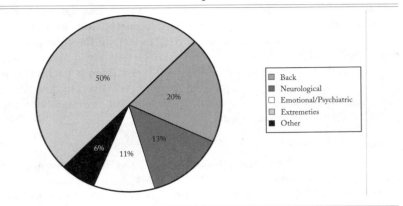

Source: West (1994).

account for slightly more than 10% of total complaints; all other impairments represent 6% or less of the total.

The ADA was passed because of the efforts of disability rights advocates who represent persons with relatively severe conditions, such as cerebral palsy, sensory impairments, and mental retardation. The advocates adopted the civil rights model used so effectively by African Americans during the 1960s. Neither the objectives of the ADA nor its implementation are directed toward the largest group of persons with disabilities, namely older, less severely disabled persons, with conditions that first occurred during middle age. The preponderance of complaints from persons who are not members of the groups traditionally represented by disability rights advocates has raised concerns regarding the population the ADA was designed to help. Some claim that "the ADA does not appear to be making a difference for persons who are not currently working and may make it even harder for those with significant disabilities to find employment," while others are worried that the ADA will be "trivialized" (West 1994).

Although most disabling health conditions are less severe than the stereotypical example of a person in a wheelchair, persons with disabilities face considerable hardships in the labor market. The following section provides some evidence on the relative employment and earnings of disabled and nondisabled workers.

Employment Statistics

According to the CPS, 8.6% of the U.S. population were work disabled in 1988 (Bennefield and McNeil 1989: Table E). The CPS is a general survey that places no special emphasis on health and disability questions. Work disability status is measured on the basis of screening questions asked of a single household respondent.[8] As a result, CPS estimates tend to underestimate the prevalence of work disability in the population relative to other sources such as the SIPP (Bennefield and McNeil 1989). The statistics reported below should be interpreted with this in mind.

As shown in Figures 3 and 4, the employment rates and earnings of workers with disabilities are substantially lower than the employment rates and earnings of nondisabled workers. In 1988, only 23% of men with work disabilities were employed full-time (Figure 3), compared to 75% of nondisabled men (Bennefield and McNeil 1989: Table 4). Employment rates for women with disabilities were even lower: 13% of disabled women worked full-time compared to 47% of nondisabled women. The unemployment rates for disabled men and women are more than double the unemployment rates for their nondisabled counterparts (14% vs. 6% for men and 15% vs. 5% for women) (Bennefield and McNeil 1989: Table 4).

Among those disabled workers who are employed, average earnings are considerably lower than average earnings for nondisabled workers.

FIGURE 3

Employment of Disabled and Nondisabled Workers

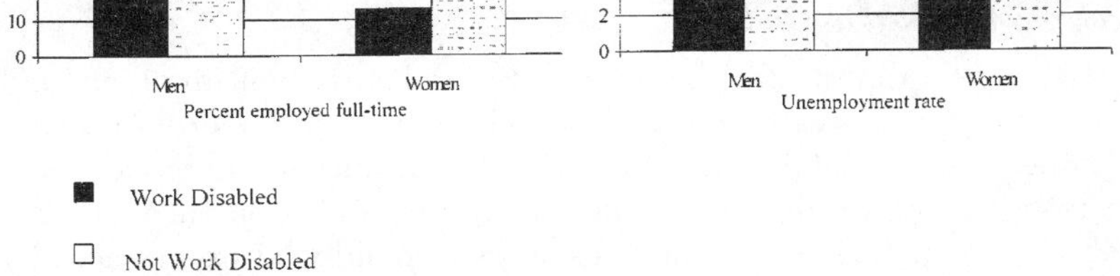

Men   Women
Percent employed full-time

Men   Women
Unemployment rate

■   Work Disabled

□   Not Work Disabled

Source: Census (1989), Table 4.

FIGURE 4

Annual Earnings of Full-time Disabled and Nondisabled Workers

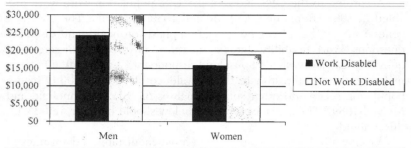

Source: Census (1989), Table D.

The disabled-nondisabled earnings ratio was 64% for men and 62% for women in 1987, decreasing from 77% and 69% respectively in 1980 (Bennefield and McNeil 1989: Table D). The earnings differential is partly explained by differences between disabled and nondisabled workers in the number of hours worked. Among full-time year-round workers (Figure 4), the disabled-nondisabled earnings ratios increase to 81% for men and 84% for women (Bennefield and McNeil 1989: Table D).

Men and women with disabilities are at a clear disadvantage in the labor market. Labor market problems for minority workers usually include disadvantages encountered early in life, but for most persons with disabilities this is not the case. In the next section we consider the experience of disability over the life cycle.

Onset of Disability

The population of persons with disabilities can be divided into two groups: persons who are disabled during childhood and persons who are disabled after completing their education.[9] The two groups encounter different problems in the workplace and require different programs and policies to improve their employment outcomes.

Persons Disabled as Children

The group most often represented in debates about disability and work are persons with conditions, such as blindness, cerebral palsy, deafness, and mental retardation, that begin during childhood. Such persons experience discrimination in education and upon entry into the labor market. Indeed, personal accounts of childhood experiences by persons with disabilities and representations in literature and the news media document the intensity of prejudice and hostility toward children and young adults with certain types of disabling conditions (Biklen 1987; Rousso 1988).

Individual examples of success notwithstanding, the process of maturing in a hostile and restricted environment imposes limitations on opportunities and on an individual's view of the world that are difficult to escape. The impact of discrimination on schooling, socialization, access to employment, and the process of "growing up disabled" parallels the experiences of African Americans and other minorities in general, even if the specifics differ.

The goals of this segment of the disabled population are to achieve legislative guarantees of their civil rights similar to the legislation that protects the rights of other minority groups. Specifically, they seek to realize fully their potential as participants in society and to guarantee the same opportunity to disabled children in the future. The ADA was enacted primarily to promote the goals of this segment of the disabled population, and in fact, they are the ones we most often envision when we consider the problem of disability and work. They do not, however, represent the majority of persons with disabilities.

Persons Disabled as Adults

The larger segment of the disabled population consists of persons with impairments that originated with illnesses or injuries occurring during adulthood, most often in middle age.[10] Such persons are not limited in their educational opportunities by disability-related discrimination, neither do they face discriminatory obstacles to employment on entry to the labor force or during their pre-onset work experience.

Consider, for example, a 55-year-old worker with a high school education and long work history, who is displaced from his job because of an episode of back pain. The profile is not uncharacteristic of the segment of the disabled population who are disabled as adults but is very different from the profile of persons who are disabled as children. The employment problem most often encountered by persons who are disabled as adults is obtaining the right to return to work after an illness or injury displaces them from their job, sometimes after a relatively lengthy work absence to recover from the acute effects of their conditions.

Burkhauser and Daly (1996) describe the post-onset labor market outcomes of the group who transitions into disability as adults. After the onset of disability there is a decline in average work hours and labor earnings. Within five years after onset nearly 50% of persons have experienced at least one year of not working. Among younger persons (below age 50), three-fifths of those who are out of work one year are able to return to work after the spell of absence, but among older persons (age 51 to 61) less than one-third return.

The Burkhauser-Daly results emphasize the heterogeneous nature of the disability experience. Within five years after onset, one in five persons with disability have experienced a spell in which family income is below the poverty line, one in two have received transfer payments for disability, but one in ten have recovered from their disability. Thus, for persons with chronic health conditions that begin in adulthood, the work disability problem is more subtle and complex than is usually perceived.

The Return to Work Myth

A common misconception, for example, is that the first return to work after a health-related work absence marks the end of the problem of work disability. The return to work measure has been used for many years by vocational rehabilitation agencies and is an increasingly popular measure of the effectiveness of medical care. Several recent studies, however, indicate that return to work measures can substantially misrepresent returns to stable employment for workers with permanent impairments.

The studies examine post-injury employment patterns among samples of Ontario workers' compensation claimants with permanent partial impairments resulting from work-related injuries (Butler, Johnson, and Baldwin 1995; Johnson, Baldwin, and Butler 1998). Four distinct post-injury employment patterns are identified: (1) the first return to work is successful (i.e., the worker remains in the job until the time of interview 3-15 years later or leaves the job for reasons unrelated to his health condition); (2) the first return to work is unsuccessful (i.e., the worker leaves the job for reasons related to his health condition); (3) the worker experiences multiple episodes of work and work absence, ending in a successful return to work; (4) the worker experiences multiple episodes of work and work absence, ending in an unsuccessful return to work. Figure 5 shows the distribution of all claimants and the subset with back injuries across the four employment patterns.

If we only considered first returns to work, we would conclude that 85% of workers in the all-injury group recovered from their injuries because they returned to work. In fact, almost 60% of those who returned

FIGURE 5

Distribution across Post-Injury Employment Patterns

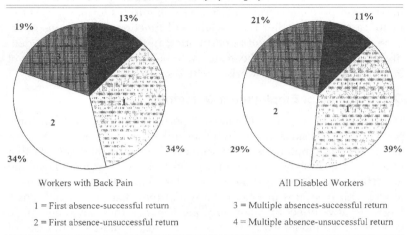

Workers with Back Pain   All Disabled Workers

1 = First absence-successful return   3 = Multiple absences-successful return

2 = First absence-unsuccessful return   4 = Multiple absence-unsuccessful return

Source: Butler, Johnson and Baldwin (1995); Johnson, Baldwin and Butler (1998).

to work had one or more subsequent injury-related work absences. Of those workers who initially returned to work, 40% were not employed at the time of interview because of the effects of their injuries, demonstrating that work disability is a persistent problem in four cases out of ten.

Focusing on the subset of workers with back injuries, the error of using first return to work as a measure of the end of work disability is even more apparent. Two-thirds of workers with back injuries who returned to work had subsequent injury-related work absences, and nearly half the workers who initially returned to work were not employed at the time of interview for reasons related to their injury.

The persistent employment problems of workers with chronic health conditions suggest that the goals of this segment of the disabled population are likely to differ from the goals of those disabled as children. Those disabled later in life are likely to be focused more on economic objectives than civil rights. The most important objectives will be access to jobs, rights to return to a job after health-related work absences, job accommodations to facilitate returns to work, and adequate compensatory incomes when returns to work are not feasible.

Clearly, access to employment is a key to economic security for persons with disabilities. Most disabled persons are able to perform some type of work and have employment histories prior to the onset of disability. In some cases the functional limitations associated with an impairment preclude a worker from returning to his former job, but in many cases factors other than health and functional limitations intervene to restrict employment opportunities. In the next section we identify those factors that have been shown to be important determinants of employment outcomes for workers with disabilities.

Determinants of Employment Outcomes

Health status is one of the most important predictors of labor force participation decisions. Stern (1989) includes measures of health status and functional limitations in an employment model and reports that both are strong, significant predictors of negative outcomes. Diamond and Hausman (1984) estimate a standard labor force participation model with measures of health status and find that poor health has a larger negative effect on labor force participation than any other single variable in the model. Nevertheless, in all but the most severe cases of disability, health status alone does not preclude employment.

Other factors, such as economic incentives and shifts in labor demand, have been shown to be significant determinants of employment among workers with disabilities (Johnson, Baldwin, and Butler 1998; Butler, Johnson, and Baldwin 1995). Some workers may choose not to work even when they are physically able to do so, because of the disincentive effects of disability benefit payments. Other workers who want to work may be forced to renegotiate employment contracts with former employers or to seek new jobs under conditions that have changed since they became disabled (Butler, Johnson, and Baldwin 1995). Employers may have hired replacement workers or reduced their demand for labor during a worker's absence. Such factors combine with the residual effects of functional limitations to determine employment outcomes for disabled workers (Johnson, Baldwin, and Butler 1998; Butler, Johnson, and Baldwin 1995).

Much of the evidence on determinants of employment for workers with disabilities comes from studies of the return to work decisions of workers' compensation claimants (e.g., Fenn 1981; Curington 1994; Johnson 1983; Butler and Worrall 1985; Johnson and Ondrich 1990; Johnson, Butler, and Baldwin 1995). Introduced in the early 1900s, workers' compensation laws guarantee compensation for workers who experience job-related injuries, whether or not the injury was caused by employer negligence. In exchange for guaranteed compensation, workers forfeit the right to sue employers and must rely on workers' compensation benefits to pay medical expenses and replace lost wages. Workers' compensation programs provide first-dollar coverage for health care (a practice that has disappeared from other forms of health insurance) and indemnity payments (approximately two-thirds of the pre-injury wage) until an injured worker returns to work. Studies of return to work among workers' compensation recipients consistently find that indemnity payments create strong work disincentives and that other socioeconomic factors also have a significant influence on the decision to return to work.

The studies focus on first return to work and do not adequately describe the long-term effects of disability.[11] The research does, however, identify important determinants of return to work that may also have longer-term effects:

1. Demographic Characteristics
   - Gender: men are more likely to return to work than women.
   - Age: the probability of return to work decreases with age.
   - Race: African Americans are less likely to return to work than white Americans.
   - Marital status: married men (unmarried women) are more likely to return to work than unmarried men (married women).

2. Human Capital Characteristics
   - Education: the probability of return to work increases with education.
   - Experience: the probability of return to work increases with work experience prior to injury.

3. Economic Incentives
   - Wages: the higher the expected wage, the higher the probability of return to work.
   - Replacement rate: the probability of return to work decreases as the ratio of indemnity benefits to pre-injury wages increases. Estimates of the benefit elasticity, however, are inconsistent across studies.

To our knowledge, the only research on employment outcomes after the first return to work are studies using a unique data set, sponsored by the Workers' Compensation Board of Ontario, Canada, that collected information on the post-injury employment and earnings of 11,000 workers with permanent partial impairments (Butler, Johnson, and Baldwin 1995; Hyatt 1996; Johnson, Baldwin, and Butler 1998). The

Hyatt study examines the impact of workers' compensation benefits and expected earnings on employment status at the point of maximum medical improvement. Consistent with the studies of first returns to work, he reports that higher benefits are associated with lower probabilities of post-injury employment, while higher expected earnings increase the probability of post-injury employment.

The other studies identify specific post-injury employment patterns after the first return to work (as described above) and analyze factors that determine which pattern an injured worker will experience. Many of the characteristics that influence first return to work are also found to be important determinants of post-return employment stability (e.g., age, education, gender).

Job accommodations, which have only been examined for workers with a first return to work, are important determinants of long-term employment. In particular, workers who receive reduced hours, light workloads, or modified equipment are less likely to experience multiple spells of injury-related work absence than other workers (Butler, Johnson, and Baldwin 1995). Burkhauser, Butler, and Kim (1995) estimate that workplace accommodations extend the average duration of employment for disabled workers by nearly five years. Gunderson and Hyatt (1996), however, show that some injured workers pay for their job accommodations in the form of lower wages.

The workers' compensation research dispels the notion that health status alone determines employment outcomes for workers with disabilities. Characteristics of the disabled worker, economic factors, and characteristics of the work environment are all important determinants of the degree of work disability associated with an impairment. There remains the important question of the extent to which employer discrimination limits the wages and employment opportunities of workers with disabilities. That issue is addressed in the following section.

Employer Discrimination vs. Productivity Differentials

Workers with disabilities earn lower wages, on average, than nondisabled workers. This fact is undisputed, but there is considerable disagreement regarding the reasons for the wage differential. One view is that "of course" workers with disabilities earn less than nondisabled workers because the functional limitations associated with impairments make disabled workers less productive in the workplace. The opposite view is that functional limitations are irrelevant: with appropriate accommodations disabled workers can be as productive as nondisabled workers. Advocates of the first view contend that disabled-nondisabled wage differentials are completely explained by productivity differentials, while advocates of the second view argue that wage differentials are completely explained by employer discrimination and unwillingness to provide suitable job accommodations.

Our research suggests that both views are based on misconceptions. Advocates of the productivity explanation ignore the fact that most men and women with disabilities are physically able to work and their functional limitations do not usually decrease their productivity in all types of work. Yet functional limitations can limit productivity in many jobs. Advocates of the discrimination explanation ignore the fact that accommodations can be costly, and wage differentials that reflect cost differentials do not represent discrimination in the economists' sense of the term. Yet there is considerable evidence that persons with disabilities are subject to prejudice and negative attitudes (Yuker 1987; Hahn 1987). Thus it is likely that both employer discrimination and productivity differences contribute to the low wages of workers with disabilities (Baldwin and Johnson 1994a, 1995). The challenge is to determine the relative importance of the two.

In a series of studies of labor market outcomes for disabled workers, we have applied the techniques economists use to study discrimination against blacks, women, and other minorities in the labor market (Oaxaca 1973; Reimers 1983) to the problem of explaining disabled-nondisabled wage differentials. The studies control for the effects of functional limitations on worker productivity by including summary measures of functional limitations as explanatory variables in the wage equation. Although the limitations variables control for differences in a number of physical and sensory limitations, they do not adequately capture correlations between the limiting effects of impairments and the requirements of a particular job.[12] The results should be viewed with this caveat in mind.

Table 1 summarizes the results of the wage discrimination studies (Johnson and Lambnnos 1985; Baldwin and Johnson 1994a, 1995, 1996).[13] The results separate differences in employer wage offers to disabled and nondisabled workers into three parts: a part attributed to productivity differentials associated with functional limitations, a part attributed to productivity differentials associated with other factors (such as differences in education and work experience), and a part unexplained by measured productivity differentials and attributed to employer discrimination.[14] The discriminatory or unexplained part of the

TABLE 1

Studies of Wage Discrimination against Workers with Disabilities

Sample	Data	Offer Wage Differential	Results % Functional Limitations	% Other Factors	% Discrimination
Men	1972 SSD	0.166	-39	41	98
Men	1984 SIPP				
More Prejudice		0.332	30	26	44
Less Prejudice		0.061	85	-177	193
Men	1990 SIPP				
More prejudice		0.295	23	2	75
Less prejudice		0.182	21	-7	86
Women	1972 SSD	0.791	7	17	77
Women	1984 SIPP	0.117	6	38	56

Source: SIPP, Wave III (1984, 1990); Social Security Survey of Disabled and Non-disabled Adults (1972).

Note: For complete decompositions refer to Baldwin and Johnson (1994, 1995, 1996).

wage differential also includes residual effects, that is, differences in wages attributed to differences in productivity that have not been adequately measured in the wage equations. The data for the discrimination studies do not, for example, include information on job accommodations. If workers pay part or all of the cost of job accommodations in the form of lower wages (Gunderson and Hyatt 1996), this may explain part of the disabled-nondisabled wage differential that is being attributed to discrimination. Because of the omitted variables problem, the unexplained component should be viewed as an upper bound estimate of discrimination, a flaw common to all studies of labor market discrimination using this technique.

Results of Discrimination Studies

With this in mind, note that the studies consider two groups of men with disabilities: men with impairments subject to more prejudice (MP), as measured by rankings of negative attitudes toward persons with disabilities (Yuker 1987; Tringo 1970), and men with impairments subject to less prejudice (LP). Impairments that evoke more prejudice include, for example, mental illness, paralysis, and epilepsy, while impairments that evoke less prejudice include diabetes, back problems, and arthritis. Some impairments subject to less prejudice can be severely disabling (such as arthritis), while other impairments subject to relatively strong prejudice are only mildly disabling. Epilepsy, for example, evokes strong negative attitudes despite the fact that in most cases seizures are completely controlled by medication and functional limitations are minimal.

The results from both 1984 and 1990 suggest that productivity differentials associated with functional limitations are an important factor contributing to the low wages of men with disabilities (Baldwin and Johnson 1994a, 1996). In general, differences in functional limitations explain 20% to 30% of the disabled-nondisabled offer wage differential. Among workers subject to more prejudice, other factors (education and occupation) also contribute to the explained part of the wage differential. Among workers subject to less prejudice, the negative sign on the component explained by other factors implies that workers with disabilities would, in the absence of discrimination, earn more than nondisabled workers, primarily because the disabled group has more work experience.

The results show that for both LP and MP groups a large part of the disabled-nondisabled offer wage differential remains unexplained. The unexplained component is larger for LP men in percentage terms but larger for MP men in absolute terms. Although the unexplained component must be viewed as an upper bound estimate of employer discrimination against men with disabilities, the results suggest that men with disabilities are subject to discrimination in the labor market and that discrimination is greater against the group subject to more prejudice.

There are too few working women with disabilities in the SIPP samples to provide separate analyses for MP and LP groups. Results from the 1984 study comparing all women with disabilities to nondisabled women show that differences in functional limitations explain a smaller part (6%) of the disabled-nondisabled offer wage differential for women than for men (Baldwin and Johnson 1995). Employment rates for women with disabilities are, however, considerably lower than employment rates for men with disabilities (13% of disabled women are employed full-time compared to 23% of disabled men—Figure 3), suggesting that only the least limited women with disabilities are employed. Differences in other productivity-related characteristics, namely education, occupational distributions and part-time employment, explain about one-third of the offer wage differential for women. The unexplained component, 56%, is attributed to discrimination and residual effects.

Statistical Discrimination

There is another possible explanation for the wage differentials between disabled and nondisabled workers in addition to the two extreme positions we have defined (discrimination based on prejudice and productivity differentials resulting from functional limitations). When employers do not have sufficient information to assess the productivity of job applicants accurately, they may use the attributes of a group, defined by race, sex, or the presence of an impairment, as a proxy for information on the productivity of individual workers within the group (Phelps 1972). This so-called statistical discrimination may be particularly important for workers with disabilities because the small size and heterogeneous nature of the disabled population suggest that employers will lack experience hiring from this group (Johnson 1986).

We are not aware of studies that test the hypothesis of statistical discrimination against workers with disabilities. However, in a study of the correlations between unexplained wage differentials and rankings of health conditions by severity of prejudice, we discovered the strongest correlations between wage differentials and employers' rankings of the employability of persons with particular health conditions (Baldwin and Johnson 1994b). This suggests that improving employer information on the productivity of workers with disabilities may be as important a policy goal as the enforcement of antidiscrimination laws.

Implications for Disability Policy

There are at least two groups within the population of persons with work disabilities that differ from one another in the problems they encounter in the labor market, the social costs associated with those problems, and the policies that may be required to overcome or compensate for disadvantages in the labor market.

The smaller group includes persons with illnesses or injuries that occur at birth or early in life. Mental or emotional conditions, sensory, and mobility limitations are characteristic of this group. It is also the group likely to face the most severe prejudice and discrimination in the labor market. The individual costs of work disability for members of this group are higher than for other groups of workers with disabilities, but aggregate costs are relatively low because of low prevalence rates.

The larger group is composed of persons for whom the onset of a disabling illness or injury typically occurs in middle age. Characteristic conditions for this group include arthritis, cardiovascular disease, and a variety of musculoskeletal conditions, including back pain. It is among workers in this group that differences in age, experience, skills, and economic incentives have the strongest influence on employment rates and wages. Individual costs of work disability vary with the severity of the underlying conditions but are small relative to the group of more severely disabled persons who compose our first group. Aggregate costs are relatively high, however, because prevalence rates are high.

The research summarized in this article suggests that public policies designed to increase the employment rates and relative earnings of workers with disabilities should differ across the two groups according to the particular problems they encounter in the labor market. Those disabled as children are likely to be best served by enforcement of anti-discrimination policies to counteract the stigma associated with their impairments and to improve their access to quality education and entry-level jobs. Those disabled as adults need policies designed to protect their rights to return to work, ensure appropriate job accommodations, and maintain adequate incomes during periods of work absence.

The distinctions between the two groups are essential to understanding the nature of work disability. Simplistic portrayals of the problem of work disability as totally caused by discrimination obscure the problems of the large number of workers for whom discrimination is not the most serious problem, instead of tailoring policy to fit the different needs of the groups that make up the population of persons with work disabilities. The distinctions between the two groups also predict that the aging of the "baby boomers" will create an enormous increase in the size of the population of persons with work disabilities.

The portrait of work disability cannot be painted as a single picture. It is, instead, a panel of pictures representing distinct groups that differ in the nature of disabling conditions, the magnitude of the costs associated with those conditions, and the extent to which labor market discrimination is an obstacle to economic independence.

Endnotes

[1] Our definitions combine concepts from Nagi (1969) and the World Health Organization (WHO 1980).

[2] The information presented in this section comes from a GAO (1993) report on eligibility for vocational rehabilitation services but was originally presented in two separate reports (LaPlante 1988; HHS 1989).

[3] The SIPP, administered by the Census Bureau, is a longitudinal survey designed to collect information on respondents' amounts and sources of income and participation in various cash and noncash benefit programs. The 1984 panel consists of nine interviews with a sample of approximately 56,000 persons. The questions on disability were included in a supplemental survey administered during the third interview.

The NHIS is administered by the National Center for Health Statistics and collects data on health and disability from a continuous weekly sampling of the target population. The data reported here are based on interviews with approximately 105,000 persons in each of the years 1983 and 1984 and 92,000 persons in 1985.

[4] The specific questions from the SIPP are "Does your health or condition limit the kind or amount of work you can do? Does your health or condition prevent you from working at a job or business?" On the NHIS the corresponding questions are "Are you limited in the kind or amount of work you can do because of any impairment or health problem? Does any impairment or health problem keep you from working at a job or business?" Persons who respond affirmatively are asked to identify the health condition that is the cause of their limitation.

[5] These surveys are the best single source of information on disabling conditions, but they do not distinguish between permanent and temporary disabilities. Thus the estimates from any one year are a mix of temporary and permanent conditions.

[6] The costs include lost wages and productivity ($63 billion), medical costs ($22 billion), administrative costs ($15 billion), and costs to the employer such as time lost by other workers or time to investigate the accident ($10 billion), damage to motor vehicles ($3 billion), and fire losses ($3 billion) (NSC 1993).

[7] Because back pain affects eight out of ten Americans during their lifetimes, there is considerable uncertainty regarding the classification of back pain as an "injury" rather than the expression of a chronic degenerative disease process (Johnson, Baldwin, and Butler 1998).

[8] A person is considered disabled if he or she satisfies at least one of the following criteria: (1) identified by the questions, "Does anyone in this household have a health problem or disability which prevents them from working or which limits the kind or amount of work they can do?" or "Is there anyone in this household who ever retired or left a job for health reasons?"; (2) did not work in the survey week because of long-term illness or disability; (3) did not work in the survey year because of illness or disability; (4) is under 65 and covered by Medicare or SSDI (Bennefield and McNeil 1989).

[9] Some of the material in this section appears in Johnson (1997).

[10] With the exception of mental illness, incidence rates for the most prevalent disabling conditions—arthritis, cardiovascular disease, and chronic back pain—are relatively constant until middle age and increase sharply with age thereafter.

[11] This section is based on the summary presented in Johnson, Baldwin, and Butler (1995).

[12] The limitations variables are constructed from self-reported data indicating limits on endurance and strength; limits on carrying, climbing, and lifting; and limits on hearing, seeing, and speaking. Stern (1989) has shown that such self-reported data are reasonably accurate and exogenous measures of health.

[13] The data come from the 1984 and 1990 panels of the Survey of Income and Program Participation (SIPP). The SIPP includes detailed information on employment, wages and earnings sources, as well as information on functional limitations and health conditions.

[14] The difference in employer wage offers is estimated by correcting the log wage differential for sample selection bias, the bias that results because we cannot observe wage offers to nonworkers.

References

Baldwin, Marjorie L., and William G. Johnson. 1994a. "Labor Market Discrimination against Men with Disabilities." *Journal of Human Resources*, Vol. 29, no. 1 (Winter), pp. 1-19.

_____. 1994b. "The Sources of Employment Discrimination: Prejudice or Poor Information?" In David M. Saunders, ed., *New Approaches to Employee Management*, Vol. 2. Greenwich: JAI Press, pp. 163-80.

_____. 1995. "Labor Market Discrimination against Women with Disabilities." *Industrial Relations*, Vol. 34, no. 4 (October), pp. 555-77.

_____. 1996. "Labor Market Discrimination against Men with Disabilities in the Year of the ADA." Unpublished paper, East Carolina University.

Bennefield, Robert L., and John M. McNeil. 1989. *Labor Force Status and Other Characteristics of Persons with a Work Disability: 1981 to 1988.* Current Population Reports, Special Studies, Series P-23, No. 160. Washington, DC: U.S. Department of Commerce, Bureau of the Census.

Biklen, Douglas. 1987. "The Culture of Policy: Disability Images and Their Analogues in Public Policy." *Policy Studies Journal*, Vol. 15, no. 3 (March), pp. 515-36.

Burkhauser, Richard V., J. S. Butler, and Yang Woo Kim. 1995. "The Importance of Employer Accommodation on the Job Duration of Workers with Disabilities: A Hazard Model Approach." *Labor Economics*, Vol. 3, no. 1 (June), pp. 109-30.

Burkhauser, Richard V., and Mary C. Daly. 1996. "Employment and Economic Well-Being Following the Onset of a Disability." In Jerry L. Mashaw, et al., eds., *Disability, Work and Cash Benefits.* Kalamazoo, MI: W.E. Upjohn Institute, pp. 59-101.

Butler, Richard J., William G. Johnson, and Marjorie L. Baldwin. 1995. "Managing Work Disability: Why First Return to Work Is Not a Measure of Success." *Industrial and Labor Relations Review*, Vol. 48, no. 3 (April), pp. 452-69.

Butler, Richard J., and John D. Worrall. 1985. "Work Injury Compensation and the Duration of Nonwork Spells." *Economic Journal*, Vol. 95, no. 379 (September), pp. 714-24.

Chirikos, Thomas, and Gilbert Nestel. 1984. "Economic Determinants and Consequences of Self-Reported Work Disability." *Journal of Health Economics*, Vol. 3, no. 2 (August), pp. 61-69.

Curington, William P. 1994. "Compensation for Permanent Impairment and the Duration of Work Absence: Evidence from Four Natural Experiments." *Journal of Human Resources*, Vol. 29, no. 3 (Summer), pp. 888-910.

Diamond, Peter A., and Jerry A. Hausman. 1984. "The Retirement and Unemployment Behavior of Older Men." In Henry Aaron and Gary Burtless, eds., *Retirement and Economic Behavior.* Washington, DC: The Brookings Institution, pp. 97-134.

EEOC. 1997. "Cumulative ADA Charge Data." Compiled by the Office of Program Operations from EEOC's Charge Data Systems National Data Base.

Fenn, Paul. 1981. "Sickness Duration, Residual Disability and Income Replacement: An Empirical Analysis." *Economic Journal*, Vol. 91, no. 361 (March), pp. 158-73.

GAO. 1993. *Vocational Rehabilitation: Evidence for Federal Program's Effectiveness Is Mixed.* (GAO/PEMD-93-19, August 27).

Gunderson, Morley, and Douglas Hyatt. 1996. "Do Injured Workers Pay for Reasonable Accommodation?" *Industrial and Labor Relations Review*, Vol. 50, no. 1 (October), pp. 92-104.

Hahn, Harlan. 1987. "Advertising the Acceptably Employable Image: Disability and Capitalism." *Policy Studies Journal*, Vol. 15, no. 3 (March), pp. 551-70.

HHS. 1989. *Task 1: Population Profiles of Disability*. Washington, DC: Assistant Secretary for Planning and Evaluation, Department of Health and Human Services.

Hyatt, Douglas E. 1996. "Work Disincentives of Workers' Compensation Permanent Partial Disability Benefits: Evidence for Canada." *Canadian Journal of Economics*, Vol. 29, no. 2 (May), pp. 289-308.

Johnson, William G. 1983. "The Disincentive Effects of Workers' Compensation Insurance." In John D. Worrall, ed., *Safety and the Work Force: Incentives and Disincentives in Workers' Compensation Insurance*. Ithaca, NY: Cornell University ILR Press, pp. 138-53.

_____. 1986. "The Rehabilitation Act and Discrimination against Handicapped Workers." In Monroe Berkowitz and M. Anne Hill, eds., *Disability and the Labor Market*. Ithaca, NY: Cornell University ILR Press, pp. 241-61.

_____. 1997. "The Future of Disability Policy: Benefit Payments or Civil Rights? The Americans with Disabilities Act: Social Contract of Special Privilege?" Special issue of *The Annals of the American Academy of Political and Social Science*, Vol. 549 (January 1997), pp. 160-72.

Johnson, William G., and James Lambrinos. 1985. "Wage Discrimination against Handicapped Men and Women." *Journal of Human Resources*, Vol. 20, no. 2 (Spring), pp. 264-77.

Johnson, William G., and Jan Ondrich. 1990. "The Duration of Post-Injury Absences from Work." *Review of Economics and Statistics*, Vol. 72, no. 4 (November), pp. 578-86.

Johnson, William G., Marjorie L. Baldwin, and Richard J. Butler. 1995. "First Spells of Work Absences among Ontario Workers." In Terry Thomason and Richard P. Chaykowsi, eds., *Research in Canadian Workers' Compensation*. Kingston, Ontario: Queens University IRC Press, pp. 72-84.

_____. 1998. "Back Pain and Work Disability: The Need for a New Paradigm." *Industrial Relations*, Vol. 37, no. 1, pp. 9-34.

Kaye, H. Stephen, Mitchell P. LaPlante, Dawn Carlson, and Barbara L. Wenger. 1996. "Trends in Disability Rates in the United States, 1970-1994." *Disability Statistics Abstract*, No. 17 (November).

LaPlante, Mitchell P. 1988. *Data on Disability from the National Health Interview Survey, 1983-1985*. Washington, DC: National Institute on Disability and Rehabilitation Research.

Nagi, Saad. 1969. *Disability and Rehabilitation: Legal, Clinical, and Self-Concepts and Measurement*. Columbus: Ohio State University Press.

NSC. 1993. *Accident Facts*. Itaska, IL: National Safety Council.

Oaxaca, Ronald L. 1973. "Male-Female Wage Differentials in Urban Labor Markets." *International Economic Review*, Vol. 14, no. 3 (October), pp. 693-709.

Piacentini, Joseph S., and Timothy J. Cerino. 1990. *EBRI Databook on Employee Benefits*. Washington, DC: Employee Benefit Research Institute.

Phelps, Edmund S. 1972. "The Statistical Theory of Racism and Sexism." *American Economic Review*, Vol. 62, no. 4 (September), pp. 659-61.

Reimers, Cordelia W. 1983. "Labor Market Discrimination against Hispanic and Black Men." *Review of Economics and Statistics*, Vol. 65, no. 4 (November), pp. 570-79.

Rousso, Harilyn. 1988. "Daughters with Disabilities: Defective Women or Minority Women?" In Michelle Fine and Adrienne Asch, eds., *Women with Disabilities*. Philadelphia: Temple University Press, pp. 139-71.

Stern, Steven. 1989. "Measuring the Effect of Disability on Labor Force Participation." *Journal of Human Resources*, Vol. 24, no. 3 (Summer), pp. 361-93.

Tringo, John L. 1970. "The Hierarchy of Preferences toward Disability Groups." *Journal of Special Education*, Vol. 4 (Summer/Fall), pp. 295-306.

U.S. Bureau of the Census. 1991. *Money Income of Households, Families, and Persons in the United States, 1990*. Series P-60, No. 174. Washington, DC: U.S. Government Printing Office.

Welch, Edward M. 1996. "Disability Trends: More Mental Disabilities." *On Workers' Compensation*, Vol. 6, no. 5 (June), p. 88.

West, Jane. 1994. *Federal Implementation of the Americans with Disabilities Act, 1991-94*. New York: Millbank Memorial Fund.

WHO. 1980. *International Classification of Impairments, Disabilities and Handicaps*. Geneva: World Health Organization.

Yelin, Edward H. 1992. *Disability and the Displaced Worker*. New Brunswick, NJ: Rutgers University Press.

Yuker, Harold E. 1987. "The Disability Hierarchies: Comparative Reactions to Various Types of Physical and Mental Disabilities." Unpublished paper, Hofstra University.

CHAPTER 3

Prevention of Disability from Work-related Sources: The Roles of Risk Management, Government Intervention, and Insurance

DAVID DURBIN
SwissRe of North America

RICHARD J. BUTLER
University of Minnesota

Since the late nineteenth century, most industrialized countries have developed a variety of social, legal, and market-based mechanisms for promoting and financing workplace safety. Among the more common are tort liability, no-fault insurance, government intervention, and use of the labor market, including the payment of compensating wage differentials for riskier employment. In addition, in the 1990s there is also a burgeoning market for various loss control, safety, and cost containment services offered directly by the marketplace.

Yet, as Burton and Chelius (1997) observe in a recent review of the underlying economic and legal theories justifying the various mechanisms, while there may be articulate (and sometimes passionate) views on the optimal mix of strategies to promote workplace safety, it has only been during the past twenty years that credible empirical evidence has emerged evaluating various safety strategies. While still evolving, the available research suggests that since the turn of the twentieth century, workplaces have gotten safer with many factors contributing to the improvement. In general, this research suggests that market-based approaches, notably the introduction of workers' compensation insurance, have had a larger impact on workplace safety than other strategies including most governmental intervention strategies. This includes the 1970 enactment of the landmark Occupational Safety and Health Act (OSHA).

Workplace Safety and Incentive Disconnect: Workplace Accident Data Do Not Always Reflect Safety Changes

For a variety of reasons related to (1) the structure of labor markets, (2) economic incentives facing employers and employees, (3) the availability and quality of empirically sound data, and (4) the specific types of governmental intervention, evaluating or designing the optimal mix of workplace safety strategies remains difficult. One of the largest fundamental issues facing those interested in workplace safety involves its measurement. On the surface this might not seem to be such a large problem. Certainly, information is available from various government agencies at both the state and federal level on the number and costs of workplace accidents. In addition, workers' compensation insurance premium and cost information are also available.

It is widely known, for example, that over the past few decades there has been a general escalation in the costs of workplace accidents. Since 1960, the costs of workers' compensation insurance—the major financial vehicle through which employers fund the costs of industrial accidents—have increased from .93% of payroll to approximately 2.5% of payroll in 1994. Consistent with this cost growth, both the frequency and severity of injuries compensated through the workers' compensation system have also increased. Since 1980, claim frequency has increased 25.4%, while claim severity has increased almost 150% for indemnity (wage replacement) costs and 350% for medical costs.[1]

However, underlying these numbers is an incentive disconnect between employers and workers that in some ways contaminates their use as measures of workplace safety. The problem is that workers' compensation costs and workplace accident data typically reported by the Bureau of Labor Statistics reflect both intrinsic workplace safety and the financial incentives to report claims generated by the existence of workers' compensation benefits and the availability of insurance coverage. These financial incentives create an "incentive disconnect" that makes workers' compensation costs and accident data unreliable measures of workplace safety.

Our goal in this chapter is to identify and discuss some of the inherent difficulties in measuring workplace safety, especially in the context of the incentive disconnect. This discussion will be guided by the currently available research with reference to the underlying economic theories. Based on two new sets of data, we will offer new tests of factors affecting workplace safety. The empirical work concentrates on refining estimates of the true safety effects of workers' compensation insurance versus possible contributions of government intervention. We will also offer some observations about the long-run improvement in workplace safety.

Conceptual Framework: Incentives and Moral Hazard

A number of researchers (among which are Butler, Hartwig, and Gardner 1997; Durbin 1992; and Krueger 1990) have investigated how behavior changes in the face of insurance benefits. To summarize the relevant workplace safety research, from the individual worker's perspective there are three important behavioral predictions. First, the safety efforts of individual workers are a decreasing function of expected workers' compensation benefits: as benefits increase workers will pay less attention to safety.[2] Second, since higher benefits decrease safety effort and less safety effort increases the risk of injury, higher benefits increase injury risk. Finally, the probability of injury is a decreasing function of wages: as wages increase the probability of an injury decreases.

A number of researchers have observed that the intuition behind the economic models relates to opportunity costs. As benefits increase, all else the same, the cost to being disabled decreases (the loss from not pursuing safety diminishes), and both the probability of injury and participation in the workers' compensation program increases because of moral hazard responses. Stated differently, the existence of workers' compensation benefits may induce risk-taking behavior which may give rise to additional injuries: Workers who know they are "covered" may actually have more injuries. This has been called "risk-bearing" moral hazard by Butler and Worrall (1991).[3] "Risk-bearing" moral hazard may be operative for employers as well, especially those who self insure or who are experience rated (to be discussed below). However, the incentives that employers face as benefits increase are opposite those of employees: Since insurance shifts some of the costs of injuries to firms,[4] insured firms will have more incentives to decrease injury risk in the workplace.

A second way that insurance benefits change behavior is through reporting effects. Workers may claim that a condition arose from a job injury when it may not qualify for disability benefits or where an employer may not provide health benefits. Workers may also file a workplace injury claim to gain the indemnity or lost wage benefits in response to changing economic conditions, if, for example, they fear immediate job layoff[5] (Hartwig et al. 1996). These behaviors are fundamentally different from the ex ante risk-bearing changes discussed in the previous paragraphs as they represent changes in the propensity to report a claim, holding risk levels constant. Such changes in reporting behavior, induced by changes in insurance coverage, are known as "claims-reporting" moral hazard. As in the "risk-bearing" model above, the key incentive response in claims-reporting moral hazard is that higher insurance benefits lowers the opportunity cost of filing a claim.

Additional claim filing by employees is just one avenue through which claims-reporting moral hazard works. Claims-reporting moral hazard also increases observed claim severity where workers extend claim duration when benefits are higher. Managers or employers may also choose to channel a management or productivity problem into the workers' compensation system (Butler and Gardner 1994). These all represent types of "claims-reporting" moral hazard.

Moral hazard does not relate to ethics per se; rather, it relates to problems that arise when information asymmetries are used for personal gain. More precisely, in the present context, moral hazard refers to the extra costs incurred due to the increased use of the disability system by an individual. These additional costs are indirectly borne by all other workers and employers through higher costs for health and insurance benefits and offsetting reductions in wages and profitability.[6]

The extant social science literature is quite convincing that workers in particular respond to the economic incentives provided by the cash or indemnity benefits. The empirical research exploits (at least until the early 1990s) the secular increase in indemnity benefits which occurred since the early 1970s, in part as a result of the recommendations of the National Commission on State Workers' Compensation Laws. Without moral hazard, changes in indemnity benefits should not cause systematic change in claims. Instead, what has been observed is that both claim frequency (as measured on a per capita or per dollar of payroll basis) and severity (duration of disability) increase as benefits increase. The evidence indicates that claim frequency rises from 3% to 8% every time there is a 10% increase in the real level of benefits.

Taken together, the available research suggests that there may be a divergence between reported workers' compensation costs and the intrinsic level of safety whenever claims-reporting moral hazard is important. This possibility is examined in Table 1, where workers' compensation costs and several safety indices are charted over time. Safety indices include real workplace fatality rates per 100,000 employees (from the National Safety Council) and non-lost work time OSHA-reported injuries (BLS). Fatalities are a good measure of safety since they are readily measured and difficult to disregard or fake. Non-lost workday injury rates, while imperfect, also provide information on safety since they are not as susceptible to disability pay incentives which affect claims with lost workdays (and are subject to moral hazard behavior induced by disability pay and workers' compensation benefits).[7]

If claims-reporting moral hazard dominates in this data, then it could be the case that workers' compensation costs will increase even as workplace safety increases. Claims-reporting moral hazard would cause the "incentive disconnect" between safety and workers' compensation costs. Indeed, it appears that the incentive disconnect is operative over the period indicated in Table 1. Workers' compensation costs, given in the left-hand column, increase throughout the period even though the "safety proxies" in the right hand columns are improving. While workers' compensation costs have shown a steady increase (more than doubling over the time period), fatal injuries have dropped throughout the period, falling by more than 50% for mining, construction, manufacturing, and the service sector, and falling by at least a third in the other sectors. Non-lost workday injury rates also generally decline throughout the period, although injury rates for agricultural, trade, and service sectors have been relatively flat throughout the period. It is likely that the agricultural, trade, and service sectors show the smallest decline since they are disproportionately populated with smaller firms and are less likely to be experience rated under workers' compensation. This reduces employers' incentives to provide workplace safety, as discussed below.

Changes in statutory benefits cannot fully account for the cost increase in workers' compensation,[8] and since the real intrinsic safety environment in every industry seems to be getting no worse, the workers' compensation cost increases would appear to result from moral hazard reporting responses.

Consequently, in order to be informative, measurement of workplace safety must somehow deal with the potential confounding influence of claims-reporting moral hazard responses.[9] There are a number of institutional features of the workers' compensation insurance pricing model that may be examined to disentangle these conflicting responses. "Manual rating," "experience rating," and partial insurance "deductibles" are three workers' compensation insurance mechanisms designed to promote workplace safety and, hence, prevent occupational injuries. The next section reviews how these mechanisms promote safety and discusses how empirical estimates of their effects have dealt with the confounding influence of claims-reporting moral hazard.

TABLE 1

Workers' Compensation Costs vs. Safety Trends

year	WC	Work injury deaths per 100,000 workers							Non-lost work day injury rates per 100 employees						
		ag	min	cons	man	tran	trd	ser	ag	min	cons	man	tran	trd	serv
1975	.83	58	63	61	8	33	6	9	6.0	5.4	10.4	8.5	4.7	4.7	3.5
1976	.87	54	63	57	9	31	6	9	6.3	5.1	9.8	8.3	4.8	4.6	3.3
1977	.92	51	63	47	9	32	6	8	6.3	4.9	9.6	8.0	4.3	4.8	3.3
1978	.94	52	56	48	9	29	7	7	6.2	5.0	9.6	7.6	4.3	4.7	3.1
1979	1.01	54	56	46	8	30	6	8	5.9	4.6	9.3	7.4	4.1	4.6	3.0
1980	1.07	56	50	45	8	30	6	7	6.1	4.6	9.1	6.8	3.8	4.2	2.9
1981	1.08	54	55	42	7	31	5	7	6.3	5.3	8.8	6.4	3.7	4.1	2.6
1982	1.16	52	50	40	6	28	6	7	5.9	5.0	8.6	5.8	3.6	4.1	2.6
1983	1.17	52	50	39	6	28	5	7	5.8	3.9	8.5	5.7	3.5	4.1	2.7
1984	1.21	49	50	39	6	29	5	7	5.9	4.3	8.6	5.9	3.6	4.2	2.7
1985	1.30	41	40	40	6	27	5	6	5.6	3.6	8.4	5.8	3.6	4.2	2.8
1986	1.37	55	38	37	5	29	4	5	5.6	3.2	8.3	5.9	3.4	4.3	2.7
1987	1.43	53	38	33	5	26	5	6	5.5	3.6	7.9	6.7	3.5	4.3	2.8
1988	1.49	48	38	34	6	26	4	5	5.2	3.6	7.7	7.3	3.8	4.3	2.8
1989	1.58	42	43	32	5	25	4	5	5.2	3.7	7.5	7.3	3.9	4.4	2.8
1990	1.66	42	43	33	4	20	3	4	5.7	3.3	7.5	7.3	4.0	4.4	3.2
1991	1.79	37	43	31	4	22	4	4	5.3	2.8	6.9	7.1	3.9	4.1	3.3
1992	1.82	31	29	24	4	23	4	3	6.2	3.3	7.3	7.1	4.0	4.9	4.2
1993	1.68	35	33	22	4	20	4	3	6.2	2.9	6.7	6.8	4.1	4.7	3.9
% change 1993-1975	102.4	-39.7	-47.6	-63.9	-50.0	-39.4	-33.3	-66.7	3.3	-46.3	-35.6	-20.0	-12.7	0	11.4

Note: WC = benefits paid as a percent of covered payroll (from *Social Security Bulletin, Annual Statistical Supplement*). The column headings indicate 1-digit SIC industries: ag = agricultural, min = mining, cons = construction, man = durable and nondurable manufacturing, tran = transportation, trd = retail and wholesale trade, and ser = services. Other data come from various issues of *Accident Facts* (National Safety Council).

Market-based Safety Mechanisms: Manual Rating, Experience Rating, and Deductibles

While experience rating has been viewed as the principal means through which safety incentives are provided in workers' compensation insurance, even in its absence, safety in the aggregate may be affected by the "manual" or baseline rates set for each individual industry group. Manual rates are set for each industry category to be actuarially fair in the sense that the rates are self-financing. The manual-rating process ensures that the most dangerous sectors, with the highest accident costs, also have higher labor costs. Since the cost of using labor is higher, there will be incentives both to reduce output and otherwise substitute away from the more expensive labor input. This should contribute to an *economywide* increase in safety as labor is reallocated from these more dangerous employers to less dangerous employers.

The use of risk categorization via the classification system has obvious policy implications. Specifically, questions regarding the optimal allocation of resources including the use and distribution of employment are of considerable interest in the global marketplace. However, tests of the "manual rating" effect in the United States have never been made. Using data from the Canadian province of Quebec, Lanoie (1992) proxied the manual-rate effect by looking at the number of risk classes per worker in a given industry. His idea was that the more risk classes, the greater this reallocation will be and the lower will be the resulting injury rates. His specification supports this finding at the 10% level of significance.[10]

As suggested above, experience rating is an important insurance pricing mechanism for promoting safety. Since experience rating ties a firm's benefit costs to its premiums, experience rating should induce firms to invest in safety in order to lower their insurance costs. A naive approach to estimating experience-rating impact would be to see whether claims fell (representing potential employer costs) as statutory benefit levels rose. This naive approach is fatally flawed because the "moral hazard" incentive disconnect, discussed above, ensures that workers' compensation claims will be a poor indicator of workplace safety. There have been a number of studies that have examined experience-rating effects in workers' compensation, many of which have tried to explicitly deal with the incentive disconnect. Besides manual rating and experience rating, there are several other pricing programs which may be employed to further adjust the final net cost to the workers' compensation insurance policyholder. Expense constants, premium discounts, and scheduled credits are ex ante programs which reflect either economies of scale for carriers in writing and servicing the insurance policy or special loss prevention programs/safety equipment the individual employer might use. Policy-holder dividends are typically ex post pricing adjustments that provide rebates for fewer than expected accidents and lower costs.

Partial insurance is currently used for both employees (through the use of the "waiting period" and wage replacement rates of two-thirds of wages subject to a maximum weekly benefit) and employers (through the use of newer, deductible insurance contracts). Generally, the available research suggests, as expected, that increases in the waiting and retroactive periods decrease the frequency of claims and total claim costs (average costs may actually increase since only the more serious injuries will qualify for benefits, see Butler [1994]).

Partial insurance arrangements are more complicated for permanent disability claims. Designing adequate and equitable benefits for workers with permanent injuries has probably been the single most vexing issue historically for workers' compensation. There are a number of differences in the design of permanent benefits across states.

Taken together, the design of workers' compensation benefit structures, while inconsistent across states, contemplates a variety of partial insurance arrangements. Some of these—such as benefit replacement rates that are less than one and longer waiting and retroactive periods—are designed to help reduce potential moral hazard problems.

The first two studies shown in Figure 1 (Russell 1974 and Harrington 1988) do not address the "moral hazard" response problem but simply try to make the link between firm size and safety incentives generated by experience rating. (A "+" indicates statistical evidence of an experience-rating effect, a "0" indicates no evidence.) Russell (1974) interprets lower injury rates among the largest firms as evidence of experience rating. Harrington (1988) finds that the actual to expected loss ratio falls as firm size increases, again consistent with an experience-rating effect. However, the theory about how firm size affects accident rates in the absence of workers' compensation is not well specified, so these findings may be indicative of effects other than experience rating. For example, these results are consistent with the hypothesis that there are economies of scale in the provision of safety, even in the absence of an experience-rating effect.

The most credible analyses of experience rating in workers' compensation have not used insurance claims or insurance costs as a measure of safety. They have taken one of three approaches to measuring the effect of experience rating: (1) they have looked at *benefit-firm size interactions*;

FIGURE 1
Prior Studies of the Impact of Experience Rating on Accident Rates

		Dependent Variables		
		BLS Accid.	Ins. Costs	A/E Losses
I n d e p e n d e n t	Size	Russell (74) -- +		Harrington (88) -- +
V a r I a b l e s	Size* Benefit	Chelius & Smith (83) -- **0** Ruser (85) -- + Ruser (91) -- + Ruser (90) -- +/**0**	Butler & Worrall (88) -- + Worrall & Butler (88) -- +/0 Butler, Appel, & Worrall (91) -- +	
	Natural "experiments"	Chelius & Smith (93) -- **0** Workers' Comp Board of Ontario (90) -- +/0 Moore & Viscusi (89) -- + Bruce & Atkins (93) -- +		

(2) they have relied upon *natural experiments*; or (3) they have employed *fatality rates to measure safety* and have examined how workers' compensation costs impacted fatality rates.

In the *"benefit-firm size" approach*, researchers have relied on some index of firm size to approximate the firms' financial incentives under workers' compensation. Since the premiums of the smallest, manually rated firms do not vary with their claims experience, they have no incentive to enhance safety as indemnity benefits rise. The premiums of larger firms that qualify for experience rating do vary with their claims experience; thus these firms have incentives to increase safety as indemnity benefits increase. Since the moral hazard effect is the same for workers in both large and small firms, the difference between the large- and the small-firm response to benefit increases should be a reflection of the effect of experience rating.

Chelius and Smith (1983) were the first to implement the approach that compares the relative benefit responses of large and small firms as a way of examining the effect of experience rating on safety incentives. They found no experience-rating effect. Unfortunately, some technical problems with the way they measured benefits cloud the interpretation of their results.[11]

More recent research uses slightly more sophisticated statistical techniques than the Chelius and Smith approach. Typically, some measure of injury rates or claims costs is evaluated as a function of expected benefits (to control moral hazard effects), firm size (to control for economies of scale in safety technology) and a benefit-firm size interaction to measure the Chelius/Smith effect. Using this approach, Ruser (1985, 1991, 1993); Butler and Worrall (1988); Worrall and Butler (1988); and Butler, Appel and Worrall (1991) all generally find statistically significant evidence of experience-rating effects.

Besides looking for "benefit-firm size" interaction effects to measure experience rating, researchers have looked for so-called "natural experiments" to analyze. Chelius and Smith (1993) and the Workers' Compensation Board of Ontario (1990) take this approach. Chelius and Smith (1993) note that small companies in Washington State are entitled to sizable premium discounts if they have no compensable claims during the first three of the last four years. They reason that if experience rating were effective, then claims rates for small firms in Washington State ought to be lower than claims rates in other states. They find just the opposite and conclude that there is no evidence of an experience-rating effect. However, they did not control for benefit effects in their specification.

The Workers' Compensation Board of Ontario (1990) examined the impact of the 1984 shift in Ontario from a strict manual-rating system to an experience-rated system for high accident industries. If experience rating were effective, then one would expect that injury rates would fall, holding severity constant, or severity would fall, holding the injury rate constant. If injury rates and severity both change, the experience-rating impact on measured severity is indeterminate since an effective experience-rating system may differentially reduce less serious or short-duration claims. This leaves a larger proportion of relatively long-termed claims in the resulting distribution, and average severity could rise even though experience rating is effective. The Workers' Compensation Board study (1990) finds that injury rates fall.

The effect of workers' compensation costs on workplace fatalities (as a better proxy for safety) has also been recently employed in a number of studies. Moore and Viscusi (1989) argue that fatality rates are a better proxy for safety in the workplace than insurance claims, since "reporting" type moral hazard problems are not likely to be significant. They find that higher workers' compensation benefits actually lower the death rate, suggesting that higher benefits may increase workplace safety.[12]

Bruce and Atkins (1993) test for experience-rating effects by combining the use of fatality rates with the "natural experiment" of the 1984 shift in Ontario from manual rating to experience rating in the construction and forestry industries. They note that "the construction industry fatality rate dropped from .72 to .32 over the 1951-89 period, while in the forestry industry it declined from 1.77 to .57 over the same period." During this same period, real benefits trended upwards. After controlling for baseline trends in fatalities as well as benefits and the shift to experience rating, Bruce and Atkins conclude that experience rating significantly reduced the number of fatal injuries. The death rate fell by 40% in forestry and by 20% in construction due to the shift to experience rating.

The possibility that higher indemnity benefits (greater costs of workers' compensation insurance) induce firms to increase safety is compatible with the finding that higher benefits also disproportionately increase workers' compensation costs, if moral hazard effects are large. If the workers' compensation system, either through "manual rating" effects or through "experience rating" effects, has had an impact on workplace safety, then we ought to have seen the real level of workplace safety improve as costs rose.

Legislative and Regulatory Safety Mechanisms

There is a small but growing literature investigating the efficacy of legislative solutions on promoting workplace safety (see Viscusi 1992, 1993; Burton and Chelius 1997). In particular, this research considers the impact of the establishment of the Occupational Safety and Health Administration (OSHA) and the effectiveness of a number of its strategies. These strategies typically take one of three forms: (1) direct intervention via guidelines and standards for use of safety equipment and hazardous materials, (2) policing/deterrent mechanisms through inspections and fines, and (3) educational programs. Very often existing research evaluates OSHA activities in cost/benefit terms. That is, specific standards/guidelines are evaluated in terms of the potential savings resulting from a reduction in accidents and illnesses versus the costs of compliance.

Measurement issues are again important. For reasons discussed above, traditional workplace safety measures are affected by the incentive disconnect. In addition, a full appraisal of the benefits associated with any standard should also consider the gains in productivity, morale, lower job turnover, and retraining costs associated with preventing an injury or illness. Measuring compliance costs, both in terms of physical capital and human capital, also presents challenges. By their very nature these costs and benefits are often difficult to measure. Further, government intervention and compliance with rules and regulations is often politically charged.

Labor market issues further complicate measurement of the net gain (losses) to society. It has long been observed (Smith 1937) that workers are at least partially compensated for risky and dangerous working conditions through higher wages. In a world of perfectly competitive labor markets where information on job risk is known with certainty by both workers and employers, and where there is complete freedom to contract over working conditions, workers will be indifferent whether working condition standards existed. If standards did not exist, they will be completely compensated for the extra risk through higher wages. Stated differently, workers would "pay" for extra safety resulting from OSHA interventions through lower wages.

While there is considerable evidence that compensating wage differentials exist (Viscusi 1993 and cites therein), the available research is ambiguous as to whether they fully compensate workers for the adverse conditions. Consequently, it appears that not only do workers pay for safety (and for that matter workers' compensation insurance) through lower wages, they may also pay through reduced employment. Firm profitability may similarly be adversely affected (Chelius and Burton 1994, Durbin 1993).

Taken together, the available research has not found consistent evidence that OSH legislation and regulation passes the cost/benefit tests; the evidence with respect to workplace safety is also inconclusive. These findings are particularly the case for OSH activities immediately preceding the 1970 OSHA enabling legislation.

A number of explanations (see Burton and Chelius 1997 for a more detailed discussion) have been offered for the apparent failure of OSH activities. These include the empirical observation that most workplace fatalities come from automobile accidents or violent activities that are unlikely to be greatly affected by inspections. Also a significant percentage of the workforce is self-employed and thus exempt from OSHA activities. Further, OSHA worksite inspections are pretty rare: the average establishment can expect to be inspected once every eighty-four years. Reviews of the literature by Burton and Chelius (1997), Kneisser and Leeth (1995, 1989) and Smith (1992) found that at best OSHA activities have had a modest impact on injury rates (from 2% to perhaps 15%), but that in many of the specific studies the results were statistically insignificant.

More recent research cited by Burton and Chelius (1997) finds some possible OSHA success stories for specific standards or firms with multiple inspections, but again the findings are statistically weak. Some observers have noted that part of the ineffectiveness of OSHA may be that the expected costs of a violation or infraction are so low rendering the economic incentives almost meaningless. Combined with the low inspection probability, the fines themselves are often not significant. As Kneisser and Leeth (1995) point out, in 1993 firms paid out more than $55 billion for workers' compensation premiums and $200 billion for compensating wage differentials. In contrast OSHA fines totaled approximately $160 million. Economic incentives are clearly larger for the market-based approaches to workplace safety.

Notwithstanding the lack of strong evidence that government-based approaches significantly improve workplace safety, many states continue to enact specific workplace safety legislation. States have also enacted a number of changes and reforms to the workers' compensation insurance programs. These have sought to tighten compensability conditions, eliminate or reduce inequities, promote quicker return to work, and reduce litigation. Table 2 lists some broad categories of reforms and the number of states enacting legislation in 1995 and 1996.

Currently, very little substantive research exists on the effectiveness of the specific reform components. Collectively, the available data suggest that premium and loss trends have declined across the board during

TABLE 2

Statutory Reforms in Workers' Compensation: 1995 and 1996

Topic	Number of States
Alcohol and Substance Abuse	10
Agency Studies	16
Attorney Fees	15
Benefits/Wage Calculations	34
Compensability	15
Coverage/Definition	33
Dispute Resolution/Appeals	23
Employee Leasing Companies/Limited Liability Companies/ Independent Contracts	24
Fraud	31
Liability/Litigation/Exclusive Remedy	18
Managed Care/Utilization Review/Case Management	18
Medical Issues	36
Occupational Disease	5
Policy Issues	14
Rates and Premium Issues/Rating Organizations	33
Report of Injuries	9
Residual Market	9
Return to Work	7
Safety	24
Second Injury Funds	12
Self-Insurance	25
State Funds	12
24-Hour Coverage	6
Uninsured Employers	9
Vocational Rehabilitation	6
Workers Compensation Administrative Issues	33
Miscellaneous	26

the 1990s in workers' compensation and that the decline has been more significant in states that have enacted statutory reforms. (See National Council on Compensation Insurance 1997.) Parsing out the effect of specific reforms from general business cycle and other inflationary effects is difficult especially since not enough time has passed post-reform in many states to provide meaningful data for analysis.

Experience Rating, Manual Rating, and OSHA: Effects in the Postwar U.S.

To measure changes in aggregate riskiness, we form an index of "risky employment" by multiplying the employment shares in each industry by the industry-specific 1990 death rates. As shown in Table 1, the relative differences in death rates across industries have remained mostly stable despite sharp secular declines in the death rates of all industries.[13]

As employment shares in the construction and transportation industries have fallen over time, so too has the numerical value of the risky employment index. As workers' compensation costs have risen, the value of the risky employment index and aggregate death rates have both fallen as can be seen in Figure 2. Workers' compensation costs, as a percent of payroll, have increased on average 2.3% per year over the whole period. At the same time, the risky employment index has declined .4% per year, while the overall workplace death rate declined at 2.7% per year.

While the trends in Figure 2 suggest a relationship between workers' compensation and safety, this graphical "proof" suffers from three shortcomings. First, the data are aggregated and potentially mask a myriad of changes at the firm and industry level. Second, they provide no quantitative indication of the relative importance of manual rating relative to experience-rating effects. Finally, other trends were also at work

FIGURE 2

Workers' Comp. Cost, Workplace Fatality Rates, and Risky Employment

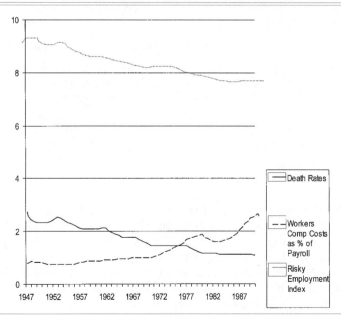

that ought to be considered in an analysis of workplace safety: business cycle and OSHA effects may have also played a major role in the reduction of job risk.

Given the questions that we are addressing and the problems inherent with insurance claims data (as a measure of safety), aggregate workplace death rates are the best available information metric for this analysis.[14]

Fatality Rate Analyses: Countrywide Experience, 1947-90, and Individual State Experience, 1983-92

In order to disentangle the effects of the other forces at work that potentially affect workplace safety, we performed two sets of statistical analyses. The results are summarized below in Table 3.[15] Panel A contains the results from models investigating the national trends in fatality rates (as shown in Figure 2). Panel B contains the results from individual state data from 1983 to 1992.

TABLE 3

A. COUNTRYWIDE WORKPLACE FATALITY ANALYSIS: 1947-1990
Percentage Response in Death Rate to 10% Increase In Workers' Compensation Costs and Enactment of OSHA

Experience Rating Effect	12.3%° decrease
Manual Rating Effect	.6%° decrease
Total Insurance Effect	12.9%° decrease
OSHA Effect	.6% increase

B. INDIVIDUAL STATE WORKPLACE FATALITY ANALYSIS: 1983-1992
Percentage Response in Death Rate to Introduction of
Deductible Programs and Changes to Experience Rating

Small Deductible	3.2% decrease
Large Deductible	10.0%°°decrease
Change in Experience Rating	16.9%° decrease

° significant at .05
°° significant at .10

For the countrywide analysis we sought to explore the relative impacts of increases in workers' compensation costs through manual rating and experience rating on fatalities. The models also considered general economic and business cycle factors including unemployment rates and the proportion of employment in risky industries. An OSHA variable was also introduced. This variable measures the impact of the enactment of the OSHA legislation on fatality rates.

Although not shown, our analysis confirms the finding of earlier research (Smith 1992 and Chelius 1977) that death rates seem to be procyclical. As business activity increases, many new workers are added to the payroll. These inexperienced workers are more likely to be seriously injured on the job. Hence, as the unemployment rate drops and new hires are added, injuries—including fatalities—rise. In general, a 10% increase in the unemployment rate leads to about a .5% decrease in the death rate.

In terms of examining the relative impact of market-based versus government interventions, our analysis suggests that market-based activities in the form of workers' compensation insurance pricing effects have a much greater effect on workplace safety. Indeed, in total, a 10% increase in workers' compensation costs implies a 12.9% decrease in fatalities as employers seek to invest in safety to reduce their insurance liabilities. The majority of this decline is through experience rating: 12.3% of this effect is attributable to this pricing program.

Similar to previous research, and as seen in Figure 2, there is no appreciable statistically significant OSHA effect. In fact, the analysis indicates that OSHA may perversely increase death rates, but again this result is not materially different from zero. Since death rates actually fell by 124% during the 1947-90 period (as measured by log differences), the analysis suggests that the direct, experience-rating effect accounts for one-quarter of the reduction in death rates.[16]

It is important to note that the aggregate measure of workers' compensation costs may not capture secular trends in interindustry manual rates, and the impact of the manual-rating effect on safety may be significantly understated.[17] Even so, the estimated overall impact of the workers' compensation system—mostly through the estimated experience-rating effect—is substantial.

As another test of the safety effects of workers' compensation insurance, individual state fatality data were compiled from 1983-92. During this period there were a number of changes to the workers' compensation pricing model discussed earlier. First and most significantly, in the early 1990s states began to permit employers to use deductible programs for their workers' compensation insurance. While there are differences across states in the permissible deductible parameters (in terms of whether per claim or per occurrence deductibles and the dollar amounts), there are generally two different deductible programs per state: small and large programs.

Small deductible programs are typically with specific dollar limits for each claim. Most states allow small deductibles of $100 per claim increasing up to as much as $2,500 and cover both the medical and indemnity components of workers' compensation claim costs. A few states (e.g., Florida, Indiana, Texas) also allow coinsurance up to a specific loss limit. Large deductible programs may be on a per claim or per policy basis. In many states they are only permitted if the total policy premium exceeds a certain, generally large (greater than $100,000 or $500,000) amount.[18] Although information is sparse, evidence compiled by the insurance industry is that there has been tremendous growth in the use of the deductible programs. Since their inception in 1989, deductibles are estimated to have grown from $800 million in 1990, to $8.8 billion in 1995 (National Council on Compensation Insurance, 1996 Annual Issues Report).

In addition to the allowance of deductibles, there have been modifications to the experience-rating formulas used by the states—specifically, threshold levels for inclusion in the experience-rating program change, sometimes yearly. In a number of states, there has been a push to lower the experience-rating thresholds to allow more employers to participate in the program. Other states have allowed the threshold levels to trend upwards in nominal terms to keep constant the proportion of employers that qualify for experience rating.

Use of deductibles and reductions in experience-rating thresholds give employers a more direct financial incentive to control compensation costs. Everything else the same, including benefits and industrial mix, these programs should provide additional safety incentives to employers without affecting worker incentives. To test this hypothesis, by-state fatality rates were regressed against controls for the small and large deductible programs and changes in the experience-rating thresholds.

The models perform pretty much as expected; results are presented in Panel B of Table 3.[19] The introduction of deductible programs appear to have contributed to declines in fatality rates: small (large) deductible programs reduce fatalities by 3.2% (10%). Although it should be noted that the small deductible program effect was not statistically significant.

The estimated experience-rating effect is strongly significant, and as expected, the effect of a decline in the threshold decreases fatalities. As more firms qualify for experience rating and thus have more direct incentives to control costs, fatalities should decline. Our analysis suggests that these changes have reduced fatalities by 16.9%.

Asymmetrical information and moral hazard responses in workers' compensation pose significant challenges to analysts and policymakers seeking to reduce the magnitude and costs of workplace accidents while providing adequate and equitable benefits to those workers who suffer injuries. A look back at the history of workers' compensation suggests a social insurance program that periodically undergoes a series of reforms. In the 1970s and 1980s, mostly in response to the work and recommendations of the National Commission on State Workers' Compensation Laws, benefit levels increased substantially. Not surprisingly, workers' compensation costs also increased. However, costs and use of the system increased disproportionately to the benefit increases driven by the moral hazard responses of employees. The research suggests that employee moral hazard responses dominated incentives by firms to invest more in safety.

Yet it is also clear that the "true" level of workplace safety may have actually increased. We believe that this, at least in part, is due to the pricing incentives built into the workers' compensation system. Policymakers have grappled with the problems of optimal benefit and financial structures in the presence of moral hazard since the inception of the first workers' compensation program. Many of these programmatic features were developed in the context of trying to define adequate and equitable benefits, while at the same time internalizing the costs of workplace accidents to employers. The aim of insurance pricing is to incorporate the appropriate safety incentives without significant subsidization across firms. The objective was to build a pricing model in which a firm's premiums reflect its own accident costs. Specific mechanisms designed to encourage optimal safety behavior in the presence of imperfect information and moral hazard include (a) partial insurance ("deductibles"), (b) government regulation (such as OSHA), (c) risk categorization, and (d) experience rating. The empirical analysis presented here suggests that a 10% increase in workers' compensation costs may reduce fatality rates by 4.1% to 15.4% and that changes in the workers' compensation pricing model, particularly the use of deductibles and changes to experience rating, have also had beneficial effects.

As is perhaps predictable, the pendulum may have swung the other way in workers' compensation at least in terms of legislative reforms. Since 1990 many states have enacted legislation restricting compensability and, in some cases, compensation levels for workplace injuries. While the ultimate effects remain unknown, it is clear that for the first time in more than twenty years workers' compensation costs are stabilizing, and in many states premium levels have fallen in nominal and real terms during 1994-96.

However, it is important to note that the extant empirical research and its moral hazard and safety implications draw on time periods of significantly increasing costs. As costs mitigate, future research will need to determine whether the moral hazard and safety responses are symmetric or whether different mechanisms/incentives will influence workers' compensation claim costs and outcomes.

Endnotes

[1] Growth in claim frequency and severity calculated from data provided by the National Council on Compensation Insurance, 1996 Annual Issues Report.

[2] This assumes that workers' compensation statutory benefits are exogenous to the individual worker.

[3] When work supervisors, health care practitioners, workers, etc., undertake activities that may affect a firm's insurance liability (and hence affect workers' compensation insurance cost data) because the firm cannot readily monitor their behavior, then there is "moral hazard" problem. There is ample evidence that moral hazard problems abound in workers' compensation and that these problems drive a wedge between the actual level of safety and claims costs.

[4] The amount of shifting depends in part on what happens to risk premia for injured workers: in a perfect information world, workers' wages may simply shift from ex ante compensation for risk to ex post compensation for injuries. That firms do respond to increased costs via experience rating is suggested by the research of Hyatt and Kralj (1995). That is, they find evidence that experience-rated employers respond to incentives to engage in claim control activities including appealing workers' compensation decisions.

[5] Workers' compensation benefits are generally not taxed and extend for a much longer (in some cases indefinite) duration than unemployment benefits.

[6] There is a considerable economics literature about the tradeoff, or compensating wage differential, between quasi-fixed labor costs such as health and workers' compensation benefits and wages (Smith 1992). To the extent that any compensating wage differentials may be imperfect, there may also be reductions in employment.

[7] In fact, there may be some bias in the non-lost days series to the extent that higher statutory weekly benefits increase the migration of claims from non-lost workday to lost day claims, the decline in non-lost day claims will be overstated during periods when real disability benefits are increasing.

[8] See Butler and Appel (1990) for a discussion of statutory benefit changes and their impact on expected workers' compensation costs.

[9] Risk-bearing moral hazard also increases workers' compensation costs but does so by changing the intrinsic level of risk by inducing changes in the risk-taking behavior of workers, rather than just the reporting of those changes. Where we estimate safety responses (such as through fatality rates) below, it will represent the net effects of changes in employer and employee behavior.

[10] He reports frequency and severity regressions separately. He finds that frequency is lowered, while severity increases. Measured severity appears to increase since the incidence of short-term claims falls more than the incidence of long-term

claims. This relative truncation of small claims leaves a disproportionate share of larger claims behind, so that average severity of the remaining claims increases. This apparent truncation is reflected in a frequency elasticity (-.06) that dominates the severity elasticity (.02): the overall impact is that an increase in the manual-rating classes is to decrease accident costs per employee.

Incidentally, Lanoie also finds significant positive benefit effects (the "incentive disconnect") for his Canadian sample, parallel to those estimated on U.S. data.

[11] On the one hand, their construction of expected benefits was relatively crude and did not fully integrate parameters of the workers' compensation system with the implied wage distribution that they used. This suggests that their benefits variable is measured with error, and their estimated benefits coefficient is biased towards zero. On the other hand, if injury rates are a linear function of benefits for both large and small firms and if expected benefits are identical for employees in both large and small firms (since employees of large firms tend to have higher wages than employees of small firms), then by an omitted variables bias argument it can be shown that the estimated benefits effect in Chelius-Smith equation 6.2 is biased in the opposite direction of the large firm benefit effect.

[12] As pointed out by both Boden (1994) and Smith (1992), the level of aggregation used for the fatality measure in the Moore and Viscusi study casts some doubt on the generality of their findings.

[13] This suggests that the use of 1990 as the "normalization" year for the index is inconsequential since changes in the risky employment index will be driven by changes in employment shares.

[14] As the appropriate micro-data becomes accessible, future research will be able to employ more disaggregated information and be able to make much cleaner tests of the hypotheses explored here.

[15] Additional details on the specific statistical techniques used and full model specifications are available from the authors upon request.

[16] Since agricultural has generally been excluded from workers' compensation until the most recent years, an additional test of the causality of the relationship between workers' compensation costs and safety can be made by examining death rates in agricultural. Unlike the trends presented in Figure 2, which show a steady post-World War II decline in all workplace death rates, agricultural death rates rose steadily until 1969 and then began to drop. So while the nonagricultural death rates are negatively correlated with workers' compensation costs as reflected in Figure 2, workplace agricultural death rates are not, except in recent years as more farm labor has been covered by the various state workers' compensation laws. Moreover, when we make workplace agricultural death rates the dependent variable, the estimated coefficients change considerably. In particular, in the difference specifications in columns 2 and 4, the estimated workers' compensation elasticities (and their associated absolute t-statistics) are -.102 (.47) and -.474 (1.06), respectively.

[17] To fully capture the dynamics of the manual-rating effect and cleanly separate it from industry shifts within and between states, we would need an extensive panel data set by state. Such an analysis will be pursued in the future, but is beyond the scope of this chapter.

[18] Available upon request, the authors have a listing of the small and large deductible program characteristics by state.

[19] The models also control for exogenous business cycle and other industrial mix issues unrelated to the deductible and experience-rating variables.

References

Accident Facts. 1991. Chicago: National Safety Council.

Baldwin, Marjorie, and William G. Johnson. 1990. "Ontario's New Experimental Experience Rating Plan," unpublished manuscript, Syracuse University.

Boden, Les. 1994. "Workers' Compensation in the United States: High Costs, Low Benefits," unpublished manuscript, Workers' Compensation Research Institute, Cambridge, MA.

Bruce, Christopher J., and Frank J. Atkins. 1993. "Efficiency Effects of Premium-setting Regimes under Workers' Compensation: Canada and the United States." *Journal of Labor Economics*, Vol. 11, no. 1, pt. 2, pp. S38-S69.

Burton, John F., and James Chelius. 1997. "Workplace Safety and Health Regulations: Rationale and Results." In Bruce E. Kaufman, ed., *Government Regulation of the Employment Relationship*. Madison, WI: Industrial Relations Research Association, pp. 253-93.

Butler, Richard J. 1994. "The Economic Determinants of Workers' Compensation Trends." *Journal of Risk and Insurance* (Sept.), pp. 1-19.

Butler, Richard J., and David Appel. 1990. "Benefit Increases in Workers' Compensation." *Southern Economic Journal*, Vol. 56, pp. 594-606.

Butler, Richard J., and Harold Gardner. 1994. "Worker Productivity Failure and Disability," unpublished manuscript, Industrial Relations Center, University of Minnesota.

Butler, Richard J., and John D. Worrall. 1988. "Labor Market Theory and the Distribution of Workers' Compensation Losses." In David Appel and Philip Borba, eds., *Workers' Compensation Insurance Pricing: Current Programs and Proposed Reforms*. Boston: Kluwer Academic Publishers.

_____. 1991. "Claims Reporting and Risk Bearing Moral Hazard in Workers' Compensation." *Journal of Risk and Insurance.* Vol. 53, pp. 191-204.

Butler, Richard J., David Appel, and John D. Worrall. 1991. "Firm Size and Financial Incentives in Workers' Compensation Insurance," unpublished manuscript.

Butler, Richard J., Robert Hartwig, and Harold Gardner. 1997. "HMOs, Moral Hazard, and Cost Shifting in Workers' Compensation." *Journal of Health Economics*, Vol. 16, no. 2 (April), pp. 191-206.

Chelius, James R. 1977. *Workplace Safety and Health*. Washington, DC: American Enterprise Institute.

_____. 1982. "The Influence of Workers' Compensation on Safety Incentives." *Industrial and Labor Relations Review*, Vol. 35, pp. 235-42.

Chelius, James R., and John F. Burton. 1994. "Who Actually Pays for Workers' Compensation?" In John F. Burton, Jr. and Timothy P. Schmidle, eds., *1995 Workers' Compensation Yearbook*. Horsham, PA: LRP Publications, pp. I-146-59.

Chelius, James R., and Robert S. Smith. 1983. "Experience Rating and Injury Prevention." In John D. Worrall, ed., *Safety and the Workforce*. Ithaca, NY: ILR Press.

_____. 1993. "The Impact of Experience Rating on Employer Behavior: The Case of Washington State." In David Durbin and Philip S. Borba, eds., *Workers' Compensation Insurance: Claim Costs, Prices and Regulation*. Boston: Kluwer Academic Publishers.

Durbin, David. 1991. "Alcohol Consumption and Workplace Accidents." Ph.D. dissertation, City University of New York.

_____. 1993. "Workers' Compensation: Business at Risk." *NCCI Digest*, Vol. 8, no. 1 (May), pp. 23-42.

Handbook of Labor Statistics. 1989. Washington, DC: Bureau of Labor Statistics.

Harrington, Scott E. 1988. "The Relationship between Standard Premium, Loss Ratios and Firm Size in Workers' Compensation Insurance." In David Appel and Philip Borba, eds., *Workers' Compensation Insurance Pricing: Current Programs and Proposed Reforms*. Boston: Kluwer Academic Publishers.

Hartwig, Robert P., Ronald Retterah, Tanya Restrepo, and William J. Kahley. 1996. "Workers' Compensation and Economic Cycles: A Longitudinal Approach." *Proceedings of the Casualty Actuarial Society*.

Hyatt, Douglas E., and Boris Kralj. 1995. "The Impact of Workers' Compensation Experience Rating on Employer Appeals Activity." *Industrial Relations*, Vol. 34, pp. 95-106.

Kniesner, Thomas J., and John D. Leeth. 1989. "Separating the Reporting Effects from the Injury Rate Effects of Workers' Compensation Insurance: A Hedonic Simulation." *Industrial and Labor Relations Review*, Vol. 42, pp. 280-93.

_____. 1995. *Simulating Workplace Safety Policy*. Boston, MA: Kluwer Academic Publishers.

Krueger, Alan B. 1990. "Incentive Effects of Workers' Compensation Insurance." *Journal of Public Economics*. Vol. 41 (February), pp. 73-99.

Lanoie, Paul. 1992. "The Impact of Occupational Safety and Health Regulation on the Risk of Workplace Accidents: Quebec, 1983-87." *Journal of Human Resources*, Vol. 27 (Fall), pp. 643-60.

Moore, Michael J., and W. Kip Viscusi. 1989. "Promoting Safety through Workers' Compensation: The Efficacy and Net Wage Costs of Injury Insurance." *Rand Journal of Economics*, Vol. 20 (Winter), pp. 499-515.

_____. 1990. *Compensation Mechanisms for Job Risks: Wages, Workers' Compensation, and Product Liability*. Princeton, NJ: Princeton University Press, Chapter 4.

National Council on Compensation Insurance. 1997. *1996 Annual Issues Report*. Boca Raton, FL: NCCI Publications.

_____. 1996. *1995 Annual Issues Report*. Boca Raton, FL: NCCI Publications.

Ruser, John W. 1985. "Workers' Compensation Insurance, Experience Rating, and Occupational Injuries." *Rand Journal of Economics*, Vol. 16, pp. 487-503.

_____. 1991. "Workers' Compensation and Occupational Injuries and Illnesses." *Journal of Labor Economics*, Vol. 9, no. 4, pp. 325-50.

_____. 1993. "Workers' Compensation and the Distribution of Occupational Injuries." *Journal of Human Resources*, Vol. 20, no. 3 (Summer), pp. 593-617.

Russell, Louise B. 1974. "Safety Incentives in Workmen's Compensation." *Journal of Human Resources*, Vol. 9, pp. 361-75.

Smith, Adam. 1937 [1776]. *The Wealth of Nations*. New York: Random House.

Smith, Robert S. 1992. "Have OSHA and Workers' Compensation Made the Workplace Safer?" *Research Frontiers in Industrial Relations and Human Resources.* Madison, WI: Industrial Relations Research Association, pp. 557-86.

Social Security Bulletin, Annual Statistical Supplement. 1993. Washington, DC: Social Security Administration.

Statistical Abstract of the United States. Various years. Washington, DC: Bureau of Statistics.

Victor, Richard B. 1983. "Experience Rating and Workplace Safety: The Nature of Employer Incentives." Santa Monica, CA: The Rand Corporation.

_____. 1985. "Experience Rating and Workplace Safety." In John D. Worrall and David Appel, eds., *Workers' Compensation Benefits: Adequacy, Equity and Efficiency.* Ithaca, NY: ILR Press.

Viscusi, W. Kip. 1992. *Fatal Tradeoffs: Public and Private Responsibilities for Risk.* New York: Oxford University Press.

_____. 1993. "The Value of Risks to Life and Health." *Journal of Economic Literature,"* Vol. 31, no. 4 (December), pp. 1912-46.

Workers' Compensation Board of Ontario. 1990. "New Experimental Experience Rating (NEER) Program Evaluation Study: Report of Research Findings and Discussion of Future Issues," unpublished manuscript, Workers' Compensation Board of Ontario.

Worrall, John D., and Richard J. Butler. 1988. "Experience Rating Matters." In David Appel and Philip Borba, eds., *Workers' Compensation Insurance Pricing: Current Programs and Proposed Reforms.* Boston: Kluwer Academic Publisher.

CHAPTER 4

The Prevention of Behavioral Disabilities from Nonwork Sources: Employee Assistance Programs and Related Strategies

PAUL M. ROMAN
University of Georgia

TERRY C. BLUM
Georgia Institute of Technology

In this chapter we examine how American workplaces use interventions to prevent disabilities associated with behavior disorders. We focus upon behavior disorders stemming from nonwork sources. We first review a number of conceptual issues that help define the empirical terrain. We then turn to a review of the historical evolution of employers' efforts to reduce disabilities associated with employees' behavior disorders. Considerable attention is given to the nature of the main intervention, employee assistance programs, and we review research and evaluative data about these programs. We then examine this kind of programming in union and other occupationally dominated work settings. Finally, attention turns to interventions that may be alternatives or complements in preventing workplace behavioral disabilities, and we close with some general observations.

Behavior Disorders and the Process of Medicalization

Behavior disorders have assumed a prominent place among publicly defined social problems of Western societies. Common across this broad category of phenomena is the inability to perform expected social roles, including sporadic and unpredictable role performances. In some instances, persons in these categories act aggressively toward others or harm themselves. These individuals' behavior generates organized social responses in families, communities, schools, and workplaces. The focus of this chapter is on work-based efforts to prevent these kinds of disabilities through mechanisms that are designed to preserve employment. For several reasons that are examined in this chapter, most of these behavior disorders are believed to originate outside the work environment.

Behavior disorders have existed in various forms since the beginning of recorded history. Persons with these patterns of aberrant behavior often were social outcasts, but in some eras they were recipients of community care, albeit custodial rather than remedial care (Rothman 1971). Through a series of relatively recent institutional processes, behavior disorders have come to be defined more or less as subcategories within emergent concepts of disability and disease. Notions of disability and functional disease (without an organic basis) in turn reflect significant symbolic and organizational transformations, collectively labeled "medicalization" (Conrad and Schneider 1980).

Medicalization is an ideology that involves the intended humane management of persons who repeatedly manifest various deviant behaviors; these behavior patterns are defined as illnesses rather than as sins, immoralities, or crimes. Ideally, persons with these patterns are identified and placed in treatment or rehabilitation settings where they are subject to interventions that are supposedly derived from scientific experiment and research, as opposed to moral beliefs or ideologies.

These interventions are administered by specialists who strive to identify themselves as professionals and as legitimate participants in the medical care delivery community (Abbott 1988). Interventions are geared toward behavior change, with outcome criteria typically emphasizing improved functioning, a diminution of the disordered behaviors, and improved health. While undergoing these treatments, persons with behavior disorders are temporarily relieved of social expectations as occupants of the "sick role" (Parsons 1951).

Concepts of Workplace Disabilities Associated with Behavior Disorders

Early identification of persons with behavior disorders is believed to facilitate "secondary prevention" (Caplan 1964), wherein behavioral changes and/or "successful" treatments allow them to return to normal functioning. In instances where identification is delayed, behavioral patterns may become irreversible (i.e., unresponsive to attempted interventions). Another possible consequence of late identification is that undesirable behavioral patterns will result in secondary physical or psychological impairments. These may preclude participation in the intervention and/or resumption of normal role functioning regardless of the motivation to participate.

These latter cases have been traditionally defined as "disabled," wherein individuals are allowed more or less permanent assignment to a "sick role" or are led to function in roles where expectations are specifically limited. Over the past decade, dramatic changes have occurred around the concept of disability, changes that have moved in what may be contradictory directions. On one hand, a series of legislative and symbolic efforts have been directed toward the normalization of disability, reflected in the "mainstreaming" of persons with disabilities into occupational and community life and into full social participation. These efforts, involving both physical and symbolic changes in the environment, are centered on de-stigmatization. They emphasize the abilities of the disabled to function fully in most social roles if opportunities are provided and barriers are removed.

A potentially contradictory theme is an expansion of the definition of disability to encompass more people. Perhaps this has a normalizing intent as well, as it increases the disabled population and thus theoretically reduces the social distance between disabled and nondisabled. This trend has been particularly marked in the arena of behavior disorders. Provisions in the Americans with Disabilities Act (ADA) mandate actions to assure full access to employment as well as other rights for those who have been diagnosed and treated for behavior disorders.

Contradiction of the first intent of normalization occurs when an expansion in the definition of disability concept is coupled with a highlighting of the disabled as a special minority group. This may call attention to claims for rights to full access and social accommodation. Such change may be interpreted as exceptional and preferential rather than "normal" and integrating. A range of complicated sociopolitical issues around notions of "preventing disability" is raised by these changes, some of which are discussed in this chapter.

There can be little doubt that persons with manifest disabilities associated with behavior disorders have been disadvantaged in employment on the basis of stigma and, in many cases, deliberately excluded from full participation in work organizations in the United States. To an extent, such exclusion is embedded in the historical concept and definition of disability, which itself may have been developed to serve as an exclusionary concept.

While American workplaces have historically tended to exclude from employment those with behavioral disabilities, many, if not most, employers have been concerned about impairments and disabilities related to behavior disorders among their employees. This concern may be split into two categories of behavioral disorders or disabilities: those that are alleged to result from the conditions of work and those that are the consequence of forces or factors outside the workplace.

This chapter focuses on the second category. However, behavior disorders caused by work-based factors are also interesting, since they are linked to the definition of disorders caused by factors external to work. Historically, workers' compensation protections and awards were limited to physical trauma and disabilities resulting from accidents and injuries. However, in the 1960s, modest attention was focused on psychiatric disabilities resulting from work, including the famed case of *Carter vs. General Motors* (Trice and Belasco 1966) in which an auto worker claimed that working conditions drove him to psychosis. Such claims for work-based etiology of behavior disorders may have been nascent from the 1960s to the 1990s (cf. Leedy 1971) when provisions of the ADA evidently stimulated large numbers of claims against employers for the consequences of work-induced stress.

Externalization of the Causes of Employees' Behavior Disorders

Aside from this very recent trend, most behavior disorders paradigms place their etiology well outside the work context. The ideology of medicalization has strongly supported the pursuit of biological causes for mental illness and substance abuse disorders. Symbolically, medicalization presses toward biomedical explanations (Roman 1988a). There are institutional supports as well. For example, through a set of political maneuvers within the scientific community, the three federal research institutes focused on behavior disorders (National Institutes of Mental Health, of Drug Abuse, and of Alcohol Abuse and Alcoholism) all became components of the National Institutes of Health in 1992. As a result, pressure for a biomedical orientation in etiological research has been increasingly driven and supported by organizational and legislative forces.

The alleged responsibility of the workplace for physical illness and injury has long been a battleground between employers and regulatory agencies (Pavalko 1989). Usually the central issue is the etiological role of workplace factors in employee illness, injury, or disability. Thus as might be expected, employers have solid reasons for supporting a biomedical orientation toward the etiology of behavior disorders rather than encouraging a focus on workplace processes as potential causal agents. Thus workplace experiences with issues of employer liability, coupled with sociocultural forces supporting the medicalization of behavior disorders, work together to encourage the idea that the etiology of behavior disorders lies outside the work environment.

However, there is a solid tradition of research linking employees' psychological well-being with working conditions, including a landmark study by Arthur Kornhauser (1965). Research in that general tradition has continued, with considerable involvement by sociologists and social psychologists. Many of these studies overlap with research concerns in organizational behavior about employees' satisfactions, commitments, and overall life happiness. This overlap and its linkage to general managerial concerns may have "defused" potential allegations that "work drives people crazy." At the same time, none of these studies has individually, or through replication, designated distinctive work-based factors in the etiology of psychiatric disorder, save for repeatedly clear up data about the adverse psychological impacts of unemployment (Dooley and Catalano 1988).

A smaller but again solid tradition of suggestive etiological work has also emerged linking work factors to substance abuse behaviors. (For examples, see Parker and Brody 1982; Martin, Roman, and Blum 1996; Greenberg and Grunberg 1994; Richman 1992; Wilsnack and Wilsnack 1992; Roman 1990; Seeman, Seeman, and Budros 1988.) When these studies have focused on the "spillover" effects of job conditions upon behavior off the job, a fairly robust association between work-based stress and problem drinking is found.

The Focus of Workplace Interventions: Disability Management

Despite attention that might be focused on employer responsibility for employee behavior disorders, the interests in workers' behavioral disability are largely centered on its amelioration rather than on changing the workplace to reduce the incidence of disability. Furthermore, employer interest in the primary prevention of behavioral disability is very likely focused on changing workers rather than changing the workplace environment or organization. Thus mechanisms such as stress management programs become solutions for stress-related problems as opposed to pursuit of the sources of stress.

It is important to note that the arena of concern in this chapter is not identical to the emerging paradigm of "disability management" (Smith 1997). Disability management has long-term roots in vocational rehabilitation and more recent roots in employer concerns about "risk management," in this instance controlling organizational losses associated with compensation for disabilities.

Of note is the marked degree of social distance between employee assistance programming, the primary mechanism directed toward workers with behavioral health problems, and vocational rehabilitation, with its concerns centered on the employment or reemployment of workers with a range of physical and mental disabilities. As discussed below, EAPs' origins derive almost entirely from interests in providing aid to employees with behavioral problems that emerge following employment.

But these activities may partially merge in the near future. The contemporary version of disability management does not appear to make a sharp demarcation around employees' behavior disorders but instead has a generic focus on disability (Smith 1997). Thus as this paradigm moves toward prevention and early identification, the potential for overlap with EAPs' programmatic designs appears considerable. While a necessarily equivocal observation, the apparent parallels between these two paradigms may represent the collision of two occupational groups with common worksite commitments but different socio-historical roots. At present, there is no clear evidence of "turf conflict" between the two groups. However, despite the potential for merged interests, it is also clear that there is real potential for confusion between these parallel missions when human resource managers are faced with resource allocation decisions.

The Logic of Secondary Prevention

Work-based interventions that address behavioral disabilities through secondary prevention have a more complex conceptual foundation than might initially appear. Definitions of many behavior disorders are relatively vague, and it is clear that moral judgments and other normative concepts can easily influence what appear to be "objective" diagnoses. Further, the boundary between normal and impaired, as well as between impaired and disabled, becomes increasingly vague as measures of symptoms and measures of role performance abilities intermingle. Finally, employers' reactions to these problems and subsequent investment in interventions may be heavily influenced by assumptions about the origins, course, and prognoses associated with particular behavioral problems.

It should be emphasized that the concept of disability and its prevention is not central to the logic that guides workplace interventions directed toward behavior disorders. Rather the focus is primarily upon (1) preserving the employment relationship by increasing the probability of adequate job performance and (2) reducing the probability of discipline or dismissal for inadequate performance. Outcomes where employees are unable to continue employment due to disability are generally viewed as failures in the operation of most of the interventions discussed in this chapter.

Socio-Historical Context of Employers' Attention to Behavior Disorders

To return to our primary focus, our operating definition of behavioral disability centers on psychiatric disorder or substance abuse that has the potential to follow a path of chronicity such that the employee is no longer able to do his or her job. Employers have obvious and strong practical interests in preventing employees from becoming behaviorally disabled (Blum and Roman 1989).

It is likely that unless these employees are identified, their job performance will decline and productivity will be reduced or lost. Further, it is likely that their behavior will disrupt the work of others. Supervisor efforts in managing these troubled individuals may be especially costly. Their use of expensive health care may escalate. Dismissal may not be a ready option, and even so, the employer must consider training and development investments as well as the obvious replacement costs. Finally, while it is difficult to produce hard evidence, many employers may have a moral commitment to prevent behavioral disabilities independent of economic considerations. By dealing with these problems as promptly as possible, multiple goals may be achieved.

The history of an organized interest by employers in behavior disorders is relatively recent. There are three somewhat distinct historical streams leading to employers' programming to prevent disabilities from psychiatric disorder and related issues, from alcoholism and from drug abuse.

Employers' attention to the broad and generic category of psychiatric disorder (and commonly associated "family problems") probably has its oldest roots in "welfare work" that spread throughout American workplaces in the late 19th and early 20th century (Brandes 1976). Before 1920, Metropolitan Life Insurance employed a "house mother" whose primary role was to aid in the work adjustment of women employees. In the 1930s, the R.H. Macy Company employed a psychiatrist for the express purpose of dealing with emotional problems among the department store's large workforce (Sonnenstuhl 1986).

Welfare capitalism generally faded during the 1920s, and there is little evidence that the concept of workplace psychiatry widely diffused from Macy's example. While industrial psychiatry became modestly ascendant in the 1940s and 1950s and is an identifiable, albeit somewhat obscure, specialty today, the development that most directly influences current employer efforts to prevent disability linked to behavior disorders was the emergence of the human relations paradigm.

This innovative set of concepts, developed in large part by Elton Mayo, drew attention to workers' behavior and attitudes beyond their immediately observed job performances. It highlighted the significance of social interaction in the workplace and drew attention to the socio-emotional dimensions of supervision (Landsberger 1958). When coupled with the widespread interpretation of the experimental data from the Hawthorne experiments, Mayo's notions set the stage for fundamental ideas about employees' potential maladjustments and their impact on work performance (Gillespie 1991). These led directly to the formation of the Counseling Department at Western Electric designed to reduce employees' personal problems, a program that persisted for several decades (Dickson and Roethlisberger 1966). Perhaps more important, emphasis on the importance of supervisory and peer relations at work helped set in motion models of human resource management that are dramatically influential in the American workplace today (Jacoby 1985). For the concerns of this discussion, the paradigm originating with Mayo and the interpretations of the Hawthorne data eventually elevated the importance of providing both attention and assistance to employees who bring psychological troubles to the job.

While in its original form the human relations paradigm emphasized work dynamics as the source of individual maladjustment, emerging models of assistance slowly turned away from this focus toward one that individualizes and externalizes the causes of employees' emotional disorders. Beginning in the 1930s, the strategy of the counseling program intervention in Western Electric made a subtle but distinct assumption that employees' troubles largely came from off-job sources. This idea in turn is supported by employers' experience with industrial welfare work, where attention (and sometimes coercion) centered on home, family, and personal adjustment was the model for producing the well-socialized, productive, and loyal employee.

Alcohol Abuse and Alcoholism

A small number of formally structured programs to rehabilitate alcoholic employees emerged in the 1940s and 1950s (Trice and Schonbrunn 1981). The DuPont Company's program of 1942 is typically regarded as the first formal program, but informal efforts at other companies extended back into the 1930s. Following the 1930s, slow but gradual changes in institutional responses to alcohol problem issues became evident. Discomfiture associated with cultural residue from the Temperance and Prohibition movements yielded to a new focus and definition of the nation's "alcohol problem." This change gained great impetus with the invention of Alcoholics Anonymous (AA), wherein a new focus on changing the alcoholic replaced that of changing the nation's drinking behavior. AA very quickly diffused as a successful recovery modality. While it took several decades, the preeminence of the AA model and its subsequent incorporation into medically based treatment essentially allowed the alcoholic to replace the drinker as the focal actor for efforts to deal with the "alcohol problem."

One of the fascinating ironies of the "folk" or "layperson's" strategy of AA is its reliance on what would seem to be the exclusive property of professionals, namely the medical model of alcoholism (Trice and Roman 1970). This attachment to a medicalized concept of alcoholism has been critical in creating AA's institutional legitimacy and was important for the diffusion of its methodology into the workplace. As should be evident, this model also externalizes the causes of employee alcoholism, typically regarding them as some form of individual biomedical abnormality related to alcohol's effects on the various organ systems of the body.

While one of AA's strong traditions precludes member involvement in political or promotional activities related to alcohol issues, a few AA members were able to politicize their new vision of alcoholism by banding together in 1943 to form the National Council on Alcoholism (NCA). This organization focuses its efforts on educating the public about the treatability of alcoholism. From its earliest days, NCA's activities included the promotion of the workplace as a setting for alcoholism rehabilitation (Presnall 1981; Trice and Schonbrunn 1981). This campaign enjoyed only modest success over the following decades, with perhaps twenty-five major companies adopting programs to identify and rehabilitate alcoholic employees.

But this diffusion apparently laid some important foundations. In addition to generating interest among some industrial executives, representatives of organized labor were mobilized into the activities of NCA at both the national and local level. There can be no doubt that labor's early efforts at some bargaining tables to provide coverage for alcoholism treatment created an impetus for efforts which were to follow (Trice and Roman 1972).

The turning point for this small social movement came in 1970 with the establishment of a federal agency, the National Institute on Alcohol

Abuse and Alcoholism (Roman and Blum 1987). Not only did the enabling legislation provide funding for alcohol-related programming, but it was based on a "new epidemiology" of alcohol problems designed to supplant the temperance-based idea that alcohol's victims were primarily down-and-out homeless men who inhabited the "Skid Rows" of American cities. Instead, the new model emphasized the widespread nature of "hidden" alcohol problems up and down the social structure. An implicit assumption was that because of its biological origins, alcoholism could affect anyone, regardless of sociodemographic or personal characteristics.

In a symbolic sense, this new epidemiology instantly placed millions of alcoholics within the walls of America's workplaces. Drawing upon the earlier efforts to launch industrial alcoholism programs, NIAAA's initiatives emphasized the urgent need for employers to curb the tremendous losses exacted by hidden alcoholics on company payrolls. At the same time, the workplace-oriented campaign emphasized the business wisdom of rehabilitating rather than dismissing these workers or ultimately being forced to place them on disability benefits (Roman 1975, 1981).

Through a nationwide network of federally supported "consultants," NIAAA endeavored to spread the word and launch what were then called "occupational alcoholism programs" in all private and public work settings (Roman 1975). The diffusion effort was not initially successful.

There were two major barriers: first, the adoption of such a program within the workplace required willingness to admit the presence of workplace alcohol problems, and second, the suggested design implied that supervisors needed diagnostic skills to accurately identify the alcoholic employee. Neither the admission of a corporate alcoholism problem or the delicate task of deciding who was and who was not an alcoholic was attractive to organizational decision makers.

In what proved to be a landmark conceptual breakthrough, NIAAA moved in the mid-1970s toward the promotion of a concept that ultimately became embellished as the philosophy of the EAP (Roman 1975, 1981, 1988b; Roman and Trice 1976). Of importance for present concerns, this change succeeded in subsuming psychiatric problems, family disruptions, and drug dependence in an umbrella program oriented toward preserving employment and preventing disability.

This new programming strategy de-emphasized the substance-abusing employee per se. It instead suggested that work settings are characterized by costly disruptions and productivity loss due to a wide variety of "behavioral-medical problems," of which substance abuse is only one category, albeit a very significant category. In terms of "selling" this program concept, it might be easy for an employer to deny the presence of alcoholic employees. However, it is much less credible to claim that none of these disruptive and difficult-to-handle "behavioral-medical" problems are represented in a workforce of any significant size.

To sidestep employers' problems with empowering their supervisors to identify alcoholism within the workforce, the EAP strategy firmly stated that problem employees were to be identified on the basis of performance problems, not behavioral symptoms. Within the EAP philosophy, the emphasis moved away from the supervisor's knowledge of the signs and symptoms of alcoholism. Substituted was help for supervisors, managers, union reps, and employees in sorting out proper EAP referrals. This was afforded through professional expertise in the workplace capable of specifying and diagnosing the nature of employee problems that underlay the job performance problems. These experts could be company staff or external contractors. Upon receiving a referral, the EAP expert assessed, motivated, and directed those employees to community treatment resources most appropriate for their needs. This program coordinator was then in an ideal position to maintain treatment gains through post-treatment follow-up and support within the work setting. Such a model clearly describes proactive disability prevention.

Drug Abuse and Drug Dependence

Employers' constructive attention to employee drug abuse as a behavior disorder has a different history and is an arena where policy is still developing. Workplaces are central stages for the acting out of tensions in American culture over the use of punishment versus treatment in response to drug abusers (Roman and Blum 1992, 1995). In a manner reminiscent of NIAAA's promulgation of a new epidemiology of alcohol problems in the early 1970s, the federal government promoted in the early 1980s the concept that drug abuse was rife among employed persons, as well as among persons seeking employment. Beyond this, the parallels between the two campaigns diminish. The actions suggested by the new epidemiology of drug abuse were punitive and exclusionary, contrasting sharply with the move toward increasing access to treatment for employed persons with drinking problems that was suggested by the NIAAA campaign.

Formal efforts to prevent disability and conserve employment among workers with drug problems had an important symbolic beginning in

1973, when a drug abuse policy was adopted by the U. S. Civil Service Commission (now the Office of Personnel Management), covering all civilian federal employees exclusive of high security operations. This idea slowly diffused into the community of EAP workers where patterns of drug abuse often turned up among EAP referrals in accompaniment with alcohol or psychiatric problems. These constructive efforts occurred in parallel with the adoption of urine-based drug screening of job applicants in a great many settings and, to a lesser degree, adoption of drug screening of current employees.

While only recently documented, workplace managers do not fully welcome the adversarial and punitive tone implied by the introduction of random or for-cause drug screening among current employees. For both humanitarian and practical reasons, survey data indicate that managers prefer to offer opportunities for treatment to persons with apparent drug dependencies (Roman and Blum 1995). This provides a ready linkage between employee drug problems and EAPs.

Employee Assistance Programs

The EAP is by far the most widespread method of preventing employee disability associated with behavior disorders. As is described in more detail below, about 50% of American workplaces provide employees with access to a version of a formalized EAP.

EAP implementation rests upon supervisory or peer identification of job performance deterioration which cannot be explained by the conditions of work. Supervisors are urged to consult with EAP staff before taking action. Procedures call for supervisors to utilize some form of constructive confrontation when employees deny their performance problems or when there is no willingness to take corrective action. Should the employee elect to use the company program, the EAP coordinator conducts an assessment or arranges for a diagnosis of the individual's problem. The coordinator or diagnostic agent will then offer referral advice as to how the problem might be dealt with. Utilization of such assistance is the option of the employee, although it is evident that coercive pressure can characterize both the encounters with the EAP as well as earlier encounters with supervisors. Should the individual be able to resume job performance after this intervention, routine follow-up occurs for a prescribed period and the case is closed. Should performance remain below standards, disciplinary action and dismissal may be ultimate outcomes.

In practice, most referral processes are informal rather than formal, and actual staged confrontations are rare. However, research reveals

(Blum, Roman, and Harwood 1995) that the "self-referral" label used to describe the majority of referrals in most EAPs is very misleading, for considerable social interaction and discussion precedes EAP referrals, often involving an employee's supervisor. For largely self-evident reasons, both supervisors and subordinates prefer these informal procedures. While flexibility is increased when informal means are employed, equity protections provided by bureaucratic procedure may be lost, i.e., "flexibility" can be used to the advantage of multiple parties in these transactions. But it is important to emphasize that while most self-referrals appear to embody the principles and assumptions underlying EAP practice, they do not involve the legalistic documentation and staged events suggested by the formal guidelines. These facts may set the stage for later conflicts if the employee's problem resolution is unsatisfactory.

Core Technology of Employee Assistance Programs

The key components and "core technology" of EAPs (Roman 1989; Blum and Roman 1989) can be summarized in four categories. To a considerable extent, these categories embody the technical program standards advanced by the national association of EAP workers, the Employee Assistance Professionals Association.

First, there should be a written policy clearly based on job performance. Such a statement should indicate that employees' behaviors are significant to the employer to the extent that they impinge on job performance. EAP policy does not supersede preexisting rules of conduct or fitness for duty policies. EAP policies do not provide employees with "excuses" for continuing substandard performance. Supervisors' responsibility is to document performance problems, with an eye toward an eventual confrontation if they accumulate.

Second, the EAP should be staffed with appropriate expertise and be directly and immediately accessible to supervisors and employees. Whether company or contract employees, EAP coordinators should be integrated into the workplace so that supervisors and employees respect their competencies vis-à-vis knowledge of the workplace. The coordinator should be readily available to provide consultative assistance to supervisors on how to appropriately deal with employees suspected to have EAP-relevant problems.

Third, supervisors, employees, and union representatives should be knowledgeable about the strategy of constructive confrontation. When documented evidence of performance problems has exceeded standards of acceptable work behavior and the employee does not volunteer to participate in guided behavioral change, constructive confrontation is implemented. Constructive confrontation is centered on evidence of performance problems and presents disciplinary steps that will be taken unless performance is improved. The context includes the supportive assistance of the company to suspend discipline and guide the employee to appropriate counseling or treatment.

Fourth, the EAP coordinator links employees with appropriate professional resources for assistance, engages in case management through the treatment period, and implements long-term follow-up based in the workplace. Resources are selected on the basis of established effectiveness, and referrals should be consistent with employees' health insurance coverage, job demands, and career contingencies. The EAP coordinator monitors compliance and participates in workplace reentry. In this process the coordinator involves the supervisor as appropriate, generates post-treatment support linkage, and engages in work-based supportive follow-up for 36 months or longer.

Core Functions of Employee Assistance Programs

An understanding of employer adoption, maintenance, and support of EAPs may be gained by a review of the "functions" that they serve for the workplace, i.e., the several "payoffs" that are involved. These functions elaborate the assertion basic to this chapter that employers desire to prevent the disabilities associated with employees' behavior disorders.

First, EAPs aid employers in retaining the services of employees in whom the organization has a substantial training commitment. Turnover and replacement costs can be very high, the events are typically disruptive to the flow of work, and turnover may have severe morale impacts on "survivors." Further, there is a clear humanitarian dimension. To the extent that employees' use of the EAP becomes known (and they do become known!), the employer's supportive efforts to recognize the individual's need for help and the "suspension of the rules" while help is sought can have positive morale impacts. Other employees often see such actions as acknowledging and rewarding fellow employees' investment, commitments, and contributions to the work organization.

A second function is reducing supervisory and managerial involvement in counseling employees with behavior disorders (Roman 1988b). Without an EAP, counseling responsibilities are assigned by default to supervisors, managers, and where a union is present, to union shop stewards. While often well-intended, such amateur counseling efforts are notably inefficient and may be dangerous. While some managers think they have natural talents in this arena, many others welcome the opportunity to refer or suggest that subordinates seek qualified assistance that is readily available through company auspices.

In this context, Phillips and Older (1977) articulated the concept of the "troubled supervisor." They observed that supervisors attempting to deal with a troubled employee often find themselves frustrated and confused. They observed supervisors who manifested a parallel troubled behavior pattern, reflecting the doubts and ambivalence that arise in attempting to "do the right thing" for the troubled employee. Phillips and Older indicated that the behaviors of the troubled supervisor could be as costly to the organization as those of the troubled employee and that an EAP intervention could, in a single step, resolve both behavioral problems.

A third function centers on legal protections that have developed around the employment setting, on the content of collective bargaining agreements, and on the organization's own guidelines in the implementation of progressive discipline. Implementation of the EAP policy provides for due process for those employees whose personal troubles may be affecting their work. It may protect the employer against subsequent legal action, while at the same time avoiding situations where an employee or union representative would be pressed to file a lawsuit or grievances. Equitable and consistent implementation of the EAP policy fosters an atmosphere in which unions can work supportively with management in EAP implementation (Trice and Roman 1972).

In general, review of court cases indicates that employers are protected by documentation of constructive attempts to provide assistance to employees whose personal problems are affecting work performance (Denenberg and Denenberg 1983; Coulson and Goldberg 1987). This orientation is not altogether different from "reasonable accommodation" concepts incorporated in the ADA.

Fourth, it is clear that EAPs enhance employers' efforts to control employee health care costs. Evidence has accumulated that employees with alcohol problems are heavy users of health care services as are the families of these employees (Holder and Hallan 1986; Holder 1987; Holder, Lennox, and Blose 1992). Data indicate further that health care utilization declines markedly following successful alcohol abuse interventions. Parallel data support the impact of intervention in reducing health care usage among employees with psychiatric problems (Jones and Vischi 1979). Thus while the initial treatment investment for substance abuse or psychiatric problems may appear high, follow-up studies indicate that these investments ultimately contain health care costs.

Related, but distinctively different, is a fifth function wherein EAPs provide a gatekeeping service that incorporates the positive ingredients of the controversial set of activities known as managed behavioral health care. Representatives of managed care contractors, who are by definition outside the workplace, likely have few insights into the work-related nature of particular employees' problems and have gained the reputation for being much more oriented toward cost containment than quality care provision.

In theory, managed care can direct a person to the care best suited for their needs. Few employees know how to select health care services for substance abuse, psychiatric, and family problems. EAP personnel, however, have access to criteria by which they can select the most effective providers for these services. Their local knowledge, coupled with intimate information about employee clients, may be considerably superior to the information possessed by large corporate managed care organizations. Advice and direction by the EAP about employees' behavioral health resources use can result in more efficient use of more effective services, resulting in cost savings for the employer as well as for the employee when copayments are involved.

A sixth payoff of EAPs is that they can enhance employee morale. Since the resolution of behavior disorders is in the interests of both the employer and the employee (as well as the union, if it is present), and since none of these parties possesses the technology to resolve behavior disorders, EAPs may be at the nexus of an "all-win" type of intervention. This can make for a smoother functioning and even for a "caring" workplace. However, such a rosy description assumes that EAP functionaries operate in a fully professional manner and avoid using their services in ways that inappropriately advantage (or disadvantage) either employers or employees.

EAP Distribution

One of the remarkable features of EAPs is their rapid diffusion across American workplaces. Data on EAP prevalence were initially focused on major corporations (Roman 1982). In 1972, 25% of the "Fortune 1000" had some type of program to provide constructive assistance to problem-drinking employees. Subsequent surveys revealed this proportion grew to 34% in 1974, 50% in 1976, and 57% in 1979, by which point the survey was querying specifically about the presence of EAPs (Roman 1982). There are no post-1979 national survey data on the prevalence of EAPs among the Fortune 1000 corporations. Commentary in practitioner publications based on informal surveys indicates that coverage is nearly complete today. However, the data do not account for program quality, and it is evident that there is great variation in EAP investment levels among firms.

The present authors have directed two major projects that provide insights about EAP distribution. One is a longitudinal analysis of a representative sample of private companies in Georgia (Blum, Milne, and Maddela 1996). The other is an ongoing repeated panel study of national samples of employed workers begun in 1992 (Blum, Roman, and Martin 1992; Roman and Blum 1995). These studies provide a number of insights about where EAPs have been adopted.

At present, it appears that about 50% of the American workforce have access to EAP services via their workplace. This figure is fairly consistent across studies that use employees for their respondents (our national surveys) versus those that query human resource managers (our Georgia project and a carefully executed study of a national organizational sample [Hartwell, Steele, French, Potter, Rodman and Zarkin 1996]). It is possible that the employee coverage figure is somewhat higher if one counts employed persons who can access their spouses' EAP services in their status as employee dependents. It is notable that this total coverage figure has remained fairly stable across our surveys and in other reported studies, varying from 45% to 55%. From an innovation diffusion perspective, it may be that this intervention has diffused about as far as it will, unless legal mandates come to require wider adoption, a possibility that is not imminent at present.

We know little about the establishments that do not adopt EAPs, except for a common characterization that they report adequate informal procedures to deal with the problems targeted by EAPs. While not a complete generalization, there is fairly substantial statistical evidence of an association between an EAP presence and the increasing sophistication and comprehensiveness of human resource management systems (Blum et al. 1996). However, it also appears that EAP development may be a "latter stage" human resources practice, one that is put in place after other more fundamental human resource management needs are met.

In the early years of EAP development, they were much more common in manufacturing than in the nonmanufacturing sector. Over time, that pattern has become reversed, reflecting both the transformation of manufacturing as well as the declining centrality of alcohol problems in EAPs, a pattern that may account for their initial popularity in manufacturing firms. But work organization affects EAP adoption as well: construction and mining industries (characterized by dispersed and shifting workers and work groups) have consistently shown the lowest adoption rates and the least extensive coverage. The sector with most extensive coverage is communications, utilities, and transportation (Hartwell et al. 1996).

Over time, we have seen a consistently strong positive association between organizational size and EAP presence. While larger organizations are much more likely to have EAPs, most employees work in smaller establishments. This may bolster concern about effective means for introducing EAPs into smaller establishments. A caution must be added, however, about the meaning of organizational size in today's U.S. economy. A great proportion of seemingly small establishments are actually units or subsidiaries of larger organizations, and their human resources practices may be a reflection or extension of those of the parent company. Thus considerations of size and ownership together are important in looking at EAP coverage in these very prevalent, small-sized settings. Unfortunately, few survey techniques lend themselves to efficiently obtaining detailed ownership data from adequately sized and representative samples of organizations.

EAP diffusion is not limited to the private sector. In the early 1970s, the federal government mandated alcohol/drug interventions—that evolved into EAPs—for all its civilian employees. Two research studies, involving on-site assessments and interviews of the nature of these programs in samples of federal installations, revealed uneven implementation (Beyer and Trice 1978; Hoffman and Roman 1984a, 1984b). While federal civilian employees are supposed to be covered by EAPs, each federal department or agency is responsible for finding the funds to provide these services, and enthusiasm for EAPs varies across departments, agencies, and central administrations.

Much of the growth in EAPs over the past fifteen years is in externally contracted services. A recent national survey (Hartwell et al. 1996) reveals that fully 81% of the reported programs to be externally contracted. As might be expected, there is a strong negative association between organizational size and the presence of externally contracted EAP services. However, many large employment settings have shifted from internal to external program design or have initially adopted an external program. The survey found that in settings with over 1,000 employees, 58% of the EAPs were externally contracted.

Contract fees for external programs are generally calculated on a per capita basis and are thus affordable to settings of any size. However, there is great variability in service arrangements and access to services across contract settings. While EAPs are widely diffused, there has been minimal diffusion of standards to evaluate program quality and to assess the pros and cons of alternative structures. Employers purchasing EAP services typically have access to little, if any, information about the appropriate program design save for that provided by the vendor offering the service!

Patterns of EAP Utilization

Data from a study of 439 internal and external EAPs indicated that an average of 5% of employees used the EAP in each site during the 12 months prior to data collection, which occurred in 1984-85 (Blum et al. 1992). In another study directed by the present authors nearly a decade later, an almost identical proportion of annual utilization was found from referral data collected at 81 EAP sites (Blum et al. 1995).

Assuming low turnover and relatively low reutilization of the EAP by the same employees, a substantial proportion of employees at a given site use an EAP over a several-year period. This widespread use at present probably affects future utilization. Indeed, our more recent data indicated substantial influence from peers among EAP users' reported reasons for going to the EAP (Blum et al. 1995). In terms of the bases for utilization, approximately 30% of the cases involved substance abuse, and 50% involved combinations of family and mental health problems.

Our own analyses of data collected in 1988 from 1,961 managers in a southeastern organization with 55,000 employees indicated that 37% of the supervisors have formally referred an employee to the EAP at least once during the EAP's 12-year existence (Blum 1989). An additional 20% suggested that an employee use the EAP, without making a formal, documented referral.

Supervisory referrals of subordinates were significantly more likely when the managers perceived top management support for the EAP, perceived EAP support by their immediate supervisors when they believed the EAP helped improve organizational productivity, when they believed that the EAP was an integral part of the company, and when they were familiar with policies related to the EAP and discipline (Blum 1989). The importance of these factors in enhancing utilization has been confirmed by a number of studies representing a wide range of employment settings (Blum and Roman 1995; Roman and Blum 1996).

Efficacy of EAPs

Probably the most commonly asked question about EAPs is their efficacy. There is no single study or set of studies that can answer this question. It would be nearly impossible, if not inappropriate, to attempt a meta-analysis of the totality of EAP evaluations that have been reported in outlets ranging from unpublished reports to published journal articles (Kurtz, Googins, and Howard 1984). Even when the effort is restricted to journal articles subject to peer review, the methodological variation is daunting (Roman and Blum 1996). The problem is that nearly each evaluation is unique, having been sponsored by a different host organization with a unique intent and thus a different research design.

Two conclusions may elucidate issues of EAP efficacy. First, EAPs serve different purposes for different organizations. This is demonstrated in their widespread adoption and maintenance among a very diverse population of workplaces. Second, regardless of how one might assess EAP effectiveness, there is no alternative that provides a systematic and constructive means for identifying and attempting deliberate employment conservation among employees who develop psychiatric problems or psychoactive substance dependence or who are preoccupied by family disintegration and disorder.

The generic efficacy of the EAP model may be a misplaced concern. It approaches EAPs as if they were a treatment modality, which they distinctively are not. The individual behavioral outcomes of most referrals to EAPs are tied to the treatment and aftercare, provided independent of EAP auspices. Thus examining individual "outcomes" associated with EAPs is to focus on the consequences of multiple inputs wherein it is close to impossible to disentangle the positive or negative influences of EAP inputs, treatment inputs, or after-care/follow-up inputs.

As it is typically posed, the efficacy question also presumes that the ongoing daily activity of EAP staff is primarily focused on sessions with individual clients. Research indicates that EAP personnel spend substantial amounts of their time resolving problems between supervisors and subordinates that do not lead to referral, giving advice to individuals that is not recorded in case records, or attempting to motivate providers to upgrade the quality of treatment services in order to improve treatment efficacy (Blum and Roman 1989; Blum et al. 1992). Further, for EAP implementation to be sustained, it is critical that EAP personnel orient, train, and educate supervisors as well as maintain program awareness among nonsupervisory employees.

Despite these caveats, data that examine individual outcomes are impressive. A few examples are illustrative. The data from our study of 439 organizations indicated that an average of 80% of the employees who had used the EAP for problems that were not substance abuse-related were on the job with adequate job performance one year after initial contact with the EAP (Blum et al. 1992). The comparable rate for alcohol and other drug problems was 66%.

Blum et al. (1995) used a somewhat stricter methodology to measure outcomes where data on EAP processes were gathered from multiple respondents at 81 different sites. These data revealed that 67% of the women and 74% of the men who had utilized the EAP were still employed at the same company one year after they had utilized the EAP (Blum et al. 1995). In terms of preventing behavioral disability, these figures should be impressive, especially compared to the sharply lower 30% rehabilitation rates commonly reported in one-year follow-up data from treatment programs.

From the perspectives of our foregoing discussion about EAP efficacy, these data can be challenged on many grounds. Most important is the fact that the clients represent only those who "got to" the EAP service. These individuals were somehow successfully motivated to become EAP intakes. These "success" data say nothing about the potential clients who remained at their jobs, quit, were fired, or died without an EAP intervention. Likewise, data indicating a high level of efficacy for constructive confrontation (Trice and Beyer 1984) are based only on those clients that "got to" that point in the EAP process. Perhaps this subgroup was substantially "ready" compared to those whose recalcitrance prevented them from entering the system in the first place or who dropped out at a point prior to formal confrontation.

Further, it must be recognized that there is little standardization in design and process across EAPs for two very basic reasons. First, EAPs must be adapted to both the workforces they serve and the workplaces within which they are developed, defying standardization in either structure or process. Second, with the exception of the transportation and nuclear power industries in the U.S., which must provide EAP-like structures as a result of federal legislation, EAPs are implemented voluntarily by employers who make independent decisions about the level of investment in their respective programs. Thus while there is pressure to conform to standards developed by EAP personnel, such conformity will be almost totally voluntary for the foreseeable future. An approximate description of the features of "typical" and "ideal" EAPs is found in Table 1.

There is another outcome criterion of considerable significance. Recalling the orientation of this chapter to the prevention of disabilities associated with employees' behavior disorders, there are no known data on disability-related outcomes associated with EAP interventions. Specifically, we do not know how many persons who receive EAP services

TABLE 1
Typical and Ideal Services Provided by EAPs

Service dimension	"Typical" EAP	"Ideal" EAP
Covered Population	Employees and dependents	Employees, dependents, and retirees
Staffing External Provider System	Rotated among staff	Specifically designated staff
Internal System	One M.A. FTE/4000 persons no backup staff	One Ph.D. FTE/2000 persons with backup clerical staff
Available Consultation	Off-site on 24-hour phone or on-site during 8-5 shift	On-site during all work shifts
Managerial Training	One 2-hour session provided during managerial career	All new supervisors provided with 2-hour training; annual 1-hour refresher
Employee Education	Brochures and posters	Mandatory education sessions
Counseling	5-8 Sessions provided, external referrals only when necessary	All final diagnoses and treatment provided by external vendors
Client Follow-up	Brief contact for 3 months following use of external vendor services	Long-term follow-up based on severity of case; minimum 12 mos.
Program Evaluation	Records developed at staff discretion	Professional external audit

end up (in the short or long run) unable to work or, in many instances, eligible for disability retirement. Understandably, EAP evaluations focus on success characteristics, i.e., those still employed after a given number of months or years. While some studies attempt to assess the quality of job performance at various post-intervention points, such measures are fraught with the typical difficulties in obtaining valid job performance measures. Thus on the assumption of rational management, evidence of continued employment is typically used as a proxy measure for adequate job performance.

However, an understanding of EAP efficacy would be advanced by exploring the common characteristics of those who are not responsive to interventions, since these outcomes may be especially costly to employers. Of course, care must be taken to assure that the EAP is not seen as solely responsible for these failures, just as it cannot be entirely credited for all positive outcomes.

Less directly linked with EAP efficacy is the broader contextual question of an organization's overall rates of disability associated with behavior disorders. It is unreasonable to expect that all employees affected by behavior disorders will be referred to EAP services or will utilize such services when recommended. Indeed, several of the more influential evaluations have based their conclusions about EAP efficacy on comparisons between employees with behavior disorders who did and who did not utilize EAP services (Blum and Roman 1995).

The significance of how behavior disorders are managed outside an EAP when EAP services are available may be reflected in overall rates and patterns of disability or disability retirement benefits associated with behavior disorders, comparing different levels of EAP utilization. This offers a different perspective on the actual impact of EAP intervention on the types of disability at issue. It should be noted that while data on patterns of disability retirement would seem relatively easy to collect compared to other types of outcome data, EAP evaluations rarely include it in their outcome analyses or even report such information.

The Limits of Employee Assistance Programs and Consideration of Alternatives

Given the dominance and visibility of EAPs as strategies to address the secondary prevention of workplace behavioral disabilities, it is sometimes difficult to recognize that there are alternatives to EAPs, several of which are very well established. In reality, these alternatives are not competitive but complementary, and none has been suggested as a substitute for EAPs. But it is clear that nearly half of the workforce does not have access to EAPs. Some proportion of this group likely has access to these alternative services. Further, these efforts may have important (but largely undocumented) impacts on disability prevention.

A central consideration is the clear fact that employers differentially devote resources to various interventions. While EAPs may be present along with complementary interventions, in some settings the alternatives receive more resources, more attention, and more support from top management. Understanding the reasons for these different intervention patterns is an important challenge for research. In this section, we examine the four major alternatives of prohibition, testing, health promotion and stress management, and programs directed toward peer and occupational groups.

Workplace Prohibition of Psychoactive Substance Use

Prohibition is not an intervention but is better defined as a passive primary prevention strategy. By reducing or eliminating their exposure to a particular causal factor, employers do not mandate that their employees "do anything" but instead that they not perform particular acts that in themselves are not directly linked to work. While the noxious factors that lead to mental health problems and family discord cannot be "prohibited," the key ingredients in alcohol and drug abuse are consumption and use of alcohol and drugs.

Alcohol and drug prohibition rules are found in nearly all workplaces. Widespread alcohol prohibition predates national Prohibition (Staudenmeier 1989). With the emergence of attention to illegal drugs, these too were specified among "intoxicating substances" and added to prohibition policy statements in most workplaces, beginning about twenty-five years ago.

While these norms are so well institutionalized that they often escape recognition, alcohol and work have not always been segregated. Drinking breaks and on-the-job drinking were historically part of many occupational settings, with the provision of alcohol by employers in some instances an accepted "right" of employment (Ames 1989). Industrialists' interests and capitalist economic growth in 19th and early 20th century America broke many time-honored links between alcohol and work and might be viewed as part of a broader paradigm shift in employers' control of employees (Clark 1976; Rumbarger 1989).

Perhaps because workplace prohibition was so thoroughly institutionalized before research on the effectiveness of human resource management began, it is not seen as an option for employers and is therefore not evaluated. Even without data, it seems reasonable to conclude that many accidents and injuries would occur were alcohol and drugs intermingled with today's work technologies, and dramatic episodes in the transportation industry seem to confirm this intuition. Widespread availability of alcohol and/or drugs in the workplace would surely increase risks of developing chemical dependencies among workers. Thus what may be in reality a major contribution to the prevention of disabilities associated with behavior disorders in the workplace is a device that is institutionalized to the point that it is practically invisible.

Psychoactive Substance-Use Testing of Job Applicants and Current Employees

There is a conceptual linkage between prohibition and testing of employees as strategies of primary prevention. Urine-based testing has been validated as a method of identifying job applicants who have used certain illegal drugs in the recent past (Macdonald and Roman 1995).

The appropriateness or effectiveness of drug screening has been the subject of much discussion and debate. Despite the furor, the majority of large workplaces and many smaller workplaces have adopted such policies, and their implementation has generally proceeded smoothly.

At issue is whether preemployment screening identifies persons with drug problems and whether it is an accurate predictor of job performance. The answer to both of these questions is negative: drug use does not necessarily mean the presence of a drug problem, and evidence of drug use does not necessarily mean that persons cannot perform a job.

A broader issue centers on the implications of turning drug-positive persons back into the community. Few applicants who are found positive are made aware of this reason for their not being hired. Thus without knowing why they were turned down, they continue drug use and possibly continue to be unemployable. Job applicants with positive drug screens may have drug problems, but rarely do potential employers assume any responsibility for directing such persons toward assistance. Underlying these concerns is the question of employer responsibility for taking steps that will help reduce community drug problems, as opposed to the practice of "externalizing" these issues away from the workplace and onto the community to bear potential costs and consequences.

There is no evidence that preemployment drug screening reduces the rate of workplace drug problems (Blum 1989; Roman 1989). To an extent, this finding highlights a question about the supposed intent of employers in implementing preemployment screening: is the purpose to prevent employee disability or is it to screen out deviants and law-breakers whose personal morality has allowed them to use illegal drugs (Roman and Blum 1995)? There is a strong suggestion that preemployment drug screening sends a message about workplace norms and values (Pfeffer 1981), perhaps secondary to its effectiveness in actually enhancing workplace safety or productivity.

Random drug screening of current employees might be seen as a "follow-up" to preemployment screening or possibly as a partial application of preemployment screening to employees who were hired before screening was put into place. As a prevention strategy, random drug screening raises some of the same issues as preemployment screening since it involves the same technology which neither identifies drug abusers nor performance impairment. Random screening is, however, a highly charged social ceremony. It is carried out so that it is known to the existing workforce (in contrast to the one-by-one "private" ceremonies of preemployment screening conducted among nonmembers of the organization), demonstrating both the evils of illegal drugs as well as the power of management (Pfeffer 1981).

Random testing is used in many settings primarily for its deterrent effects. Immediate dismissal can be the consequence for those who are found to be drug positive, demonstrating again how a workplace can externalize its employee drug problems to the community. However, in what appears to be a growing trend, random testing can serve potentially constructive ends for disability prevention where workplace policy calls for referral of drug positive employees to the EAP or similar service with a goal of offering treatment or rehabilitation. Rarely are such opportunities offered more than once. This use of random drug testing may contribute to disability prevention.

Another lesser-known constructive example is where random drug screening protocols are developed for individuals who have undergone treatment for drug problems under EAP auspices. Here also there may be only a single opportunity for an observed "slip," although EAP policies vary in the extent to which they consistently regard relapse as a common or even expected feature of recovery from substance dependency problems. Anecdote indicates that this use of random testing can be a very strong motivator for employees desiring to keep their jobs. Thus testing can be regarded as a contributor to disability prevention.

For-cause screening fits more closely with traditional workplace intervention approaches, and, like random screening, it is sometimes accompanied by referral to an EAP but often with the condition that such an offer of help will not be repeated. By definition, for-cause screening is linked to performance problems, which may involve accidents or injury. Once again, externalization of drug positives is a possible outcome, although instances where for-cause screening leads to offers of assistance should be seen as instances of disability prevention.

Unlike most illegal drugs, alcohol is present in the body only for hours after consumption. U.S. Department of Transportation regulations currently mandate alcohol testing, particularly after an accident. This is not an innovation. Many workplaces, as part of their "rules of conduct" or "fitness for duty" regulations, have reserved the right to test employees for alcohol either upon suspicion of intoxication or after an accident or other disruptive incident. However, a preemployment test that accurately identifies applicants with alcohol problems has not yet been developed. Such technology is being pursued but with unknown prospects for success. Such a screening device could have dramatic implications for employer investment in other preventive interventions.

Health Promotion and Stress Management

Workplace health promotion is presently of minor consequence as a strategy for the primary prevention of disabilities stemming from behavior disorders. There has been some suggestion that health promotion and wellness programs are potentially effective in the prevention of substance abuse problems, typically through measured impact of educational programs on changes in self-reported drinking behavior (Stolzfus and Benson 1994).

When health problems such as overweight, high blood pressure, or gastric problems are identified by health risk appraisal administered at the worksite, an agent with medical authority might suggest reduction in drinking as a means of alleviating the primary symptom. There is no evidence of widespread use or the impact of such a strategy on employee drinking. Alternatively, it is possible that employees undertaking exercise programs or other health-oriented leisure activities might change their drinking behavior because of the lack of "fit" between excessive drinking and their new healthy regimen. Again, while this intervention is possible, evidence is lacking.

Stress management is a widely used intervention in the workplace, typically associated with diffuse and unmeasured goals. Stress management techniques possess a high degree of face validity. Employees typically enjoy participation in stress management training and commonly report positive benefits. There is essentially no evidence that stress management has any long-term effect on the prevention of disability associated with behavior disorders. It is possible that it indirectly affects prevention by sensitizing employees to their stress reactions and possibly inducing immediate or eventual self-referral to an EAP. However, stress management ideology tends to deflect the problem of stress creation by the workplace onto the stress management abilities of employees. The need for employees to "buck up" in the face of stress is the overriding theme, in contrast to careful research that might ferret out the causes of stress and attempt to eliminate them.

Disability Prevention in Settings Dominated by Occupations: Peer and Member Assistance Programs

Since the 1970s, several professions, including medicine, law, dentistry, psychology, and nursing, have reported activities designed to resolve problems of alcohol abuse among their members through peer intervention programs. Two intertwined rationales underlie such programs.

First, most professionals are not part of a typical employment relationship; they often have considerable autonomy in determining work hours, techniques, and other aspects of work style. Indeed, independence of performance often marks highly creative or heroic accomplishments among professionals. A second feature is a strong sense of community such that members of a professional group tend to protect one another from external confrontations, interventions, or criticism. This relates to the first feature: to the extent that supervision of professionals occurs at all, it is typically one member of a profession supervising other members.

With these work characteristics, the typical organizationally based intervention for substance abuse would have a low likelihood of effectiveness. It would be expected that problem performance among professionals would be minimally visible, that they would readily "cover up" for each other, and that their power would make them highly resistant to any form of confrontation.

If anyone is aware of a professional's dramatic mood swings or drinking problem, it is likely to be a fellow professional. Further, an aspect of the community of shared interest (and shared fate!) among professionals is that the deviance, misbehavior, or malpractice of one professional may have an adverse impact on professional peers. Finally, since most professions are certified or licensed through boards composed of professional peers, the profession itself may be in a unique position to threaten sanctions against nonconforming members.

These ingredients are said to make up a peer intervention program for professionals. Such programs reportedly exist in many locations, generally lodged in the local or statewide association of the professional group. Peer intervention programs are operated and governed by members of the profession, sometimes by members who have recovered from their own substance abuse.

Evidence on how these programs work and how effective they are is largely anecdotal. As might be expected, these groups do not readily admit outsiders to carry out objective research studies on the profession, particularly studies of potentially threatening behaviors such as substance abuse. Given the nature of professional power and how it is maintained, this is certainly not surprising. Thus while there are a number of reports of the success of these programs, they are prepared by the program operatives or by others with a clear vested interest in the program's success.

There is an important second category of peer interventions. A research group at Cornell University has been examining member assistance programs (MAPs) in labor unions for more than a decade. In a first set of studies (summarized in Sonnenstuhl 1996), focus was upon a small, independent union with an intense drinking culture that included on-the-job drinking. Through the slow introduction of a union-based program to provide recovery assistance to alcoholic union members (a program manned by a union member who was a recovering alcoholic), a gradual transformation of the workplace drinking culture emerged. Recovery and abstinence became accepted lifestyle choices, and there was a diminution of the near-universal pressure to drink with work peers both on and off the job. This was a dramatic example of a change in what appeared to be deeply entrenched drinking norms, and the study is suggestive of the potential for preventing worker disability associated with substance abuse through workplace interventions directed toward cultural change.

A second set of studies by the Cornell group (Bacharach et al. 1994) focused upon member assistance programs with broader ranges of coverage. They examined programs in the railroad industry and one organized by the flight attendants in commercial air transportation. The research findings were almost uniformly positive regarding the impact of these programs. There were no means for comparing the relative efficacy of these MAPs with management-based employee assistance programs. However, from an absolute basis, the programs had an impact on the substance abuse of union members across these wide ranging settings within the transportation industry.

The focus on a single type of industry and the lack of comparison with other types of strategies are obvious limitations of this research. The applicability of the findings is also constricted by the relative small proportion of the U.S. labor force that is unionized and the apparent continuing decline of this coverage. The findings, however, offer a bright complement to ongoing evaluations of traditional, management-based EAPs.

Many prognosticators see the American workplace moving more toward a model of peer organization, accompanied by a decline in traditional patterns of top-down hierarchical management. This generic model includes many features of participative management and collective responsibility within the rank and file. Should this transformation come to pass, the model of a peer or member assistance program may have considerable applicability for dealing with employees' substance abuse. Its most attractive feature may be that it operates outside traditional definitions of authority, power, and accompanying opportunities for coercion and threat. Such features are congruent with descriptions of accepted and successful models of alcoholism treatment and sobriety maintenance.

On the other hand, we are still in the dark regarding the actual dynamics and effectiveness of peer intervention programs within groups of relatively affluent and powerful professionals. To some extent, the research on member assistance programs tends to have a working-class orientation. While the Cornell group's work offers an abundance of insights, it is remarkably uncritical, offering virtually no descriptions of program dysfunction, problematic incidents, or unsuccessful outcomes. Peer intervention has potential difficulties. By defining and implementing actions toward deviant behavior within an informal and undocumented framework, potential abuses may be greater than when power is implemented through a bureaucratic hierarchy. Many features of hierarchical bureaucracy—such as the open definition of authority, procedure, and rules—offer opportunities for equitable treatment and due process when rules are breached.

In sum, peer and member intervention programs are important new frontiers for addressing substance abuse among employed people. A good foundation has been launched with studies of member assistance programs, indicating that their success and potential are very real.

Conclusion

We have covered a broad ranging terrain in this chapter and have described a number of interventions that demonstrate strong potential for the prevention of disability among employees with behavior disorders. Research is badly needed on all types of intervention, particularly on the complementarity and synergy that is possible by having several strategies available in the same workplace. Despite the relative neglect of workplace behavior disorders by scholars and researchers, their importance cannot be underestimated. An analysis of the worldwide epidemiology of diseases, injuries, and associated risk factors reveals that mental illness and alcohol use are among the leading causes of disability in countries outside the U.S. Furthermore, it is likely that the scope and depth of these problems will increase in the future (Murray and Lopez 1996). The materials in this chapter indicate that technology has been developed to reduce the occurrence and impact of these disabilities. Future tasks include diffusion of this knowledge well beyond the borders of North America.

Acknowledgment

The authors gratefully acknowledge partial support from Grant No. R01 AA 10130 from the National Institute on Alcohol Abuse and Alcoholism and from Grant No. R01 DA 07417 from the National Institute on Drug Abuse during the preparation of this manuscript.

References

Abbott, Andrew. 1988. *The System of Professions*. Chicago: University of Chicago Press.

Ames, Genevieve. 1989. "Alcohol Related Movements and Their Effects on Drinking Policies in American Workplaces: An Historical Review." *Journal of Drug Issues*, Vol. 19, pp. 489-510.

Bacharach, Samuel B., Peter Bamberger, and William J. Sonnenstuhl. 1994. *Member Assistance Programs in the Workplace*. Ithaca, NY: ILR Press of Cornell University Press.

Beyer, Janice C. and H. M. Trice. 1978. *Implementing Change: Alcoholism Programs in Federal Agencies*. New York: The Free Press.

Blum, Terry C. 1989. "The Presence and Integration of Drug Abuse Intervention in Human Resource Management." In S. Gust and J. Walsh, eds., *Drugs in the Workplace: Research and Evaluation Data*. National Institute on Drug Abuse Research Monograph No. 91, Washington, DC: U.S. Government Printing Office, pp. 271-86.

Blum, Terry C., and Paul M. Roman. 1989. "Employee Assistance and Human Resource Management." In K. Rowland and G. Ferris, eds., *Research in Personnel and Human Resources Management*, Vol. 7. Greenwich, CT: JAI Press, 258-312.

_____. 1995. *The Cost Effectiveness and Preventive Implications of Employee Assistance Programs*. Monograph No. 5, Center for Substance Abuse Prevention. Washington, DC: Substance Abuse and Mental Health Administration, U.S. Department of Health and Human Services.

Blum, Terry C., Paul M. Roman, and Jack K. Martin. 1992. "A Research Note on EAP Prevalence, Components and Utilization." *Journal of Employee Assistance Research*, Vol. 1, pp. 209-29.

Blum, Terry C., Paul M. Roman, and Eileen Harwood. 1995. "Employed Women with Alcohol Problems Who Seek Help from Employee Assistance Programs: Description and Comparisons." In Marc Galanter, ed., *Recent Developments in Alcoholism*, Vol. 12. New York: Plenum Press, pp. 126-61.

Blum, Terry C., Stuart Milne, and Tara Maddela. 1996. *1996 Human Resource Management Report*. Atlanta: DuPree School of Management of Georgia Institute of Technology.

Brandes, Stuart D. 1976. *American Welfare Capitalism*. Chicago: University of Chicago Press.

Caplan, Gerald. 1964. *Principles of Preventive Psychiatry*. New York: Basic Books.

Clark, Norman S. 1976. *Deliver Us from Evil*. New York: W. W. Norton.

Conrad, P., and J. Schneider. 1980. *Deviance and Medicalization*. St. Louis: Mosby.

Coulson, R., and M. D. Goldberg. 1987. *Alcohol, Drugs and Arbitration*. New York: American Arbitration Association.

Denenberg, T., and R. V. Denenberg. 1983. *Alcohol and Drugs: Issues in the Workplace*. Washington, DC: Bureau of National Affairs.

Dickson, William, and Fritz Roethlisberger. 1966. *Counseling in an Organization: a Sequel to the Hawthorne Researches*. Boston: Graduate School of Business Administration of Harvard University.

Dooley, D., and R. Catalano. 1988. "Psychological Effects of Unemployment." *Journal of Social Issues*, Vol. 44, pp. 1-12.

Gillespie, Richard. 1991. *Manufacturing Knowledge: A History of the Hawthorne Experiments*. New York: Cambridge University Press.

Greenberg, E. S., and L. Grunberg. 1995. "Work Alienation and Problem Drinking Behavior." *Journal of Health and Social Behavior*, Vol. 26, pp. 83-106.

Hartwell, Tyler D., Paul Steele, Michael T. French, Frank J. Potter, Nathaniel Rodman, and Gary A. Zarkin. 1996. "Aiding Troubled Employees: The Prevalence, Cost and Characteristics of Employee Assistance Programs in the United States. *American Journal of Public Health*, Vol. 86, pp. 804-08.

Hoffman, Eric, and Paul M. Roman. 1984a. "Effects of Supervisory Style and Experiential Frames of Reference on Successful Organizational Alcoholism Policy Implementation." *Journal of Studies on Alcohol*, Vol. 45, pp. 260-67.

_____. 1984b. "The Effect of Organizational Emphasis upon the Diffusion of Information about Innovations." *Journal of Management*, Vol. 7, pp. 277-92.

Holder, H. D. 1987. "Alcoholism Treatment and Potential Health Care Cost Savings." *Medical Care*, Vol. 25, pp. 52-71.

Holder, H. D., and J. B. Hallan. 1986. "Impact of Alcoholism Treatment on Total Health Care Costs: A Six-Year Study." *Advances in Alcohol and Substance Abuse*, Vol. 6, pp. 1-15.

Holder, H. D., Richard Lennox, and James O. Blose. 1992. "The Economic Benefits of Alcoholism Treatment: A Summary of 25 Years of Research." *Journal of Employee Assistance Research*, Vol. 1, pp. 63-82.

Jacoby, Sanford M. 1985. *Employing Bureaucracy: Managers, Unions and the Transformation of Work in American Industry, 1900-1945*. New York: Columbia University Press.

Jones, K. R., and T. R. Vischi. 1979. "Impact of Alcohol, Drug Abuse and Mental Health Treatment on Care Utilization." *Medical Care*, Supplement 12.

Kornhauser, Arthur. 1965. *The Mental Health of the Industrial Worker*. New York: John Wiley.

Kurtz, Norman, Bradley Googins, and William Howard. 1984. "Measuring the Success of Occupational Alcoholism Programs." *Journal of Studies on Alcohol*, Vol. 45, pp. 33-45.

Landsberger, Henry. 1958. *Hawthorne Revisited*. Ithaca, NY: Publications Division of the New York State School of Industrial and Labor Relations at Cornell University.

Leedy, Jack J., ed. 1971. *Compensation in Psychiatric Disability and Rehabilitation*. Springfield, IL: Charles C. Thomas.

Macdonald, S., and P. Roman, eds. 1995. *Drug Testing in the Workplace*. New York: Plenum.

Martin, Jack K., Paul M. Roman, and Terry C. Blum. 1996. "Job Stress, Drinking Networks, and Social Support at Work: A Comprehensive Model of Employees' Problem Drinking Behavior." *The Sociological Quarterly*, Vol. 37, pp. 579-99.

Murray, Christopher J. L., and Alan D. Lopez, eds. 1996. *The Global Burden of Disease*. Geneva: World Health Organization.

Parker, D., and J. Brody. 1982. "Risk Factors for Alcoholism and Alcohol Problems among Employed Men and Women." In A. Pawlowski, ed., *Occupational Alcoholism: A Review of Research Issues*. National Institute on Alcohol Abuse and Alcoholism Research Monograph No. 8. Washington, DC: Government Printing Office, pp. 106-21.

Parsons, Talcott. 1951. *The Social System*. Glencoe, IL: The Free Press of Glencoe.

Pavalko, Eliza. 1989. "State Timing of Policy Adoptions: Workmen's Compensation in the United States, 1909-1929." *American Journal of Sociology*, Vol. 95, pp. 592-615.

Phillips, Donald, and Harry J. Older. 1977. "A Model for Counseling Troubled Supervisors." *Alcohol, Health and Research World*, Vol. 2, pp. 24-30.

Pfeffer, Jeffrey. 1981. "Management as Symbolic Action." In Larry Cummings and Barry Staw, eds., *Research in Organizational Behavior*, Vol. 3. Greenwich, CT: JAI Press, pp. 11-52.

Presnall, Lewis. 1981. *Occupational Counseling and Referral Systems*. Salt Lake City: Utah Alcoholism Foundation.

Richman, Judith. 1992. "Occupational Stress, Psychological Vulnerability and Alcohol-Related Problems over Time in Future Physicians." *Alcoholism: Clinical and Experimental Research*, Vol. 16, pp. 166-71.

Roman, Paul M. 1975. "Secondary Prevention of Alcoholism: Problems and Prospects in Occupational Programming." *Journal of Drug Issues*, Vol. 5, pp. 327-43.

_____. 1981. "From Employee Alcoholism to Employee Assistance: An Analysis of the De-Emphasis on Prevention and on Alcoholism Problems in Work-Based Programs." *Journal of Studies on Alcohol*, Vol. 42, pp. 244-72.

_____. 1982. "Employee Programs in Major Corporations in 1979: Scope, Change, and Receptivity." In John DeLuca, ed., *Prevention, Intervention and Treatment: Concerns and Models, Alcohol and Health*, Monograph 3. Washington: Government Printing Office, pp. 177-200.

_____. 1988a. "The Disease Concept of Alcoholism: Sociocultural and Organizational Bases of Support." *Drugs and Society*, Vol. 2, pp. 5-32.

_____. 1988b. "Growth and Transformation in Workplace Alcoholism Programming." In Marc Galanter, ed., *Recent Developments in Alcoholism*, Volume 6. New York: Plenum Press, pp. 131-58.

_____. 1989. "The Use of Employee Assistance Programs to Deal with Drug Abuse in the Workplace." In S. Guste and J. Walsh, eds., *Drugs in the Workplace: Research and Evaluation Data*. National Institute on Drug Abuse Research Monograph No. 91. Washington: U. S. Government Printing Office, pp. 271-86.

_____, ed. 1990. *Alcohol Problem Prevention in the Workplace: Employee Assistance Programs and Strategic Alternatives*. Westport, CT: Quorum.

Roman, Paul M., and Terry C. Blum. 1987. "Notes on the New Epidemiology of Alcoholism in the U.S.A." *Journal of Drug Issues*, Vol. 11, pp. 321-32.

_____. 1992. "Drugs, the Workplace, and Employee-Oriented Programming." In D. Gerstein and H. Harwood, eds., *Treating Drug Problems*. Volume 2. Washington: National Academy of Sciences Press, pp. 197-243.

_____. 1995. "Employers." In R. Coombs and D. Zedonis, eds., *Handbook on Drug Abuse*. Englewood Cliffs, NJ: Prentice Hall, pp. 129-58.

_____. 1996. "Effectiveness of Workplace Alcohol Problem Interventions." *American Journal of Health Promotion*, Vol. 11, pp. 112-28.

Roman, Paul M., and H. M. Trice. 1976. "Alcohol Abuse in Work Organizations." In Benjamin Kissin and Henri Begleiter, eds., *The Biology of Alcoholism.* Volume 4: Social Aspects of Alcoholism. New York: Plenum Press, pp. 445-518.

Rothman, David. 1971. *The Discovery of the Asylum. Social Order and Disorder in the New Republic.* Boston: Little Brown.

Rumbarger, J. J. 1989. *Power, Profits and Prohibition: Alcohol Reform and the Industrializing of America, 1800-1930.* Albany, NY: State University of New York Press.

Seeman, Melvin, Alice Seeman, and Art Burdos. 1988. "Powerlessness, Work and Community: A Longitudinal Study of Alienation and Alcohol Use." *Journal of Health and Social Behavior*, Vol. 29, pp. 185-88.

Smith, David. 1997. "Implementing Disability Management: A Review of Basic Concepts and Essential Components." *Employee Assistance Quarterly*, Vol. 12, no. 4, pp. 37-50.

Sonnenstuhl, William J. 1986. *Inside an Emotional Health Program.* Ithaca, NY: ILR Press of Cornell University Press.

_____. 1996. *Working Sober.* Ithaca, NY: ILR Press of Cornell University Press.

Staudenmaier, William J. 1989. "Contrasting Organizational Responses to Alcohol and Illegal Drug Abuse among Employees." *Journal of Drug Issues*, Vol. 19, pp. 451-72.

Stolzfus, J. A., and P. A. Benson. 1994. "The 3M Alcohol and Other Drug Prevention Program." *Journal of Primary Prevention*, Vol. 15, pp. 147-59.

Trice, H. M., and J. A. Belasco. 1966. *Emotional Health and Employer Responsibility.* Ithaca, NY: Publications Division of the New York State School of Industrial and Labor Relations at Cornell University.

Trice, H. M., and Janice C. Beyer. 1984. "Work-related Outcomes of Constructive Confrontation Strategies in a Job-based Alcoholism Program." *Journal of Studies on Alcohol*, Vol. 45, pp. 393-404.

Trice, H. M., and Paul M. Roman. 1970. "Delabeling, Relabeling and Alcoholics Anonymous." *Social Problems*, Vol. 17, pp. 468-80.

_____. 1972. *Spirits and Demons at Work: Alcohol and Other Drugs on the Job.* Ithaca, NY: ILR Press of Cornell University Press.

Trice, H. M., and M. Schonbrunn. 1981. "A History of Job-Based Alcoholism Programs, 1900-1955." *Journal of Drug Issues*, Vol. 11, pp. 171-98.

Wilsnack, Richard, and Sharon Wilsnack. 1992. "Women, Work and Alcohol: Failures of Simple Theories." *Alcoholism: Clinical and Experimental Research*, Vol. 16, pp. 172-79.

CHAPTER 5

The Role of Unions and Collective Bargaining in Preventing Work-related Disability

SUSAN J. SCHURMAN
George Meany Center for Labor Studies

DAVID WEIL
Boston University

PAUL LANDSBERGIS
Cornell University

BARBARA A. ISRAEL
University of Michigan

For most of this century, unionization has been one of the primary responses by American workers seeking to influence the terms and conditions of their employment either directly—through collective bargaining—or indirectly through collective political influence. Indeed, preventing disability or death from work-related injury or illness is among the oldest and most durable of trade union goals. From its earliest days to the present, a major purpose of organized labor has been to use collective economic and political power on behalf of workers' "health and welfare."[1] To that end unions have employed a range of strategies and tactics from direct actions in the workplace and community to collective bargaining to political and legislative pressure and consumer boycotts.

At the same time, it is also true that labor unions have sometimes traded health and safety standards for other benefits—even when faced with strident demands from their members for protection from known debilitating hazards.[2] And unions have sometimes opposed regulatory and policy changes aimed at certain kinds of health and safety risks. Unions, for example, have often opposed mandatory nonsmoking policies. However, despite these internal factors and despite the fact that

121

unions face legal and internal political difficulties in their role as advocates for increased occupational safety and health (Ashford and Katz 1977; Dorman 1996), even labor's harshest critics generally acknowledge that unions have played a significant role in the dramatic reduction in injuries and illnesses in this century.

There are several general reasons to expect that unions will increase the effectiveness of various mechanisms for promoting workplace health and safety. They may use their bargaining power to secure higher risk premiums. They also may use their expertise and comparative advantage to collect and interpret information on workplace hazards to bargain and enforce strong health and safety provisions in collective agreements. And they may use collective power to obtain contractual guarantees against unjust dismissal, which allow workers to exercise their rights under the law. As this chapter will discuss, empirical evidence generally supports these claims: unionized workers appear to have greater access to workers' compensation benefits, OSHA enforcement, more effective workplace safety committees and programs, and receive higher risk premiums for fatal injuries than their nonunion counterparts.

The goal of this chapter is to describe the general strategies unions employ in their efforts to prevent work-related disability and/or to mitigate its effects and then to examine the empirical evidence on the impact of these efforts.[3] We begin by considering theoretical arguments from different disciplines concerning the role of unions in disability prevention or compensation. We then present a conceptual framework on the process of preventing work-related injury and illness that blends economic and industrial relations systems perspectives with those of scholars and practitioners from other social, behavioral, and biological sciences and those of activists from labor, public health, and environmental movements. This framework will be used as a basis for examining union efforts to improve the health and safety aspects of work. We conclude with suggestions for how unions can further enhance their role as advocates for a safer, healthier workplace.

Theoretical Views on the Role of Unions in the Prevention of Disabilities

Economic Perspectives on the Role of Unions

Economic perspectives on the impact of interventions in the economy aimed to improve occupational safety and health form a continuum. On one end of the continuum is the pure neoclassical view, which claims that any intervention into the functioning of labor markets reduces social welfare. On the other end is the "government mandate" theory that asserts that the promulgation and enforcement of government standards is required and essential to improve workplace health and safety (Burton and Chelius 1997:32). In between are a range of theoretical positions that incorporate different degrees of intervention.

Unions are hypothesized to have different effects on health and safety outcomes along this continuum. In the strictest neoclassical economic theory the answer is simple: there is no role. Safety and health are market commodities like any other and therefore subject to the usual assumptions concerning the operation of free markets. Dangerous work will be compensated by higher wages. Unions distort the bargaining power of some workers in relation to others, between workers and employers, and among employers. They therefore impede the operation of the market and distort compensating wage differentials related to safety. The consequence is a misallocation of the distribution of safety and health costs and benefits compared with the optimum levels that the unimpeded market could provide.

Political economists, such as Commons,[4] as well as present-day labor economists (see discussion in Burton and Chelius 1997) have long criticized this view of the operation of labor markets in regard to safety and health outcomes. Mainstream economic theory and research subscribe to variants which acknowledge imperfections in market functioning such as asymmetrical information on risks, limitations in mobility within or between labor markets, distortions arising from unequal bargaining power between workers and employers, or the public good character of safety and health provision. Researchers in this "modified" position allow for certain interventions in the market to correct for these imperfections. While much of the discussion revolves around the appropriate role of public institutions, it also suggests potential roles for labor unions.

If the provision of safety and health breaks down because of information asymmetries concerning risks, unions may play a role in improving access to risk information or in educating workers about such risks at the work site. In this way, unions may improve safety and health outcomes, either by raising wage premiums or by affecting quit rates (see, for example, Viscusi 1979). Unions' role in changing relative bargaining power in the face of labor immobility, monopsonistic markets, or noncompetitive product markets (coupled with reducing the problem of information asymmetries) may similarly improve labor market outcomes related to safety and health (Olson 1981; Dickens 1984). Unions may also favorably modify labor market outcomes relating to risk due to "voice" effects

(Freeman and Medoff 1983), that is, by influencing workplace changes that lead to improved safety rather than worker exit. In a related vein, unions may provide a set of workplace public goods related to safety and health that potentially result in more optimal setting of wage and benefit policies and regulatory interventions (Kahn 1994; Weil 1998).

These perspectives provide insight into where one might expect to see different levels of union involvement as well as impacts on safety and health. For example, union/nonunion hazard pay differentials should vary on the basis of information or bargaining asymmetries. In this sense, the economic literature provides a perspective on a set of "macro-level" determinants of disabilities arising from features of the labor and product market. It does not, however, offer a full picture of the complete set of pathways that result in the wide range of disability outcomes, particularly those arising from the interaction of the individual with institutions outside of the workplace, such as the family, health care institutions, and other social support groups. Fortunately, a separate literature has focused on these aspects of the disability development process.

Social Ecology and Open Systems Theory Perspectives on the Role of Unions

In recent years, concern over trends in workplace safety and health has prompted theoretical and empirical attention by scholars from a variety of behavioral and health science disciplines as well as by labor and public health practitioners and activists. This work arises from several literatures including open systems theory (e.g., Thompson 1967) and social ecological frameworks (Bronfenbrenner 1979; Israel, Schurman, and House 1989; Stokols, Peletier, and Fielding 1996).

Drawing from this literature, several general principles are instructive in understanding the determinants of disabilities and in turn the potential role of labor unions. The first principle posits that an individual's or group's health status (dependent variable) is jointly determined by multiple personal and environmental factors (independent and intervening variables). The second emphasizes linkages between the workplace and other life settings such as family and residential environments, modes of commuting, community standards of living, and health care systems. The third principle suggests that since work-related health or illness is a multivariate phenomenon, comprehensive preventive interventions require a multidisciplinary perspective that integrates theoretical and practical knowledge as well as methods from several different fields (Stokols, Peletier, and Fielding 1996).

In contrast, the two predominant occupational health and safety intervention traditions—occupational safety and health (OSH) and workplace health promotion (WHP)—have focused heavily on the properties of either persons or their immediate physical environments as independent variables (Goldenhar and Schulte 1994; Baker, Israel, and Schurman 1996; Israel et al. 1996; Polanyi et al. 1996). OSH researchers and practitioners have concentrated primarily on the identification and reduction of toxic exposures and physical demands with less attention to the role of individual behavior (Robins and Klitzman 1988; Schurman, Silverstein, and Richards 1994). On the other hand, WHP researchers and practitioners focus primarily on the role of individual behavior with little attention to the influence of work conditions on these behaviors and on health and safety more broadly (McElroy, Bibeau, Steckler, and Glanz 1988). Until recently, both traditions have paid little attention to the interaction effects of persons and environments, and both had a limited conception and characterization of the role of larger social, economic, and political environments in the disability development and prevention process.

Scholars from a variety of social and health science disciplines have contributed to a growing theoretical literature based on a more systemic view of the relationships between individual and environmental factors at different levels of social aggregation (e.g., Katz and Kahn 1978; Emery and Trist 1981; McElroy et. al. 1988; Israel, Schurman and House 1989; Karesek and Theorell 1990, Karasek 1992; Landsbergis et al. 1993; Institute for Work and Health 1996). These theoretical advances have spawned a growing number of more complex worker health interventions. (See, for example, DiMartino 1992; *American Journal of Industrial Medicine* 1994; and *Health Education Quarterly* 1996 for reviews of this literature.)

A Framework for Evaluating Preventive Interventions

Figure 1 presents a conceptual framework that draws on both the economics and social ecology literatures to explain the disability development and prevention process. This framework portrays work-related disability as the outcome of the intersection of two sets of determinants. The left side of the figure depicts macro-level factors that collectively determine the nature and design of work and the set of human resource practices that, in turn, affect the likelihood and severity of workplace disabilities. These factors, which are related to the economic and industrial relations systems perspectives, include product and labor market forces, underlying production technologies, and regulatory systems. The

FIGURE 1

Conceptual Framework on Disability Development Process

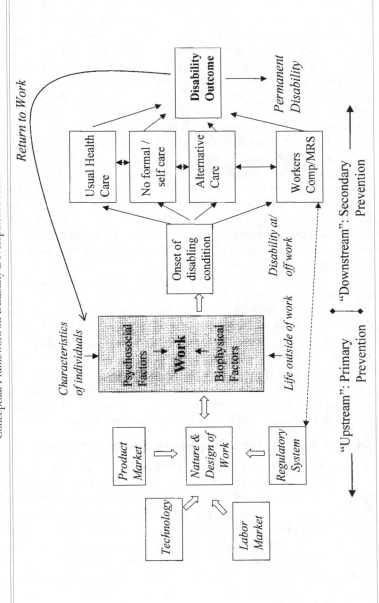

right side of the figure depicts a set of micro-level factors that influence the path of disability of development following the onset of symptoms.

The two "sides" of the framework are linked together by the work process: individual factors, workplace factors (human resource practices, job accommodations) and social systems (in particular, health care and workers' compensation systems) that influence the probability that a worker will return to work. The framework posits that every "stage" of the process is modified by factors related to individuals' biological, behavioral, and socioeconomic characteristics.

Intervening in this process in order to prevent injury or illness requires (explicitly or implicitly) identifying cause-effect pathways that make clear how the intervention is expected to affect specific health outcomes. Such analysis is difficult, especially further "upstream" in the process, since most workers are exposed to a complex interaction of work and non-work-related risk factors and there is a great deal of individual variation in both biological and behavioral responses. And given the costs associated with prevention, neither employers nor government nor workers themselves are likely to support interventions in the absence of clear evidence that establishes (a) the causal links between risks and health outcomes and (b) the efficacy of the proposed intervention. Hence there has been more attention paid recently by the occupational and workplace health and safety community to improving intervention research (see, e.g., *American Journal of Industrial Medicine Special Issue on Intervention Research* 1994).

Intervention Leverage Points: "Upstream-Downstream"

The framework in Figure 1 implies that there are certain "leverage" points in the disability development process where interventions may have significant preventive effects. The search for effective intervention and prevention extends from finding effective treatment for the acutely injured to the enactment of social policies intended to eliminate or reduce risk at the source. As the focus of prevention moves upstream in the process, it reaches a clear threshold prior to the onset of symptoms. This threshold—shown here as the midpoint in Figure 1—is the conventional dividing line between primary and secondary prevention. Downstream from this threshold, interventions focus on variations in the diagnosis and treatment of particular injuries or illnesses in order to restore health or prevent permanent disability. Increasingly, since the passage of the Americans with Disabilities Act (ADA), secondary prevention also addresses the issue of workplace accommodation of workers with physical or psychological impairments.

Immediately upstream from the threshold, primary prevention efforts lead to investigations of the health effects of variation in the nature and design of work systems. These involve understanding both the contributions of work environment variables as well as individuals' characteristics to health outcomes. Because workplace design has its roots in policy decisions influenced by the external factors affecting firm-level human resource strategy, as one proceeds further "upstream" from the threshold, the search for prevention leads to an examination of the broader set of forces that shape both the nature and design of work. These forces include the social policies governing occupational safety and health regulation as well as workers' compensation for illness or injury.

This framework suggests that attempts to intervene prior to the onset of symptoms face sharply increasing complexity of the social, economic, and political factors involved (Karasek 1992). This is particularly evident in the case of occupationally related disease as opposed to injuries since the etiology of disease is influenced by genetic and biological variables.

No example better illustrates the complexities involved in preventing occupationally related diseases than the recent class-action lawsuit against the tobacco industry by a group of nonsmoking flight attendants. The attendants claimed that inhalation of second hand cigarette smoke—a mandatory condition of employment prior to 1990 on most airlines—contributed significantly to the development of health problems ranging from lung cancer to heart disease (*New York Times*, July 17 and October 11, 1997). Though the industry settled the lawsuit by agreeing to pay $300 million for the study of tobacco-related diseases, it denied that secondhand smoke is harmful, pointing to other potential causes, such as individual biological and life style factors and other environmental hazards outside their control (e.g., high altitude radiation exposure).

This case involves conflicting interests at virtually every level of analysis, from legislators on different sides of the "tobacco question" to corporate executives (the CEO of one tobacco company testified for the flight attendants), to unions (flight attendants' unions generally favor smoking bans while the tobacco workers' unions generally oppose nonsmoking policies), and to workers themselves (smokers and nonsmokers). In this case, the major intervention—nonsmoking policies on all U.S. domestic flights—is already in place, and future research will seek to assess its impact on employee health. However, the example highlights why (in the absence of a clear theoretical framework and solid data) primary prevention remains limited in scope in occupational settings.

Variation in Union Approaches to Intervention

As suggested earlier, Figure 1 proposes a series of leverage points for preventive intervention: at the level of macro social policy, strategic firm-level policy, workplace-level policy, individual behavior, medical management policy, and so forth. Theoretically, unions might try to intervene at any or all of these leverage points, and taken as a whole, organized labor has sought to intervene at virtually all of these points. Dealing with labor's aggregate response, however, masks some important differences in strategy and tactics across individual unions and across sectors. In reality, faced with constrained resources and limited empirical data on the efficacy of various types of intervention, unions choose which interventions to pursue in their overall strategy for preventing work-related injury or illness. They must also decide where to place health and safety demands in relation to other bargaining objectives.

Compared to their counterparts in other industrialized countries, the American labor movement contains substantial variation in terms of (1) the relative bargaining power of unions vis-à-vis the employer(s) they bargain with, (2) internal decision-making structures and processes, (3) the political and technical efficacy of officers and staff, and (4) the jurisdictional basis on which individual unions seek to organize workers in particular labor markets. These differences can be expected to constrain or facilitate a given union's ability to affect workplace design and human resource choices. In addition, unions face significant differences in employers' "ability to pay" based on specific product/service market, regulatory, and technological factors in the employer's primary industry (Kochan 1980; Craypo 1986; Dunlop 1993).

In general, it can be predicted that since unions are political institutions in which leaders are elected by members, specific health and safety strategies will be based on two primary principles: providing the greatest benefit for a majority of members and reduction of the most serious risks faced by members.[5] While both principles provide strong institutional dividends to unions and political dividends to leaders, they can sometimes conflict. This is especially likely to occur in unions with multijurisdictional memberships and a heterogeneous occupational makeup. Members may disagree about the seriousness of a particular risk factor (e.g., air quality or VDT radiation) or about the proper compensation tradeoffs to be made in exchange for the risks. Or one segment of the bargaining unit may perceive that the union is devoting too large a share of resources to a different group's issues or to a risk factor of undocumented consequence in comparison to their own.

Perhaps the most typical case involves conflict between high- and low-seniority groups, since seniority is in many unionized firms the pathway to jobs with *both* more safety and health and more pay.[6] Lower seniority members are often willing to trade more risk for more pay. More senior members, however, have already achieved higher pay and less risky jobs and may be more cognizant of the consequences of health and safety hazards and/or more risk averse (see Kahn [1994]; Dorman [1996] for more detailed discussions of this issue).

Union activity on safety and health policies may also derive from its linkage with other union strategies or priorities. Northrup (1997) suggests that unions use OSHA enforcement as part of corporate campaign strategies linked to organizing and collective bargaining. While analysis of OSHA enforcement data does not support Northrup's claim in the aggregate (see below), unions have used safety and health as an organizing issue during campaigns in recent years. Canadian and U.S. unions have also advocated safety and health legislation such as mandated health and safety committees partly as a means to promote the virtues of representation in nonunion workplaces, although the Canadian experience with such committees indicates that they have only had modest impacts on expanding union representation (Bernard 1995).

Thus in formulating specific approaches to improving occupational health and safety—as with all other bargaining demands—union leaders are forced to balance competing interests of different membership groups with the union's overall institutional objectives, in the context of their perceptions of the employer's ability to pay and the union's relative power to extract payment from the employer. With this view of union bargaining power and decision making in mind, we are now in a position to examine labor's record on disability prevention.

Union Strategies for Disability Prevention: Macro-level Interventions

Unions influence safety and health outcomes through their impacts on the employment relationship. This arises in their varied roles in modifying the impact of labor and product market forces described above as well as being central actors in an industrial relations system (Dunlop 1993). Macro-level leverage points include collective bargaining, influencing political processes, and participation at various levels of the safety and health regulatory system.

Collective Bargaining Interventions

Unions pursue improved workplace safety and health through collective bargaining in four general ways. First, unions negotiate higher pay in exchange for higher risk, thereby creating or enhancing compensating wage differentials in the labor market.[7] Second, unions bargain specific contract language mandating certain policies and standards to which management agrees to adhere. Third, they negotiate health and safety committees (or other structures) through which workers may influence the employer's policies and practices to address worksite health and safety problems. Fourth, they attempt to influence higher-level management policies, such as technology choices or the design of workplace practices that have major implications on safety and health outcomes.

Wage premiums. Unions may raise wage differentials to compensate for increased exposure to risk explicitly through contract language regarding hazard pay. Hazardous work premiums are provided for in about 15% of collective agreements with the highest frequency in construction industry agreements (BNA 1995). The most common form of this type of provision requires firms to apply varying pay rates according to the type of risk or the degree of potential hazard associated with a given risk.[8]

The more fundamental impact of unions on hazard premiums arises because of their role in changing the nature of the wage bargain between workers and employers. As discussed in the previous section, this impact of unions arises from their role in improving information asymmetries, providing workplace public goods in the form of safety and health, and in their ability to offer countervailing bargaining power. As a result, unions should increase risk premiums for workers relative to those paid to comparable nonunion workers. In the long run, firms will adopt practices that balance increased costs arising from wage premiums against investments that improve safety and health conditions and will substitute capital for labor in response to the higher costs for union labor (Viscusi 1993).

The majority of studies measuring union/nonunion differences in hazard wage premiums support this expected impact of unions (for example, see Thaler and Rosen 1975; Olson 1981; Dickens 1984; Fairris 1992; Siebert and Wei 1994; Sandy and Elliott 1996). A few studies, however, find no evidence of this expected effect (see, for example, Martinello and Meng 1992).[9]

Specific safety and health provisions. The frequency of health and safety clauses in labor union agreements related to all four responses increased markedly following passage of the Occupational Safety and

Health Act (OSHA) in 1971. An examination of labor agreements negotiated between 1954 and 1981 found that the proportion of contracts containing a health and safety clause of any type increased from 63% in the period prior to OSHA passage (1954-71) to 82% afterward (Office of Technology Assessment: Table 15.1). The depth of language increased significantly, expanding from longstanding issues of bereavement funds and provision of basic safety protective gear (e.g., goggles) to more complex standards incorporating OSHA provisions, training requirements, and safety procedures.

A variety of provisions in collective agreements deal with substantive interventions relating to safety and health, including specific requirements to provide safety equipment (e.g., goggles, protective clothing, respirators) or safety training, hazard pay requirements, or the explicit incorporation of OSHA safety and health standards into the collective agreement. These provisions are often very specific, reflecting safety or health concerns particular to an industry or occupation. For example, contract clauses include provision of adequate lighting, eye and face protection, protection against noxious gases, hearing protection, guards and "lockout" procedures, and radiation protection.

While not explicitly linked to safety and health, a wide variety of collective bargaining policies relating to staffing requirements/crew size, job classification, internal promotion, layoff policies and procedures, training, and other "core" human resource practices partially shape the nature of work design as well as the characteristics of workers who staff given jobs. These characteristics of the human resource system, arising from the industrial relations system choices of unions, will in turn affect (whether intentionally or not) the likelihood and nature of disabilities.

Establishing safety and health processes. Process-related collective bargaining provisions range from a requirement that the employer provide access and pay to safety stewards (common among building trades unions) to the creation of safety and health committees. While committee requirements are quite common—provisions for joint safety and health committees are found in more than half of private sector agreements and 65% of manufacturing agreements (BNA 1995)—there is wide variance in the composition, role, and authority of the committee established by collective agreements. Many committees are advisory in nature and have limited powers to inspect or directly determine policies relating to safety and health. Other collective agreements establish committees with significant authority (e.g., UAW/General Motors, UMWA/BCOA, OCAW/petrochemical companies). Indeed, UAW contracts with the "Big Three" auto companies include the right to strike over health and safety violations, and UMWA committees may issue withdrawal and shutdown orders in the face of imminent dangers.[10]

Unions increase the likelihood that firms will have some type of joint committee structure to deal with safety and health issues in general (Planek and Kolosh 1993). The limited number of empirical studies of health and safety committees established under labor agreements have generally found them to improve health and safety outcomes (Kochan, Dyer, and Lipsky 1977; Cooke and Gautschi 1981). Two recent studies— one from the United Kingdom (Reilly, Paci, and Holl 1995) and another from Canada (Heckscher and Schurman 1997)—find that joint consultative committees, with all employee representatives appointed by unions, significantly reduce workplace injuries relative to establishments where the management alone determines health and safety arrangements.

A number of other studies demonstrate that unions have positive impacts on health and safety committee structures where mandated by law. Canadian unions seem to have increased the probability that committees will actually be formed as required by provincial law and that they adhere to key standards of practice (e.g., in regard to composition, frequency of meeting, training, etc.) once established (Bernard 1995). They also improve the performance of committees in regard to certain safety and health outcomes (Ontario Advisory Council 1986; Tuohy and Simard 1993). The gap between union and nonunion enforcement of OSHA (see below) increased appreciably following the implementation of mandated safety and health committee requirements in Oregon (Weil 1998).

Influencing strategic decisions. A more recent collective bargaining approach involves unions seeking to influence corporate policy decisions at the strategic level that have health and safety impacts but that are traditionally regarded as part of "management's right to manage." Throughout the 1980s a growing number of unions began to seek formal influence on employer decision making beyond the traditional scope of mandatory and permissible bargaining (Kochan and Osterman 1994), such as participation in technology choices. Most notable have been the United Auto Workers, the United Steel Workers of America, the Communications Workers of America, the Union of Needletrades, Industrial, and Textile Employees (UNITE), and the American Federation of Teachers.[11] For example, UNITE has become involved in major work redesign efforts at Levi Strauss at the corporate and plant level, in part fueled by the concerns of both parties over repetitive trauma syndrome related to apparel assembly and in part arising from broader strategic directions of the company.[12] A series of side-agreements between the UAW and the big-three automakers provide for consultation on technology investments with implications for worker safety or health. The UAW has also bargained to moderate the impact of Japanese intensive production methods on repetitive strain injuries at facilities such as the Mazda Flat Rock plant and the New United Motors Manufacturing Inc. (NUMMI) in California, through language on staffing, training, joint committees, election of team leaders and production standards (Adler, Goldaftas, and Levine 1997; Babson 1993; Landsbergis, Schnall, and Cahill in press).

Attempts to influence policy at the strategic level signals a departure from the "labor accord" of the past half-century in which labor accepted management's right to manage in exchange for union security and higher wages. For the most part, the rhetoric accompanying these forays into management's rights is not framed directly in terms of improved health and safety but rather addresses issues relating to employment security and the intensity of work demands. However, as we discuss below, since both employment security and work intensity have significant health effects, these changes can be assumed to potentially improve workers' health.

Legal and Regulatory Intervention

Supplementing their direct dealings with employers, unions have used their political influence to enact legislation or influence regulatory promulgation at the federal, state, or local level. To a greater degree (although far less frequently perceived), unions influence disability outcomes by acting as agents in the implementation of public policies relating to safety and health at the workplace level.

Labor (in particular, several major manufacturing unions) played a major role in the development and passage of the Occupational Safety and Health Act in 1970 (see Page and O'Brien 1973; Mintz 1984) as well as in state OSHA laws. More recently, unions have been highly active in both the appropriation process for OSHA and MSHA and in efforts to legislatively reform those agencies. For example, in 1992 the AFL-CIO and its affiliates vigorously supported Congressional efforts to reform OSHA by (among other things) increasing its enforcement authority and mandating safety and health committees (via the "Comprehensive Occupational Safety and Health Reform Act of 1992"). With equal vigor, unions also opposed bills sponsored by Representative Cass Ballenger in the 1994 Congress that would have drastically reduced the scope and enforcement authority of OSHA.[13]

Unions have also been lobbyists for and participants in federal- and state-funded research and training on safety and health (see, e.g., Kaminski, Graubarth, and Mock 1995; Merrill 1997). Over the past five years, for example, the AFL-CIO's Building Trades Department participated actively in efforts to maintain or increase funding for safety and health-related research conducted by the National Institute for Occupational Safety and Health (NIOSH). In New Jersey, labor was successful in creating a legislative set-aside clause in the state's workforce development fund of 3% to fund worker safety and health training.

Unions also participated in efforts by state legislatures across the U.S. to revise workers' compensation systems during the early and mid-1990s. As in the case of federal reform efforts, this role has varied from being vocal opponents of efforts to move away from the status quo systems to being proponents of certain types of legislative reform of state compensation systems.[14]

Unions play a direct, day-to-day role in the ongoing activities of regulatory structures established under federal and state legislation. OSHA's and MSHA's administrative structure begins with health and safety standard-setting processes where new standards are promulgated or existing standards modified. Virtually all unions representing workers in the manufacturing and construction sectors and many of the unions representing service and public sector workers maintain national-level departments for health and safety (as does the AFL-CIO). One of the major functions of these departments is to monitor and participate in the standard-setting process.

Finally, unions directly influence implementation of health and safety laws. Labor market policies, in general, and OSHA and MSHA, in particular, require that workers play a role in policy implementation through the exercise of designated employee rights. Under OSHA, for example, workers have the right to initiate inspections, participate individually or through a chosen representative in the conduct of inspections, and participate in post-inspection activities related to penalty setting and abatement planning. It can be shown that individual exercise of employee rights, however, is dependent on the presence of a collective workplace agent, like a labor union, due to the public goods character of these rights. (See Weil [1998] for a full theoretical treatment of this issue.) As a result, labor unions may exercise an ongoing role at the workplace in ensuring that workers exercise the rights provided them under OSHA and MSHA. (See Weil [1996a] for an empirical review of this issue in regards to U.S. labor policies.)[15]

Weil (1991, 1992, 1997) finds pronounced union/nonunion impacts on all aspects of OSHA and MSHA enforcement activity in a variety of sectors and over time. These results demonstrate that unions raise the probability of receiving an inspection, the intensity of inspection once initiated, the detection rate of violations, and the penalties relative to otherwise comparable nonunion workplaces. He also shows that unions appreciably increase the probability that an employer will come into compliance with specific safety and health standards subsequent to receiving an OSHA inspection (Weil 1996b).

Combining Macro-level Interventions

Unions differ in the way they combine these macro-level approaches into an overall health and safety strategy. For example, as UAW Health and Safety Director Franklin Mirer (1991:191-93) points out:

> The UAW's general approach to health and safety hazards is to seek to establish local union health and safety representatives trained to recognize hazards and recommend solutions. These safety representatives are full-time appointed officials in larger contracts but may also be part-time, or elected, or combine health and safety with other responsibilities. Contracts specify that health and safety representatives interact with management through labor management safety committees at the workplace and where appropriate at the national levels. Issues unresolved through the health and safety committee are subject to the grievance procedure that generally ends with the right to strike over health and safety. The UAW seeks joint decision making in each element of the management program, with special emphasis on training and research.

Building trades unions have also developed diverse macro-level approaches toward disability. The United Brotherhood of Carpenters, the Laborers International Union of North America, and other major construction unions have large staffs that interact with regulatory agencies at the national level and create and disseminate educational and training materials related to health and safety. At the same time, both unions have negotiated large joint labor-management health and safety funds at the national and regional levels that seek to promote better health and safety practice at the worksite, develop new approaches to prevention, and address problems related to disability and workers' compensation. Finally, the national Building Trades Department created the Center to Protect Workers Rights (CPWR) in 1990 with the express aim of undertaking primary research on all aspects of safety and health in the construction industry. CPWR, which receives a large portion of its funding from the National Institute for Occupational Safety and Health (NIOSH), sponsors research on ergonomics, injury prevention, and the economics of health and safety from a wide range of public health, occupational medicine, public policy, and economic researchers.[16]

The United Mine Workers of America has developed a highly integrated system of safety and health regulation drawing on all of the macro-level interventions discussed in this section. Specifically, the union has established extensive rights for its mine-level health and safety committees through collective bargaining.[17] These provisions establish the rights, authority, and structure for the committee, empowering them to conduct inspections, direct mine operators to make changes, and in cases of imminent danger close down mining operations. The provisions also provide for time off, training requirements, and a dispute resolution mechanism. At the same time, the union has designed an internal health and safety committee structure that parallels MSHA at the local, regional, and national level. This allows the union to leverage its privately established rights against the extensive rights provided to miners and their representatives under MSHA. See Weil (1994:195-201) for an extended description of this program and its operation.

It would be incorrect, however, to conclude that the summation of a labor union's policies in collective bargaining, political action, and regulatory involvement result in coherent safety and health policies. In fact, in the majority of cases, unions do not systematically review their chosen policies at various levels to take advantage of potential synergies across policies or activities, let alone to assure that policies are not in direct conflict with one another. Many unions have also not paid adequate attention to the relative efficacy of various macro-level interventions, as a means of focusing limited organizational resources on those activities that yield the greatest benefits in regard to disability prevention. We return to this subject in the final section of the chapter.

Union Strategies for Disability Prevention: Micro-Level Interventions

The Work Process

Returning once again to the framework in Figure 1, we now turn our attention to what is often termed the "black box" of occupational illness and injury—the work process itself. As Figure 1 shows, most of the formal characteristics of work design are the product of policy choices above the level of the workplace. It is in the actual work process, however, that the most significant interaction effects from all of the posited variable blocks (macro policy, corporate policy, individual worker characteristics, nonwork factors, treatment options) occur. For this reason we conceptualize the work process as the primary situs that links the two "sides" of the framework. This suggests that the work process is a very important leverage point for intervention.

It has long been clear that the design of the work process and working conditions play a role not only in work-related injury but also in illness. The field of epidemiology long ago established that variation in risk exists not only *between* different occupations but *within* the same general occupational title. The historic importance of workplace design to injury outcomes is examined by Fairris (1998: 201), who argues that aggregate increases in manufacturing injury rates in the 1960s can be attributed to "the institutional changes in the system of shopfloor governance (that) took place across a variety of manufacturing industries in the late 1950s and early 1960s." A recent study of lost-time claim rates for soft-tissue injuries in assembly plants of five different Canadian automobile manufacturers illustrates this point (Institute for Work and Health 1996). This study revealed a surprisingly heterogeneous pattern of injury rates among workers in the same job title. Such variation in risk within an occupation strongly points to differences in work practices, supervision, training, and engineering and administrative controls that are specific to the firm or unit of the firm and that are within the control of the firm. This finding is particularly important because, as measured by workers' compensation costs and days off from work, soft tissue and musculoskeletal injuries together account for over half of all occupational injuries in most industrial countries.

Other studies reveal clear, though often indirect, relationships between both job insecurity (see, e.g., Israel et al. 1992; Heany et al. 1993) and work intensity (e.g., Karasek and Theorell 1992) and physical and mental health outcomes. And cumulative research on the "psychosocial" characteristics of working conditions strongly suggests that the distribution of authority among jobs along with the quality of interpersonal relations (especially between supervisors and supervisees) play an important role modifying the relationship between physical and psychosocial risk factors and physical and mental health outcomes. (See Katz and Kahn [1978], House [1980], Karasek and Theorell [1990], Israel and Schurman [1992], and Baker [1994] for reviews.)

Briefly stated, this research indicates that workers who perceive themselves to have greater influence in their workplace report fewer health problems holding other factors constant. The same pattern holds with regard to supportive social relations. The implication of this evidence is that there is substantial variation in firm and facility-level practice within similar work processes and that interventions that increase workers direct influence on work process variables will have both direct and indirect positive effects on physical and mental health outcomes.

We have already outlined general union bargaining strategies in the area of work design in our earlier discussion of macro-level approaches. Here we focus on innovations that seek to expand the range and scope of workers' individual and collective influence on the day-to-day conditions within the work process. These innovations are themselves usually either the direct product of collective bargaining or of indirect process bargaining structures such as joint committees, joint training funds, and so forth.

The standard phrase "wages, hours, and working conditions" has generally been interpreted very narrowly by both unions and employers to allow union negotiators few degrees of freedom to initiate major work redesign changes. As we discussed earlier, unions can and do seek to influence virtually every aspect of the work process such as facility design, tools and technology, staffing levels, job content, training, raw materials, production standards, and so forth. However, the majority of American unions have been reluctant to propose changes that expand the scope of individual worker influence in the work process. In part this reluctance reflects a fear that such changes will lead to a return to individual-level bargaining and a weakening of the collective bargaining process (Rankin 1986). It also reflects the fact that few unions have the internal capacity to ensure that the union's institutional interests are not undermined by individual worker influence (Heckscher and Schurman in press). And unions' reluctance to initiate in this area has certainly been shaped by the fact that the vast majority of such innovations have been introduced by employers seeking to increase productivity and quality rather than health and safety (see, e.g., Cooke 1990).

In addition to these factors, there are some specific internal political difficulties confronting unions that wish to initiate changes that increase workers direct influence on the work process. The relationships between work process variables and health outcomes are both much less well established and more complicated to detect than the relationships between, for example, certain physical hazards and health. This raises what game theorists refer to as the "bright line" problem: to be workable, proposed solutions/interventions must possess clear standards that enable each individual worker, despite differences in outlook and circumstances, to determine how to apply the standards (Dorman 1996: 174-75). In comparison to acute exposure to certain hazards such as heating or ventilation problems, noise, or chemicals, where the cause-effect linkage is both directly observable and intuitively obvious to workers, the health effects of, for example, low-level chemical or VDT exposure, poor social relations, lack of decision latitude, work intensity, and job insecurity are not directly observable and must be inferred from large scale statistical studies. This absence of a "bright line," combined with labor's fear of individual or workgroup-level bargaining, pose a significant difficulty in initiating work process interventions.

Nonetheless, as we discussed earlier, an increasing number of unions are negotiating provisions that give individual workers and workgroups increased ability to influence factors in their immediate work process. This occurs within an overall framework that gives the union a strong institutional role, protects the collective bargaining process, and ensures equity among workers in different occupational titles and worksites. There has been very little research recently on the health and safety effects of these innovations, and this represents an important and fruitful area for future intervention research. (For a recent review of psychosocial interventions, see Murphy, Hurrell, Sauter, and Keiter [1995].)

Characteristics of Individuals

A large literature has established that individuals differ in their biological and behavioral responses to similar risks and hazards. Based on genetic, psychological, socioeconomic, cultural, and historical factors, individuals bring different resources to bear on their responses to risk. The Workplace Health Promotion (WHP) field has sought to prevent injury and especially illness by teaching individuals to modify their behaviors to either (1) reduce exposure to risk, (2) minimize the contribution of intervening variables, or (3) reduce the likelihood of negative responses that may exacerbate the effect of the risk or hazard. (See, for example, Baker, Israel, and Schurman [1996] for a discussion of this literature.) Unions have not been major contributors to WHP interventions, viewing them as "blame-the-victim" distractions from addressing the hazards and risks of the work environment. There have been some exceptions. For example, the UAW has participated in sponsoring "worksite wellness" programs together with the Big Three automobile companies (Erfurt and Foote 1991). In addition, many unions have co-sponsored employee assistance programs (EAPs) with employers (such as in the agreements between a number of major U.S.-based airlines and the Association of Flight Attendants and the Air Line Pilots Association). A number of unions have sponsored programs dealing with occupational stress among their members (Landsbergis, Silverman, Barrett, and Schnall 1992; Landsbergis and Cahill 1994).

Union Strategies for Disability Prevention: Treatment Interventions

Returning to the framework in Figure 1 we can examine those interventions involving unions aimed at secondary prevention factors in the disability development process (right-hand side of the figure). Specifically, these leverage points involve unions in affecting various work and nonwork arrangements that affect injured or ill workers beginning in the diagnosis and medical management stages and progressing through policies affecting return to work or compensation for ongoing disability.

Diagnosis, Medical Management, and the Availability of Care

Our framework posits that the most immediate and critical point of preventive intervention after an injury or onset of symptoms is to influence the availability of appropriate medical management and treatment. (We will discuss the issue of accommodation for temporarily or permanently disabled workers later.)

The primary means through which unions influence diagnostic and treatment practice is by increasing the accessibility and quality of such care to members. This might result from several of the macro-level avenues discussed previously: negotiating health care and medical management procedures in contracts, providing direct access to medical care under union auspices, and providing assistance to members in using health care facilities available via contractual or noncontractual avenues. It might also result from a strong presence in the workplace to support workers' individual exercise of legal and contractual rights to seek appropriate care.

The availability of comprehensive health care coverage is arguably the most important and first line of defense against work-related injury or illness because it is accessible to workers irrespective of the employers' medical management policies and practices.[18] Unions appreciably raise the probability that workers receive health care coverage relative to comparable nonunion workers. Based on data from the April 1993 Current

Population Survey, Budd (1998) finds that 57% of nonunion workers were included in an employer's health insurance plan versus 86% of workers covered by a union contract. Even after controlling for observable differences in demographics, firm size, industry, and other factors, coverage by a union contract raises the probability of receiving health care coverage by 13.5%. Budd's estimates parallel those of earlier studies (e.g., Freeman 1981).

Medical Management

The employer's medical management policies and practices can have a significant impact on immediate diagnosis, treatment, and rehabilitation time. Beginning with the immediate response of supervisors and plant/worksite nurses or physicians (where these exist) through visits to the employer's preferred clinic for return-to-work evaluation, management's orientation to injury/illness is likely to play a critical role. Unions in the U.S. and Canada have initiated or cosponsored a variety of research investigations designed to improve the outcomes of secondary prevention aimed at established injuries and illnesses as well as untangling the etiology of more complex chronic illness.[19]

The United Auto Workers has been one of the leaders in this regard in the U.S. The UAW has negotiated large jointly administered health and safety training funds with each of the Big Three auto companies. These funds have sponsored a wide variety of research as well as developed model training and other interventions. For examples of UAW-funded research and intervention, see Schurman and Israel (1990); Hugentobler, Robins, and Schurman (1992); Schurman, Silverstein, and Richards (1992).

The national network of occupational health clinics has been one of the major resources that the labor movement has developed. These clinics seek to provide comprehensive diagnostic and treatment facilities via medical staff trained in recognition of work-related diseases. They also provide resources for workers education and industrial hygiene evaluation (Tuminaro 1990; Lax 1996).[20]

Workers' Compensation, ADA, and Return to Work

A final set of micro-level interventions involves assisting workers to receive benefits in the event of disability and in assisting/fostering return to work. Like the area of work redesign, these activities represent an intersection between the macro- and micro-level policies pursued by unions. Such efforts involve both individual determinants of disability outcomes (e.g., access and quality of health care, biological factors)—and the larger set of firm practices (e.g., retraining and reassignment policies) and public policies (workers' compensation systems) that together determine the probability and characteristics of a return to work.

Workers' compensation requires injured workers covered by the program to file a claim with the designated state agency. Once filed, the designated agency determines whether the individual qualifies for benefits and, if so, the level and length of benefits. Unions potentially play the same role in this system as described in a previous section regarding regulatory intervention: by providing assistance to the injured worker in securing such compensation.

A number of studies indicate that unions increase the likelihood that an injured worker will file and receive benefits relative to comparable nonunion workers. Butler and Worrall (1983) find that a 10% increase in the proportion of unions in an industry is associated with a 10% increase in the number of workers' compensation claims filed, other factors held constant. Krueger and Burton (1990) find similar evidence of a union effect on compensation claims, even after controlling for injury and benefit rates. Hirsch, Macpherson, and DuMond (1997) find large impacts of unionization on the receipt of workers' compensation over the period of 1977-92, which they attribute to the provision of information afforded by unions to their members. Gleason and Roberts (1993) also report higher utilization of workers' compensation systems by unionized workers, based on a survey of Michigan workers injured on the job between 1984-85. While the study suggests that union workers receive higher post-accident household income than nonunion workers, it does not control for possible confounding factors that might also account for the reported differences.[21]

Unionization is also associated with higher levels of compliance with core activities mandated by the Americans with Disabilities Act (ADA). Specifically, Stern and Balser (1996) show that employers in unionized firms are far more likely to comply with a set of four ADA compliance requirements than comparable nonunion employers. These compliance requirements are (1) distributing information on ADA rights, (2) assigning a person or department to handle ADA issues, (3) sending employees for ADA-related training, and (4) developing procedures to create reasonable accommodations for people with disabilities. All of these impacts should raise the probability that a worker once disabled will eventually return to work.

Conclusions

In 1996, according to the National Institute for Occupational Safety and Health (NIOSH), one American worker was injured every five seconds on the job, and every ten seconds a worker was either temporarily or permanently disabled. An average of 16 Americans died each day from injuries on the job; an additional 137 died each day from work-related diseases (NIOSH 1996:vii).[22] The cost of these occupational injuries and illnesses in lost wages and productivity, administrative expenses, health care, and other costs was estimated at $121 billion in 1994 (NIOSH 1996:vii).

More disturbing than the actual number of cases and dollars involved is the lack of change in overall injury and illness trends in recent years. The rate of injury and illnesses in the private sector as reported by the Bureau of Labor Statistics was relatively unchanged over the decade between 1985 and 1995, beginning at 7.9 per 100 full-time workers and ending at 8.1 in 1995. In a recent review, Burton and Chelius (1997:3) assert that "at best there is no apparent overall improvement in workplace safety and health in the last twenty-five years."

Despite the stagnation in injury and illness rates over the last decade, there have been significant reductions in specific industries over this same period. Injury and illness rates have fallen appreciably in three of the most hazardous industries over the past decade. In construction industries, injury and illness rates have fallen from 15.2 per 100 full-time workers in 1985 to 10.6 in 1995. Similarly, the rate of injury and illness fell from 11.4 in 1985 to 9.7 in agriculture, forestry, and fishing and from 8.4 to 6.2 in mining, an industry that has experienced secular falls in these rates since the early 1970s (BLS 1997).

These differences are important from a policy perspective. Industry-level differences in the rate of injury reduction suggest variation in the underlying determinants of safety and health outcomes by sector. As a result, factors affecting health and safety outcomes within industries may be more useful policy variables than factors examined at an aggregated level. For example, service, retailing, and financial service industries may share common characteristics that make reduction in injury rates more difficult using traditional health and safety instruments than in industries such as construction, mining, agriculture, and fishing, where injury rate reduction has been more pronounced. Many occupations in these industries share the characteristic of "high demand-low control" (e.g., Karasek and Theorell 1990) that the occupational stress literature has identified as a significant risk factor for stress-related illness and injury. Interventions focused on the psychosocial aspects of work design may yield a major benefit in these sectors. One promising approach involves integrating traditional occupational safety and health interventions with work reorganization and health promotion interventions (e.g., Baker et al. [1996]; Sorensen, Stoddard, Ockene, Hunt, and Youngstrom [1996]). An integrated approach helps to overcome some of the political difficulties faced by unions that were discussed above by linking the psychosocial work environment to the physical work environment.

One important implication of the framework regarding the disability development process is that some of the variation in recent trends may arise from the suite of practices that unions, management, government, and the other parties that make up the "macro" and "micro" environment have chosen to use across different industries. In particular, the relative impact and importance of the "leverage points" discussed in this chapter vary widely across and within industries. This implies that from a prescriptive perspective, unions should pay greater attention to certain leverage points given characteristics of the entire set of choices depicted in Figure 1.

Analyzing opportunities for intervention among specific leverage points requires a far more systematic approach to prevention than found in the de facto policies pursued in many parts of the labor movement. It requires unions to analyze and respond to the particular set of macro- and micro-level determinants affecting the industries and occupations that they represent and weigh the benefits and costs of different intervention strategies. As a result, an optimal safety and health strategy for the labor movement could very well be one where the approach of one segment of the labor movement diverges considerably from that pursued by another or even within a single union representing a variety of occupational/industrial sectors.

This suggests that there are instances where a "labor movement" position on a policy intervention related to safety and health is not desirable. That is, efforts to improve safety and health prevention through more cooperative labor-management strategies, which have often been greeted with skepticism, may be a beneficial policy in one set of circumstances—for example, as has been found under major project agreements in the construction industry or in some psychosocial work environment experiments. Explicitly including OSHA may be more desirable in other instances where such tripartite agreements framed around particular problems may be the most fruitful avenue to reduce disabilities (e.g., in the agreements reached in the meatpacking industry regarding ergonomics). Enhancing workers' use of rights and increasing the threat of regulatory intervention might be most prudent in cases where compliance with existing standards can appreciably improve safety and health outcomes. Finally, protracted efforts by unions to improve the social network surrounding the disabled might be the most appropriate and fruitful response to disability where the causes of disabilities represent more complicated interactions of work and non-work-related problems.

Along with the need for variation in approaches, however, the framework of this chapter also raises a common issue that cuts across industries and occupations. Figure 1 places the work site as the meeting place between macro- and micro-level interventions regarding disabilities (and between primary and secondary prevention strategies). This suggests the need for a more comprehensive view of the opportunities to prevent work-related disabilities by labor unions at the job site. Unions (as well as employers and government regulators) need to consider a wider variety of tools to address safety and health than found in a narrowly focused approach to injury reduction. Thus technology choice, broader human resource policies, and the network of social service agencies available to the ill or injured need to be considered in fashioning effective safety and health policies, along with aspects of the workplace more directly tied to workplace injuries.

Endnotes

[1] The oldest example of such activity comes from the coal mining industry. "As early as 1662, it is said that 2000 colliers of Northumberland and Durham prepared a petition to the King, asking, among other things, that the mine owners should be required to provide better ventilation of the pits." In their classic studies of trade union functions, the Webbs date the first major efforts in safety and health by unions to the 1840s (Webb and Webb 1920:354-56).

[2] The history of the United Mine Workers of America is indicative of the tension between safety and health and other labor union objectives. Under John L. Lewis, safety outcomes were treated as secondary to agreements with mine operators to promote industry restructuring in order to improve productivity, force out marginal coal operators, and increase wages for the remaining unionized mineworkers. On the one hand, this policy reduced mineworker exposure to risks in small mines (which contribute disproportionately to overall fatality rates). On the other hand, it increased miner exposure to coal dust and consequently to the risk of contracting black lung disease. Inattention to this growing health problem in Lewis' later years and, more profoundly, under his successor Tony Boyle led to tremendous internal upheaval within the UMWA (see Hume 1971; Clark 1981; Smith 1987).

[3] The focus in this chapter will be limited to those disabilities in which work activity plays a significant causal role. We will not devote attention to unions' efforts (or lack thereof as the case may be) to represent the interests of persons with congenital or non-work-related disability.

[4] "Although about half of the waking hours of the ordinary wage earner are spent at his place of employment, it is one of the fundamental disharmonies of present-day industry that he has little or no control over the conditions which there surround him, and which profoundly affect his well-being and even his life. Individual complaint frequently leads to loss of employment rather than to improvement of conditions" (Commons and Andrews 1936:159).

[5] In more formal models of union behavior, union leaders respond to the preferences of the median voter in the union because of their pivotal role in election processes (see, for example, Freeman 1980). This changes the dynamics of internal political processes, as the discussion of seniority below indicates.

[6] This does not hold for all union jobs, however. For example, in building trades unions, seniority is associated with greater exposure to risk since seniority is positively related to work opportunities via the hiring hall.

[7] Unions may also negotiate benefits and programs to assist injured or ill workers, such as the provision of health benefits or sick leave and return-to-work policies. These are reviewed below.

[8] For example: "It is hereby mutually agreed by both parties that work on chimneys shall be done at a higher rate of wages than those specified herein. Should a job arise involving work on chimneys not covered in the rates listed in Section 2, a meeting shall be called, at which time the hours of work, as well as the rate of wages shall be set and agreed upon by the union" (Associated General Contractors of America, Inc. and Pennsylvania Builders Chapter Laborers [LIUNA]).

[9] Hazard pay premiums may result either from explicit wage policies (e.g., contractually specified pay for work entailing higher risks) or implicitly through the interaction of workers, unions, and firms described in the text. The empirical studies cited in the text estimate the relative size of the wage premium arising from both processes, after controlling for other factors that may also lead to systematic differences between union and nonunion workplaces.

[10] The "depth" of safety and health language in agreements negotiated by the UMWA, UAW, URA, OCAW and a number of other manufacturing unions increased significantly following passage of MSHA in 1969 and OSHA in 1971. More detailed contract language diffused more gradually to the building trades unions and even later to service and public sector unions.

[11] Recently, the Executive Council of the AFL-CIO adopted an official policy statement encouraging unions to seek such influence (AFL-CIO 1997).

[12] See "Partnership Agreement Levi Strauss & Co./UNITE."

[13] The labor movement's relative success over the past three decades in advocating for occupational safety and health legislation parallels its success in promoting social legislation that benefits workers regardless of union status (e.g., in supporting legislation related to civil rights, fair labor standards, and plant closing notification).

In contrast, labor has proved far less successful over the past twenty-five years in efforts to promote legislation deemed in the specific interest of organized labor. This included the defeat of legislation to amend labor laws in construction (Common Situs Picketing in 1974), more general reform of organizing provisions of the NLRA in 1977, and recent efforts to propose labor law reform during the first term of the Clinton administration. For a general discussion of this dichotomy, see Freeman and Medoff (1983:Chapter 13).

[14] For example, labor union involvement in worker compensation reform in the state of Oregon led to a 1991 reform bill that fundamentally restructured both the availability and generosity of workers' compensation benefits while at the same time mandating safety and health committees in workplaces with more than ten employees. (See Hecker [1994] for a discussion of the role of labor unions in this reform effort.)

[15] The role of unions in promoting the use of regulatory rights such as those provided by OSHA and MSHA also raises the potential for use of these rights in pursuit of other objectives, such as a tool for pressuring management during organizing or collective bargaining efforts (Northrup 1997). If unions systematically use OSHA for non-safety- and health-related purposes, one would expect to find that employee-initiated complaint inspections in unionized workplaces turn up a higher percentage of trivial (nonserious) violations than in comparable nonunion workplaces. In fact, a detailed analysis of OSHA inspection data for the period 1988-93 by Weil (available from the author) finds that complaint inspections in unionized establishments result in a *higher* percentage of serious violations of OSHA standards than in comparable inspections in nonunion workplaces. While these data do not completely refute Northrup's claim, the aggregate data suggest that while unions may from time to time use health and safety regulatory rights to achieve other objectives, such use does not form the balance of their behavior.

[16] CPWR has three broad goals: (1) to assure a safe and healthful workplace for every construction worker, (2) to improve the health and well-being of construction workers and their families by focusing on health problems related to construction, and (3) to enhance the productivity and economic viability of construction work. For a full description, see Center to Protect Workers Rights (1993).

[17] In contrast to more than 85% of safety and health committees established by private sector collective agreements that are joint labor-management committees, the UMWA/BCOA agreement establishes these as labor-only committees.

[18] Early union efforts in this area include those of the United Mine Workers which negotiated joint health and pension funds in their contracts with the Bituminous Coal Operators Association in the 1950s. These funds provided "nearly comprehensive medical coverage to UMWA miners for several decades" (Seltzer 1988:246).

[19] The United Rubber Workers were the pioneers in establishing joint university/labor union studies on workplace carcinogens, beginning with the formation of the Joint Occupational Health Program between Harvard University, the Rubber Workers, and the B.F. Goodrich Corporation in 1971.

[20] An example of such a joint academic-medical-union clinical effort to prevent disability is the occupational medicine program at the Union of Needletrades, Industrial,

and Textile Employees (UNITE) Union Health Center, a comprehensive health care center serving over 50,000 garment workers in New York City. The occupational medicine clinic integrates direct clinical care with worker and employer education and workplace hazard abatement (Herbert et al. 1997).

[21] A potential conflict between unions facilitating provision of workers' compensation benefits and raising the costs faced by unionized employers through payments into the workers' compensation system arises in many cases, particularly in construction. This occurs in part because of a higher likelihood that unionized contractors will correctly classify their workforce (e.g., laborer, clerical, structural steel worker) for the purpose of setting workers' compensation premiums due to provisions both of collective bargaining agreements and (in the case of public sector work) prevailing wage laws. Since employer workers' compensation premiums are partly determined by the type of work conducted and because compensation rates vary dramatically across construction occupations, unions can adversely affect the relative competitive position of contractors. The building trades and unionized contractors have recently initiated experiments with "carve out" programs to deal with this problem in Massachusetts, California, and other states. These "carve out" programs allow unionized employers and building trades to opt out of the state workers' compensation system and use internal mechanisms to both resolve disability claims on the work site and to promote the return to work.

[22] This figure is controversial due to the methodological difficulties involved in isolating the contribution of work roles to the etiology of many diseases.

References

Adler, Paul S., Barbara Goldaftas, and David I. Levine. 1997. "Ergonomics, Employer Involvement, and the Toyota Production System: A Case Study of NUM-MI's 1993 Model Introduction." *Industrial and Labor Relations Review*, Vol. 50, pp. 416-37.

AFL-CIO. 1997. "Policy on Workplace Democracy." Washington, DC: AFL-CIO.

American Journal of Industrial Medicine Special Issue on Intervention Research. 1994.

Ashford, Nicholas, and Judith Katz. 1977. "Unsafe Working Conditions: Employee Rights under the Labor Management Relations Act and the Occupational Safety and Health Act." *Notre Dame Lawyer*, Vol. 70, pp. 802-37.

Baker, Elizabeth A., Barbara A. Israel, and Susan J. Schurman. 1996. "The Integrated Model: Implications for Worksite Health Promotion and Occupational Health and Safety Practice." *Health Education Quarterly*, Vol. 23, no. 2, pp. 175-90.

Bernard, Elaine. 1995. "Canada: Joint Committees on Occupational Health and Safety." In Joel Rogers and Wolfgang Streeck, eds., *Works Councils: Consultation, Representation, and Cooperation in Industrial Relations*. Chicago, IL: University of Chicago Press, pp. 351-74.

Bronfenbrenner, Urie. 1979. *The Ecology of Human Development*. Cambridge, MA: Harvard University Press.

Budd, John. 1998. "Fringe Benefits and Union Status: Members versus Covered Nonmembers." *Proceedings of the Fiftieth Annual Meeting* (Chicago, Jan. 2-4, 1998). Madison, WI: Industrial Relations Research Association, pp. 250-58.

Bureau of Labor Statistics. 1997. "Current Labor Statistics—Occupational Injury and Illness Rates by Industry." *Monthly Labor Review* (June), pp. 100-102.

Bureau of National Affairs. 1995. *Basic Patterns in Union Contracts.* Washington, DC: BNA Inc.

Burton, John F., Jr., and James R. Chelius. 1997. "Workplace Safety and Health Regulations: Rationale and Results." In Bruce E. Kaufman, ed., *Government Regulation of the Employment Relationship.* Madison, WI: Industrial Relationship Research Association.

Butler, Richard, and John Worrall. 1983. "Workers' Compensation and Injury Claim Rates in the Seventies." *Review of Economics and Statistics,* Vol. 60, pp. 580-90.

Center for Studying Health System Change. 1997. *Issue Brief.* No. 10, June.

Center to Protect Workers Rights. 1993. *Research Project Guidelines.* Washington, DC: CPWR.

Clark, Paul. 1981. *The Miner's Fight for Democracy: Arnold Miller and the Reform of the United Mine Workers.* Ithaca, NY: ILR Press.

Commons, John, and John Andrews. 1936. *Principles of Labor Legislation.* 4th revised ed. New York: Augustus Kelley Publishers (Reprints of Economic Classics).

Cooke, William. 1990. *Labor-Management Cooperation: New Directions or Going in Circles?* Kalamazoo, MI: Upjohn.

Cooke, William, and Frederick Gautschi III. 1981. "OSHA, Plant Safety Programs, and Injury Reduction." *Industrial Relations,* Vol. 20, no. 1, pp. 245-57.

Craypo, Charles. 1986. *The Economics of Collective Bargaining.* Washington, DC: BNA.

Dickens, William. 1984. "Difference between Risk Premiums in Union and Nonunion Wages and the Case for Occupational Safety Regulation." *American Economic Review,* Vol. 74, no. 2, pp. 320-23.

Dorman, Peter. 1996. *Markets and Mortality.* Cambridge: Cambridge University Press.

Dunlop, John T. 1993. *Industrial Relations Systems.* Revised ed. Boston: Harvard Business School Press.

Emery, Fred, and Eric Trist. 1981. "The Causal Texture of Organizational Environments." In Fred Emery, ed., *Systems Thinking.* Vol. 1. London: Penguin.

Erfurt, John, and Andrea Foote. 1991. "How to Design and Implement Megabrush: The Combination of Employee Assistance and Worksite Wellness Programs in a Joint Labor-Management Environment." *Proceedings of the International Conference on Participatory Approaches to Improving Workplace Health* (June 3-5). Ann Arbor: The University of Michigan Labor Studies Center.

Fairris, David. 1992. "Compensating Payments and Hazardous Work in Union and Nonunion Settings." *Journal of Labor Research,* Vol. 13, no. 2, pp. 205-21.

_____. 1998. "Institutional Change in Shopfloor Governance and the Trajectory of Postwar Injury Rates in U.S. Manufacturing, 1946-1970." *Industrial and Labor Relations Review,* Vol. 51, no. 2, pp. 187-203.

Fishback, V. Price, and Shawn-Everett Kantor. 1995. "Did Workers Pay for the Passage of Workers' Compensation Laws?" *Quarterly Journal of Economics,* Vol. 110, no. 3, pp. 713-42.

Freeman, Richard. 1980. "The Exit-Voice Trade-off in the Labor Market: Unionism, Job Tenure, Quits, and Separations." *Quarterly Journal of Economics,* Vol. 94, no. 4, pp. 643-73.

_____. 1981. "The Effect of Unionism on Fringe Benefits." *Industrial and Labor Relations Review*, Vol. 34, no. 4, pp. 489-509.

Freeman, Richard, and James Medoff. 1983. *What Do Unions Do?* New York: Basic Books.

Gleason, Sandra, and Karen Roberts. 1993. "Worker Perceptions of Procedural Justice in Workers' Compensation Claims: Do Unions Make a Difference?" *Journal of Labor Studies*, Vol. 14, no. 1, pp. 45-58.

Goldenhar, Linda, and Paul Schulte. 1994. "Intervention Research in Occupational Health and Safety." *Journal of Occupational Medicine*, Vol. 36, pp. 763-75.

Heaney, Catherine, Barbara Israel, Susan Schurman, Elizabeth Baker, James House, and Margrit Hugentobler. 1993. "Industrial Relations, Worksite Stress Reduction and Employee Well Being: A Participatory Action Research Investigation." *Journal of Organizational Behavior*, Vol. 14, pp. 495-510.

Hecker, Steven. 1994. "Legally Mandated Joint Safety and Health Committees: The Oregon Experience in Comparative Perspective." Manuscript, University of Oregon.

Heckscher, Charles, and Sue Schurman. 1997. "Towards Jobs and Justice: Can Labor-Management Cooperation Deliver Jobs and Justice?" *Industrial Relations Journal*, Vol. 28, no. 4, pp. 323-30.

Herbert, R., B. Plattus, L. Kellogg , J. Luo, M. Marcuso, A. Mascolo, and Philip Landrigan. 1997. "The Union Health Center: A Working Model of Clinical Care Linked to Preventive Occupational Health Services." *American Journal of Industrial Medicine*, Vol. 31, pp. 263-73.

Hirsch, Barry, David Macpherson, and J. Michael Dumond. 1997. "Workers' Compensation Recipiency in Union and Nonunion Workplaces." *Industrial and Labor Relations Review*, Vol. 50, no. 2, pp. 213-36.

Hugentobler, Margrit, Thomas Robins, and Susan Schurman. 1990. "How Unions Can Improve the Outcomes of Joint Health and Safety Programs." *Labor Studies Journal*, Vol. 15, no. 4.

Hume, Brit. 1971. *Death and the Mines: Rebellion and Murder in the UMWA*. New York: Grossman.

Institute for Work and Health. 1996. *The First Five Years: A Review of the Institute's Work & Health Research Program*. Toronto: Institute for Work and Health.

Israel, Barbara A., Susan J. Schurman, and James S. House. 1989. "Action Research on Occupational Stress: Involving Workers as Researchers." *International Journal of Health Services*, Vol. 19, no. 1, pp. 135-55.

Israel, Barbara, Elizabeth Baker, Linda Goldenhar, Catherine Heaney, and Susan Schurman. 1996. "Occupational Stress and Health: Framework and Principles for Effective Prevention Interventions." *Journal of Occupational Health Psychology*, Vol. 1, no. 3, pp. 361-86.

Israel, Barbara, James House, Susan Schurman, Catherine Heaney, and Richard Mero. 1989. "The Relation of Personal Resources, Participation, Influence, Interpersonal Relationships and Coping Strategies to Occupational Stress, Job Strains and Health: a Multivariate Analysis." *Work and Stress*, Vol. 3, pp. 163-94.

Johansson, Gunn, Jeffery Johnson, and E. Hall. 1991. "Smoking and Sedentary Behavior as Related to Work Organization." *Social Science Medicine*, Vol. 32, pp. 837-46.

Kahn, Shulamit. 1990. "What Occupational Safety Tells Us about Political Power in Union Firms." *RAND Journal of Economics*, Vol. 21, no. 3, pp. 481-96.

_____. 1994. "Does Employer Monopsony Power Increase Occupational Accidents? The Case of Kentucky Coal Mines." NBER Working Paper 3897. Cambridge, MA: National Bureau of Economic Research.

Kaminski, Michele, Robin Graubarth, and Amy Mock. 1995. "Using Grant-based Training as a Vehicle for Lasting Change: Strengthening the Role of Local Health and Safety Activists." New Solutions (Winter), pp. 6-14.

Karesek, Robert. 1992. "Stress Prevention through Work Reorganization: A Summary of 19 International Cases." In V. DiMartino, ed., Preventing Stress at Work: Conditions of Work Digest. Vol. II, pp. 23-40.

Karesek, Robert, and Torres Theorell. 1990. Healthy Work. New York: Basic Books.

Katz, Dan, and Robert Kahn. 1978. The Social Psychology of Organizations. 2d ed. New York: Wiley.

Kochan, Thomas. 1980. Collective Bargaining and Industrial Relations. Homewood, IL: Richard D. Irwin, Inc.

Kochan, Thomas, and Paul Osterman. 1994. The Mutual Gains Enterprise: Forging a Winning Partnership among Labor, Management, and Government. Boston, MA: Harvard Business School Press.

Kochan, Thomas, Lee Dyer, and David Lipsky. 1977. The Effectiveness of Union-Management Safety and Health Committees. Kalamazoo, MI: Upjohn Institute of Employment Research.

Krueger, Alan, and John Burton. 1990. "The Employers' Cost of Workers' Compensation Insurance: Magnitudes, Determinants and Public Policy." The Review of Economics and Statistics, Vol. 72, no. 2, pp. 228-40.

Landsbergis, Paul, and Janet Cahill. 1994. "Labor Union Programs to Prevent Occupational Stress in the United States." International Journal of Health Services, Vol. 24, pp. 105-79.

Landsbergis, Paul, Peter Schnall, and Janet Cahill. In press. "Lean Production and Worker Health." Journal of Occupational Health Psychology.

Landsbergis, Paul, Susan Schurman, Barbara Israel, Peter Schnall, Margrit Hugentobler, Janet Cahill, and Dean Baker. 1993. "Job Stress and Heart Disease: Evidence and Strategies for Prevention." New Solutions, Vol. 3, pp. 42-58.

Landsbergis, Paul, B. Silverman, C. Barrett, and P. L. Schnall. 1992. "Union Stress Committees and Stress Reduction in Blue and White-Collar Workers in the United States." Conditions of Work Digest, Vol. 2, no. 2, pp. 144-51.

Lax, M. B. 1996. "Occupational Disease: Addressing the Problem of Under-Diagnosis." New Solutions, Vol. 6, no. 4, pp. 81-92.

Martinello, Felice, and Ronald Meng. 1992. "Workplace Risks and the Value of Hazard Avoidance." Canadian Journal of Economics, Vol. 25, no. 2, pp. 333-45.

McElroy, K. R., D. Bibeau, A. Steckler, and K. Glanz. 1988. "An Ecological Perspective on Health Promotion." Health Education Quarterly, Vol. 15, pp. 351-77.

Merrill, Michael. 1997. "National Institute of Environmental Health Sciences Worker Training Program: A State of the Art Review." Working paper. Silver Spring, MD: George Meany Center for Labor Studies.

Mintz, Benjamin. 1994. OSHA: History, Law and Policy. Washington, DC: Bureau of National Affairs.

National Institute for Occupational Safety and Health. 1996. "National Occupational Research Agenda." Washington, DC: U.S. Department of Health and Human Services.

New York Times. July 15, 1997. "Trial Begins in Class Action Suit on Secondhand Smoke."

_____. October 11, 1997. "Cigarette Makers Reach Settlement in Nonsmoker Suit."

Northrup, Herbert. 1997. "Expanding Union Power by Comprehensive Corporate Campaigns and Manipulation of the Regulatory Process." In Bruce E. Kaufman, ed., *Government Regulation of the Employment Relationship*. Madison, WI: Industrial Relationship Research Association, pp. 533-46.

Office of Technology Assessment. 1985. *Preventing Illness and Injury in the Workplace*. Washington, DC: OTA.

Olson, Craig. 1981. "An Analysis of Wage Differentials Received by Workers in Dangerous Jobs." *Journal of Human Resources*, Vol. 16, no. 3, pp. 167-85.

Ontario Advisory Council on Occupational Health and Occupational Safety. 1986. *Eighth Annual Report, April 1, 1985 to March 31, 1986*. Vols. 2, 3, and 7. Toronto: Government of Ontario.

Page, Joseph, and Mary Win-O'Brien. 1973. *Bitter Wages*. New York: Grossman Publishers.

Planek, Thomas, and Kenneth Kolosh. 1993. *Survey of Employee Participation in Safety and Health*. Itasca, IL: National Safety Council.

Rankin, Tom. 1990. *New Forms of Work Organization: The Challenge to North American Unions*. Toronto: University of Toronto Press.

Reilly, Barry, Pierella Paci, and Peter Holl. 1995. "Unions, Safety Committees and Workplace Injuries." *British Journal of Industrial Relations*, Vol. 33, no. 2, pp. 275-88.

Robins, Thomas, and Susan Klitzman. 1988. "Hazard Communication in a Large U.S. Manufacturing Program: The Ecology of Health Education in the Workplace." *Health Education Quarterly*, Vol. 15, pp. 451-72.

Sandy, Robert, and Robert Elliott. 1996. "Unions and Risk: Their Impact on the Level of Compensation for Fatal Risk." *Economica*, Vol. 63, no. 250, pp. 291-309.

Silverstein, Barbara A., Susan E. Richards, Kirsten Alscer, and Susan Schurman. 1991. "Evaluation of In-Plant Ergonomics Training." *Journal of Industrial Ergonomics*, Vol. 8, pp. 179-93.

Schurman, Susan J., and Barbara A. Israel. 1995. "Redesigning Work Systems to Reduce Stress: Participatory Action Research Approach to Creating Change." In Lawrence E. Murphy, Joseph J. Hurrell, Jr., Steven L. Sauter, and Gwendolyn Puryear Keita, eds., *Job Stress Interventions*. Washington, DC: American Psychological Association.

Schurman, Susan J., Barbara A. Silverstein, and Susan E. Richards. 1994. "Designing a Curriculum for Health Work. Reflections on the United Automobile, Aerospace and Agricultural Workers Union-General Motors Ergonomics Pilot Project." In Michael J. Colligan, ed., *Occupational Medicine State of the Art Reviews; Occupational Safety and Health Training*, Vol. 9, no. 2. Philadelphia: Hanley & Belfus.

Seltzer, Curtis. 1988. "More Dimensions of Occupational Health: The Case of the 1969 Coal Mine Health and Safety Act." In Ronald Bayer, ed., *The Health and Safety of Workers*. New York: Oxford University Press, pp. 242-70.

Siebert, W. Stanley, and X. Wei. 1994. "Compensating Wage Differentials for Workplace Accidents: Evidence for Union and Nonunion Workers in the U.K." *Journal of Risk and Uncertainty*, Vol. 9, no. 1, pp. 61-76.

Sorensen, Gloria, Anne Stoddard, Judith Ockene, Mary Kay Hunt, and Richard Youngstrom. 1996. "Worker Participation in an Integrated Health Promotional Health Protection Program: Results from the WellWorks Project." *Health Education Quarterly*, Vol. 23, no. 2, pp. 191-203.

Stern, Robert, and Deborah Balser. 1996. "Regulations, Social Control, and Institutional Perspectives: Implementing the Americans with Disabilities Act." Manuscript. Cornell University.

Stokols, Daniel, Kenneth R. Peletier, and Jonathan E. Fielding. 1996. "The Ecology of Work and Health: Research and Policy Directions for the Promotion of Employee Health." *Health Education Quarterly*, Vol. 23, no. 2, pp. 137-58.

Thaler, Richard, and Sherwin Rosen. 1975. "The Value of Saving a Life: Evidence from the Labor Markets." In Nestor Terlecky, ed., *Household Production and Consumption*. Cambridge, MA: National Bureau of Economic Research, pp. 265-98.

Thompson, James D. 1967. *Organizations in Action*. New York: McGraw-Hill.

Tuohy, Carolyn, and Marcel Simard. 1993. *The Impact of Joint Health and Safety Committees in Ontario and Quebec*. Study prepared for the Canadian Association of Administrators of Labor Law. Manuscript.

Tuminaro, Daniel. 1990. "Organizing for a Statewide Network of Occupational Disease Diagnostic Centers." *New Solutions*, Vol. 1, no. 1, pp. 18-19.

Viscusi, W. Kip. 1979. *Employment Hazards: An Investigation of Market Performance*. Cambridge, MA: Harvard University Press.

_____. 1993. "The Value of Risks to Life and Health." *Journal of Economic Literature*, Vol. 31, no. 4, pp. 1912-46.

Webb, Sidney, and Beatrice Webb. 1920. *Industrial Democracy*. Revised ed. London: Longmans, Green and Co.

Weil, David. 1991. "Enforcing OSHA: The Role of Labor Unions." *Industrial Relations*, Vol. 30, no. 1, pp. 20-36.

_____. 1992. "Building Safety: The Role of Construction Unions in the Enforcement of OSHA." *Journal of Labor Research*, Vol. 13, no. 1, pp. 121-32.

_____. 1994. *Turning the Tide: Strategic Planning for Labor Unions*. New York: Lexington Books/Macmillan.

_____. 1996a. "Regulating the Workplace: The Vexing Problem of Implementation." *Advances in Industrial and Labor Relations*, Vol. 7, pp. 247-86.

_____. 1996b. "If OSHA Is So Bad, Why Is Compliance So Good?" *The RAND Journal of Economics*, Vol. 27, no. 3, pp. 618-40.

_____. 1997. "Implementing Employment Regulations: Insights on the Determinants of Regulatory Performance." In Bruce E. Kaufman, ed., *Government Regulation of the Employment Relationship*. Madison, WI: Industrial Relationship Research Association, pp. 429-74.

_____. 1998 (forthcoming). "Are Mandated Health and Safety Committees Substitutes or Supplements to Labor Unions?" *Industrial and Labor Relations Review*.

CHAPTER 6

Reducing the Consequences of Disability: Policies to Reduce Discrimination against Disabled Workers

BARBARA A. LEE
Rutgers University

ROGER J. THOMPSON
Travelers Insurance

Previous chapters have focused on state and federal programs to encourage workplace safety, to provide compensation for workplace injuries in exchange for limiting employer liability, and to provide income replacement for individuals who are unable to work at all. This chapter focuses upon individuals with disabilities who can work and the incentives created by state and federal governments to encourage employers to hire and retain workers with disabilities, both by rewarding those that do and by providing legal and financial penalties for those that don't.

State second injury funds are addressed first, and an analysis of their purpose, effectiveness, and future status is presented. After a brief description of state laws prohibiting disability discrimination, the chapter discusses the Americans with Disabilities Act of 1990 (ADA). Comparisons of its purpose and what appears to be its effect after four years of existence are made, and an analysis of its interpretation by federal trial and appellate courts is provided. A discussion of several unresolved issues follows, as well as suggestions for further research.

State Second Injury Fund Provisions

Purpose and Scope

State workers' compensation laws were designed to compensate injured workers for the consequences of workplace injuries. In order to encourage employers to hire and retain workers with preexisting disabilities, state-specific second injury fund (SIF) provisions were added to the workers' compensation laws.

Prior to the creation of SIFs, an occupational accident resulting in further disability to a previously disabled worker would either (1) penalize the worker because compensation benefits were limited to the disability associated with the second injury or (2) penalize the employer by requiring compensation for the combined disability. The latter rule provides a strong disincentive for employers to hire or retain disabled workers. For example, under most state statutes an employee who suffers the loss of sight in both eyes is presumed totally disabled, whereas the loss of sight in one eye is considered a partial disability. There is a substantial difference in indemnity benefits awarded for these two injuries; the loss of sight of an eye may result in benefits for 100 to 200 weeks, while the loss of sight in both eyes can result in benefits paid for the remainder of the claimant's life. Employers will be reluctant to hire workers who have already lost the sight of one eye, if they are held liable for the combined disability in the event of a workplace accident. SIFs encouraged the employment of disabled workers by limiting the employers' financial exposure should a second injury occur.

New York enacted the first SIF in 1916. The law provided that if a worker who had previously incurred permanent partial disability through the loss of one hand, arm, foot, leg or eye incurred permanent total disability through the loss of another member or organ, the employer would be liable only for the second loss. Any remaining compensation due for the combined injury would be paid from a special fund. Most funds were created after World War II to provide employers with an incentive to hire disabled veterans.[1] This development was motivated by a desire to help these veterans find appropriate employment and by the realization that disabled workers, who had been employed during the war due to the existing manpower shortage, were useful and productive workers. In the majority of states SIF legislation was patterned after the New York law.

Coverage Issues

Although the early funds encouraged employers to hire and retain disabled workers, critics attacked the narrowness of their coverage, particularly the requirement of the loss of a "member" and the requirement that the individual be totally disabled. In response, states began to experiment with increasing coverage. At the same time, a group of compensation experts who convened under the auspices of the Council of State Governments was drafting the model Workmen's Compensation Act (hereafter model act), which influenced state action regarding second injury funds.

In drafting the model act SIF provisions, the work group considered the type of preexisting condition that would be required in order to obtain protection. The New York law specified a "previously incurred permanent partial disability," which implied that the second injury must be work-related. Language in the model act broadened coverage to include impairment "from any cause or origin and by defining permanent impairment as more than simply the loss of a member or organ: "(a)ny permanent condition, whether congenital or due to injury or disease, of such seriousness as to constitute a hindrance or obstacle to obtaining employment or to obtaining reemployment if the employee should become unemployed."

The model act further clarified the intent that permanent impairment be broadly defined by including a schedule of the most common prior impairments. The list included epilepsy, diabetes, cardiac disease, ruptured disc, psychoneurotic disabilities, and 21 other conditions. The list concluded with recognition for any condition that "would support a rating of disability of 200 weeks or more if evaluated in accordance with standards applied to workers' compensation cases." The intent was that if a worker had one of the conditions listed in the schedule and later suffered a second injury, the existence of the preexisting condition would be sufficient to qualify the claim for SIF relief.

Although only a few states adopted the model act's provisions, many did adopt language similar to the model act's definition of permanent impairment. A few states retain the narrower definition that requires the impairment to be "a hindrance or obstacle to employment."

Defining the Extent of "Combined Effect"

Another issue facing those states that wished to expand coverage was whether the combined effect of the first and second injuries must result in permanent and total disability. Twelve states have this requirement, which restricted the number of cases qualifying for relief because work-related injuries that result in permanent and total disability occur infrequently, even in cases where there is a preexisting impairment. The model act expanded the definition of permanent impairment by providing that the subsequent disability be "substantially greater by reason of the combined effect of the preexisting impairment and the subsequent injury or by reason of the aggravation of the preexisting impairment than that which would have resulted from the second injury alone." Many states adopted this language and faced the need to pay significantly more claims from their SIFs. Furthermore, disputes arose as to the extent of the disability associated with the original condition, frequently culminating in litigation. Expansion of the "combined effect" language also exposed the funds to claims involving disability of short duration or for minor impairments.

Recognizing the inefficiencies associated with the undefined point at which a fund's liability could begin and to prevent the fund from becoming involved in a multitude of relatively minor claims, the model act provided that the employer or his insurance carrier would be responsible only for the first 104 weeks of disability payments. Making the fund liable after 104 weeks eliminated the need to make individual determinations as to the extent of the original disability and also eliminated claims involving minor impairments or minimal periods of disability from fund liability.

Financing the Second Injury Funds

Expansion of fund utilization prompted changes in financing methods. Following the New York example, many early funds secured financing by requiring that employer make payments to the fund in death cases where there are no surviving dependents. While several states continue to use this approach, most found that this source is insufficient to finance expenditures.

The model act included a financing scheme which established a prorata share of the cost among all insurance carriers and self-insured employers based upon the prior year's payments of workers' compensation benefits. This approach was designed to ensure that adequate funding would be available each year to cover expenditures from the fund. These assessments on insurance companies were passed back to the employers through the premiums that employers paid for workers' compensation insurance. A few states used other techniques for acquiring funding, including a percentage of the premium tax insurance carriers paid to the state, additional payments to the fund where the claim resulted in the loss of major body members, and general revenues from the state.

States that lowered access thresholds significantly expanded fund utilization. For example, the second injury fund of Kentucky spent over $112 million in 1993 (or $95 per worker) compared with expenditures of $56,418 (or $0.02 per employee) by North Carolina during this same year.

The extent of fund expenditures represents a potential problem in two respects. First, assessments need to be sufficient to raise the monies necessary to cover expenditures. Secondly, because assessments are only sufficient to cover current expenditures and do not establish reserves for future liabilities, growth of these funds may create significant unfunded liabilities. Even where new claims are no longer being accepted, assessments are required to pay off previously created liabilities.

The growth in fund activity prompted a few states to consider formal certification of preexisting conditions as a method to control fund utilization. Some states enacted language permitting preexisting conditions to be certified as an effort to expedite acceptance by the fund. While certification expedites the claim acceptance process, conditions that were not certified were not precluded from seeking acceptance through traditional procedures. Other states have established a narrower rule for registration of preexisting conditions; the employer's responsibility is limited to 104 weeks of benefits where a certified "vocationally handicapped" person suffered a second injury. Additional benefits, without consideration of increased disability or permanent and total disability, are payable from the fund. This approach eliminates the need for certification after the second injury.

More recently, a growing number of states have begun to examine the original purposes for which these SIFs were established and have, in some instances, repealed such provisions for new and arising cases. For states with high access thresholds, questions arise as to whether the original purpose of such funds is being met when the potential for recovery is so limited. States with low access thresholds question whether or not their funds are becoming "dumping grounds" for problem cases rather than serving the original purpose of encouraging the hiring and retention of workers with disabilities, and several have closed their funds to new applicants.

Without addressing many of the previously noted limitations of the initial SIF laws, employers did probably look to SIFs as one inducement to hire and retain disabled workers. This encouragement applied not only to disabled veterans but also had application for individuals with non-work-related disabilities or preexisting health conditions. Workers with diabetes, epilepsy, and other congenital conditions were frequently the target of employment discrimination and benefited from these funds.

But while state SIF provisions may have initially operated to encourage the hiring of disabled workers, these laws have come to be supplanted by state and federal legislation barring employment discrimination. Replacing economic incentives for employers of disabled workers with the threat of potential legal liability for discrimination has shifted the locus of activity from state compensation boards and agencies to state and federal courts.

State Nondiscrimination Laws

Purpose and Scope

Many states have prohibited discrimination on the basis of disability for several decades. Some states have added disability to the list of other protected characteristics (i.e., race, gender, and religion) in their fair employment practices or human rights laws, while other states have passed separate laws that forbid discrimination on the basis of disability.

Although all states have some form of prohibition against discrimination on the basis of disability for certain employees, many of these state laws do not cover the employment sector or the array of disorders, nor do they require the type of accommodation specified by the ADA. For example, some state statutes only protect public sector employees, while others limit coverage to physical disabilities—thereby excluding mental disorders. Still others specifically exclude alcoholism or drug abuse. Therefore, the ADA provides more comprehensive coverage in terms of the types of disabilities that may be included within its ambit and the number of employers who must comply with the law.

Limitations and State Experience

State laws differ from the ADA in other important ways. Many do not mention reasonable accommodation, while others specify that the covered disability must be "unrelated to performance," suggesting that the individual must be able to perform job functions despite the disability. This appears to excuse the employer from the necessity of providing a reasonable accommodation for an individual whose disability affects job performance.[2] Furthermore, some state statutes have been interpreted to limit the accommodation requirement to the actual job the disabled worker holds; reassignment to a vacant position or reallocation of peripheral functions have not been acknowledged as potential accommodations (Draper 1990:316-17).

Other state laws have capped the amount that the employer must expend on the accommodation. For example, Minnesota's nondiscrimination law states that the maximum cost of a reasonable accommodation for a disabled worker is $50; Virginia law establishes a $500 limit. North Carolina law provides that an accommodation is reasonable if it does not exceed 5% of the employee's annual salary (Harger 1993:805).

Critics take issue with state disability discrimination laws for several reasons. In addition to the problems discussed above, these laws have not been aggressively enforced, leading one commentator to conclude that protection against disability discrimination provided by state statutes was "potluck" at best and ineffective in many cases (Erf 1977). Some legal scholars had recommended that "disability" be added to the list of protected characteristics in Title VII of the Civil Rights Act of 1964 (Erf 1977; Peck 1983). However, disability rights advocates pushed for a separate law that would recognize the special circumstances of individuals with disabilities, rather than treating "disability" as a unidimensional characteristic, like race or gender. This approach ultimately prevailed when Congress passed the Americans with Disabilities Act of 1990.

The Americans with Disabilities Act (ADA)

Purpose and Scope

Although the federal Rehabilitation Act had forbidden disability discrimination by federal contractors and public agencies since 1972, this law did not affect most private sector employers. The ADA was designed to integrate individuals with disabilities into American society—a society from which they had been excluded by physical and attitudinal barriers. This section of the chapter will assess to what degree the law, four years after it became effective for employers with 25 or more workers, has fulfilled its original objectives. These objectives include (1) increasing access to employment for individuals with disabilities, (2) providing effective remedies for current or potential workers with disabilities, and (3) increasing employer willingness to hire and retain workers with disabilities.

Increasing access and integration. A 1986 Harris poll reported that approximately two-thirds of people with disabilities in the U.S. were unemployed, and of those individuals, two-thirds stated that they would like to work (West 1991:5). Although the disability rights movement expected the ADA to result in better integration of individuals with disabilities into the workforce, this goal has not yet been reached. Five years after the ADA's enactment, the proportion of unemployed individuals with disabilities was identical to the 1986 figure, according to another Harris poll (Smolowe 1995:55), and the proportion of individuals with disabilities who are working actually declined between 1986 and 1994 (Holmes 1994:A18). Part of the reason for the apparent failure of the law to increase access may be traced to an economic recession in the early 1990s. However, commentators also cite employer prejudice against workers with disabilities (particularly certain disabilities, as discussed in Lee 1996); employer fears that hiring disabled workers will increase health insurance costs, workers' compensation costs, and impose high accommodation costs; and the disinclination of disabled individuals dependent upon federal disability benefits to lose them if they accept employment (Krenek 1994:1971).

Table 1, which summarizes ADA claims filed with the Equal Employment Opportunity Commission (EEOC), shows that access to employment has not been the primary focus of enforcement activity. Challenges to negative hiring decisions comprised only 10% of the disability discrimination claims filed with the EEOC between July 26, 1992 (the date the law first became effective), and March 31, 1997. As

TABLE 1

Disability Discrimination Charges Filed with the Equal Employment Opportunity Commission between July 26, 1992 and March 31, 1997.

Violation Cited	Number	Percent[1]
Discharge	42,582	52.2
Failure to provide reasonable accommodation	23,310	28.6
Harassment	10,023	12.3
Hiring	7,791	9.5
Discipline	6,487	8.0
Layoff	3,761	4.6
Promotion	3,180	3.9
Benefits	3,098	3.8
Wages	2,830	3.5
Rehire	2,736	3.4
Suspension	1,840	2.3
Total claims filed	81,595	

Impairments Claimed	Number	Percent[2]
Back Impairments	14,639	17.9
Emotional/Psychiatric Disorders	10,487	12.8
Neurological	9,095	11.1
Extremities	7,491	9.2
Heart	3,345	4.1
Diabetes	2,927	3.6
Substance Abuse	2,663	3.3
Hearing Impairments	2,303	2.8
Blood Disorders	2,312	2.6
(HIV)	(1,451)	(1.8)
Vision Impairments	2,112	2.6
Cancer	1,920	2.4
Asthma	1,400	1.7

[1,2] These figures add to more than 100% because individuals may allege multiple violations and/or multiple disabilities.

the table demonstrates, most charges involved discharge (52%) or failure to provide reasonable accommodation (29%).

Additional data from the EEOC suggest that the disabilities mentioned during congressional debates (mobility impairments, visual and hearing impairments) have not been the focus of the ADA's enforcement. Table 1 indicates that the most frequent impairment claimed by individuals alleging disability discrimination under the ADA is back impairments (18%), followed by emotional or psychiatric impairments (13%), neurological impairments (11%), impairments of the extremities (9%), and heart impairments (4%).

The EEOC data show a disconnect between the purpose of the law—to increase access to employment for individuals with disabilities—and the enforcement experience. They demonstrate that currently or previously employed workers (90% of the charges), a substantial proportion of whom may have developed disabilities during their employment,[3] are using the law to challenge perceived discrimination. These data also show that workers who have disabilities that are particularly difficult to diagnose and verify—back disorders and psychiatric impairment—account for nearly one-third of the charges.

Providing effective remedies. The ADA provides for both equitable remedies and compensatory and punitive damages for employees or applicants who can prove that a negative employment decision violated the ADA. Equitable remedies include reinstatement or hiring, an injunction forbidding future discrimination against the individual or a class of disabled individuals, promotion, access to training, or some other employment benefit that was discriminatorily denied. Compensatory and punitive damages are capped at $300,000 for employers with 500 or more employees; the caps are lower for smaller companies. Successful plaintiffs under the ADA can also be awarded backpay, frontpay, and attorney's fees.

Between July 26, 1992 (the date the law first became effective), and March 31, 1997, 81,595 charges of employment discrimination on the basis of disability were filed with the Equal Employment Opportunity Commission (EEOC 1997). Of the 70,140 charges that had been resolved by March 31, 1997, 38% were closed administratively,[4] 48% resulted in a finding of no discrimination, 6% were withdrawn with benefits, and 5% were settled. Only 2.7% resulted in a finding of reasonable cause to believe that discrimination had occurred. The EEOC reported a total of $150.5 million in monetary benefits obtained by individuals who filed claims of employment discrimination between 1992 and March 31, 1997 (EEOC 1997).

While there has been no comprehensive analysis of the success of plaintiffs in ADA litigation, the emerging case law suggests that judges are interpreting the ADA's provisions narrowly. Because of the ADA's relatively recent enactment, few cases have reached the appellate courts. Furthermore, many cases litigated under the ADA involve successful motions for summary judgment by employers, which means that no trial is held. The ADA plaintiffs who have prevailed, however, have been awarded backpay, frontpay, and attorney's fees, as well as reinstatement to their prior position (with accommodation), reassignment, or promotion (*EEOC v. AIC Security Investigations, Ltd.* 1995; *Bombrys v. City of Toledo* 1993).

Increased employer receptivity to employing individuals with disabilities. Research conducted prior to the enactment of the ADA on employer attitudes toward hiring or retaining disabled workers obtained mixed results. Although many employers reported positive attitudes toward employing disabled individuals, their actual hiring behavior often belied this response (Lyth 1973). Furthermore, many employers keep no records on the number or identity of their workers who have a disability (McFarlin, Song, and Sonntag 1991), making it difficult to collect information about employment practices with regard to these individuals. Other research demonstrates a strong size effect: respondents from small and medium-size companies are significantly more likely to state that they had no disabled workers, that they could not accommodate such workers, and that the cost of such accommodation was prohibitive (Eagleton Institute 1993; Lee 1996). Most companies have no policies regarding the hiring, evaluation, or monitoring of workers with disabilities (Gallup 1992).

Five years after the ADA's enactment, it did not appear that employer attitudes had become much more positive. A 1995 Harris survey found that the hiring rate of workers with disabilities in large companies had remained stable since 1990 and had actually decreased by six percentage points for small businesses (Smolowe 1995:55).

Research has also demonstrated that employers appear to have a hierarchy of preferences with regard to their employees' disabilities; they are more averse to disabilities that they fear may result in problematic behavior (psychiatric disorders, alcoholism, seizure disorders) than they are to other disorders, such as mobility impairments or learning disorders (Lee and Newman 1993). Other research has demonstrated that employers are more likely to hire or retain workers with physical disabilities than those with other disabilities (Combs and Omvig 1986; Greenwood, Schriner and Johnson 1991; Mancuso 1990).

The ADA has been in effect only since 1992; most companies that must comply with the law have been covered only since 1994. Litigation has focused primarily on whether the law covers the ADA plaintiff; many cases never reach the stage at which the reasonable accommodation requirement is discussed. Further research is needed on employer compliance with the law, on the cost of that compliance, and employer attitudes toward these workers before any definitive statement can be made about the law's impact on employer attitudes.

Policy Issues and Judicial Response

The ADA has been criticized by a variety of sources. The business community, and most particularly small employers, has complained that it will force them to make expensive accommodations that they are ill-equipped to make or to pay for (Janofsky 1993:A-12). On the other hand, the disability rights movement has criticized the law for not going far enough to require employers to make meaningful changes that will help integrate disabled individuals into the workplace because the law requires only that "reasonable" accommodations be made on a case-by-case basis (Krenek 1994:1983). Lawyers have criticized its lack of guidance on the scope of the reasonable accommodation requirement (Krenek 1994; Lavelle 1991), its lack of clarity in defining the term "essential function" (Arney 1992; Shaller 1991), and its amorphous definition of "undue hardship" (Epstein 1995; Harger 1993; Mastrangelo 1994). Although the ADA is still a relatively young law, some responses to these criticisms are beginning to emerge, both from research and from the courts.

Although federal courts have not been entirely consistent in their interpretation of the ADA, a body of jurisprudence developed under the Rehabilitation Act is helping the federal courts shape a relatively consistent interpretation of the ADA's four primary elements (1) that the individual have a *disability* that meets the statute's definition, (2) that the individual be *qualified* to perform the position's essential functions, (3) that the employer determine whether a *reasonable accommodation* will enable the individual to perform the job, and (4) the degree to which the accommodation requirement is limited by *undue hardship*. Analysis of judicial response to these four statutory concepts has implications both for national policy related to disability and for employment relations at the individual firm.

Scope of Coverage for Disability

The ADA defines a disability as "a physical or mental impairment that substantially limits one or more of the major life activities of such individual, a record of such an impairment, or being regarded as having such an impairment" (42 U.S.C. sec. 12102[2]). This definition is identical to the definition of disability in the Rehabilitation Act (29 U.S.C. sec. 706[B]) and encompasses a wide variety of disorders. Despite the breadth of its language, however, courts have interpreted the definition narrowly, limiting both the type of disorder that will qualify as a disability and limiting the scope of the term "substantially limited."

In interpreting the ADA, courts have required in most cases that the individual be substantially limited in his or her ability to perform a wide range of jobs, rather than being simply unable to do one or more tasks of a particular job. For example, in an often-cited case litigated under the Rehabilitation Act, *E.E. Black, Ltd. v. Marshall* (1980), the federal trial court articulated a standard that many subsequent courts have followed: the individual must be disqualified from a given occupation in the geographic area reasonably accessible to the individual (p. 1101). Because of this interpretation, which has been adopted by the EEOC, many ADA plaintiffs have been unable to meet the statutory definition. For example, in *Schwartz v. Northwest Iowa Community College* (1995), a library clerk with a visual disorder (night blindness) challenged the college's decision to transfer her to the night shift. The court noted that her visual impairment did not affect her ability to work, but only to drive at night. Nor did the disorder disqualify her from a wide range of jobs. Therefore, stated the court, she did not meet the definition of "substantially limited." Courts reached similar conclusions in *Schluter v. Industrial Coils, Inc.* (1996) (diabetes), *Matthews v. TCI of Illinois* (1996) (back disorder), and *Taylor v. Albertsons* (1996) (repetitive motion disorder).

These cases suggest that courts are interpreting the ADA's definition of "disability" very narrowly. They are excluding even those disorders that are cited in the legislative history and the regulations (for example, diabetes and back disorders) if the plaintiff cannot show that the impairment excludes him or her from a wide range of jobs or classes of jobs. This approach may result in a bifurcated group of individuals with disabilities: those whose disorders are real and require medical treatment but which preclude only certain types of work, compared with those with disorders so severe that they limit that individual's ability to do almost any type of work. Individuals in the first category may not be protected, even though their disabilities may be easier and less expensive to accommodate than those in the second category. Under current judicial interpretation of the "substantially limited" language, employers may be able to escape liability for refusing to accommodate a disabled worker who cannot perform his or her job. This is because the litigation will never reach the stage at which the accommodation issue is addressed if the case is dismissed because the plaintiff is deemed not "disabled" under the ADA's definition.

Qualification and Essential Functions

The ADA defines a qualified individual with a disability as "an individual with a disability who, with or without reasonable accommodation, can perform the essential functions of the employment position that such individual holds or desires" (42 U.S.C. sec. 12111[8]). Litigation concerning this definition has focused upon the meaning of "essential function" and a determination as to whether the individual has been, or is capable of, performing those essential functions.

The regulations define "essential function" as "the fundamental job duties of the employment position the individual with a disability holds or desires. The term . . . does not include the marginal functions of the position" (29 C.F.R. sec. 1630.2[n]). According to the regulations, the employer has the right to determine the job's essential functions (29 C.F.R. sec. 1630.2[n]). However, the court will make a factual inquiry that includes the amount of time spent on the function, whether employees in the same job category perform the function(s), and the consequences of not requiring the disabled worker to perform the function, among other criteria.

Determination of essential functions. In an often-cited case brought under the Rehabilitation Act involving the U.S. Postal Service, a federal trial court ruled that a hearing-impaired plaintiff was "qualified" for a position as a clerk-typist, despite the fact that she could not answer the telephone. The court noted that several other clerks in the work area already were answering the telephone, and it was not an essential function of the position (*Davis v. Frank* 1989). Most cases brought under the Rehabilitation Act, however, resulted in a finding that the plaintiff could not perform the essential functions of the position. For example, in *Jasany v. United States Postal Service* (1985), a federal appellate court ruled that a postal employee who could not operate a mail-sorting machine because of a visual impairment was not qualified, since using the machine was an essential function of his position. Courts interpreting the ADA have adopted Rehabilitation Act jurisprudence and have shown considerable deference to an employer's assertion that certain job tasks are essential functions. For example, in *Mancini v. General Electric* (1993), the court upheld the discharge of a production worker with "emotional problems" who was insubordinate on several occasions, saying that the ability to follow orders is an essential function of his job. And in *Misek-Falkoff v. IBM Corp.* (1994), the court accepted the company's argument that ability to work with a team, cooperation with coworkers, and reliability in getting work completed on time were essential functions of the job of an individual whose atypical trigeminal neuralgia resulted in poor attendance and numerous controversies with supervisors and coworkers.

Attendance. Many employers have claimed that regular attendance is an essential function of a wide range of positions, and the courts have typically accepted that argument when a plaintiff has claimed that a discharge for excessive absences violated the ADA because the absences were directly related to the disability. For example, in *Carr v. Reno* (1994), a federal appellate court ruled that an employee with Meuniere's Disease who was frequently absent was not qualified because the nature of the work required her to perform it at the worksite and the work had to be completed by the end of the work day. Similar results were reached in *Tyndall v. National Education Center* (1994) (lupus) and *Jackson v. Veterans Administration* (1994) (rheumatoid arthritis), and in *Whillock v. Delta Air Lines, Inc.* (1995) (chemical sensitivity).

Disability benefits. A third area of judicial activity related to the issue of employee qualification is the effect of seeking disability benefits upon a plaintiff's ability to argue that he or she is "qualified" under the ADA. In several cases, courts have ruled that a plaintiff who has applied for or is receiving disability benefits on the representation that he or she is totally disabled cannot therefore be "qualified" under the ADA (see, for example, *McNemar v. The Disney Store, Inc.* [1995] and *EEOC v. CNA Insurance Companies et al.* [1996]).

The results in these cases have important implications for the practice of negotiating "compromise and release agreements" as a method of settling a workers' compensation claim. In these settlements, the claimant agrees to accept a lump sum payment in exchange for releasing the employer from further liability for the claim. Importantly, these agreements also typically provide that the claimant will not seek reemployment or future employment with the employer. Assuming that a judge would find the particular agreement valid on the grounds that the claimant was informed as to the rights being waived and that sufficient consideration was given for the waiver, the agreement would appear to preclude subsequent litigation by the claimant under the ADA. The claimant, having voluntarily resigned from employment, could not demonstrate that he or she was an "employee" for purposes of the act.

The cases decided to date under the ADA, following in many respects jurisprudence developed under the Rehabilitation Act, demonstrate that substantial hurdles exist for plaintiffs who wish to challenge a negative employment decision under the statute. But if the plaintiff succeeds in convincing a court that the disability is covered by the law and that he or she can perform the essential functions of the position (with or without accommodation), the court must then determine whether the employer has provided, or considered, accommodations that would enable the individual to perform the job.

Boundaries of "Reasonable" Accommodation

The primary objection that employers have voiced to the ADA's reasonable accommodation requirement is its purported cost. Even prior to the law's enactment, employers reported concerns that disabled workers would be expensive to accommodate (McFarlin, Song, and Sonntag 1991). But research suggests that the cost of accommodating currently employed workers with disabilities is relatively modest.

A survey of 2,000 federal contractors in 1982 found that most accommodations made for workers with disabilities involved no cost or only a modest cost. Fifty-one percent of the accommodations cost nothing, another 30% cost less than $500, and only 8% of the accommodations cost more than $2,000 (Collignon 1986:215-16). Other pre-ADA studies have reached similar conclusions (Bureau of National Affairs 1992; Job Accommodation Network, cited in Hearne 1991:116). A pre- and post-ADA study of the cost of accommodations made by Sears, Roebuck and Company found that 69% of the accommodations involved no cost, 28% cost less than $1,000, and 3% cost more than $1,000. The average accommodation cost was $121 (Blanck 1994:12). Two years later, a follow-up survey of accommodation costs at Sears found that the average accommodation cost had dropped to $45 (Blanck 1996). Yet another study, this one of fifty New Jersey employers, found that 54% of the accommodations were cost-free, 16% cost less than $500, another 16% cost between $500 and $5,000, and 10% cost more than $5,000 (Lee and Newman 1995:219-20).

But these research results may understate the full cost of implementing the ADA's reasonable accommodation requirement. First, many accommodations involve additional supervisory time or the adoption of a flexible schedule for the worker—actions that may involve some "cost" to the employer that does not show up on a balance sheet and thus is not reported (Lee and Newman 1995). Secondly, employers may only be hiring or retaining workers with disabilities that are relatively inexpensive to accommodate; extending the accommodation requirement to workers with a wide range of disabilities or to workers with more severe work limitations could increase the cost of accommodation (Chirikos 1991).

Some evidence has emerged from research conducted in Canada on the cost of accommodating workers who suffered work-related injuries. A study found that Ontario employers who rehired their own injured workers appeared to have absorbed the full cost of accommodation, but those who hired workers injured elsewhere appeared to have responded to the accommodation requirement through lowering the pay of those workers (Gunderson and Hyatt 1996). This research was conducted prior to the passage of an Ontario law that requires employers to reemploy those workers injured at their place of business and, if necessary, to provide accommodations up to the point of undue hardship. Additional research, using national samples of private sector employers in both the U.S. and Canada, needs to be conducted to determine more precisely the cost of accommodation.

The ADA does not define the term "reasonable accommodation" but provides examples of potential reasonable accommodations. Accommodations may be necessary either to provide disabled workers with access to the employer's facilities (such as lunchrooms, restrooms, or the work area itself) or to enable the individual to perform the job. The law includes the following as reasonable accommodations:

> job restructuring, part-time or modified work schedules, reassignment to a vacant position, acquisition or modification of equipment or devices, appropriate adjustment or modifications of examinations, training materials or policies, the provision of qualified readers or interpreters, and other similar accommodations. (42 U.S.C. sec. 12111[9])

The law requires that an individualized determination be made concerning the accommodation needs of a worker with a disability.

Despite the breadth of the reasonable accommodation requirement, it does not require the employer to create a position for the disabled worker, nor does it require the employer to reassign essential functions of the position. Furthermore, it does not require the employer to promote a disabled worker nor to hire a second employee to perform most of the essential functions of the job (Shaller 1991:433). The law does not require the employer to provide personal devices, such as eyeglasses or a wheelchair. However, it may require the employer to provide adaptive equipment to modify the physical layout of the employee's workspace or to provide a modified work schedule for certain workers. This latter category could include workers who must rely on public transportation, workers who cannot work rotating shifts because of the effect of fatigue on their condition, or workers who need a special schedule for some other legitimate disability-related reason.

Despite the list of potential accommodations in the statute and the extended discussion of accommodation in the EEOC Technical Assistance manual, federal courts have interpreted the ADA's reasonable accommodation requirement rather narrowly. A review of ADA cases that reached the federal appellate courts revealed that plaintiffs were overwhelmingly unsuccessful in prevailing when they claimed that either the employer had failed to accommodate them or that the accommodations chosen by the employer were inadequate.

Additional time or training. In *Carozza v. Howard County* (1995), a clerk who had bipolar disorder claimed that her employer had insufficiently accommodated her disability. The court disagreed, noting that the county had given her additional time to learn the required word processing programs, an essential function of her position, and had provided numerous training opportunities, job counseling, and medical leave. Similarly in *Hankins v. The Gap, Inc.* (1996), an appellate court cited with approval the employer's attempts to accommodate an employee with migraine headaches by offering her sick leave, in-house medical treatment, and additional rest time.

Physical modification of the workplace. The ADA requires employers to make modifications in the physical layout of the work area or to provide technology to enable a qualified disabled worker to perform his or her job. In *Stewart v. County of Brown* (1996), the employer of a security guard with both physical and psychiatric disorders redesigned the security room in conjunction with a doctor's suggestions, gave the employee a leave of absence, installed blinds and film on windows and doors to reduce glare, and purchased an ergonomic chair. The court rejected the employee's claim that the accommodations were insufficient, saying that the ADA does not require the employer to provide accommodations that will "cure" the employee, only those that are responsive to the employee's needs.

Additional leave time. A leave of absence has typically been viewed as a potential reasonable accommodation under the Rehabilitation Act (*Walker v. Weinberger* [1985]); however, courts interpreting the ADA have been unwilling to require employers to provide a disabled worker with a leave of indefinite duration, even if the leave is unpaid. For example, in *Myers v. Hose* (1995), a federal appellate court rejected the claim of the plaintiff, a bus driver who had been disqualified under U.S. Department of Transportation regulations because of his congestive heart failure and diabetes. The plaintiff had asserted that the employer should accommodate him by providing him sufficient time to bring his diabetes under control. A similar result was reached in *Hudson v. MCI Telecommunications Corp.* (1996) (carpal tunnel syndrome).

Working at home. Because some disabilities make it difficult for an individual to get to work, either because of transportation problems (lack of public transportation, for example) or because of the nature of the disability itself, some plaintiffs have requested the accommodation of working at home. Although the courts have been willing to consider working at home as a potential accommodation, the predominant judicial response to this request has been negative. For example, in *Van de Zande v. State of Wisconsin Department of Administration* (1995), the court rejected the plaintiff's request, noting that her position required her to function with other employees as a team; furthermore, she could not be supervised if she worked at home, said the court. Another federal appellate court reached a similar conclusion in *Whillock v. Delta Air Lines, Inc.* (1995) (multiple chemical sensitivity).

Special considerations. The reasonable accommodation requirement may require the employer to provide a disabled worker with a device or some other assistance that nondisabled employees are not given. For example, a visually impaired worker may need a part-time reader; courts have found an aide or assistant to be a reasonable accommodation under the Rehabilitation Act (*Nelson v. Thornburgh* [1984]). Again, the courts have been willing to consider a plaintiff's argument that special consideration of some type is required as a reasonable accommodation, but results have been mixed. For example, in *Lyons v. The Legal Aid Society* (1995), an appellate court ordered the trial court to hold a hearing to determine whether an employer-paid parking space was a reasonable accommodation for an employee with serious mobility impairments. And in *Borkowski v. Valley Central School District* (1994), a panel of appellate judges in the same circuit held that the trial court must determine whether the school district must provide a teacher with cognitive difficulties associated with head trauma with a teacher's aide as a reasonable accommodation. But in *Kennedy v. Chemical Waste Management* (1996), an employer had initially accommodated a unionized, disabled worker by transferring him to a position outside the bargaining unit. After several years, the worker reassumed his old position but lost his previous seniority. The court rejected the plaintiff's claim that reasonable accommodation required restoration of seniority since the company's policy of treating the plaintiff like a new employee for seniority purposes was applied neutrally and since the restoration of seniority was not necessary to accommodate the worker's disability.

Reassignment to a vacant position. The ADA lists reassignment as a potential reasonable accommodation, yet the courts have not been consistent in their interpretation of this type of accommodation, particularly when other employees have prior claims on the position, either through seniority or through the provisions of a collective bargaining agreement. Some courts have read the statutory language literally and have required the employer to explain why vacant positions are not suitable for the disabled worker. For example, in *Benson v. Northwest Airlines* (1995), an appellate court reversed a summary judgment award to the employer because the plaintiff had claimed that several vacant positions were available that he could perform, despite the fact that he could no longer perform his original job as an airplane mechanic. But in *Myers v. Hose* (1995) the court, seemingly ignoring the ADA's inclusion of reassignment as a form of reasonable accommodation, stated that "the duty of reasonable accommodation does not encompass a responsibility to provide a disabled employee with alternative employment when the employee is unable to meet the demands of his present position" (p. 283). This interpretation appears to flatly contradict the statutory language of the ADA, since an employee who could meet the demands of his or her present position would not need to be reassigned to a different job.

Employers who are subject to a collective bargaining agreement may face particularly complex problems if a requested reassignment or transfer would be a reasonable accommodation but would violate the provisions of a collective bargaining agreement. The legislative history of the

ADA addresses this issue obliquely; it says that a collective bargaining agreement "may be evidence" of an undue hardship, but would not necessarily make the accommodation unreasonable as a matter of law (U.S. House of Representatives 1990:63). Legal commentators differ as to whether the individual's right to accommodation would supersede the collective rights of the workers protected by the agreement. Some commentators believe that courts will apply the Rehabilitation Act jurisprudence that elevated the collective agreement over the rights of the individual worker (Smith 1992). However, most believe that courts will be reluctant to find that the parties can effectively negotiate a private agreement that exempts them from complying with the ADA (Ervin 1991; Hodges 1994; O'Melveny 1994; Pritchard 1995; Shaller 1991). Unfortunately, the two federal agencies that enforce the federal laws that are in conflict—the National Labor Relations Act and the ADA—have been unable to agree on how this conundrum should be resolved. To date, the two agencies have only been able to agree to coordinate their enforcement efforts where there is a conflict between the laws. This includes cases where an ADA accommodation violates the NLRA's prohibitions of unfair labor practices (an NLRA claim) and cases where the employer insists on honoring the collective agreement and thereby refuses to accommodate a qualified disabled worker (an ADA claim). This agreement to coordinate enforcement deals only with procedure; the substantive issues of which law takes precedence remain unresolved ("NLRB, EEOC Memo of Understanding" 1993).

One federal appellate court has addressed this issue squarely under the ADA and has ruled that the seniority rights of other workers are superior to a disabled worker's right to reassignment. In *Eckles v. Consolidated Rail Corporation* (1996), the court stated that the ADA does not require an employer to bump a more senior worker from a position in order to accommodate a less-senior worker with a disability. However, the court was careful to limit its ruling to cases involving seniority rights and took no position on the conflict between other provisions of a collective bargaining agreement and the ADA.

Summary. This brief review of federal appellate opinions suggests that the fears of employers that the courts will require expensive, disruptive, or inappropriate accommodations are exaggerated. On the contrary, several of the opinions suggest that federal courts are reluctant to require employers to provide even those accommodations that the statutory language requires.

The reasonable accommodation requirement is limited, by statutory language, to those accommodations that do not pose undue hardship for the employer. The undue hardship defense has been an area of some judicial activity, under both the Rehabilitation Act and the ADA.

Determination of Undue Hardship

The limitation on the employer's duty to accommodate a worker with a disability is the "undue hardship" doctrine. This term is defined very broadly in the legislation as "an action requiring significant difficulty or expense" (42 U.S.C. sec. 12111[9]). The statute includes suggested factors for determining undue hardship, such as the nature and cost of the accommodation, overall financial resources of the facility and/or the covered entity, and the type of operation of the covered entity.

Cost of accommodation. The statute does not contain a monetary cap for reasonable accommodations. Prior to the ADA's passage, efforts by some legislators to impose a cap (such as a percentage of the employee's annual wage, as is the case in some state civil rights laws) were defeated.[5] Given the broad statutory language and the lack of real clarification of this concept in the ADA regulations, legal commentators have developed several proposals in response to the problem of accommodation cost. These proposals range from repealing the employment provisions of the ADA altogether (Epstein 1992:488; Mashaw 1994:231) to a requirement that the employer demonstrate that the cost of the accommodation would require a reduction in the workforce (Cooper 1991:1454).

Few courts had reviewed claims of *financial* hardship under the Rehabilitation Act, since most employer-defendants were public agencies. In addition, Rehabilitation Act jurisprudence regarding undue hardship can be best characterized as a "mish-mash" (Epstein 1995:440). As a result, the parameters of the undue hardship concept will have to be determined on a case-by-case basis as ADA cases reach federal courts. To date, appellate courts have disqualified most ADA plaintiffs from coverage by the law either because their disorder does not meet the ADA definition or because they cannot perform the job's essential functions. The courts have yet to squarely address the issue of how to define "significant expense."

The safety defense. Although the ADA regulations state that co-worker morale problems resulting from some accommodation are not an undue hardship (29 C.F.R. sec. 1630.15[d]), safety concerns may limit an employer's duty to accommodate a worker with a disability. The concern must be real, however; speculation as to potential safety hazards, unconnected to an individualized assessment of the job requirements and the worker's limitations, will not constitute an undue hardship defense.

The ADA regulations state that the employer must demonstrate that accommodating the worker will pose a "direct threat." Direct threat is defined as "a significant risk of substantial harm to the health or safety of the individual or others that cannot be eliminated or reduced by reasonable accommodation" (29 C.F.R. sec. 1630.2[r]). The regulations require the employer to make an individualized determination based on the applicant or worker's "present ability to safely perform the essential functions of the job." The determination must be made on the basis of "a reasonable medical judgment that relies on the most current medical knowledge and/or on the best available objective evidence" (29 C.F.R. sec. 1630.2[r]).

In *Rizzo v. Children's World Learning Center* (1996), a federal appellate court chided the employer for assuming that a hearing-impaired bus driver was a "direct threat" because she could not "hear a choking child." Characterizing the employer's argument as speculative, the court stated that the employer must make a factual demonstration that the ability to hear "a choking child" was an essential function of the job. Furthermore, the court stated that the employer would need to demonstrate that an individual who was not hearing-impaired would be able to hear the child and thus that the plaintiff's hearing loss made her a "direct threat." On the other hand, a federal trial court sided with the employer of a police officer with uncontrolled diabetes. The court ruled that the officer's severe hypoglycemic reaction while driving a police car made him a direct threat to the safety of the public and his fellow officers (*Sifkin v. Village of Arlington Heights* 1994).

Disruption or "significant difficulty." Another category of undue hardship involves disruption of work. Although the regulations are silent on the issue of whether disruptive misconduct related to a disability poses an undue hardship for the employer, courts have addressed this issue on numerous occasions under the Rehabilitation Act. And reviewing courts in subsequent cases brought under the ADA have relied upon Rehabilitation Act precedent. There is little consensus, however, on how a claim that disability-related misconduct (for example, aggression linked to alcoholism or a psychiatric disorder) should be reviewed. It is also unclear whether the employer should be required to demonstrate that even absent the disability-related misconduct, the same employment decision would have been made (see, for example, *Teahan v. Metro-North Commuter Railroad Co.* 1991). As with the financial limitations of the undue hardship defense, the parameters of the "disruption" defense remain to be established.

Courts have shown little sympathy to employees who were discharged or disciplined for disruptive behavior, even if the behavior was a manifestation of the disability. For example, in *Allen v. Stone* (1992), a nursing supervisor at Walter Reed Hospital with a personality disorder was rude and disruptive, claiming that supervision exacerbated her disorder. Her suggested accommodation was transfer away from any supervision and no criticism of her work. The court ruled that her request was unreasonable and that her disruptiveness, albeit related to her disability, justified her termination. Similarly, the court upheld the discharge of a mail handler with a psychiatric disorder who had a history of disruptive behavior and brought a stun gun to work, stating that it is not reasonable to require the employer to "indulge a propensity for violence" (*Gordon v. Runyon* 1994). Similar results have occurred when employees with alcoholism have been discharged for work misconduct (see, for example, *Williams v. Widnall* 1996).

Although the courts appear to be quite deferential to an employer's assertion that accommodation poses an undue hardship, the hardship must be supported by clear evidence of a burden either on the employer's efficiency or its finances. Employers, who do not provide such evidence, even in a situation where the facts seem to preclude accommodation, will likely not win a summary judgment motion.[6]

Summary. Given the evidence that the ADA has not appreciably increased the proportion of disabled workers and the continuing uncertainties about compliance costs and the limits of the employer's duty to accommodate, it is clear that the body of ADA jurisprudence must be further developed. Although it is too early to judge the law's success or the quality of the courts' interpretive guidance for employers and policymakers, courts have tended to interpret the law narrowly and to place a heavy evidentiary burden on plaintiffs. This burden includes the requirement that plaintiffs make the threshold showing of the "proper" disability as well as a showing that they are able to perform the essential functions of the job. This suggests that the law will be ineffective in assisting many individuals with genuine physical or mental disorders to obtain or keep a job.

Conclusions and Suggestions for Future Research

Given the states' reliance on nondiscrimination laws to provide access to employment for individuals with disabilities, rather than continuing the financial incentives represented by second injury funds, it is reasonable to ask whether the enforcement of state and federal nondiscrimination laws has been effective. Although it is too soon to evaluate the effectiveness of the ADA, some trends are emerging that, if they continue, suggest that the ADA has not yet resulted in the opening of employers' doors to individuals with disabilities.

The EEOC data on charges filed over nearly a four-year period are perplexing, since relatively few individuals have challenged an employer's failure to hire them. Given the Harris Poll data cited earlier in the chapter that found the proportion of disabled workers to be the same in 1993 as prior to the act's enactment, it is unlikely that employers have increased their recruitment and hiring of individuals with disabilities. Thus either disabled individuals are not seeking employment, or they are not challenging negative hiring decisions. In either case, the ADA has not increased access for these individuals in the way that was anticipated by supporters of the legislation.

For those individuals who do file an ADA claim, the road to victory is filled with hurdles. Although it is impossible to know how many ADA lawsuits were settled before trial or how many plaintiffs dropped their legal claims, written court opinions, both published and unpublished, suggest that the federal courts are interpreting the ADA very narrowly and are excluding many individuals who have a physical or mental disorder from the protection of the law. While this strict interpretation of the term "disability" tends to protect individuals with severe or pervasive impairments, it leaves many individuals with genuine impairments that interfere with their current job unprotected. Policymakers need to consider whether this category of individuals, many of whom could be accommodated relatively easily and inexpensively, need some other form of protection, or whether the law should be amended to include these individuals within its ambit.

It is certainly too early to brand the ADA a failure. More research needs to be conducted to ascertain the level of employer compliance, the experience of employers who have hired or retained disabled workers, and the real costs of accommodation. Policymakers need to use these data to reassure employers that disabled workers represent a safe, reliable, and usually inexpensive potential pool of human resources from which to recruit. And the courts need to recognize the social policy behind the law and follow its language and its spirit somewhat more closely, while crafting clearer rules for defining what the employer's accommodation requirement is and how it will be evaluated.

Endnotes

[1] Prior to 1940 only 12 states had some form of second injury fund, while by 1950 only 7 states operated without a fund.

[2] This is in direct contrast to the ADA's definition of a "qualified individual with a disability," which specifies that the individual must be able to perform the essential functions of the position "with or without reasonable accommodation."

[3] The EEOC data do not differentiate between individuals whose disabilities were acquired prior to employment and those who became disabled after being employed.

[4] Administrative closure may occur for several reasons, including a finding that the charging party has abandoned the claim or a request by the charging party to obtain a right-to-sue letter after 300 days have elapsed.

[5] The House Judiciary Committee rejected a proposed amendment that would have fixed a ceiling of 10% of the employee's salary as the maximum cost of an accommodation; a higher cost would have been an "undue hardship" had the amendment been approved (U.S. House of Representatives 1990:41).

[6] For example, in *Hindman v. GTE Data Services* (1994), a federal trial court refused to award summary judgment to the employer of a worker who was fired for bringing a gun to work. The employee had told the employer he had a psychiatric disorder; the employer made no attempt to ascertain whether the claim was true and did not perform the reasonable accommodation analysis required by the ADA.

References

Allen v. Stone, 1992 U.S. Dist. LEXIS 1008 (D.D.C. 1992).

Arney, D. Todd. 1992. "Note: Survey of the Americans with Disabilities Act, Title I: With the Final Regulations In, Are the Criticisms Out?" *Washburn Law Journal*, Vol. 31, pp. 522-43.

Benson v. Northwest Airlines, 62 F.3d 1108 (8th Cir. 1995).

Blanck, Peter David. 1994. *Communicating the Americans with Disabilities Act, Transcending Compliance: A Case Report on Sears, Roebuck and Co*. Washington, DC: The Annenberg Washington Program in Communications Policy Studies of Northwestern University.

_____. 1996. *The Americans with Disabilities Act, Transcending Compliance: 1996 Follow-up Report*. Washington, DC: The Annenberg Washington Program in Communications Policy Studies of Northwestern University.

Bombrys v. City of Toledo, 849 F. Supp. 1210 (N.D. Ohio 1993).

Borkowski v. Valley Central School District, 63 F.3d 131 (2d Cir. 1994).

Bureau of National Affairs. 1992. *The Americans with Disabilities Act: A Practice and Legal Guide to Impact, Enforcement and Compliance*. Washington, DC: BNA.

Carozza v. Howard County, 1995 U.S. App. LEXIS 387 (4th Cir. 1995) (unpublished).
Carr v. Reno, 3 Americans with Disabilities Cases 434 (D.C. Cir. 1994).
Chirikos, Thomas N. 1991. "The Economics of Employment." In Jane West, ed., *The Americans with Disabilities Act: From Policy to Practice*. New York: Milbank Memorial Fund, pp. 150-79.
Collignon, Frederick C. 1986. "The Role of Reasonable Accommodation in Employing Disabled Persons in Private Industry." In Monroe Berkowitz and M. Anne Hill, eds., *Disability and the Labor Market*. Ithaca, NY: ILR Press, pp. 196-241.
Combs, Ira, and Clayton R. Omvig. 1986. "Accommodation of Disabled People into Employment: Perceptions of Employers." *Journal of Rehabilitation*, Vol. 52, pp. 42-45.
Cooper, Jeffrey O. 1991. "Overcoming Barriers to Employment: The Meaning of Reasonable Accommodation and Undue Hardship in the Americans with Disabilities Act." *University of Pennsylvania Law Review*, Vol. 139, pp. 1423-68.
Davis v. Frank, 711 F. Supp. 447 (N.D. Ill. 1989).
Draper, Jane M. 1990. Annotation: "Accommodation Requirements under State Legislation Forbidding Job Discrimination on Account of Handicap." *American Law Reports*, 4th Series, Vol. 74, pp. 265-327.
Eagleton Institute of Politics. 1993. "Employing People with Disabilities: The Employer's Perspective—Quantitative Survey." New Brunswick, NJ: Eagleton Institute of Politics, Rutgers University.
E. E. Black Ltd. v. Marshall, 497 F. Supp. 1088 (D. Haw. 1980).
Eckles v. Consolidated Rail Corporation, 94 F.3d 1041 (7th Cir. 1996).
EEOC v. AIC Security Systems, Ltd., 1995 U.S. App. LEXIS 12139 (7th Cir. 1995).
Epstein, Richard A. 1992. *Forbidden Grounds: The Case against Employment Discrimination Law*. Cambridge: Harvard University Press.
Epstein, Steven B. 1995. "In Search of a Bright Line: Determining When an Employer's Financial Hardship Becomes 'Undue' under the Americans with Disabilities Act." *Vanderbilt Law Review*, Vol. 48, pp. 392-478.
Equal Employment Opportunity Commission. June 1997. "Cumulative ADA Charge Data for the July 26, 1992–March 31, 1997 Reporting Period." Washington, DC: EEOC.
Erf, Stephen D. 1977. "Potluck Protections for Handicapped Discriminatees: The Need to Amend Title VII to Prohibit Discrimination on the Basis of Disability." *Loyola Univ. (Chicago) Law Journal*, Vol. 8, pp. 814-45.
Ervin, Joanne Jocha. 1991. "Reasonable Accommodation and the Collective Bargaining Agreement under the Americans with Disabilities Act of 1990." *Detroit College of Law Review*, Vol. 3, pp. 925-72.
Gallup Organization. 1992. "Baseline Study to Determine Business' Attitudes, Awareness and Reaction to the Americans with Disabilities Act." Washington, DC: Electronic Industries Foundation.
Gordon v. Runyon, 3 Americans with Disabilities Cases 284 (E.D. Pa. 1994).
Greenwood, Reed, Kay F. Schriner, and V. Johnson. 1991. "Employer Concerns Regarding Workers with Disabilities and the Business-Rehabilitation Partnership: The PWI Practitioners' Perspective." *Journal of Rehabilitation*, Vol. 57, pp. 21-25.
Gunderson, Morley, and Douglas Hyatt. 1996. "Do Injured Workers Pay for Reasonable Accommodation?" *Industrial and Labor Relations Review*, Vol. 50, pp. 92-104.

Hankins v. The Gap, Inc., 84 F.3d 797 (6th Cir. 1996).

Harger, David. 1993. "Drawing the Line between Reasonable Accommodation and Undue Hardships under the Americans with Disabilities Act: Reducing the Effects of Ambiguity on Small Businesses." *Kansas Law Review*, Vol. 41, pp. 783-807.

Hearne, Paul G. 1991. "Employment Strategies for People with Disabilities: A Prescription for Change." In Jane West, ed., *The Americans with Disabilities Act: From Policy to Practice*. New York: Milbank Memorial Fund, pp. 111-29.

Hindman v. GTE Data Services, 1994 U.S. Dist. LEXIS 9522 (N.D. Fla. 1994).

Hodges, Ann C. 1994. "The Americans with Disabilities Act in the Unionized Workplace." *University of Miami Law Review*, Vol. 48, pp. 567-625.

Holmes, Steven A. 1994. "In 4 Years, Disabilities Act Hasn't Improved Jobs Rate," *New York Times*, October 23, A18.

Hudson v. MCI Telecommunications Corp., 1996 U.S. App. LEXIS 15821 (10th Cir. 1996).

Jackson v. Veterans Administration, 22 F.3d 277 (11th Cir. 1994).

Janofsky, Julie C. 1993. "Whoever Wrote ADA Regs Never Ran a Business." *Wall Street Journal*, March 15, A-12.

Jasany v. United States Postal Service, 755 F.2d 1244 (6th Cir. 1985).

Krenek, Sue A. 1994. "Beyond Reasonable Accommodation." *Texas Law Review*, Vol. 72, pp. 1969-2014.

Lavelle, Lisa A. 1991. "The Duty to Accommodate: Will Title I of the Americans with Disabilities Act Emancipate Individuals with Disabilities Only to Disable Small Businesses?" *Notre Dame Law Review*, Vol. 66, pp. 1135-94.

Lee, Barbara A. 1996. "Legal Requirements and Employer Responses to Accommodating Employees with Disabilities." *Human Resource Management Review*, Vol. 6, pp. 231-51.

Lee, Barbara A., and Karen A. Newman. 1995. "Employer Response to Disability: Preliminary Evidence and a Research Agenda." *Employee Responsibilities and Rights Journal*, Vol. 8, pp. 209-29.

_____. 1993. "Attitudes of New Jersey Employers toward Employing Individuals with Disabilities." Research report to the New Jersey Developmental Disabilities Council, Trenton, New Jersey.

Lyons v. The Legal Aid Society, 68 F.3d 1512 (2d Cir. 1995).

Lyth, Margaret. 1973. "Employers' Attitudes to the Employment of the Disabled." *Occupational Psychology*, Vol. 47, pp. 67-70.

McFarlin, Dean B., James Song, and Michelle Sonntag. 1991. "Integrating the Disabled into the Work Force: A Survey of Fortune 500 Company Attitudes and Practices." *Employee Responsibilities and Rights Journal*, Vol. 4, pp. 107-23.

McNemar v. The Disney Store, Inc., 4 Americans with Disabilities Cases 897 (E.D. Pa. 1995).

Mancini v. General Electric, 2 Americans with Disabilities Cases 764 (D. Vt. 1993).

Mancuso, Laura. 1990. "Reasonable Accommodation for Workers with Psychiatric Disabilities." *Psychosocial Rehabilitation Journal*, Vol. 14, pp. 3-19.

Mashaw, Jerry L. 1994. "Against First Principles." *San Diego Law Review*, Vol. 31, pp. 211-39.

Mastrangelo, Rebecca. 1994. "Does the Americans with Disabilities Act of 1990 Impose an Undue Burden on Employers?" *Duquesne Law Review*, Vol. 32, pp. 269-84.

Matthews v. TCI of Illinois, 1996 U.S. Dist. LEXIS 8274 (N.D. Ill. 1996).
Misek-Falkoff v. IBM Corp., 3 Americans with Disabilities Cases 449 (S.D.N.Y. 1994).
Myers v. Hose, 50 F.3d 278 (4th Cir. 1995).
"NLRB, EEOC Memo of Understanding on Procedure for Coordinating ADA, NLRA." 1993. *Daily Labor Report* (BNA), No. 220, November 17, D-24.
Nelson v. Thornburgh, 732 F. 2d 146 (3d Cir. 1984).
O'Melveny, Mary K. 1994. "The Americans with Disabilities Act and Collective Bargaining Agreements: Reasonable Accommodation or Irreconcilable Conflicts?" *Kentucky Law Journal*, Vol. 82, pp. 219-48.
Peck, Cornelius J. 1983. "Employment Problems of the Handicapped: Would Title VII Remedies Be Appropriate and Effective?" *University of Michigan Journal of Legislative Reform*, Vol. 16, pp. 343-85.
Pritchard, Robert W. 1995. "Avoiding the Inevitable: Resolving the Conflicts between the ADA and the NLRA." *The Labor Lawyer*, Vol. 11, pp. 375-414.
Rizzo v. Children's World Learning Center, 84 F.3d 758 (5th Cir. 1996).
Schwartz v. Northwest Iowa Community College, 881 F. Supp. 1323 (N.D. Iowa 1995).
Schluter v. Industrial Coils, Inc., 1996 U.S. Dist. LEXIS 8962 (W.D. Wisc. 1996).
Shaller, Elliot H. 1991. "'Reasonable Accommodation' under the Americans with Disabilities Act—What Does It Mean?" *Employee Relations Law Journal*, Vol. 16, pp. 431-47.
Sifkin v. Village of Arlington Heights, 1994 U.S. Dist. LEXIS 13015 (E.D. Ill. 1994).
Smith, Jules L. 1992. "Accommodating the Americans with Disabilities Act to Collective Bargaining Obligations under the NLRA." *Employee Relations Law Journal*, Vol. 18, pp. 273-85.
Smolowe, Jill. 1995. "Noble Aims, Mixed Results." *Time*, July 31, pp. 54-55.
Stewart v. County of Brown, 86 F.3d 107 (7th Cir. 1996).
Taylor v. Albertsons, 886 F. Supp. 819 (W.D. Okla. 1995).
Teahan v. Metro-North Commuter Railroad Co., 951 F.2d 511 (2d Cir.1991).
Tyndall v. National Education Center, 31 F.3d 209 (4th Cir. 1994).
U. S. House of Representatives. 1990. *House of Representatives Report No. 485*, 101st Congress, 2d Session, part 2.
U. S. Senate. 1990. *Senate Report No. 116*, 101st Congress, 2d Session.
Van de Zande v. State of Wisconsin Dept. of Administration, 44 F.3d 538 (7th Cir. 1995).
Walker v. Weinberger, 600 F. Supp. 757 (D.D.C. 1985).
West, Jane. 1991. "The Social and Policy Context of the Act." In Jane West, ed., *The Americans with Disabilities Act: From Policy to Practice*. New York: Milbank Memorial Fund, pp. 3-24.
_____, ed. 1991. *The Americans with Disabilities Act: From Policy to Practice*. New York: Milbank Memorial Fund.
Whillock v. Delta Air Lines, Inc., 1995 U.S. Dist. LEXIS 20928 (N.D. Ga. 1995).
Williams v. Widnall, 79 F.3d 1003 (10th Cir. 1996).

CHAPTER 7

Facilitating Employment through Vocational Rehabilitation

MONROE BERKOWITZ
Rutgers University

DAVID DEAN
University of Richmond

A national vocational rehabilitation "system" began in the United States after World War I and was targeted primarily to persons with work injuries. In the past seventy-five years a patchwork of programs has developed at the national and state levels, encompassing both the public and, more recently, the private sector. National programs in the current schema are the joint federal-state Vocational Rehabilitation Program, including rehabilitation through Social Security Disability Insurance and the Veterans' Rehabilitation Program. At the state level, various workers' compensation agencies may administer public sector rehabilitation programs for injured workers. Increasingly, however, rehabilitation for injured workers is provided by the private sector. Private sector providers also serve persons with off-the-job injuries and illnesses.

This chapter will examine the institutional framework and rationale for these programs. The sense in which we are using the term "rehabilitation" refers to a process whereby persons with mental or physical impairments and disparate work experience are provided services designed to improve their vocational status. These services vary considerably across individuals and programs. They range from a minimal evaluation of job readiness capacity to a comprehensive restoration, schooling, job-training, and placement package. Some of the confusion surrounding the term "rehabilitation" can be avoided if there is a common understanding of the reasons why rehabilitation programs differ.

The answers to four basic questions distinguish rehabilitation programs. First, who organizes the administration of services? Second, what types of services are provided? Third, who receives services? And finally, who pays? We address each of these in turn, while recognizing the interrelationships among them. Needless to say, the effectiveness of rehabilitation programs varies and depends on many complicating factors. The remainder of this chapter offers evidence on the efficacy of public and, to the extent possible, private sector rehabilitation initiatives.

Who Organizes the Administration of Services?

A broad distinction concerning the organization of rehabilitation programs is between public and private sectors. There are three principal public sector programs: (1) the federal-state vocational rehabilitation partnership that we refer to as the VR program, (2) the rehabilitation program for veterans of the armed forces, and (3) rehabilitation activities undertaken by state workers' compensation agencies.

Private sector rehabilitation services are primarily provided by private employers and insurers, usually in connection with the payment of some sort of disability benefits. These benefits may be workers' compensation benefits for work-related disability or short-term or long-term disability benefits for either work or non-work-related illnesses and injuries. In addition, individuals may purchase rehabilitation services to aid them in their recovery from a disabling illness or injury.

The distinction between public and private sectors is fundamental. By and large, private sector providers operate for-profit businesses or are employed as staff of a private insurer or employer who is in business to maximize profits. Presumably, they only rehabilitate persons when the cost of rehabilitation services is less than savings gained by the restoration of the disabled worker to the payroll or by his or her removal from the insurer's obligation. If private sector providers are inefficient or fail to satisfy their clients, they will go out of business. Public sector providers, for the most part, do not face this market test.

Another difference between public and private sector agencies is the degree of flexibility and discretion that each has over its clientele. Increasingly, public sector agencies, particularly the VR program, must select clients in accordance with priorities established by legislation. Priorities change as different disability groups vie for congressional or presidential attention. President Kennedy was responsible for an emphasis on mentally retarded clients, a disability group that had not been served extensively under the federal-state public program in prior years. In President Johnson's drive for the Great Society, attention was paid to the economically disadvantaged. In recent years, the emphasis has been on severely disabled persons, and labor market tests have been considerably weakened to allow for less restrictive eligibility criteria.

Although the distinction between private and public sector is fundamental, there are many similarities between the two sectors. They employ staff with similar professional qualifications and purchase the same types of services from vendors. For instance, both sectors employ counselors who are certified, licensed, or registered in one of the rehabilitation specialties. In addition, both sectors buy "work evaluation" services or psychological examinations from the same sources.

Types of Services Provided

A broad distinction here is between medical and vocational rehabilitation. Medical rehabilitation involves the provision of medical services, possibly under the direction of a physician who leads a rehabilitation team of physical therapists, occupational therapists, and rehabilitation nurses. Vocational rehabilitation involves the delivery of services designed to restore the disabled worker to the labor market. Increasingly today, as persons with mental retardation become clients, the objective may be to prepare the disabled to enter the labor market for the first time.

For the most part, the distinction between medical and vocational rehabilitation is clear, although each blends into the other. For example, in the VR program, the state agency may offer medical restoration as part of its services. In addition, some advocates declare that rehabilitation is a seamless web and that in the case of an industrial injury, the rehabilitation process must begin in the hospital before the blood has dried on the wound. Accepted wisdom is that early intervention is the key to successful rehabilitation, so that a return to work is facilitated if the worker realizes, at the time of injury, that a job awaits upon recovery. In spite of these interrelationships, there are distinct differences between medical and vocational rehabilitation. The process of vocational rehabilitation in the form of services designed to return the worker to the job or to a state of optimal functioning begins in earnest after the person has reached what in workers' compensation parlance is called "maximum medical recovery."

Another distinction arises from the markedly different rehabilitation objectives of the public and private sectors. The public sector VR program is charged with the goal of maximizing the vocational potential of a client—the individual applying for services. Often this entails a regimen of formal training or schooling. The mission of private sector rehabilitation is usually much narrower—to return the person to work as expeditiously as possible. Frequently, the "client" is an employer or insurance carrier who is necessarily concerned with cost minimization. Consequently, private sector providers are more apt to prescribe job modification and/or placement services rather than more costly training and education. Three general types of services are provided under the public sector VR program. Virtually all eligible client/consumers are first provided a medical diagnosis and vocational assessment in preparation for the development of a rehabilitation plan. Next, clients receive some form of "human capital" enhancement. Roughly one-third of all state VR clients receive some physical and/or mental restoration intended to permit them to achieve the equivalent of "maximum medical improvement." In half the cases the person is given a training regimen, ranging from university education to on-the-job or personal and vocational adjustment training (GAO 1993:41). Finally, the VR agency provides job referral and placement along with ancillary services such as a maintenance stipend, transportation, and support for other family members.

Public sector VR counselors, who are usually civil service employees, make eligibility decisions, arrange for the delivery of services, and offer clients counseling and guidance. However, most of the other services provided—evaluation, restoration, training, etc.—are purchased from a private sector vendor. Such services are usually, but not always, funded by public money. The counselor is instructed to search for alternative sources of payment, such as other state or private agencies, for which the client may be eligible.

In short, these public VR counselors operate in much the same way as private sector providers and may, in fact, purchase services from the same set of vendors. Again, differences between private and public providers lie in the presence or absence of market tests.

Who Receives Services?

Obviously, the answer to this question depends upon the program under discussion and the period under consideration. The nature of the clientele of the public VR program has changed dramatically over the years. When it began in 1920, Congress stated that it was to provide services to persons disabled in industry and the relationship with workers' compensation was quite close and coordinated (Berkowitz 1979:44-45). That relationship has eroded over time as Congress has specified other priorities and as emphasis has shifted to more severely disabled persons who have a more tenuous labor force attachment. For instance, public sector VR serves disabled recipients of Supplemental Security Income (SSI), a program federalized in 1974 from state initiatives serving the "permanently and totally disabled."

The characteristics of the persons flowing into the VR system will greatly influence its outcomes. The proportion of incoming clients who meet the definition of program success, i.e., "persons rehabilitated," has fallen in the past two decades. This is primarily due to a legislatively mandated shift in emphasis from persons most likely to benefit from service provision to those persons with severe disabilities.

The Department of Veterans' Affairs (VA) program's clients are exclusively veterans of the armed forces. In certain cases the VA may coordinate service provision through the state VR program.

Workers' compensation programs serve persons with some work-related injury or illness. Two related issues arise under these programs. First, which cases, among all those injured, will receive services? Second, among rehabilitation recipients, what level of services (which can range from formal education or training to simple and less-costly job evaluation) will be provided to which claimants? There is substantial variation across state compensation programs with respect to the administration and provision of rehabilitation services. For instance, Florida is one of eighteen states that provides formal training initiatives to eligible work-injury claimants through a separate funding mechanism such as an assessment on workers' compensation premiums. In contrast, several states make no mention of VR in their workers' compensation statutes (King and Hadley 1995:9-10).

Finally, sweeping changes have occurred in private sector clientele. With the revolution in health care, managed care has emerged as a technique to ensure efficiency and contain increasing health care costs in the workplace. One aspect of managed care is "disability management" in which the treatment of disabled persons is monitored and attention is given to medical regimens and the duration of absence. Rehabilitation becomes part of the monitoring process and is purchased by the firm or supplied by on-staff rehabilitation personnel on an as-needed basis (Akabas, Gates, and Galvin 1992:Chapter 1).

Monitoring may be a continuous process that begins at the time of injury or onset of an illness. A member of the disability management team reviews the planned treatment by the physician and suggests changes if the plan varies from accepted practice. The duration of absence is carefully watched and compared to duration guidelines established on the basis of appropriate cases. If the claimant is referred to rehabilitation, the rehabilitation counselor documents the appropriate way to return the worker to the job.

In companies where disability management is not practiced intensively, the rehabilitation counselor, concerned with return to work, may become more involved in the monitoring function. The counselor may inquire about medical treatment and monitor the duration of absence as recommendations are made for further training or workplace accommodations.

Who Pays for Rehabilitation Services?

Although some persons, as a sequel to debilitating illness or injury, may initiate and pay for their own rehabilitation services, that would be unusual. Like health services, rehabilitation is usually funded by third-party payers. In some cases, health insurers pay for services through individual or employer-provided health care plans. More often, employer payments are made under a disability benefit plan. That is, employers provide rehabilitation services to employees who are absent for an extended period of time under a sick leave (short-term or long-term) disability benefits program on a voluntary basis.

The situation may be different when it comes to work injuries since employers may be compelled to pay for rehabilitation services under the provisions of state workers' compensation laws. As noted below, the requirement to provide services varies from state to state. However, if the law requires the provision of services, it also makes payment the responsibility of the employer or insurance carrier. The situation is different for nonwork injuries or illnesses. Disability insurers provide services on a voluntary basis; there is no legal requirement for payment.

Federal rehabilitation programs are funded by taxpayers through general obligations of the U.S. Treasury. Services under the VA program are provided at no cost to veterans. Under the federal-state VR program, individual clients are not charged for counseling services, although other services may be provided on a cost-sharing basis according to the client's ability to pay. As noted above, counselors purchase services and are instructed to seek alternative sources for payment, although interestingly enough, the amount of these "similar benefits" payments is not tracked in the evaluation studies.

In the next section, we examine evidence on the effectiveness of various public sector VR programs, including rehabilitation under the Social Security Disability Insurance program, the Veterans' Administration rehabilitation program, and rehabilitation under the state workers' compensation programs, and private sector VR efforts.

Public Sector VR

The nation's largest public sector, vocational rehabilitation venture is the basic federal-state program, which began shortly after World War I. This program is a partnership between the Rehabilitation Services Administration (RSA) and some 83 state and territorial agencies (with 26 states having separate agencies serving persons with visual impairments).[1] Incurred expenses are split on a roughly 80/20 basis between the RSA and the various state agencies. In fiscal year 1994, some $2 billion in federal funding was spent, along with an additional $0.5 billion in state matching funds (U.S. Department of Education 1994a:Tables B-1 and D-1). In any given year slightly less than one million persons are served by state VR agencies. The agency subsequently "successfully rehabilitates"—that is, finds suitable employment for a period of at least two months—about 200,000 persons annually.

To qualify for public sector VR, individuals first must be referred or apply to the VR program. At the point of contact they are judged eligible or ineligible for services on the basis of the following admissions criteria: (1) the presence of a physical or mental disability, (2) the existence of a substantial impediment to employment, and (3) a reasonable expectation that vocational rehabilitation services will increase the individual's employability (U.S Department of Education, Rehabilitation Services Manual 1994b:5).

The 1992 Amendments to the Rehabilitation Act of 1973 modified the last criterion. The burden of proof is now on the agency to determine that service provision cannot ultimately help a person gain substantial employment. The Rehabilitation Act also mandates that state agencies serve persons with severe disabilities. Roughly two-thirds of those served meet the RSA-designation of "severe disability."

Once a client/consumer is accepted for services, the client and counselor meet to work out an individual written rehabilitation plan (IWRP) that spells out the services the client is to receive and the results to be expected. As noted above, the services prescribed for consumers are extremely varied. Counseling, guidance, and job placement services are usually provided through an in-house staff of rehabilitation counselors. A comprehensive range of purchased services, including medical restoration, education, and training, is also available. The value of purchased services for all VR-eligible clients terminated in 1980 averaged under $1,600 per client (GAO 1993:3). This figure has remained relatively constant for the past fifteen years.

Clients are classified as "successfully rehabilitated" if they achieve any one of a number of outcomes. These outcomes include being placed in the competitive labor market, self-employment, or sheltered work or being placed as homemakers or unpaid family workers. While persons whose cases are closed as "not rehabilitated" may eventually become engaged in gainful activity, the state agency cannot claim credit for a successful rehabilitation.

Given the long history of the VR program, numerous studies have been undertaken to estimate its effect. These have differed markedly in level of sophistication and model assumptions as well as the conclusions that were drawn from them. All have used a variation of the mandated reporting system (the RSA-911) as the basis for their evaluation. This standardized form records demographic information, data on the receipt and duration of VR services, as well as information on limited earnings profiles for clients terminated from state agency rolls during a given fiscal year. Unfortunately, these data are collected primarily for administrative and not evaluative purposes. For example, earnings are only reported for a few weeks prior to referral for services and three months after termination. Moreover, post-earnings data are only available for roughly one-quarter of the annual program "closures" who are successfully rehabilitated; post-program earnings are not recorded for ineligibles, program dropouts, and clients who were not rehabilitated.

However, these analyses can be distinguished on the basis of the unit of analysis employed (aggregate versus individual) and subsequent statistical tests of program impact that were conducted. Another distinction involves whether and what type of comparison group is used to gauge program effects.

This standardized database led to some early attempts to use benefit-cost analysis to gauge VR program impacts. These initial efforts were flawed in that they utilize a univariate framework wherein all benefits were attributed to the VR intervention. Moreover, the evaluative methodologies were constrained by the limited earnings profile. Program benefits were measured by subtracting earnings in the week prior to referral from earnings reported in the week of closure. Since most clients were unemployed prior to application for services, pre-referral earnings were assumed to be zero. In the absence of longitudinal earnings data, post-program earnings were assumed to continue for the remainder of the worker's career. Not surprisingly, these first-generation studies cast VR in an extremely favorable light. Benefit-cost ratios of ten to one were not uncommon (Berkowitz 1988).

Most of these initial studies have been largely discredited. Later studies used multivariate techniques to control for the influence of various demographic attributes across clients (Bellante 1972; Worrall 1978). However, problems remained in that complete earnings profiles were still only available for successfully rehabilitated clients. This limitation did not allow for the construction of the necessary comparison groups to estimate program impacts in the absence of VR intervention. Subsequently, the lack of longitudinal earnings for all program participants made it impossible to test for and correct possible selection bias. This is an inherent problem in most manpower training evaluation studies due to the correlation between factors affecting the decision to participate in a program and subsequent earnings levels.

The General Accounting Office (GAO 1993) conducted a recent evaluation of the public sector VR program's efficacy. This study is noteworthy in that it used a large-scale national VR database containing longitudinal earnings data necessary to estimate program impacts. The GAO study found that earnings gains for successfully rehabilitated clients were "modest," particularly when compared to claims made by previous analyses (GAO 1993:57). Unfortunately, this study, while acknowledging the problem, did not undertake requisite tests of the statistical validity of the comparison group used to gauge program impacts. This unique data set was subsequently reanalyzed using the appropriate tests to detect and then correct for the presence of selection bias in the comparison group (Dean and Schmidt 1997). Earnings effects were then estimated according to numerous gender/disability stratifications. VR program impacts were generally found to be positive, statistically significant, and sustained over an eight-year, post-program period, when compared to eligible clients who had dropped out prior to service provision.

The VR-SSA Connection

The United States has a long history of efforts to link this federal-state VR program with income maintenance/pension programs run by the Social Security Administration (SSA) for persons with disabilities. This relationship was finally formalized in 1965 through the establishment of the Beneficiary Rehabilitation Program (BRP) for Disability Insurance (DI) beneficiaries. The BRP provided DI trust funds for rehabilitation services for eligible beneficiaries on a prospective payment basis to state VR agencies. Combined with the explosive growth in the DI caseload and in program expenditures, the BRP grew into a significant subsidy to the VR program. By 1979, the BRP provided services to some 95,000 DI beneficiaries at an average value of $7,673 per rehabilitant; total expenditure exceeded $102 million (McManus 1981:20). Unfortunately, a study by the GAO (1987) found that only one out of every thousand DI beneficiaries rehabilitated to the extent that they could leave the DI rolls.

Dissatisfaction with the efficacy of the BRP led to an overhaul. The successor to the BRP, while much more efficient, has not improved the rehabilitation rate of DI beneficiaries. SSA is expending considerably less in the aggregate for reimbursement to state VR agencies for DI beneficiaries. In real terms (1987 dollars), the 1992 aggregate expenditure was only one-third the 1979 level. The number of claims allowed annually from 1991 through 1993 was less than half the number SSA reimbursed through the BRP in the latter part of the 1970s. At some 6,000 claims allowed for reimbursement in 1993, the program is in danger of being marginalized (Berkowitz and Dean 1996:237).

Meanwhile, the number of persons awarded DI benefits continues to grow, exceeding 636,000 in 1992. In response, the SSA has placed renewed emphasis on return-to-work initiatives, resulting in "Developing a World Class Employment Strategy for People with Disabilities" (SSA 1994). Moreover, skepticism over findings from previous "quasi-experimental" evaluations of VR efficacy has led the SSA to conduct the largest controlled experiment ever undertaken of "case-managed" VR service provision for DI beneficiaries and/or SSI recipients. A final report providing separate cost-benefit analyses for each of four distinct return-to-work models is due in 1998.

Veterans' Administration VR

Another federal initiative is the Department of Veterans Affairs rehabilitation program, which dates back to World War I in its present form. Indeed, some VA activities can be traced back to the beginnings of the nation. As early as 1776, the Continental Congress provided pensions for wounded veterans of the Revolutionary War. Importantly, VA rehabilitation provided the model for the public sector VR program.

The VA advertises that its rehabilitation program is designed to prepare the veteran for a suitable job, to help the veteran get and keep the job, and to assist in making the veteran fully productive and independent (Department of Veteran Affairs 1994). Services include evaluation, counseling, training, education financial assistance, medical, and dental treatment. To qualify, the veteran must have a combined VA compensable disability rating of at least 20% as a result of active service on or after September 16, 1940. In addition, they must have received a discharge or release from duty under other than dishonorable conditions.

A profile of VA participants shows that the average age of rehabilitation applicants is 41 with an average educational level of 12.5 years.[2] A little less than half of all applicants have joint/bone/muscle disorders. Veterans from the pre-Vietnam Era comprise 8.3% of applicants; and Vietnam-Era veterans account for 27.4% of the applicant pool. In fiscal year 1995, a total of $300 million was spent to provide services to about 48,000 veterans.

The VA tracks the outcomes and efficacy of its program to some degree. Slightly more than 6,000 veterans were rehabilitated in 1995, a number that increased to 7,395 in 1996 and is projected to increase to about 9,000 in 1997. The VA points out that the average pre-program income was $4,506 in 1996 compared to an average post-program income of $21,994.

These and other data supplied by the Department of Veterans Affairs are hardly convincing as to the effectiveness of services provided. A recent GAO report (1996) offers a critical appraisal of the program. This study notes that Congress changed the focus of the program in 1980 from just providing training to improving the employability of veterans by helping them find and maintain suitable jobs. The GAO also found that the characteristics of program participants are changing. Only about one in four veterans in the vocational rehabilitation program has a serious employment handicap, and this ratio has been declining in recent years.

The GAO concluded that the VA places few veterans in jobs. Over the five-year period from 1991-95, only about 8% of approximately 74,000 veterans found eligible for services were placed in jobs. A review of 100 case files determined that the VA spent, on average, about $20,000 for each veteran who gained employment and about $10,000 for each veteran who dropped out of the program. Program emphasis remains on training rather than job placement.

In general, the GAO finds fault with the VA program's emphasis on education and that a large proportion of the rehabilitation dollar was spent in providing higher education to disabled veterans. They found about 91% of such veterans were enrolled in a university or college. The remaining 9% were enrolled in vocational/technical schools or participated in other types of training programs such as apprenticeships or on-the-job training. One of the reasons cited for the expenditure of such a large proportion of funds on higher education was that counselors lacked expertise in job counseling and placement.

Workers' Compensation Rehabilitation Programs

Although its origins can be traced to earlier legislation that was later declared unconstitutional, the workers' compensation program in the United States can be dated as beginning in 1911, when several states, including Wisconsin and New Jersey, passed laws (Berkowitz 1987:15). These no-fault laws provided that workers injured in accidents that "arose out of and in the course of employment" were to be paid specified weekly benefits and were to be provided medical care necessary "to relieve and cure" the effects of their injuries. From the very beginning, administrators of the laws talked about the virtues of rehabilitation and how the objective of the laws was to restore the worker to the job. The earliest meetings of the International Association of Industrial Accident Boards and Commissions (IAIABC), the professional organization of the administrators, devoted sessions to encouraging rehabilitation. Each year at the annual meetings the rehabilitation committee reported on its progress in encouraging the use of rehabilitation.[3]

Performance never quite lived up to aspirations in this regard. Medical rehabilitation was seen as a logical extension of the obligation placed on employers under these laws to provide medical care. Once a worker reached "maximum medical improvement" and could not return to the old job and had no immediate job prospects, the question was whether the employer was obligated to pay for training or an alternative vocational rehabilitation plan. For the most part, this issue was resolved on a case-by-case basis, although some states inserted specific rehabilitation provisions into their statutes.

According to the General Accounting Office, as of 1993, 43 state workers' compensation statutes specifically addressed vocational rehabilitation (GAO 1996:62). There is much diversity in rehabilitation provisions among states. In some states—such as Washington and West Virginia—insurance is provided by an exclusive state fund, which operates like a private insurance carrier and presumably has the same set of incentives to minimize liability. If rehabilitation will get the worker back to a job and obviate some payments, the state fund has an incentive to measure the costs and benefits and to act on the basis of the results. In contrast, in states where private insurers primarily provide compensation insurance, the state agency administering the program operates quite differently.[4] It has several choices when it comes to rehabilitation.

One of the key differences among states that are involved in vocational rehabilitation efforts is with regard to the referral. The workers' compensation program is faced with a perplexing question: When and under what conditions should the agency require that the worker be referred to VR? It is sometimes said that states requiring referral have systems of mandatory rehabilitation. However, the referral requirement can be for evaluation purposes to develop a plan of services or the actual provision of service. Despite the exact nature of requirements, funds must be expended, and in many cases these funds will have been expended without any discernible benefit. In essence, the agencies are establishing criteria that require referrals of some, perhaps many, persons who would have returned to work in the normal course of events without any intervention.

As we seek evidence of the effectiveness of rehabilitation in the workers' compensation arena, we have to distinguish between two sometimes quite separate activities. On the one hand, we can evaluate the effectiveness of the arrangements for referral or the monitoring of cases that may require rehabilitation.[5] On the other hand, we can measure the effectiveness of whatever rehabilitation actually takes place. If the latter is our objective, then we are forced back to the position that these decisions are in the hands of self-insurers or private carriers except in the case of the exclusive state funds.[6] We are back to the notion that an insurer will not voluntarily purchase rehabilitation services unless it believes that these expenditures will pay off. The return may be in lowered indemnity payments or lower medical care costs.

The return that insurers will gain depends on the provisions of the state workers' compensation laws. The insurer can possibly gain if periods of temporary total disability are shortened. Alternatively, the insurer may be better off if a worker receiving permanent total disability benefits is restored to a measure of independence and the insurer is relieved of payments for personal assistance. For workers receiving permanent partial benefits, the insurer's return varies depending on the basis of the permanent partial benefits. If benefits are based on actual wage loss, an earlier return to work will reduce insurer payments. If benefits are based on the extent of physical impairment, returns will be possible only if the rehabilitation results in a reduction in the impairment level. If the basis of payment is loss of wage-earning capacity, then rehabilitation, if successful, may result in lower permanent partial disability benefits.

There is plentiful information about what state agencies require in the way of rehabilitation but little about the rehabilitation process.

Process details can be found in the statutes and the annual reports and special reports that state agencies make when they report on their rehabilitation activities from time to time. The Workers' Compensation Research Institute has published a series of Administrative Inventories.[7] Each has some information about rehabilitation provisions. For the most part, these summaries corroborate the finding that state laws attempt to specify the process that the parties are required to follow, but few, if any, require information about outcomes.

One of the earliest attempts to deal with rehabilitation within a workers' compensation statute is found in New York. Carriers are required to notify the state agency in every case in which rehabilitation has been instituted, where rehabilitation has been deemed necessary but not instituted, or where the worker has lost eight weeks from the job. This filing requirement does not obligate the carrier or self-insurer to provide vocational rehabilitation, but it presumably forces them to consider the need for such services. The Board's Vocational Rehabilitation Bureau evaluates vocational rehabilitation needs from the forms it receives. However, as the WCRI study indicates, the board's data system does not allow routine claim monitoring since it cannot identify claims reaching the eight-week time period (Ballantyne and Telles 1992:21).

In many ways, the New York system is typical in that it imposes a strict regimen on employers—in this case to file a form at a specified time—and it has no way to determine whether the statutory requirement is obeyed. And even if the insurer adheres to the statute and the form is filed in a timely manner, there is no requirement that anything be done and certainly no requirement that the whole process be evaluated in terms of outcomes.

This experience can be repeated in state after state where there is a statutorily imposed rehabilitation requirement. It may require a referral after a period of time, an evaluation by rehabilitation personnel under specified circumstances, or in some instances, a rehabilitation services plan. However, there is very little in the way of follow-up to determine what happens to the persons involved and, in particular, what happens to their earnings. There have been a few ad hoc studies in which workers' compensation claims data have been linked to unemployment insurance earnings records, but these have not been followed through on any consistent basis (see, for example, Harris [1996]).

An alternative that has been proposed but not adopted is to free the statutes from these largely meaningless references to the process of rehabilitation and to judge employers and insurance carriers by results

(Berkowitz 1988; Berkowitz, Burton, Chelius, and Dean 1995). Such a system of macro-monitoring would allow comparisons among carriers and could be used to stimulate best practices among insurers.

Workers' compensation started in the U.S. with high hopes and ambitions for making rehabilitation a primary goal of the system. What happened to defeat that objective was that the system, perhaps of necessity, had to pay attention to its primary goal of providing benefits to injured workers. That task, for better or worse, involved workers' compensation agencies in a litigious atmosphere where most of the administrators' time and energy was devoted to settling disputes between the parties over liability for injury and the quantum of the awards that were appropriate in the case of permanent partial injuries (Berkowitz and Burton 1987). The legal atmosphere crowded out the more clinical approach demanded of rehabilitation, and programs lost sight of the primary goal of making return to work. To make matters worse, when rehabilitation was made a matter of right in compulsory rehabilitation states, rehabilitation, especially when accompanied by cash benefits, became entangled in disputes between claimants and insurers/employers.

It is disheartening to end this section on such a pessimistic note. If it is any comfort, the problems of integrating a system of rehabilitation with a benefit payment are not confined to workers' compensation. Certainly equally intractable problems are faced by the Social Security Administration's Disability Insurance program (Mashaw and Reno 1996) and many of the same problems have been encountered in work disability programs abroad (Chelius, Berkowitz, and Burton 1997).

Rehabilitation in the Private Sector

Private sector rehabilitation faces a market test with all of its attendant advantages and disadvantages. We can look at private sector activities and examine the same set of questions as we posed concerning public sector programs.

Who is selected for receiving rehabilitation services? Leaving aside the demand for rehabilitation services exercised by persons who pay for their own services, rehabilitation services are paid for by employers and insurers, and they select the persons who will receive such services. There may well be exceptions to this selection method since some plans allow injured or ill persons the right to choose whether to receive services, and receipt of services may be viewed as a right under the plan. However, the general rule is that the payer chooses when services are to be offered and who will receive them. If one accepts the proposition that the rational insurer or employer will not proffer such services unless advantageous, then we have a market test functioning as a substitute for any measure of effectiveness.

We have not been able to discover any comprehensive impartial studies of the functioning of rehabilitation or return-to-work programs in the private sector. There have been isolated studies of small groups. In their volume on disability management, Akabas et al. (1992) cite the case of the Buick, Oldsmobile, and Cadillac divisions of General Motors. In 1987 a team of researchers from Michigan State University conducted a small-scale evaluation of the B-O-C disability management program. Twenty disabled workers who returned to work in 1984 prior to the establishment of the company's disability management program were compared to fifty employees who returned to work in 1985-86 after the program was established. They found that disability duration had shrunk dramatically under the new program. The average time between injury and the return to work had been reduced from four years to ten months. The average cost of rehabilitation had risen, but the significant reduction in time off the job more than offset these increased costs.

Needless to say, without additional data the study does not reveal a great deal about the effectiveness of the company's program. The authors also cite the case of the Long Island Rail Road. They claim that reports show that through an aggressive, team-oriented approach, the LIRR was able to return hundreds of disabled employees to productive work and simultaneously reduce costs associated with disabling injuries by more than $6 million a year. They also cite the Weyerhauser Company's experience with a disability management program that substantially reduced workers' compensation costs and reduced lost workdays due to disabling absences. Other case studies are also reported, but for the most part, these deal with a program of disability management, and rehabilitation is but a piece in the overall program. Also, the evidence borders on the anecdotal, although there are some data on reductions in benefit payments from one period to another.

In tracing the growth of private sector rehabilitation in the U.S., there is an implicit assumption that services provided are, in some sense, cost beneficial. Matkin (1985) dates the real expansion of private sector rehabilitation to California's 1975 law mandating rehabilitation for workers' compensation beneficiaries but notes that the use of private sector providers by insurance carriers antedates these provisions. He notes that since the 1940s, insurance carriers such as Liberty Mutual had been using rehabilitation nurses to assist industrially injured workers to return to employment. He claims that their use was based on three factors: (1) the cost-savings induced by providing prompt services to injured workers, (2) the inflexibility of the public program, and (3) the reluctance of workers to be stigmatized by the use of the public rehabilitation program.

It is also Matkin's contention that private sector providers had an advantage over the public program in that the objective of the private sector programs was unambiguously the return to work. The public program may have had the objective of restoring the worker to the best condition possible or some other more laudatory goal, that possibly requires more time-consuming and expensive procedures. Matkin views this return-to-work philosophy as being of primary importance.

Conclusions

Our objective has been to provide a rationale and institutional overview of the system of rehabilitation in the United States. We have identified the principal programs in the U.S.: the public federal-state Vocational Rehabilitation program, the rehabilitation program administered by the Department of Veterans Affairs, rehabilitation under workers' compensation, and the private sector rehabilitation efforts.

Comparing and measuring the effectiveness of these programs is a difficult business. Obviously, governmentally financed and administered programs such as the VR program and the veterans' program operate quite apart from any market tests. It is here that one would expect inquiries and investigations concerning program efficiency and effectiveness. The federal-state VR program has prided itself on its cost effectiveness from its very beginning. The idea that the program returned benefits to the taxpayer was the flag under which the program was launched and the rallying cry used to justify its continued existence. Claims of program effectiveness were based on fine rhetoric but quite thin evidence.

One of the difficulties with these evaluations is that the results obtained bear little relationship to the funding of the state agency or to any other measure of immediate concern to the agency. Data, for the most part, are collected by the federal agency that presumably oversees operations at the state level. However, there is no indication that evaluation results influence state funding. In all fairness to the Rehabilitation Services Administration, the federal body in question, funding decisions are governed by a formula that is the product of legislative enactment and are not something over which the RSA can exercise much discretion.

The VR program, whatever can be said of the results, deserves high marks for trying. That cannot be said of the VA program, which has not been characterized by any great search for measures of effectiveness. From the limited evidence at hand, it is a program that apparently has concentrated on providing eligible veterans opportunities for enrolling in higher education but has neglected placement and other remedial programs.

Workers' compensation return-to-work programs face different problems. Most cases arise under private insurance arrangements, and presumably referral to rehabilitation services is governed by the private insurer's cost-benefit analysis. The difficulty with any analysis of rehabilitation activities under workers' compensation is that the agencies have attempted to regulate "process" and have not been overly concerned with outcomes. Thus we have New York mandating that carriers file forms after employees have been off work for a certain period. Other states mandate referral to some sort of rehabilitation activity after so many days off work or after a particular type of injury. Where these programs are mandatory, as they were in California beginning in 1975, they force the parties through a lock-step procedure in each case that comes under the rules, regardless of whether the claimant needs the services or not. At the very least, this procedure is expensive and at its worst, it may interfere with other return-to-work efforts. For the most part, such mandatory rehabilitation laws have been repealed, but the emphasis of state agencies is still on process rather than results. A suggested alternative is to have state agencies monitor the overall performances of insurers and large employers, evaluating them by their return-to-work results.

When it comes to private sector rehabilitation, it is probably wise to distinguish among rehabilitation activities according to their sponsor. If a private insurer retains a private rehabilitation provider, rehabilitation becomes a market-driven decision, and it is not likely that any superimposed evaluation will be a better guide than the market. However, when the client receives benefits from a public program, the demand situation is different. As experience with the workers' compensation program illustrates, there are great difficulties in setting forth rules and regulations that mandate when rehabilitation services should be provided. And that is only the beginning. The agency providing benefits may feel obliged to regulate fees and possibly prescribe utilization criteria. The difficulty is that astute private providers become proficient in obeying these rules and regulations and in using them to maximize their incomes. The objective of the whole process, returning the injured worker to gainful employment, becomes a secondary matter.

An alternative, which is now under active discussion in the case of the Social Security Disability Insurance rehabilitation or return-to-work program, is to pay providers according to results. The idea is that the provider is paid for services only after the beneficiary is back at work and off the benefit rolls. The amount paid to providers under the proposed scheme would be set according to agency savings in benefit costs and would bear no necessary relationship to the costs incurred by the provider. Establishing reimbursement schedules in this fashion eliminates the need for the agency to negotiate or establish fee schedules and utilization protocols. Some private insurers pay providers on such a contingency basis, and such a system could be adapted to workers' compensation, but as far as we are aware, no state is currently contemplating such a change in their law.

Endnotes

[1] This agency is housed in the Office of Special Education and Rehabilitation Services (OSERS) within the cabinet-level Department of Education. The RSA is responsible for administering the federal-state vocational rehabilitation (VR) system through ten regional offices. It also monitors ongoing and discretionary grant programs funded under the Rehabilitation Act of 1973.

[2] The information about the program and characteristics of its participants comes from unpublished information supplied by the Department of Veterans Affairs, June 24, 1997. The material, according to Jeffrey T. Goetz, Acting Director, Vocational Rehabilitation and Counseling Service, was prepared for a congressional hearing.

[3] As early as 1916, the IAIABC annual meetings were being advised that rehabilitation of injured persons and the readaptation of dependents in fatal cases should be the first concern of the program (Donoghue 1917:212).

[4] The contrast here is between the incentives and activities of state agencies in these two types of jurisdictions. In states where there is a private insurance option, state agencies lack motivation to remove claimants from disability rolls. Of course, private carriers in nonexclusive state fund jurisdictions may also actively pursue rehabilitation options as they seek to maximize profits.

[5] Once a claimant is accepted for VR services, the state workers' compensation law may provide that the worker is eligible for continued indemnity benefits.

[6] We are considering the competitive state funds as operating in much the same manner as private insurance carriers.

[7] Thus far, administrative inventories have been published by the WCRI for the following states: California, Colorado, Connecticut, Georgia, Illinois, Maine, Michigan, Minnesota, Missouri, New Jersey, New York, North Carolina, Oregon, Pennsylvania, Texas, Virginia, Washington, and Wisconsin.

References

Akabas, Sheila H., Lauren B. Gates, and Donald E. Galvin. 1992. *Disability Management*. New York: American Management Association.

Ballantyne, Duncan S., and Carol A. Telles. 1992. *Workers' Compensation in New York: Administrative Inventory.* Cambridge, MA: Workers' Compensation Research Institute.

Bellante, Donald. 1972. "A Multivariate Analysis of a Vocational Rehabilitation Program." *Journal of Human Resources,* Volume 7, no. 2 (Spring).

Berkowitz, Edward D. 1979. "The American Disability System in Historical Perspective." In Edward D. Berkowitz, ed., *Programs Disability Policies and Government.* New York: Praeger Scientific.

_____. 1987. *Disabled Policy.* New York: Cambridge University Press.

_____. 1988. "The Cost Benefit Tradition in Vocational Rehabilitation." In Monroe Berkowitz, ed., *Measuring the Efficiency of Public Programs: Costs and Benefits in Vocational Rehabilitation.* Philadelphia, PA: Temple University Press.

Berkowitz, Edward, and David Dean. 1996. "Vocational Rehabilitation/Social Security Administration Experience." In Jerry Mashaw et al., eds., *Disability, Work and Cash Benefits.* Kalamazoo, MI: Upjohn Institute.

Berkowitz, Monroe. 1988. "Preliminary Overview of Rehabilitation Systems." Research Report prepared for the Subcommittee on Rehabilitation, Maine State Legislature.

Berkowitz, Monroe, and John F. Burton, Jr. 1987. *Permanent Partial Disability and Workers' Compensation.* Kalamazoo, MI: W.E. Upjohn Institute for Rehabilitation.

Berkowitz, Monroe, John F. Burton, Jr., James Chelius, and David H. Dean. 1995. "Development of a Three-Year Plan to Guide Future Policies and Operations of the Division of Workers' Compensation." Research Report prepared for the Florida Division of Workers' Compensation.

Chelius, James R., Monroe Berkowitz, and John F. Burton, Jr. 1997. "Workers' Compensation Insurance: Fundamental Issues in the North American Context." Report prepared for Victorian Work Cover Authority, Melbourne, Australia.

Dean, David H., Robert Dolan, and Robert Schmidt. 1997. "Estimating Longitudinal Earnings Impacts for the VR Program." In submission at *Evaluation Review.*

Department of Veterans Affairs. 1997. Unpublished information supplied on June 24, 1997 by Jeffrey T. Goetz, Acting Director, Vocational Rehabilitation and Counseling Service, Washington, DC.

Department of Veterans Affairs. 1994. "Vocational Rehabilitation—Making It All Possible." VA Pamphlet 28-82-1. Washington, DC: Veterans Benefits Administration.

Donoghue, Francis D. 1917. "Restoring the Injured Employee to Work." *IAIABC Proceedings,* 1916. US Department of Labor, Bureau of Labor Statistics, Bulletin 210, p. 212.

General Accounting Office. 1996a. *Workers' Compensation: Selected Comparisons of Federal and State Laws.* GAO/GGD-96-76. Washington, DC: Government Printing Office.

_____. 1996b. *Vocational Rehabilitation—VA Continues to Place Few Disabled Veterans in Jobs.* GAO/HEHS-96-155. Washington, DC: Government Printing Office.

_____. 1993. *Vocational Rehabilitation: Evidence for Federal Program's Effectiveness Is Mixed.* GAO 93-19. Washington, DC: Government Printing Office.

_____. 1987. *Social Security—Little Success Achieved in Rehabilitating Disabled Beneficiaries.* Washington, DC: Government Printing Office.

Harris, Kay. 1996. *Defining, Measuring and Predicting Return to Work in Florida*. Tallahassee, FL: Division of Workers' Compensation, Florida Department of Labor and Employment Security.

King, Christopher T., and Susan J. Hadley. 1995. "Return-To-Work Programs for Texas Workers' Compensation Claimants: Suggested Design Parameters." Report prepared for Texas Workers' Compensation Research Center, Austin, TX.

Mashaw, Jerry L., and Virginia P. Reno, eds. 1996. *Balancing Security and Opportunity: The Challenge of Disability Income Policy*. Washington, DC: National Academy of Social Insurance.

Matkin, Ralph E. 1985. "The State of Private Sector Rehabilitation." In Lewis J. Taylor, Marjorie Golter, Gary Golter, and Thomas E. Backer, eds., *Handbook of Private Sector Rehabilitation*. New York: Springer Publishing Company.

McManus, Leo. 1981. "Evaluation of Disability Insurance Savings Due to Beneficiary Rehabilitation." *Social Security Bulletin*, Vol. 44. no. 2.

Social Security Administration. 1994. "Developing a World-Class Strategy for People with Disabilities." A Briefing for Commissioner Chater and Principal Deputy Commissioner Thompson (August 5).

U.S. Department of Education, Office of Special Education and Rehabilitative Services, Rehabilitation Services Administration. 1994a. *Annual Report to the President and to the Congress, Fiscal Year 1994*. Washington, DC: Government Printing Office.

_____. 1994b. *Rehabilitation Services Manual*. Washington, DC: Government Printing Office.

Worrall, John D. 1978. "A Benefit-Cost Analysis of the Vocational Rehabilitation Program." *Journal of Human Resources*, Vol. 13, no. 2.

CHAPTER 8

Compensation for Disabled Workers: Workers' Compensation

EMILY A. SPIELER
West Virginia University

JOHN F. BURTON, JR.
Rutgers University

Workers' compensation statutes require employers to provide cash benefits, medical care, and rehabilitation services to workers who experience work-related injuries and diseases. This chapter begins with an overview of the history, scope, and critical recent developments in the program.

Historical Origins

Prior to the passage of workers' compensation laws, injured employees were often without any recourse when disabled by work. The law of the 19th century generally precluded successful negligence lawsuits against employers. When employees did win these lawsuits, however, employers sometimes had to pay substantial cash awards. The result was essentially unsatisfactory for everyone: employers confronted potentially large and uncertain financial risk while at the same time workers faced destitution as a result of occupational injuries.

Workers' compensation was designed to overcome these deficiencies of the common law by reliance on two principles. First, adequate (albeit limited) benefits are provided to workers under a no-fault approach in which the worker only has to show that the injury is work-related—not that the employer was negligent—in order to qualify for benefits. Second, the program provides limited liability for employers, who are required to pay for benefits prescribed by statute but are insulated from negligence suits. Workers' compensation was also intended to make employers' costs of providing benefits predictable, manageable, and insurable and to curtail the delays and expenses of lawsuits.

Workers' compensation laws were passed with strong support from both business and labor in most states during the decade after 1910. At that time the Supreme Court's interpretation of the U.S. Constitution precluded federal legislation for most private sector workers. This pattern of state control has persisted with minor exceptions until today. The state-based nature of this program gives it its special character: programs vary substantially among states; political battles over benefit adequacy, eligibility, and costs are fought at the state—not the federal—level; and political arguments often focus on whether a particular state's program is either too expansive or too restrictive compared with neighboring states' programs.

Coverage

Today most workers—about 97% to 98% of employees (Schmulowitz 1997:10-11)—are covered by the program. However, even when employed in industries or occupations covered by workers' compensation statutes, workers in most states must meet four legal tests to receive benefits: (1) there must be a *personal injury*, which is sometimes interpreted to exclude mental disorders; (2) that results from an *accident*, which historically was interpreted by many states to exclude injuries that develop over a long period of time, as opposed to those resulting from a traumatic incident; (3) that must *arise out of employment*, which means that the source of the injury must be related to the job (if you have a personal quarrel with a neighbor who stalks you to the job and shoots you there, this is unlikely to meet the arising-out-of-employment test); and (4) that must occur during the *course of employment*, which normally requires that the injury occur on the employer's premises during working hours. Most work-related injuries can meet these four tests, although there are numerous exceptions.

Coverage of work-related diseases has been more problematic. Many diseases could not meet the accident test because they developed over a prolonged period. In addition, the statutes historically contained limited lists of diseases that were compensable. Fortunately, these lists have now been abandoned in all jurisdictions. Nonetheless, restrictions in language pertaining to work-related diseases are still found in many laws, such as statutes of limitations that require the claim to be filed within a limited period after the last exposure to the substance causing the disease, even if the disease did not manifest itself for a prolonged period. These statutory restrictions are compounded by difficulties in medical diagnosis and complicated questions regarding occupational causation of common diseases.[1]

Benefits

Most state workers' compensation laws require the employer to provide full medical benefits, including medical rehabilitation, without cost to the workers. However, many states do not provide vocational rehabilitation services that may be necessary before the injured worker can handle a new job.

Cash benefits include temporary total disability benefits, temporary partial disability benefits, permanent partial disability benefits (PPD), permanent total disability benefits, and death benefits.

Temporary total disability benefits are paid to an injured employee who is completely but temporarily unable to work. Benefits continue until he or she returns to work or recovers as fully as can be expected from the injury. This point is commonly referred to as the date of maximum medical improvement (MMI). The weekly benefit is two-thirds of the preinjury wage in most states, subject to maximum and minimum amounts, which are generally set as percentages of the state's average weekly wage. For example, in 1998 the Wisconsin temporary total disability benefit was 66 2/3% of preinjury wages, subject to maximum and minimum weekly benefits of $523 and $30. Maximum weekly benefits in 1998 varied from $903 in Iowa to $279.78 in Mississippi.[2]

Temporary partial disability benefits are paid to a worker who has returned to work prior to the date of MMI, but at a reduced wage. This benefit may rise in importance as disability management programs (discussed below) encourage workers to return to work more quickly after injury. The weekly benefit in most states is two-thirds of the difference between pre- and postinjury earnings, again subject to a maximum weekly amount.

Permanent partial disability (PPD) benefits are paid to workers who have permanent consequences due to their injury or disease that are not totally disabling. There are two general approaches: scheduled and unscheduled benefits.

Scheduled PPD benefits are paid for those injuries included in a list found in the workers' compensation statute. In Wisconsin, for example, 100% loss of an arm entitles the worker to 500 weeks of benefits. Schedules also apply to partial loss, so that a 50% loss of an arm is worth 250 weeks in Wisconsin. Normally the schedule is limited to extremities such as arms, legs, fingers, and toes, as well as the eyes and ears. The actual amount of compensation for loss of a particular scheduled body part varies substantially from one state to another.

Nonscheduled PPD benefits, which are paid for injuries not on the schedule (such as back cases), are handled in three different ways, depending on the state. Some states use an "impairment approach" which looks only at the medical consequences of the injury. For example, in New Jersey, 25% of loss of the whole person in a medical sense translates into 25% of 600 weeks, or 150 weeks of benefits. In states that use the "loss of earning capacity approach," disability evaluation considers medical consequences as well as factors such as age, education, and job experience that affect the worker's earning capacity. For an injured worker in Wisconsin assessed under the earning capacity approach, 25% of loss of earning capacity translates into 25% of 1,000 weeks or 250 weeks of benefits.

Under the third approach, termed "wage-loss," benefits are only paid if the worker also has actual wage loss due to work injury. For example, the weekly nonscheduled PPD benefit in New York is 66 2/3% of the difference between the worker's earnings after the date of MMI minus the worker's earnings prior to the injury, subject to a maximum weekly amount ($400 as of 1998). In New York these nonscheduled PPD benefits can continue for as long as the worker has earnings loss due to the work-related injury.

Permanent total disability benefits are paid to an injured worker who is unable to work after the date of MMI. These benefits are rarely awarded. The weekly benefit is normally two-thirds of the preinjury wage, subject to maximum and minimum amounts. In most states, permanent total benefits are paid for the duration of disability or for life. Some states, however, have arbitrary limits on total dollar amounts or duration of permanent disability benefits.

Death benefits are paid to the survivor(s) of a worker killed on the job. In many jurisdictions the weekly benefit depends on the number of survivors. For example, a widow might receive a benefit that is 50% of the deceased worker's wage, while a widow with a child might receive a weekly benefit that is 66 2/3% of the deceased worker's wage. Benefits are subject to minimum and maximum weekly amounts. Most states provide benefits for the period of dependency, which for a widow or widower is until death or remarriage and for a child is until age 21. However, there are a number of states that limit benefit duration.

Financing of Benefits

Workers' compensation laws assign responsibility for providing benefits to employers, who in turn can provide benefits by one of three mechanisms (depending on the state in which they are located): They can purchase insurance from a private insurance carrier or from a state workers' compensation fund, or they can self-insure and pay employees directly.

Some states, such as New York, have a "three-way system" in which all three options are available. A few states, such as Ohio, restrict choices to the state fund (known as an exclusive or monopolistic state fund) or self-insurance. Still other states, such as Wisconsin, restrict the choice to private insurance carriers or self-insurance. Nationally, about 50% of all benefits are paid by private insurance carriers, with self-insurance and state funds accounting for about 25% each (Burton and Schmidle 1996:I-7).

Workers' compensation insurance is experience-rated, which means that the premium depends on the level of benefits paid to injured workers. Firms that experience more frequent and more serious injuries pay higher rates. There are two possible steps in the experience rating process, beginning with industry-level experience rating. Employers are assigned to a particular insurance classification, and an initial rate (termed the "manual rate") is based on the average experience of all employers in the class. In addition, medium or large employers are eligible for firm-level experience rating and pay more or less than the manual rate, depending on their own experience relative to other firms in the class.

Goals of Workers' Compensation

The basic goals of the workers' compensation are those shared with the other programs in the workers' disability system considered in this volume. The goals are, first, the *prevention* of injuries and illnesses; second, the *compensation* of workers when they do become injured or ill, including provision of both cash benefits and medical care; and third, the *rehabilitation* of disabled workers, including return to work.

Traditionally, prevention has been promoted through experience rating and other insurance rating mechanisms, which provide incentives for employers to reduce insurance premiums by improving workplace safety. Empirical evidence regarding the success of experience rating is mixed: some studies support the theory that experience rating promotes safety, but others do not.[3] Recent legislative changes have broadened the focus on prevention; some states require employers to engage in loss prevention activities, develop safety plans, or create joint labor-management committees. We do not explore prevention further because it is examined in another chapter.

Rehabilitation is a more recent and important focus for workers' compensation programs. As rehabilitation in workers' compensation is likewise examined in another chapter, we only explore one important recent development—disability management.

Our primary focus is on the compensation goal for workers' compensation, which we evaluate using two criteria: (1) the benefits should be adequate, and (2) the costs should be affordable.[4]

Adequacy

At a conceptual level, a program can be considered adequate if it delivers sufficient benefits and services to meet its goals. Workers' compensation generally uses the economic losses suffered by injured workers as a benchmark for determining benefit adequacy. The operational basis we use to evaluate the adequacy of cash benefits is the generosity of a state's benefits compared to the benefits recommended by the 1974 edition of the *Workmen's Compensation and Rehabilitation Law* (generally referred to as the Model Act) published by the Council of State Governments. The Model Act incorporates the 84 recommendations contained in *The Report of the National Commission on State Workmen's Compensation Laws* (National Commission 1972). Since both documents reflected unanimous agreement among representatives of all the interests involved in workers' compensation, the prescribed cash benefits provide an unambiguous standard for assessing adequacy. To evaluate medical benefits adequacy, we use the recommendations of the National Commission, particularly Recommendation 4.2, which states there should be no statutory limits of time or dollar amount for medical care or physical rehabilitation services.

Affordability

At a conceptual level, a program is affordable if benefits and services are provided without serious adverse consequences for employers, workers, and the public, such as loss of jobs. We examine the affordability criteria in greater detail in our conclusions.

The history of workers' compensation shows that adequacy and affordability are often in a particularly virulent form of conflict. Without federal mandates, arguments regarding costs and adequacy occur at the state level, where interest groups engage in pitched battle over the program parameters. This tension between affordability and adequacy provides an organizing theme for much of our analysis.

An Overview of Costs and Benefits since 1960

Costs to employers and benefits paid to workers as a percent of payroll fluctuated significantly from 1960 to 1995, as shown in Figure A and Table 1. The data pertain to all states and all types of insurance arrangements, including self-insuring employers. Employers' costs have ranged from a low of 0.93% of payroll in 1960 to a high of 2.17% in 1993, followed by a decline to 1.83% in 1995. Even prior to the 1990s, there were significant variations in the rates of increase or decrease of workers' compensation costs.

The data in Table 1 also show the average (mean) cost of workers' compensation insurance rates as well as a measure of dispersion of states around the mean (the standard deviation). Data are available for 1975 to 1995 for 71 types of employers in 42 jurisdictions (including the District of Columbia). Average insurance costs have a pattern over time similar to the costs for all employers (Figure A), with an initial peak in 1980, a subsequent trough in 1984, a new peak in 1993, and a subsequent decline in costs. We have divided the post-1960 experience into subperiods based on whether total program costs were rising on average by less than or more than 10% a year. Analysis of these subperiods allows us to identify the dynamics of the last forty years that still affect program developments.[5]

The Tranquillity Era: 1960-71

The period from 1960 through 1971 was an era of relative tranquillity in terms of costs and benefits: national costs of the workers' compensation program increased from 0.93% of payroll in 1960 to 1.11% in 1971, while benefits increased from 0.59% of payroll in 1960 to 0.67% in 1971 (Figure A). During the 1960s, however, workers' compensation programs were increasingly criticized for failing to provide adequate benefits and coverage. Maximum weekly benefits had not been amended during and after World War II to keep up with increases in the average wage, and in most jurisdictions the maximums were lower relative to wages in the 1960s than in 1940.[6] Indeed, as of 1972 the maximum weekly benefit for temporary total disability in more than half the states was less than $79.56, the national poverty level for a nonfarm family of four (National Commission 1972:61). The extent of workers covered by workers' compensation did not match the coverage of other social insurance programs, including the Social Security (OASDHI) and unemployment insurance.

Other related developments in this era soon affected the compensation programs. The number of disabling work injuries increased in the

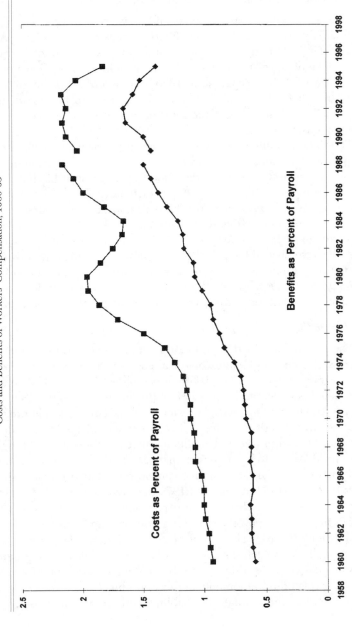

FIGURE A

Costs and Benefits of Workers' Compensation, 1960-95

Source: Table 1, col. (1) - (2)

TABLE 1

Workers' Compensation Costs and Benefits, 1975-95

	SSA/NASI Data as Percentage of Payroll		Insurance Rates as Percentage of Payroll		Changes in Benefits Paid (Percent)			Statutory Cash Benefits Average Stated as Percentage of Payroll
	Benefits (1)	Costs (2)	Mean (3)	Standard Deviation (4)	Cash (5)	Medical (6)	Total (7)	(8)
1960	0.59	0.93						
1961	0.61	0.95						
1962	0.62	0.96						
1963	0.62	0.99						
1964	0.63	1.00						
1965	0.61	1.00						
1966	0.61	1.02						
1967	0.63	1.07						
1968	0.62	1.07						
1969	0.62	1.08						
1970	0.66	1.11						
1971	0.67	1.11						
1972	0.68	1.14						39.6
1973	0.70	1.17						44.3
1974	0.75	1.24						44.7
1975	0.83	1.32	0.908	0.378				45.4
1976	0.87	1.49	1.101	0.446				49.4
1977	0.92	1.71	1.257	0.527				49.6
1978	0.94	1.86	1.448	0.624				48.9
1979	1.01	1.95	1.576	0.656				50.4
1980	1.07	1.96	1.655	0.681				50.3
1981	1.08	1.85	1.599	0.615				49.3
1982	1.16	1.75	1.475	0.524				49.7
1983	1.17	1.67	1.387	0.501				50.7
1984	1.21	1.66	1.371	0.491				50.7
1985	1.30	1.82	1.551	0.562				50.5
1986	1.37	1.99	1.807	0.628				50.1
1987	1.43	2.07	1.920	0.634	11.0	7.3	9.5	50.6
1988	1.49	2.16	2.176	0.720	10.8	10.7	10.8	50.1
1989	1.43	2.04	2.277	0.772	11.5	18.8	14.3	51.0
1990	1.49	2.13	2.597	1.014	13.9	15.6	14.6	50.1
1991	1.64	2.16	2.758	0.859	2.2	12.5	6.3	49.9
1992	1.66	2.13	3.020	0.979	-11.3	3.9	-4.8	48.9
1993	1.58	2.17	3.178	1.018	-15.2	-9.9	-12.7	50.0
1994	1.52	2.05	3.114	0.792	-10.5	-6.5	-8.7	49.3
1995	1.39	1.83	3.040	0.839	-2.6	-0.6	-1.6	49.1

Source: Columns (1)-(2): 1960-88 data: Social Security Bulletin, Annual Statistical Supplement (1995: Table 9.B1); 1989-95 data: Schmulowitz (1997: Table 11).
Columns (3), (4), and (8): Preliminary data from Thomason, Schmidle, and Burton (1998).
Columns (5)-(7): Data from National Council on Compensation Insurance, *Annual Statistical Bulletin*, 1988-98 eds. Calculations by Florence Blum and John F. Burton, Jr.

1960s, resulting in more deaths, permanent disabilities, and temporary total disabilities (Williams and Barth 1973:3). A 1968 explosion in a West Virginia coal mine served as the catalyst for the enactment of the federal Coal Mine Health and Safety Act of 1969, which *inter alia* provided benefits to disabled coal miners and their survivors (Barth 1987: 12-13). Many viewed this law as an indicator of increased federal concern regarding inadequacy of state compensation for occupational diseases and as a harbinger of increased federal involvement in the workers' compensation arena.

The Era of Reform: 1972-79

One result of the concern about deteriorating workplace safety and the increasing criticism of the workers' compensation program was the creation of the National Commission on State Workmen's Compensation Laws as part of the Occupational Safety and Health Act of 1970. The commission (1972:119) concluded that state laws "in general are inadequate and inequitable." The commission made 84 recommendations, designated 19 of the recommendations as essential, and urged Congress to enact federal minimum standards incorporating the essential recommendations if the states did not improve their laws by 1975.

Congress did not enact federal standards. One reason is that state laws were significantly improved in the 1970s in response to the threat of federal intrusion. For example, average cash benefits increased from 39.6% of the benefits prescribed by the Model Act in 1972 to 50.4% of the prescribed benefits by 1979 (Table 1).[7] The compliance score for the recommendation that full medical benefits be provided without arbitrary limits on time or dollar amount increased from 36 jurisdictions in 1972 to 50 in 1979.[8]

Changes in statutory benefits translated into higher benefit payments to workers. Benefits rose from 0.67% of payroll in 1971 to 1.01% in 1979 (Figure A). Costs to all types of employers increased from 1.11% of payroll in 1971 to 1.95% in 1979 (Figure A).

The Squeeze of Benefits and Costs: 1980-84

A deceleration in workers' compensation benefit payments occurred in the early 1980s, in part reflecting the slower pace of state reform as the threat of federal standards vanished in wake of the 1980 election of President Reagan. Benefits as a percent of payroll increased from 1.01% to 1.21% between 1979 and 1984. Costs of workers' compensation for all types of employers grew at a much more modest rate, not even matching total payroll growth. As a result, costs plummeted from 1.95% of payroll in 1979 to 1.66% in 1984 (Figure A).

The squeeze between costs and benefits in workers' compensation can be explained by macroeconomic developments. High inflation in the late 1970s and early 1980s led to high interest rates and bond yields. One consequence was that workers' compensation insurance carriers experienced higher returns on their investments, allowing them to compete for business by lowering insurance rates, despite increasing benefit payments. Since insurance premiums are collected at the beginning of a policy period, while benefits are paid over the course of several years, insurers earn investment income on reserves. For most of the period, the strategy worked: from 1979 to 1983 workers' compensation was a profitable line of insurance.

The Seeds for Neo-Reform Are Sown: 1985-91

Compensation benefits increased during this period from 1.21% of payroll in 1984 to 1.64% in 1991 (Figure A). Medical benefits increased at 15.6% per year between 1984 and 1991, more rapidly than both the annual increase of 10.8% in cash benefits and the generally high rate of medical cost inflation. Costs also increased rapidly, rising from 1.66% of payroll in 1984 to 2.16% in 1991 (Figure A). Insurance premiums doubled: from 1.37% of payroll in 1984 to 2.76% in 1991 (Table 1).

As this period progressed, the workers' compensation insurance industry declared itself in a crisis mode. Several factors contributed to the industry's problems. Benefit payments continued to increase rapidly, but in many states carriers were unable to gain approval from regulators for rate filings with significant premium increases that the industry felt were justified. As a result, the industry lost money in every year between 1984 and 1991, even considering investment income.

The Neo-Reform Era: 1992-98

During the most recent period, both benefits and costs declined substantially. Benefits peaked at 1.66% of payroll in 1992 and then declined until reaching 1.39% in 1995 (Figure A). The multiyear decline in benefits relative to payroll is unprecedented in duration and magnitude since at least 1960. During the same interval, employer costs peaked in 1993 and then declined significantly (Table 1). Despite the recent drop, costs as a percent of payroll for all employers were roughly twice as high in 1995 as in 1960; insurance costs as a percent of payroll more than tripled from 1975 to 1995.

As benefits and costs declined in the 1990s, insurer profitability quickly improved. The period from 1994 to 1997 was the most profitable period in at least twenty years for workers' compensation insurance.

Significant Developments: Causes and Consequences

Escalating costs in the period from 1985 to 1991 galvanized political opposition from employers and insurers to compensation programs that had been liberalized in the wake of the National Commission's Report. Over half of state legislatures passed major amendments to workers' compensation laws during the period 1989 to 1996, generally reducing benefits and attempting to contain health care costs.[9] This retrenchment in benefit generosity provides the context for our examination of five significant recent developments in workers' compensation.

First, we examine the reduction in the statutory level of cash benefits that has occurred in a number of jurisdictions, particularly with regard to permanent partial disability benefits. Second, we look at the contracting availability of workers' compensation benefits due to the changing rules of compensability. The more stringent eligibility rules and the reduced statutory benefits contributed to the rapid decline in cash benefits paid to workers in the 1990s.

Third, we explore the transformation of the health care delivery system, including the introduction of managed care. Although the causes are not entirely clear, the medical benefits actually paid to workers have also declined substantially in the 1990s. Changes in the health care delivery system affect both health care costs as well as the evaluation of workers for cash benefits. In relation to this, our fourth focus is on the rise of disability management, which is intertwined both with cost reductions and changes in health care delivery. Finally, we examine challenges to the exclusive remedy doctrine, caused in part by greater limitations on the availability of compensation benefits.

We examine these five recent developments, while recognizing that other important changes are affecting the program. For example, the reported injury rate declined in the 1990s according to Bureau of Labor Statistics data. Determining the extent to which the improved safety record is due to increased effectiveness of OSHA enforcement activities, to the greater impact of experience rating in workers' compensation as average premium levels have increased, or to more effort at prevention by employers involves issues beyond the scope of this chapter. There can be no question, however, that a reduction in injuries may have contributed substantially to reductions in aggregate costs in this period.

Important changes in insurance arrangements that have occurred in recent decades are also not examined. Since 1980 several states have established new state funds, while a few others have increased the role of private carriers in their compensation insurance markets. In addition, most states with private carriers have deregulated their workers' compensation insurance markets since 1970.[10]

Finally, a third important issue not discussed here is the rising concern about adjudication of workers' compensation claims. Originally conceived as an administratively simple program, complex hearing and appeal procedures have led to significant delays in many states, contributing to claimants mistrust of these programs. Attempts to develop new and more efficient mechanisms for dispute resolution—and accompanying attempts to restrict the access of claimants to lawyers—are important developments discussed in Chapter 10.

While we make no pretense of having captured every recent significant development in workers' compensation, the five developments we have chosen to examine capture critical changes occurring in this volatile program.

Significant Development One: Reductions in Cash Benefits

The contrasting record of benefits paid to workers in the 1980s and 1990s is illustrated by Figure B, which provides information on benefits paid to employees whose employers purchase insurance from private carriers or competitive state funds. While cash benefits per 100,000 employees were increasing at double-digit rates from 1986-87 to 1989-90, a quick reversal saw aggregate cash benefits decline at double-digit rates from 1991-92 to 1993-94.

Not all benefits came under challenge in the 1990s. For example, maximum weekly benefits for total disability were not scaled back in many jurisdictions, in large part because most states now provide that the maximum is tied to the state's average weekly cap. In January 1990, 32 of 51 jurisdictions (including the District of Columbia) had maximum weekly benefits for temporary total disability that were at least 100% of the average weekly wage; by January 1998, 34 states met this standard. On the other hand, several states reduced the maximum number of weeks of temporary total disability benefits (usually to a limit of 104 weeks). In addition, Massachusetts cut the nominal replacement rate for temporary total disability benefits from 66.67% to 60% of the worker's preinjury rate.[11]

Many states also now mandate that permanent total disability benefits be reduced by other income, most commonly Social Security Old

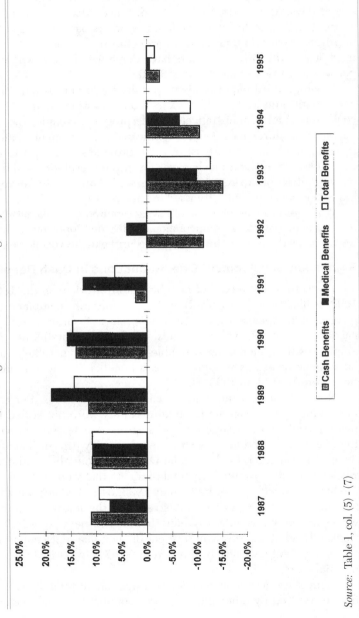

FIGURE B

Changes in Benefits Paid per 100,000 Workers
(Percentage Increases from Preceding Policy Year)

Source: Table 1, col. (5) - (7)

Age benefits, or be terminated when the claimant reaches a particular age or becomes eligible to collect alternative benefits. These provisions generally make inadequate allowance for the reduction in retirement income resulting from lost wages due to disability. Although these restrictions have been challenged in many states, only one court has held the reduction of workers' compensation benefits by benefits received from the Social Security Old Age program to be unlawful.[12]

The primary target for reform in the 1990s has been permanent partial disability benefits, which typically account for most benefit payments. Three patterns of PPD reform are evident. First, there are reductions in the duration and/or weekly amount of the PPD benefits. Thus in Connecticut a 27% reduction in PPD benefits was achieved in 1993 by reducing the nominal replacement rate from 80% to 75% of spendable earnings; by reducing the duration for scheduled injuries (e.g., the number of weeks for loss of a leg was reduced from 238 to 155 weeks); and by reducing the maximum duration of nonscheduled PPD benefits from 780 to 520 weeks. These changes reduce both the duration of compensation awards in more serious cases and the value of claims settled early in litigation.

A second pattern in PPD reform in the 1990s was the substantial curtailment of the wage-loss approach to benefits. Pennsylvania enacted legislation in 1996 that reduced the employer's obligation to offer employment to avoid responsibility for wage-loss benefits. Florida had been viewed as a pioneer in 1979 when it introduced a two-track system for PPD benefits: impairment benefits for workers who experienced actual physical loss of body members and concurrent wage loss benefits for workers with actual earnings losses due to their injuries. During the 1980s the maximum duration for the wage-loss benefits was 525 weeks. In 1990 the duration of wage-loss benefits was seriously curtailed (reducing the actuarial valuation of the PPD benefits by 48.4%). In 1994 impairment benefits were eliminated, wage-loss benefits were restricted to a few workers with very serious injuries, and the overall duration for all benefits in PPD cases was limited to 401 weeks. The actuarial valuation indicated these 1994 reforms reduced the Florida PPD benefits by another 16.7% (NCCI 1998:99).

A third pattern in PPD reform in the 1990s was to move toward benefits based on the extent of impairment, rather than on the extent of loss of earning capacity. The rationale was that the impairment ratings were more objective and thus less prone to litigation. In practice, the reform was often accompanied by reductions in maximum duration, as in Texas.

Despite these examples, the primary explanation for the recent decline in total benefits paid to workers (shown in Figure B) is not that the level of statutory cash benefits were slashed drastically in the 1990s. Cash benefits provided by the average state statute declined from 49.9% of the benefits prescribed by the Model Act in 1991 to 49.1% in 1995 (Table 1), which can hardly explain the magnitude of the decline in benefits paid. Part of the explanation for the steep decline in benefits paid is that the legal requirements for obtaining workers' compensation benefits have been significantly tightened in many jurisdictions.

Significant Development Two: Changing Rules of Compensability

More restrictive rules governing benefit eligibility have played a critical role in the declining workers' compensation cost in the 1990s. Since each state's program is an interdependent system with its own history of tradeoffs among key provisions, it is important to be careful in making generalizations about trends. Some of the more common types of changes in the availability of benefits are, however, apparent.

Changes in Compensability of Particular Conditions

One of the most obvious constraints on benefit availability involves statutory or regulatory changes that explicitly limit the compensability of claims involving particular medical diagnoses. Not surprisingly, the focus has been on health conditions that are potentially most costly to a compensation program.

For example, many states substantially restricted the right of workers to make claims for psychological injuries resulting from a mental stimulus in the absence of a physical injury (so-called "mental-mental" claims). In a much smaller number of states, restrictions on compensation for psychological injury even includes those that develop as a result of a physical injury. These restrictions have been designed in a number of ways. Some state laws simply make mental-mental claims noncompensable. A second approach imposes heightened standards of causation or increased burdens of proof. A third reduces the amount of benefits: in Colorado benefits for mental injury are now limited to twelve weeks, with a maximum weekly benefit of 50% of the state's average weekly wage. Several states explicitly limit mental-mental claims to situations not involving lawful personnel actions or to situations involving extraordinary or unusual circumstances. Psychological reactions to stressful work situations that are not illegal or unusual are therefore noncompensable in these states.

California provides an interesting case study. Psychological claims had been compensable based upon the worker's subjective perception of work stressors. Associated costs were rising, and so between 1989 and 1993 the state legislature clamped down. The statute was changed to preclude mental injury claims resulting from good faith personnel actions, to require that employment be the predominant cause of injury and that mental claims be proved by a preponderance of the evidence, and to restrict compensability of claims at the beginning of employment and after separation from employment.

The motivation for these limitations is clear. Psychological harm from work may be common, but workers' responses to work stressors are both very individualized and subject to serious measurement problems. Costs are therefore both potentially huge and uncertain. Stress claims were a relatively new phenomenon and appeared to be growing quickly in some jurisdictions. There was substantial disagreement between those who believe this increase reflected changes in management practices that resulted in actual increased stress at work and those who believe that the increase was simply a reporting phenomenon.

By changing the legal rules, claims are made to "disappear" from workers' compensation programs. Despite the strong economic rationale for this solution, it is nevertheless troubling in light of the growing recognition of the seriousness of mental illness and the requirement under federal law that group health insurance plans must provide "mental health equity." This is likely to increase cost-shifting from workers' compensation to general health plans.

Injuries caused by repetitive trauma, such as carpal tunnel syndrome and noise-induced hearing loss, present a similar picture. As the incidence of these claims sky-rocketed, state legislatures responded by tightening eligibility standards, using the same mechanisms used to limit compensability of stress claims. In Virginia the state's supreme court ruled that repetitive injury claims were noncompensable under the language of the state statute. In response to criticism of these decisions, the Virginia legislature amended the workers' compensation statute to provide nominal, but very narrow, coverage for these conditions.[13]

Limitations on Coverage When the Injury Involves Aggravation of a Preexisting Condition

Other changes are subtler than explicit restrictions on the compensability of specific conditions. Traditionally, employers were said to "take workers as they found them." This meant that workers with preexisting conditions were not barred from coverage for work injuries, even if the underlying condition contributed to the occurrence of the injury or to the extent of the resulting disability. Through a variety of legislative and judicial changes, rules governing compensation for preexisting conditions or aggravation have been tightened in many jurisdictions.

For example, second injury funds historically provided insurance coverage for disability that resulted from the combined effects of a new injury and past disabilities. Pressure on second injury funds has mounted over the last decade. Costs associated with second injuries rose, and employers and insurers had little incentive to defend against claims that would be charged to the funds. Recently formulated accounting principles forced states to recognize the magnitude of unfunded liabilities. Private insurers led a lobbying campaign to eliminate the funds, resulting in the abolition or severe restriction of second injury funds in several states. To the extent that the disability discrimination laws result in increased hiring of previously injured workers, elimination of the financial protection offered by second injury funds means that employers may face increased liability for aggravation of old injuries. As a result, employers have more incentive both to fight individual claims and to argue in the political arena for reduced workers' compensation coverage for injuries previously compensated by these funds.

And although not specifically the result of the elimination of second injury funds, both state courts and legislatures have moved to restrict compensation of injuries involving aggravation of preexisting conditions. Most significantly, several states now limit compensation when the current injury is not the sole or major cause of disability. These limitations come in a variety of forms: excluding injuries or resulting disabilities if they are the effects of "the natural aging process," requiring that work be the "major" or "predominant" cause or "the major contributing factor" of any disability, and excluding injuries for which current work is merely the triggering factor. These changes are reinforced by heightened evidentiary standards for claimants, including requirements of "objective medical evidence" (discussed below), and by stricter rules and shorter time limits for reopening prior claims when progression of a condition occurs.

Judicial application of these statutory developments illustrates their effects on workers. For example, the Oregon rule requiring that work be the predominant cause of the injury resulted in a finding that when a preexisting condition predisposed a worker to airway irritation, the resulting, occupationally caused lung disease was not compensable.[14] In Illinois a reviewing court denied benefits for occupational lung disease to a coal miner who presented medical evidence of occupational lung disease and who had worked for twenty-five years in underground mines where he was "continually exposed to coal dust"; the court nevertheless found, despite a statutory presumption of causation in cases involving miners' lung diseases, that his claim was appropriately denied, based upon the claimant's smoking history and conflicting medical testimony.[15]

Restrictions on Compensability of Permanent Total Disability Cases

Efforts to reduce costs has also been directed at what actuaries call the "long tail" of workers' compensation claims—those with benefits that may continue for years. Statutory reductions in benefit duration, as described in the preceding section, are part of this trend. In addition, there has been a particularly strong assault in some states on eligibility criteria for permanent total disability benefits.

Prior to recent developments, many states had adopted the "odd lot" doctrine, considering not only the extent of injury but the claimant's age, education, and skills in determining eligibility. State legislatures have moved away from this concept. Some, like Florida, now require a "catastrophic" injury before a worker can be considered for a PTD award. Others, including West Virginia, have established impairment thresholds requiring the injury to result in a very high level of functional impairment before a worker can be considered for a PTD award. Many states have narrowed the definition of PTD by abandoning the claimant's prior work as a reference point: for example, in Minnesota, injured workers must be incapable of working at any occupation that produces income.

The results have sometimes been startling. For example, in West Virginia, adoption of a threshold requirement that a claimant have at least 50% functional impairment (within the restrictive definition in the American Medical Association's *Guides for the Evaluation of Permanent Impairment*) resulted in a 97% reduction in the rate of PTD awards, from 117 to 5.8 per 100,000 workers (BNA 1997:276).

The combined effects of the changes in the duration of permanent disability benefits are two-sided. On the one hand, costs are reduced. On the other hand, many states appear to be abandoning any attempt to relate these benefits to the economic losses of claimants. The tension between affordability and adequacy is apparent.

Procedural and Evidentiary Changes in Claims Processing That Restrict Compensability

Finally, statutory and administrative changes in procedural rules and evidentiary standards are resulting in restrictions on the number of compensable claims in many programs. For example, statutory changes in a number of states now require a claimant to prove both that the injury was primarily work-related and that the resulting medical condition can be documented by "objective medical" evidence. The requirement for objective evidence excludes claims based upon subjective reports of patients that cannot be substantiated by objective evidence, including debilitating musculoskeletal injuries that involve soft tissue damage and reports of pain and psychological impairment. These heightened requirements appear to be rooted both in a desire to save money and in a distrust of subjective injury reports.

In addition, claimants are sometimes asked to meet increasingly strict burdens of proof. In a landmark case under the federal black lung compensation law, the U.S. Supreme Court threw out the Department of Labor's "true doubt rule." Under this rule, claimants win if the medical evidence offered by the claimant and the coal operator are equal in weight. The court ruled that due to requirements in the Administrative Procedures Act, claimants must prove their cases by a "preponderance of the evidence."[16] The result was a reduction in the number of approved claims. Amendments to some state statutes now require, either in all claims or for specifically delineated ones, that claimants meet this "preponderance" standard or, for some injuries or diseases, the even more difficult standard of "clear and convincing evidence." Because many workers' compensation programs gave claimants the benefit of the doubt in close cases in the past, these changes are significant.

The general tightening of eligibility standards has a predictable but difficult to quantify effect on the handling of claims. All over the country, claimants and their representatives assert that insurance carriers are more likely to controvert or contest claims and less likely to offer reasonable settlements. The Workers' Compensation Research Institute report regarding Massachusetts' experience supports this claim (Gardner et al. 1996). A study in New York City found that 81% of workers diagnosed with occupational cumulative trauma disorders had their claims contested or received no response from the insurance carrier when their claims were filed (Herbert et al. 1997). Thus even in jurisdictions that nominally compensate these injuries, many claims go uncompensated.

Significant Development Three: Transformation of the Health Care Component

Annual rates of change in the cost of medical benefits paid per 100,000 workers are shown in Figure B. After soaring in excess of 10% a year from 1986-87 to 1990-91, there was a sharp deceleration from policy years 1990-91 to 1991-92, followed by three years of decline. What explains this sharp reversal of fortunes?

Several other developments discussed in this chapter play a part in the decline of medical costs. Falling injury rates and tightening eligibility standards during the 1990s mean fewer claims were filed and approved, affecting both cash and medical benefits. However, factors peculiar to the workers' compensation health care system also played a role.[17]

The relatively rapid increases in workers' compensation health care costs in the 1980s were in part due to developments in other parts of the health care system. Group health plans for nonoccupational injuries and illnesses became increasingly restrictive during this period and attempted to cut costs through reliance on cost-sharing mechanisms (such as deductibles and coinsurance payments) as well as increased use of managed care strategies, including fee regulation, utilization review, and various forms of provider networks. At the same time, workers' compensation health care continued to be paid entirely by the employer and to rely primarily on fee-for-service reimbursement arrangements with medical practitioners.

Such disparities provided an incentive for providers to classify marginal conditions (such as backs) as work-related in order to receive higher payments. As a result, medical expenses for comparable conditions were considerably higher in workers' compensation than in the general health care system. For example, Johnson, Baldwin, and Burton (1996) examined 1991-93 data on health care payments in California and found that the ratio of workers' compensation to nonoccupational health insurance payments for comparable injuries ranged from 4.2 for backs to 1.7 for fractures. Workers also had greater incentive to have marginal conditions treated as work-related so as to avoid the increasingly unattractive financial arrangements for group health care plans. Thus some of the rapid increase in health care costs in workers' compensation in the late 1980s was probably due to cost shifting from the rest of the health care system.[18]

Since about 1990, due to a perception that workers' compensation was experiencing inordinate increases in health care costs, many states changed the health care component of their compensation programs. Some changes represented increased reliance on traditional approaches to limiting health care costs, namely fee schedules, limits on the choice of treating physicians, and limits on the amount or duration of health care. Other changes were designed to emulate the managed care developments in nonoccupational health care plans in part to reduce the extent of cost shifting to workers' compensation.

Increased Reliance on Traditional Health Care Cost Containment Methods

Medical payment limits. In 1972 the National Commission recommended that medical care should be provided with no statutory limits of time or dollar amount. In 1980 all 51 jurisdictions were considered to be in compliance with this recommendation by the U.S Department of Labor; in 1998, 6 jurisdictions were no longer in compliance, in most instances because of statutory changes in the 1990s. Two states require worker copayments, while four limit medical benefits unless the workers' compensation agency specifically approves additional payments.[19]

Fee schedules. Medical fee schedules specify maximum reimbursement rates for services supplied by hospitals, physicians, and other health care providers. According to a recent review by the Workers Compensation Research Institute (WCRI), the number of jurisdictions using fee schedules for workers' compensation health care increased from 27 in 1991 to 40 by 1995 (Eccleston and Yeager 1997:24).

The obvious purpose of fee schedules is to restrict health care providers' fees and thus reduce costs, but the evidence of the actual effect is limited and inconclusive. For example, Boden and Fleischman (1989) computed the average annual growth rate in workers' compensation medical costs for twenty years (1965-85) for 41 states, of which 12 had a fee schedule in effect for at least fifteen years during this period. The correlation between the presence of a fee schedule and the average annual growth rate was very low (-0.08). In contrast, Durbin and Appel (1991), examined medical cost data from 33 states for the period 1964-84 and found that fee schedules reduced medical costs between 3.5% and 5.4%.

Several recent studies have examined the effect of fee schedules using data on individual workers (rather than state-level data). Pozzebon (1993:20) examined data from 17 states for workers injured between 1979 and 1987 and concluded that "the effect of fee schedules on moderating the rate of increase in medical prices is modest at best." In contrast, Levy and Miller (1996:43) using similar data found that fee schedules were associated with substantially lower medical care costs.

Johnson, Baldwin, and Burton (1996) examined California data and found that for three out of four injury groups, average unit charges were higher for general health care cases than for workers' compensation cases, which suggests that the California fee schedule was effective in holding down unit charges. However, average total charges (which is the product of the average unit charges and the number of units of care) were from 1.7 (fractures) to 4.2 (backs) greater for work injuries than for comparable, non-work-related injuries. As the authors observed (1996:62), "When, as in California, the fee schedule applies to nearly every service but does not control the utilization of services, overutilization of services becomes the strategy of choice for providers who want to maximize revenues." The ability of medical practitioners to counteract fee schedules by increasing the quantity of services has not deterred most states from pursuing this cost containment strategy.[20]

Limitation on employees' choice of provider. Employers and carriers assert that injured workers who control the choice of providers may overutilize medical services and select physicians who prescribe excessive diagnosis and treatments. Pressure to restrict employee choice of physicians is also fueled by another concern: in workers' compensation, medical practitioners play multiple roles. They not only provide treatment, they also assess the extent of permanent disability and influence the timing of a worker's return to work. The selection of the physician, therefore, may have significant impact on both cash and medical benefit costs. Not surprisingly, organized labor and many workers argue that restrictions on employee choice of providers have an adverse impact on the injured worker, damage the provider-patient relationship, and lead to inferior treatment and premature return to work.

The WCRI survey indicated that as of 1997, workers' compensation programs in 14 states gave employees an unrestricted initial choice of the treating provider; the number of jurisdictions providing such a choice that has been virtually cut in half in the last decade (Eccleston and Yeager 1997:41). Again, only a few empirical studies have investigated the impact of limiting the employees' choice of physician on health care costs, and again the findings are inconsistent. Boden and Fleischman (1989) concluded that employee choice had no discernible effect on workers' compensation medical costs. In contrast, studies by Victor and Fleischman (1990) and Durbin and Appel (1991) found that limiting employee choice decreased medical costs. All these studies used state-level aggregated data. Pozzebon (1993) used information on individual workers' compensation claims and found that medical benefits were 5% to 15% *more* costly in states limiting the employee's initial choice of provider than in jurisdictions without such limits.

New Approaches for Health Care Cost Containment

Most workers' compensation programs now use some of the cost containment approaches that are widely used in the general health care system, including HMOs and PPOs (or, more generally, Managed Care Organizations (MCOs)).[21] As of 1997, 6 jurisdictions mandated the use of managed care organizations (Eccleston and Yeager 1997:13-15). But this number is misleading. One reason is that 12 other jurisdictions provide that when an MCO exists, the employee must choose a treating physician from the MCO. Moreover, in some states, employers long had the legal right to choose the treating physicians but in practice allowed employees to choose the doctors; in the 1990s employers in those states began to require injured workers to use MCOs.

This transformation of the workers' compensation health care delivery system proceeded despite the paucity of evidence on the impact of managed care on the costs, quality, and satisfaction of health care. Dembe (1998) conducted a careful review of the studies of managed care and found numerous reports issued by employers and health plans that in general had not been conducted by independent researchers and lacked methodological rigor. Dembe did find five credible studies which he concluded suggest that the introduction of managed care can, on average, reduce total workers' compensation claims costs by about 20%-30% compared to unmanaged fee-for-service arrangements, with savings resulting from a combination of the introduction of discounted medical fees, decreased utilization of medial services, and a lower frequency and duration of cash benefit claims. These studies do not assess the adequacy of the reduced cash benefits paid to workers, nor do they look carefully at the other effects of disability management discussed in the next section.

Although Dembe reports little difference in medical or functional outcomes between workers' compensation patients treated under managed care and those receiving medical care under traditional arrangements, he notes that the studies demonstrate the managed care patients are consistently less satisfied with their care. Dembe adds a further note of caution to his findings on cost savings: elimination of unnecessary or inappropriate medical services can produce a rapid cost decline compared to previous unmanaged fee-for-service contexts, but once new treatment norms are established, additional cost reductions may be difficult to achieve. Also, two of the credible studies were done in Florida, where medical benefits paid per 100,000 workers have been at least 50% above the national average in most years in the 1990s (Burton and Blum

1996:22). As Dembe indicates, the effects of discounted fee schedules (a component of the managed care projects in Florida) can expect to be the greatest in states that have relatively high medical costs prior to establishment of the managed care program.

Assessment of the Medical Care Cost Containment Strategies

The sparse available research suggests the following. First, two of the traditional strategies used to reduce health care costs in workers' compensation—fee schedules and limits on the employee choice of physician—are of limited value or may even be counterproductive. Second, managed care may reduce costs but at the expense of greater worker dissatisfaction. Further studies clearly are needed to determine whether managed care arrangements can improve the quality of medical care while also achieving cost reductions.

A facile conclusion would be that the transformation of the workers' compensation health care delivery system during the 1990s is causally related to the significant reduction in health care benefits paid to workers during the 1990s shown in Figure B. We resist that conclusion for two reasons. First, the magnitude of the decline seems disproportionate to the extent of changes in the workers' compensation health care delivery system. Second, as previously noted, other significant changes in workers' compensation during the 1990s also probably had a major impact on medical benefits. These include the increasing restrictiveness of eligibility rules and the greater attention to disability management by employers. It is too soon to sort out these causes of the decline in medical benefits paid to workers in the 1990s.

Significant Development Four: The Rise of Disability Management

Increased employer control over medical management of injured workers through managed care networks and choice of physician is inextricably linked to increased interest in reduction of costs through "disability management." Perhaps the most remarkable change in workers' compensation over the past twenty years has been the shift to a focus on disability management and "return to work" for injured workers. In the past, the decision to return a disabled worker to his or her old job or to any job at all was solely within the discretion of employers and was not viewed as the concern of workers' compensation programs.[22]

In contrast, current law, economics, and medical management all encourage work participation by disabled workers. Insurance carriers, employers, and workers' compensation administrators now routinely refer to workers' compensation as a "disability management program"— not a compensation program. Why? Because disability management can accomplish two critical goals: it can limit costs by reducing both the duration of absence from work and the permanent disability rating (especially any psychological "overlay" resulting from prolonged absence), and it can improve the quality of life for workers by increasing successful postinjury work participation.

Not surprisingly, the strong motivation for insurers and employers to promote rapid return to work makes many labor union officials and injured workers' groups wary. In most states an accepted or spurned job offer, even before the worker has reached maximum medical improvement, will lead to termination of temporary total disability benefits; in some states the job offer may limit permanent disability benefits as well. Not all states require that the job offer be appropriate for the worker. Workers and their unions have charged that injured workers are asked to resume duties they are not yet physically capable of performing.

Legal Changes Supporting Increased Disability Management

Legal changes have both supported and reflected this shift toward disability management. Some are internal to workers' compensation statutes: expanding rehabilitation opportunities, making retaliation for filing workers' compensation actionable, and establishing both incentives and requirements for returning an injured worker to work. For example, quite a few state laws now explicitly provide that if the injured worker refuses either to cooperate in a job placement process or fails to accept a job, the benefits will be terminated or substantially reduced. Other states have moved toward similar policies administratively. Only a few of these statutory or administrative policies protect workers with regard to the pay or nature of the job that must be accepted. Other states require participation in rehabilitation efforts before a claimant can be considered for permanent total disability benefits.

Employers and insurers are also required or encouraged to participate in this process. For example, several states provide financial incentives for employers to reemploy injured workers by reducing the amount of the award charged to an employer's account or by reimbursing the employer from the second injury fund for some of the disability award. Some states require reemployment and penalize noncomplying employers.

Often, statutory changes that focus on reemployment were passed as part of a legislative package with other major amendments (some described earlier in this chapter) that changed the eligibility rules for benefits. Sometimes, restrictions on compensability or reductions in benefits have been justified under the rubric of encouraging people to work. According to Governor Chiles of Florida, "The theory was that if you tell somebody that you have to be off the system at a certain time, they will do what needs to be done to move ahead." A Florida claimant's attorney characterized this incentive another way: "If we starve them, they'll go back to work."[23]

Other legal developments outside of the workers' compensation laws have both encouraged and reinforced these trends. Most importantly, the Americans with Disabilities Act and state disability discrimination laws and the Family and Medical Leave Act, described in Chapter 6, now regulate employers' treatment of injured workers. Workers with disabilities caused by work-related injuries and diseases in principle receive the protection of these new laws. The ADA, at least on its surface, clearly supports the return-to-work concepts now espoused in workers' compensation.[24] For example, pursuant to the policy statements issued by the EEOC, an employee who is off work due to a work-related disability is entitled to return to his/her same position unless the employer demonstrates either that holding open the position would impose an undue hardship or that the injured employee cannot perform the essential functions of the job with reasonable accommodation.

While some employers object to the policy statements as intrusive, most have applauded the EEOC's willingness to support their efforts to bring workers with compensable injuries back to work in light duty jobs. The agency's published guidance, for example, specifically permits (but does not require) employers to establish light duty programs targeted at employees with occupational injuries. This is the first time that the EEOC has recognized that employers may, for economic reasons, choose to treat occupationally injured employees differently from other employees with disabilities.

The effectiveness of the ADA in promoting reemployment of occupationally injured workers is not yet clear. In the majority of complaints filed with the EEOC under the ADA, employees claim that their employers discharged or disciplined or failed to rehire or accommodate them.[25] Many of these claims may therefore involve disabilities caused by or aggravated by work; unfortunately, the agency does not keep data on the etiology of the claimed disability. As the number of reported decisions in litigated cases has grown, it has become increasingly obvious that many federal judges are reluctant to extend the protections of the ADA to workers with common occupational musculoskeletal or respiratory conditions. For example, most federal courts have held that workers with common restrictions (such as "no lifting over [25] pounds; no bending") or with repetitive trauma disorders are not "disabled" because their condition is not sufficiently impairing.[26] One federal appellate court held "as a matter of law, that a twenty-five pound lifting limitation—particularly when compared to an average person's abilities—does not constitute a significant restriction on one's ability to lift, work, or perform any other major life activity."[27] Although not all courts agree, there is a growing feeling that the ADA does not provide the strong incentive to reemploy occupationally injured workers that some initially predicted.

Occupational Medicine and Disability Management

The shift toward disability management is also supported by evolving views about the role of occupational physicians, who have moved from diagnosis and treatment of disease or injury into a role as advisor to both employers and employees in the return-to-work process. This focus on disability management leads to increased communication between the health care provider and the insurer or employer and often to speedier and more successful return to work for an injured worker.

From the standpoint of workers, this has both positive and negative ramifications. On the one hand, physicians are often eager to assist patients to maintain a self-sufficient economic life and can provide invaluable assistance to employers and workers in defining appropriate return-to-work solutions. On the other hand, some physicians may see their role as working with the insurer or employer to manage the worker's disability; to the extent this occurs, the physicians' loyalty may be influenced by the economic motivations of employers to limit workers' compensation costs. This interplay of motives can result in both appropriate and inappropriate job placements.

Moreover, enhanced communication between physicians and employers can both provide necessary information to employers and result in the erosion of patient-provider confidentiality. Filing a workers' compensation claim now legally constitutes a blanket waiver of medical confidentiality; in some states this includes both the transfer of medical records and oral communications between medical providers and employers or insurers. If this communication excludes the injured worker and if the employer is solely motivated by a desire to save costs, the result can be troubling in the long term: both the employment relationship and the worker's long-term participation in the labor market may be damaged. The requirement in many states that injured workers see physicians chosen by their employers enhances communication between physician and employer and increases worker distrust.

In summary, disability management unquestionably contributes to the reduction in compensation costs. Arguably, the reduction is a win-win situation: employers benefit both from the continuing productivity of experienced workers and the reduction in compensation costs, while employees benefit from amelioration in the economic consequences of postinjury disability. But disability management can go awry, as when workers are forced into inappropriate jobs or are denied benefits based upon a presumed but inaccurate perception that appropriate work is available in the labor market.

Significant Development Five: Challenges to Exclusivity

Workers' compensation benefits were explicitly designed as the exclusive remedy for work-related injuries. The exclusivity principle is the quid pro quo for employers who must pay benefits to injured workers on a no-fault basis. Not surprisingly, as workers' dissatisfaction with the adequacy of workers' compensation benefits increased in the 1990s, the impetus to challenge the exclusivity doctrine has likewise grown. When coupled with the creativity and increasing supply of personal injury lawyers and the growing availability of other remedies for workplace harms to workers, it is not surprising that lawsuits have aggressively tested the boundaries of the exclusivity doctrine.

Attacks on the exclusivity doctrine cause considerable consternation among employers and their associations, whose attempts to raise exclusivity as a defense to the civil actions brought by injured workers seeking remedies other than workers' compensation benefits have met with varying success. Employers have raised substantial concern that the exclusivity doctrine has been improperly eroded by this onslaught of litigation. Not infrequently, employers have successfully brought their concerns to state legislatures, which in several states have responded by strengthening the exclusivity protections.

To what extent are employer concerns valid? Workers' compensation was primarily designed to compensate workers for physical injuries (and diseases) that are work-related. Today physical injuries caused by negligently caused job-related incidents continue to be viewed in every state as exclusively within the parameters of workers' compensation. Nevertheless, four developments appear to have reduced the scope of employers' immunity from civil law suits: (1) some states have expanded the right of workers to sue for "intentional torts" or for actions by the employer that follow the occurrence of the compensable injury;[28] (2) the exclusivity doctrine has not expanded to cover the broad array of new rights for at-will employees with nonphysical injuries, including rights against discrimination and harassment under federal employment laws and many state provisions;[29] (3) more workers are pursuing remedies for nonphysical injuries that were never covered by the exclusivity doctrine (such as fraud, invasion of privacy, loss of reputation and dignity);[30] and (4) contractions in the availability of benefits for some injuries and illnesses have resulted in expanded tort suits against employers for these injuries. We provide closer examination only of this fourth development because it relates directly to the conflict between affordability and adequacy, the main theme of this chapter.

The exclusivity doctrine does not generally shield employers from lawsuits involving injuries or illnesses that are explicitly outside the scope of injuries covered by workers' compensation. This is an age-old premise, rooted in the idea that if the condition is not compensable, then the employee has received nothing and the employer has given nothing: the quid pro quo premise underlying the workers' compensation deal is simply missing.

In recent years, as legislatures and courts have narrowed definitions of compensability, workers have relied on this concept to press for the expansion of common law liability of employers. For example, the statutory exclusion of psychological claims which are not sequelae of physical injuries may mean that these claims may be pursued by the worker under civil personal injury law. As a result, a number of states have allowed workers to bring tort actions ranging from claims involving generic common law negligence to negligent or intentional infliction of emotional distress to sexual harassment, precisely because of the explicit statutory exclusion of these "mental-mental" claims from the compensation system.[31]

Similarly, as discussed above, in some states injuries are now only compensable if a work exposure is the major cause of the health condition. Faced with an apparent reduction in the scope of compensable injuries, injured workers have brought legal actions against employers for negligently caused health conditions not covered by the workers' compensation. For example, the court in Oregon allowed a steelworker with a preexisting condition, whose breathing difficulties were exacerbated by exposures at work, to maintain a common law action against his employer; the compensation bureau had denied him workers' compensation benefits because "his work was not the 'major cause' of his condition and, thus, he did not suffer 'compensable injury' within meaning of exclusivity provision."[32]

Employers have no doubt been startled to discover that their successful lobbying for the exclusion of cónditions from workers' compensation can result in substantially expanded liability for negligent failure to maintain safe conditions in the workplace. In Oregon the legislature responded quickly to employers' concerns, passing a revised state statute which extends exclusivity "to all injuries and to diseases, symptom complexes or similar conditions" arising out of employment "whether or not they are determined to be compensable under this chapter."[33] This legislative response means that some workers in Oregon will be barred both from workers' compensation benefits and civil lawsuit damages.

In contrast to the potential expansion of civil liability when conditions are explicitly excluded from workers' compensation coverage, provision of low or inadequate benefits to a worker for a compensable injury will not remove the mantle of exclusivity. Most state courts have rejected constitutional and policy challenges to benefits set by state legislatures while continuing to endorse the application of exclusivity, even when those benefits have been substantially curtailed. Not surprisingly, in light of the growing restrictions on benefit availability described above, this is currently a hotly contested area.

Analysis and Conclusions

The history of workers' compensation over the past forty years is largely a history of the conflicting goals of adequacy and affordability. In 1972 the National Commission concluded that state laws were inadequate and inequitable and recommended federal standards if state programs did not quickly improve (National Commission 1972:127). The threat of federal involvement soon led to improvements in the adequacy of benefits in most state statutes. The higher levels of statutory benefits enacted during the 1970s were sustained through the 1980s and to a large extent even the 1990s.

Concerns about adequacy fueled the expansion of benefits in the 1970s. But the push for adequacy was never entirely successful: at no time did the states come close to achieving adequate cash benefits as measured by the consensus standards contained in the 1974 Model Act.[34] Due to inadequate statutory benefits and underreporting of claims, it is likely that workers' economic losses associated with occupational injury and illnesses have never been appropriately compensated by most state workers' compensation programs.

Nevertheless, higher statutory benefits enacted in the 1970s soon translated into higher benefit payments and higher costs to employers. The magnitude of the underlying cost increases was masked in the early 1980s, when high interest rates produced earnings on reserves that allowed insurance carriers to cut premium rates. From the mid-1980s to the early 1990s, however, benefits payments continued to increase and costs to employers soared.

The combination of rapidly increasing costs to employers and unprofitability for carriers beginning in the mid-1980s resulted in a backlash: affordability became the dominating criterion for reform during the 1990s. Employers and insurers mounted successful political campaigns to reduce costs. We have documented the consequences in terms of cutbacks in benefits, tougher eligibility standards, and new approaches to medical care and disability management.

The Lessons

We draw five lessons concerning adequacy and affordability from this history. First, there is ultimately an inevitable conflict between adequacy and affordability. In the short run, such as in the early 1980s when high interest rates produced earnings on reserves that allowed insurance carriers to cut rates, the conflict may be masked. And there are some aspects of reform—such as disability management or successful safety initiatives—where adequacy and affordability are both served if proper policies are developed. But most workers' compensation "reforms" constitute gains for one party at the expense of the other, which helps explain the intensity of the political struggles over workers' compensation.

Second, the concern over affordability usually focuses on the costs to employers of insurance premiums or the equivalent expenditures by self-insuring employers. This focus is misleading, however, in the degree of attention given to employers' costs. Employers are likely to bear much of the cost of higher workers' compensation premiums in the short run in the form of lower profits. In the long run, however, the cost of higher workers' compensation benefits and premiums is shared three ways: by employers, who are likely to experience some reduction in profits; by consumers, who pay part of the cost in the form of higher prices and reduced consumption; and by workers, who bear part of the cost in the form of lower wages and lower employment. In fact, empirical evidence suggests that in the long run, workers bear most of the costs of higher benefits in the form of lower wages (Chelius and Burton 1994).

This point is worth emphasizing because debates over workers' compensation reform are generally cast as a trade-off between adequacy (which presumably is primarily of interest to workers) and affordability (which presumably is primarily of interest to employers). In fact, there are positive aspects for employers of more adequate benefits (including higher morale and greater productivity among workers who feel they are treated fairly), and there are negative aspects for workers from higher benefits (including loss of jobs and lower wages).

If the costs of higher workers' compensation benefits are largely paid by employees in the form of lower wages and reduced employment, then why do employers place so much emphasis on the affordability criterion when workers' compensation reforms are undertaken? One reason is that employers are not aware of or do not believe this postulated relationship. Another is that in the short run, the costs of higher workers' compensation are largely borne by employers in the form of lower profits, and the short run appears to be the maximum planning horizon for many firms. And if employees pay for higher benefits with lower wages, why do workers place so much emphasis on adequacy? Again, one reason is that employees are not aware of or do not believe this relationship. Another is that workers may prefer workers' compensation benefits, which focus the provision of benefits on injured and impaired workers, to an equivalent value of higher wages, which will provide inadequate replacement of lost wages for those workers who are injured.[35]

The third lesson is that the affordability issue does not just involve employers and workers in the U.S. workers' compensation programs but also involves private carriers. Much of the zeal for reform of workers' compensation in the 1990s can be traced to the significant underwriting losses that carriers experienced in the 1980s and early 1990s. Whatever advantages may accrue to employees and employers from more adequate benefits, much of the higher cost of the program was borne by carriers. These carriers found it was easier to restore profitability by supporting legislative reforms that reduced benefits than by obtaining higher insurance rates from employers and regulators.

Fourth, concern over affordability is a reaction both to the national average for costs of the program and to the relative costs among states. The lesson we draw is that the decentralized nature of workers' compensation contributes to the downward pressure on costs and thereby benefits, thus jeopardizing adequacy. The importance of this threat to adequacy was recognized by the National Commission (1972:125), which concluded:

It seems likely that many States have been dissuaded from reform of their workmen's compensation statute because of the specter of the vanishing employer, even if that apparition is a product of fancy not fact. A few States have achieved genuine reform, but most suffer with inadequate laws because of the drag of laws in competing States.

Because of this "drag" created by interstate comparisons, the commission recommended federal standards if states did not rapidly improve their laws. It is ironic that the response of states to this threat led to increased adequacy and increased costs. In turn, opposition to the resulting costs now means that affordability has become the cornerstone of legislative reform in the 1990s. At the same time, differences among states in the costs of workers' compensation insurance widened between 1975 and 1990 (Table 1), deepening the threat of interstate competition and the concern for affordability.

Fifth, the dominance of the affordability criterion in the 1990s resulted in reforms that reduced average costs and apparently to some degree the magnitude of the growing interstate differences in costs. Nevertheless, recent reform cannot be understood as a rational effort to reduce dispersion among states by reining in high-cost states. For example, the Kansas legislature reduced medical and cash benefits of its workers' compensation program by over 11% in 1993 at a time when its insurance costs were below the national average.[36] The political onslaught against benefit adequacy and in favor of reducing costs appears to have taken on a life of its own.

Prognostications

The history of the workers' compensation program since 1960, in terms of achieving the compensation goal, has shown a variation through time in the relative importance of the adequacy and affordability criteria. Adequacy received the most attention in the 1970s, and concerns for adequacy and affordability were roughly in balance during most of the 1980s. The 1990s have been dominated by efforts to achieve affordability. While reform efforts to reduce costs have waned in intensity as the decade ends, renewed attention to affordability seems likely to reemerge if costs again start to climb, perhaps due to a rekindling of medical inflation, or if profits start to slip for private carriers. The general dominance of affordability as a basis for reform that has characterized the 1990s is likely to continue, without regard to whether benefits provided to injured workers meet a standard of adequacy.

Endnotes

[1] Whether all workers who legally qualify for workers' compensation actually receive benefits is an important question. A recent study provides a partial answer: only 9.6% to 45.6% of workers with known or suspected cases of occupational illness filed for workers' compensation cash benefits in Michigan during the period 1992-94 (Biddle et al. 1998). If workers do not file legitimate claims for workers' compensation benefits, then the costs of occupational injuries and illnesses are likely to be externalized from workers' compensation and borne by other health and disability insurance programs or by injured workers themselves.

[2] There is also a waiting period (three days in Wisconsin) during which the worker receives no benefits. However, if the worker is still disabled beyond a specified date, known as the retroactive date (seven days in Wisconsin), then the benefits for the waiting period are paid on a retroactive basis.

[3] Burton and Chelius (1997:266) endorsed a view that experience rating "has had at least some role in improving safety for large firms." Spieler (1994) concluded, before some recent studies were completed, that experience rating made little or no contribution to improving workplace safety.

[4] Other criteria for evaluating workers' compensation, including equity and delivery system efficiency, are examined in Chapter 1 of this volume.

[5] Additional data and analysis on the costs and benefits in the workers' compensation program since 1960 are included in Thomason, Schmidle, and Burton (1998:Chapter 1).

[6] In 1940 the maximum weekly benefit for temporary total disability benefits was at least 66.7% of the state's average weekly wage in 38 jurisdictions. In 1966, only three jurisdictions met this standard (National Commission 1972:61).

[7] The Model Act incorporated the recommendations of the National Commission, such as the recommendation that the maximum weekly benefit for temporary total disability be at least 100% of the state's average weekly wage: in 1972, 1 state complied with this recommendation; by 1979, 28 states complied.

[8] Montana, the only jurisdiction not in compliance as of 1979, achieved compliance the following year.

[9] The examination of developments in the 1990s is based in part on Tinsley (1990, 1991); Berreth (1992, 1994, 1996, 1997); and Brown (1993, 1995).

[10] The developments involving insurance arrangements are examined in Thomason, Schmidle, and Burton (1998).

[11] According to a study by the Workers Compensation Research Institute, these and related changes in Massachusetts reduced the average number of temporary total disability weeks in claims from 24 to 18 and drove the average lump-sum settlement from $27,040 to $18,860 (Gardner et al. 1996:101, 98).

[12] *State of West Virginia ex rel. Boan v. Richardson*, 482 S.E.2d 162 (W.Va. 1996).

[13] *Stench Group v. Gamut*, 467 S.E.2d 795 (Va. 1996) (carpal tunnel); *Allied Fibers v. Rhodes*, 23 Va. 101, 474 S.E.2d 829 (Va. 1996) (noise induced hearing loss). The amended statute is Virginia Code Sec. 65.2-400(c) and 65.2-401.

[14] *Errand v. Cascade Steel Rolling Mills*, 888 P.2d 544 (Ore. 1994).

[15] *Freeman United Coal Mining Co. v. Industrial Commission*, 286 Ill.App.3d 1098, 677 N.E.2d 1005 (1997).

[16] *Director, OWCP v. Greenwich Collieries*, 114 S.Ct. 2251 (1994).

[17] Burton (1997) provides a more extensive examination of the topics in this section.

[18] Health care expenditures increased 15.2% a year in workers' compensation between 1985-90, while health care expenditures in the general health care system increased 9.5% annually during the period (Burton 1994:I-47). While these data are consistent with cost shifting, Levy and Miller (1996:44) found no evidence of cost shifting from Medicare to workers' compensation after the introduction of a prospective payment system into Medicare in 1983.

[19] The information in this paragraph relies in part on U.S. Department of Labor 1998a and 1998b.

[20] Durbin, Corro, and Helvacian (1996) found no evidence that health care providers charge workers' compensation claimants any differently than patients covered by group health insurance but did find dramatic differences in total medical costs for the two groups, which they concluded can entirely be explained by a greater utilization of services and a different mix of medical care providers.

[21] Another strategy in workers' compensation in the 1990s designed in part to reduce the costs of medical care in workers' compensation is twenty-four-hour coverage. Burton (1997:141-48) examines the four primary variants of twenty-four-hour coverage: (1) integration within self-insuring employers; (2) integration of benefits and services in insurance policies; (3) integration of benefits and services by expanding workers' compensation; and (4) integration of benefits and services through general health care reform.

[22] See, for example, a famous case, *United Steel Workers of America v. American Mfg. Co.* 363 U.S. 564 (1960), in which the claim of a grievant that he should be entitled to reinstatement after receiving a permanent partial disability settlement was characterized as frivolous by the courts.

[23] Governor Chiles and the Florida attorney are quoted in Larson (1996:11).

[24] See particularly, EEOC Enforcement Guidance: Workers' Compensation and the Americans with Disabilities Act, Reasonable Accommodation (9/3/96).

[25] EEOC charge data are available at http://www.eeoc.gov/stats/ada.html. Charges brought under the Americans with Disabilities Act, cumulative for 1992-97, indicate that back and extremity impairments represented 26.8% of total charges; psychiatric and neurological impairments were another 24.2%. The two most common types of complaints alleged illegal discharges (52.2% of complaints) and failure to provide reasonable accommodation (28.9% of complaints). Only 9.4% of charges raised the issue of failure to hire.

[26] See, for example, *Wooten v. Farmland Foods*, 58 F.3d 382 (8th Cir. 1995) (employee who suffered from bilateral carpal tunnel syndrome and inflammation of left hand and shoulder and who was restricted from lifting more than 20 pounds and who was terminated was not substantially limited in performing major life activities).

[27] *Williams v. Channel Master Satellite Systems*, 101 F.3d 346, 349 (4th Cir. 1996).

[28] Some states established a new test which allows intentional tort cases against employers who create conditions which are substantially certain to lead to serious injury. See, for example, *Beauchamp v. Dow Chem Co.*, 398 N.W.2d 882 (Mich. 1986) (civil liability lies if employer knew that the injury was substantially certain to occur and intended the act which caused the injury). The legislatures in Michigan as well as in Ohio and West Virginia subsequently tightened the exception for intentional torts and resulted in challenges to the new legislation.

[29] Employers are not, for example, immune from workers' lawsuits brought under federal employment regulation statutes (such as Title VII of the Civil Rights Act, the Americans with Disabilities Act, the Family and Medical Leave Act, or the Employee Retirement Income Security Act). Absent specific statutory language that state workers' compensation law overrides the federal statute, courts have consistently upheld the right of workers to pursue these federal civil claims. See *Varner v. National Super Markets, Inc.*, 94 F.3d 1209 (8th Cir. 1996) (state workers' compensation exclusivity provision cannot preempt an employee's federally created right to recover damages under Title VII."); *Adams Fruit Co., Inc. v. Barrett*, 494 U.S. 638, 110 S.Ct. 1384 (1990). States have almost universally also upheld the right of injured workers to pursue rights under state antidiscrimination and antiretaliatory provisions. A recent example is *City of Moorpark v. Superior Court of Ventura County*, 959 P.2d 752 (Calif. 1998).

[30] See, for example, *Persinger v. Peabody Coal Co.*, 474 S.E.2d 887 (W.Va. 1996) (holding West Virginia Code Section 23-2-6 [1994] does not preclude an employee from maintaining a separate and distinct cause of action against an employer for damages as a result of the employer knowingly and intentionally fraudulently misrepresenting facts to the Workers' Compensation Fund that are not only in opposition to the employee's claim but are made with the intention of depriving the employee of benefits rightfully due him.) The West Virginia court followed other courts which upheld the right of a worker to assert a separate claim for tortious conduct occurring outside the employment relationship and during the processing and settlement of a workers' compensation claim. Of course, not all courts follow this rule. See, for example, *Doss v. Food Lion Inc.*, 477 S.E. 2d 577 (Ga. 1996) (in which the Georgia Supreme Court refused to allow a separate action for an employers' or insurers' intentional delay in authorizing medical treatment).

[31] A case in which a mental injury was held to be actionable under common law is *Stratemeyer v. Lincoln County*, 915 P.2d 175 (Mont. 1996) (holding that a sheriff's noncompensable claim for post-traumatic stress disorder could give rise to a common law tort claim against the employing county).

[32] *Errand v. Cascade Steel Rolling Mills, Inc.*, 888 P.2d 544 (Oregon 1995).

[33] 1996 Oregon Rev. Statutes, Title 51, Section 656.018.

[34] The average state's statutory cash benefits as a proportion of the cash benefits prescribed by the Model Act varied from 49% to 51% between 1979 to 1996 (Table 1).

[35] For a discussion of risk premiums and risk-averse workers, see Burton and Chelius (1997:258-59).

[36] The actuarial evaluations of the 1993 legislation are in NCCI (1998:106). Thomason, Schmidle, and Burton (1998) report that a representative set of Kansas employers spent 2.869% of payroll on workers' compensation insurance in 1993; the national average for comparable employers was 3.178% of payroll.

References

Barth, Peter S. 1987. *The Tragedy of Black Lung: Federal Compensation for Occupational Disease*. Kalamazoo, MI: W.E. Upjohn Institute for Employment Research.

Berreth, Charles A. 1992. "Workers' Compensation; State Enactments in 1991." *Monthly Labor Review*, Vol. 115, no. 1 (Jan.), pp. 56-63.

_____. 1994. "Workers' Compensation Laws: Significant Changes in 1993." *Monthly Labor Review*, Vol. 116, no. 1 (Jan.), pp. 53-64.

_____. 1996. "Workers' Compensation Laws Enacted in 1995." *Monthly Labor Review*, Vol. 118, no. 1 (Jan./Feb.), pp. 59-72.

_____. 1997. "State Workers' Compensation Legislation Enacted in 1996." *Monthly Labor Review*, Vol. 119, no. 1 (Jan.), pp. 43-50.

Biddle, Jeff, Karen Roberts, Kenneth D. Rosenman, and Edward M. Welch. 1998. "What Percentage of Workers with Work-related Illnesses Receive Workers' Compensation Benefits?" *Journal of Occupational and Environmental Medicine*, Vol. 40, no. 4 (April), pp. 325-31.

Boden, Leslie I., and Charles A. Fleischman. 1989. *Medical Costs in Workers' Compensation: Trends and Interstate Comparisons*. Cambridge, MA: Workers' Compensation Research Institute.

Brown, Ruth A. 1993. "Workers' Compensation: State Enactments in 1992." *Monthly Labor Review*, Vol. 116, no. 1 (Jan.), pp. 50-55.

_____. 1995. "Workers' Compensation Laws: Enactments in 1994." *Monthly Labor Review*, Vol. 117, no. 1 (Jan.), pp. 53-59.

Bureau of National Affairs (BNA). 1997. "Permanent Total Disability Awards Fell by 97% under New Law." *BNA's Workers' Compensation Report*, Vol. 8, no. 11 (May 26), pp. 276-77.

Burton, John F., Jr. 1994. "National Health Care Reform and Workers' Compensation." In John F. Burton, Jr. and Timothy P. Schmidle, eds., *1995 Workers' Compensation Year Book*. Horsham, PA: LRP Publications, pp. I-45-I-55.

_____. 1997. "Workers' Compensation, Twenty-Four-Hour Coverage, and Managed Care." In Virginia P. Reno, Jerry L. Mashaw, and Bill Gradison, eds., *Disability: Challenges for Social Insurance, Health Care Financing, and Labor Market Policy*. Washington, DC: National Academy of Social Insurance, pp. 129-49.

Burton, John F,. Jr., and Florence Blum. 1996. "Workers' Compensation Benefits Paid to Workers: The 1996 Update." *Workers' Compensation Monitor*, Vol. 9, no. 6 (November/December), pp. 13-27.

Burton, John F., Jr., and James R. Chelius. 1997. "Workplace Safety and Health Regulations: Rationale and Results." In Bruce E. Kaufman, ed., *Government Regulation of the Employment Relationship*. Madison, WI: Industrial Relations Research Association, pp. 253-93.

Burton, John F., Jr., and Timothy P. Schmidle, eds. 1996. *1996 Workers' Compensation Year Book*. Horsham, PA: LRP Publications.

Chelius, James R., and John F. Burton, Jr. 1994. "Who Actually Pays for Workers' Compensation? The Empirical Evidence." In John F. Burton, Jr. and Timothy P. Schmidle, eds., *1995 Workers' Compensation Year Book*. Horsham, PA: LRP Publications.

Council of State Governments. 1974. *Workmen's Compensation and Rehabilitation Law (Revised)*. Lexington, KY: Council of State Governments.

Dembe, Allard E. Forthcoming. "Evaluating the Impact of Managed Health Care in Workers' Compensation." In Jeffrey Harris, ed., *Managed Care in Occupational Medicine*. Hanley & Belfus Publishers.

Durbin, David L., and David Appel. 1991. "The Impact of Fee Schedules and Employer Choice of Physician." *NCCI Digest*, Vol. 6, no. 3, pp. 45-47.

Durbin, David L., Dan Corro, and Nurhan Helvacian. 1996. "Workers' Compensation Medical Expenditures: Price vs. Quantity." *The Journal of Risk and Insurance*, Vol. 63, no. 1, pp. 13-33.

Eccleston, Stacey M., and Carter M. Yeager. 1997. *Managed Care and Medical Cost Containment in Workers' Compensation: A National Inventory, 1997-98*. Cambridge, MA: Workers Compensation Research Institute.

Gardner, John A., Carol A. Telles, and Gretchen A. Moss. 1996. *The 1991 Reforms in Massachusetts: An Assessment of Impact*. Cambridge, MA: Workers Compensation Research Institute.

Herbert, Robin, K. Janeway, and C. Schechter. 1997. "Carpal Tunnel Syndrome and Workers' Compensation in New York." Under review at *American Journal of Industrial Medicine*.

Johnson, William G., Marjorie L. Baldwin, and John F. Burton, Jr. 1996. "Why Is the Treatment of Work-related Injuries So Costly? New Evidence from California." *Inquiry*, Vol. 33 (Spring), pp. 53-65.

Larson, Lex K. 1996. "Special Report: A Workers' Compensation Murder." *Larson's Workers' Compensation News*, Vol. 1, no. 2 (October), pp. 9-13.

Levy, David T., and Ted R. Miller. 1996. "Rate Regulations and Medical Payments in Workers' Compensation." *The Journal of Risk and Insurance*, Vol. 63, no. 1, pp. 35-47.

National Commission on State Workmen's Compensation Laws. 1972. *The Report of the National Commission on State Workmen's Compensation Laws*. Washington, DC: Government Printing Office.

National Council on Compensation Insurance (NCCI). 1998. *Annual Statistical Bulletin*. Boca Raton, FL: NCCI

Pozzebon, Silvana. 1993. "Do Traditional Health Care Cost Containment Practices Really Work?" *Workers' Compensation Monitor*, Vol. 6, no. 3, pp. 17-22.

Schmulowitz, Jack. 1997. *Workers' Compensation: Benefits, Coverage, and Costs, 1994-95*. Washington, DC: National Academy of Social Insurance.

Spieler, Emily A. 1994. "Perpetuating Risk? Workers' Compensation and the Persistence of Occupational Injuries." *Houston Law Review*, Vol. 31, no. 1 (Symposium), pp. 119-264.

Thomason, Terry, Timothy P. Schmidle, and John F. Burton, Jr. 1998. *Workers' Compensation: A Comparative Analysis of System Costs under Alternative Insurance Arrangements*. Draft version of manuscript scheduled to be published by the W.E. Upjohn Institute of Employment Research in 1999.

Tinsley, LaVerne C. 1990. "State Workers' Compensation: Significant Legislation in 1989." *Monthly Labor Review*, Vol. 113, no. 1 (Jan.), pp. 57-63.

_____. 1991. "State Workers' Compensation: Legislation Enacted in 1990." *Monthly Labor Review*, Vol. 114, no. 1 (Jan.), pp. 57-62.

U.S. Department of Labor. 1998a. *State Workers' Compensation Laws in Effect on January 1, 1998 Compared with the 19 Essential Recommendations of the National Commission on State Workmen's Compensation Laws*. Washington, DC: U.S. Department of Labor, Employment Standards Administration, Office of Workers' Compensation Programs.

_____. 1998b. *State Workers' Compensation Laws*. Washington, DC: U.S. Department of Labor, Employment Standards Administration, Office of Workers' Compensation Programs.

Victor, Richard B., and Charles A. Fleischman. 1990. *How Choice of Provider and Recessions Affect Medical Costs in Workers' Compensation*. Cambridge, MA: Workers Compensation Research Institute.

Williams, C. Arthur, Jr., and Peter S. Barth. 1973. *Compendium on Workmen's Compensation*. Washington, DC: National Commission on State Workmen's Compensation Laws and Government Printing Office.

CHAPTER 9

Social Security Disability Insurance: A Policy Review

JERRY L. MASHAW
Yale University

VIRGINIA RENO
National Academy of Social Insurance

Disability insurance (DI)—a part of the Old-Age, Survivors and Disability Insurance program, better known as Social Security—is an earnings replacement program that provides benefits for workers and their families when severe, long-term disability interrupts the worker's ability to earn a living. Eligibility is based on prior work from which Social Security tax contributions were paid. Benefits are calculated to replicate the pension that a worker having a similar work history (uninterrupted by disability) would have received under the retirement benefit program.

DI was added to the program of old-age pensions in 1957 (for workers age 50 and older) and was extended to workers of all ages in 1960. Today, it pays benefits to 4.5 million disabled workers, about 20% of whom had dependent children or spouses who also received benefits (SSA 1997, 1998). The average monthly benefit for disabled workers was $722 in December 1997 (SSA 1998). Total annual benefits in 1996 were about $44.2 billion. Social Security is financed mainly by a tax on wages paid by workers and matched by employers. They each pay 6.2% of earnings up to a limit ($68,400 in 1998) for the total Social Security program, of which 0.85 percentage points each are earmarked for disability benefits.

DI has episodically appeared on the national agenda, usually when unexpected growth in the benefit rolls caused policymakers to worry about the cost of the program. Typically, unexpected growth has coincided with economic recessions, sometimes accompanied by subtle changes in policies for determining eligibility for benefits and/or a shortage of administrative resources to make disability determinations.[1] This was the case in the late 1970s. In the early 1980s Congress and the administration adopted retrenchment policies that brought a precipitous drop in the disability rolls as more new claims were denied and benefits of many of those on the rolls were terminated under strict reviews of beneficiaries' continuing eligibility. Public reaction to the hardship these policies imposed on disabled individuals resulted in 1984 legislation that undid some of the retrenchment policies.

The rest of the 1980s were a period of relative stability in the DI program. At that time, national attention on disability policy centered on civil rights and culminated in the Americans with Disabilities Act of 1990. The presumption underlying the civil rights approach (that persons with disabilities could work if given appropriate accommodations) appeared to be in conflict with the fundamental purpose of the DI program—that is, to pay benefits that partially replace past earnings for workers who are no longer able to work because of the onset of a disabling impairment.

In 1991 the chairmen of the House Ways and Means Committee and its Social Security Subcommittee asked the National Academy of Social Insurance to undertake a comprehensive review of the Social Security disability insurance program to help sort out this dilemma. The academy convened a panel of experts—economists, rehabilitation specialists, doctors, lawyers, and members of the disability community—to respond to the questions the chairmen raised about the DI program and the companion assistance program, Supplemental Security Income (SSI):[2]

- Do benefits provided by the DI and SSI programs pose strong disincentives for workers to remain in or reenter the workforce?

- Can rehabilitation be built into these programs without (1) greatly increasing costs or (2) undermining benefit security?

- Can changes in income support policy be made that will better promote work?

While these questions seem relatively straightforward, they reflect a sophisticated understanding of disability cash benefits programs and their history. The first question recognizes that any cash benefits program will provide some disincentive to remain in or reenter the workforce. It is precisely the purpose of cash benefits to allow some workers to substitute benefits for wages when their personal circumstances make workforce participation too difficult.

The second question further recognizes that there are serious trade-offs among the objectives of increasing rehabilitation and return to work, running programs at acceptable budgetary cost, and maintaining benefit security for those who require cash benefits. A single-minded focus on rehabilitation and return to work, for example, is likely to be very costly in a target population that has relatively modest prospects for self-support. Moreover, if pursued aggressively with respect to that whole population, activities designed to promote work by deterring benefit receipt can result in delay in providing needed benefits or unwarranted termination of benefits for those who are entitled to them. This latter possibility was exemplified in the unhappy history of the continuing disability review initiatives implemented in the DI and SSI programs in the early 1980s (Mashaw 1988; Goldman and Gattozzi 1988).

Finally, the third question recognizes that promoting work through the alteration of income support programs is a problematic enterprise. Not only do work incentives structured into such programs have a checkered history as effective means for promoting work, the promotion of work effort may be better accomplished by changes in public policy outside of rather than within income support programs.

The Work Disincentive Effects of DI and SSI Are Modest

Empirical research attempting to measure the effects of disability payments on labor force participation rates reaches differing conclusions that are highly sensitive to the assumptions and methodologies used and to the time period under study. Observations of trends in the 1970s found a correlation between the growth in the DI rolls and legislated increases in benefits during the period (Parsons 1988; Leonard 1979). Congress lowered DI benefits for future claimants in 1977 and capped payments to those with dependents in 1980. Other studies concluded that reducing benefits was unlikely to lead to significant increases in work effort and productivity (Haveman, Wolfe, and Warlick 1984). If benefits are a strong deterrent to work, one might expect to find high levels of employment among those denied benefits. The panel reviewed various studies over the past three decades that tracked the experience of persons denied DI benefits. They consistently found modest levels of employment and high rates of poor health and poverty among those denied benefits (Mashaw and Reno 1996a; U.S. General Accounting Office 1989; Bound 1989; Smith and Lilienfield 1971).[3]

Given these mixed findings, the Disability Policy Panel looked at the question of benefits and incentives in ways that go beyond standard economic studies. Approached from any of four differing perspectives, the panel concluded that DI and SSI payments were likely to provide modest work disincentives.

Definitional Stringency

The definition of work incapacity in the DI and SSI programs is among the strictest used in any public or private program in the United States. In order to qualify, a beneficiary must be unable to engage in any substantial gainful activity (currently defined as work producing earnings of $500 per month) that is available in significant numbers in the national economy. If a claimant could do any such work, he or she is ineligible whether or not jobs exist in the area in which he or she lives or whether he or she would be hired. The medically determinable impairment that causes the work incapacity must be expected to last at least twelve months or to result in prior death. Furthermore, there is a five-month waiting period after the onset of disability before DI benefits begin and another twenty-four-month waiting period for Medicare eligibility.

Given this definition, it is not surprising that DI and SSI benefits are paid only to those with the most severe work disabilities. Indeed, when the number of DI and SSI disability beneficiaries are compared to the much larger number of working-aged persons with any sort of disability, we find that nearly three in four such persons do not receive benefits. About 30 million working-aged Americans have some sort of disability. They include those limited in their ability to see, hear, speak, lift, climb stairs, walk, or to work, do housework or perform other activities of living, according to the Survey of Income and Program Participation (U.S. Bureau of the Census 1993). Nearly 17 million Americans have a work disability that limits the kind or amount of work they can do, according to the Current Population Survey (U.S. Bureau of the Census 1995). In contrast, about 7 million working-aged persons received DI or SSI benefits at the end of 1994. They include about 4 million disabled workers receiving DI, another 0.7 million who get Social Security disability benefits as widow(er)s or adult children with disabilities; and 2.3 million persons who get only SSI benefits[4] (Social Security Administration 1995a).

Benefit Levels Are Modest

The degree to which persons are likely to accept DI or SSI benefits rather than continuing to work is obviously affected by the relationship between benefit levels and what could be earned in the private market. For SSI recipients, who normally have a limited work history, it is difficult to estimate what their earnings would be but for their disability. Nevertheless, the level of SSI benefits is not a very attractive alternative to work. The federal SSI payment is $484 a month in 1997. This is about 70% of the poverty threshold for a nonelderly person living alone.

For disability insurance beneficiaries who do have a substantial prior work history, one can compare disability benefits with prior earnings. The ratio of benefits to prior earnings is called the "replacement rate." Studies generally find that replacement rates of 70% to 80% are needed to match a worker's prior level of living[5] (Palmer 1994). By that standard, DI replacement rates are quite modest. A disabled worker in 1995 with prior earnings of $15,000 would receive benefits replacing 51% of those earnings. The replacement rate drops rapidly at higher earnings levels. At $25,000 it is 43%; at $40,000 it is 37%; and at $60,000 it is 26%. These replacement rates are increased somewhat for a minority of beneficiaries (about 18%) who also receive dependents' benefits (Social Security Administration 1995a).

The Path from Work to Disability Benefits

The panel relied on both longitudinal survey research and focus group interviews with recent entrants to the disability benefit rolls to explore the experience of workers after the onset of a disability. By pooling twenty years of data from the Panel Study of Income Dynamics from 1970 through 1989, Burkhauser and Daly examined the employment of workers after their first onset of disability. They found that most workers remain in the workforce after disability onset. As Table 1 illustrates, even five years after the onset of a work disability, most people aged 25 to 50 were still employed and a bare majority of those between 51 and 61 were not working. This pattern seems to suggest that disability benefits are not a strong attraction for persons who are in the workforce. People generally do not turn to disability benefits immediately after the onset of an injury or illness that causes impairment. Instead, they keep working, often at reduced wages or reduced hours. Over time as family income deteriorates, more and more of them turn to disability benefits.

These findings are consistent with what the panel heard in interviews with disability beneficiaries around the country. The panel sponsored focus group interviews with recent entrants to the DI and SSI benefit rolls in four sites—Iowa, New York, Oregon, and Virginia. Participants were selected to include people with three broad categories of impairments proportional to their representation on the benefit rolls— musculoskeletal impairments; mental disorders; and cardiac, respiratory

TABLE 1

Percent of Workers Not Employed after Disability Onset:
Workers with a Disability Onset in 1970-89,
Panel Study of Income Dynamics

Years after disability onset	Age at Disability	
	25-50	51-61
	Percent not employed	
1 year	15	24
2 years	26	35
3 years	32	42
4 years	38	49
5 years	44	53

Source: Burkhauser and Daly 1996.

and other diseases. Beneficiaries typically reported they had stayed on their jobs months or years after the onset of their injury or diagnosis, determined to "beat the odds" of their condition. Many had accommodations—a change in duties or help from coworkers—before they or their employers determined they could no longer function at work. By the time they turned to Social Security, they had experienced the loss of their health, their livelihood, the psychological rewards of productive employment, and their hopes for ending their work lives with a comfortable retirement. This anecdotal evidence suggests that beneficiaries turned to cash benefits as a last resort (Mashaw and Reno 1996b:Appendix A).

Cross-National Comparisons

The panel also considered whether U.S. spending on long-term disability benefits is out of line with that of other countries, particularly those that have a reputation for aggressive return-to-work policies for disabled workers. If U.S. spending were high in relation to other countries, it would suggest that we were spending too much on benefits and too little on return-to-work policies.

But comparison with other industrialized countries suggests that U.S. spending on public long-term disability benefits is relatively low (Table 2). Other countries have more comprehensive supports for ill or disadvantaged workers, including national health insurance, short-term disability benefits, and universal assistance for the poor. In their disability policy, both Germany and Sweden have a reputation for early intervention and aggressive rehabilitation and return-to-work policies. Sweden emphasizes public sector employment, including sheltered employment, while

TABLE 2
Spending on Long-Term Disability Benefits as a
Percent of Gross Domestic Product (GDP), 1991

Country	Percent of GDP
United States	0.7[a]
United Kingdom	1.9
Germany	2.0
Sweden	3.3
The Netherlands	4.6[b]

[a] Includes DI and SSI. U.S. spending was 0.9% in 1995.
[b] Includes work-injury benefits.
Source: Arts and de Jong, 1996.

Germany promotes private employment through hiring quotas, tax penalties, and subsidies for employers who accommodate workers who are listed on a disability register. The United Kingdom has a relatively strict disability pension program, uses employer subsidies, sheltered employment, and has employer quotas that are not diligently enforced. As shown in Table 2, German and U.K. spending on public long-term disability benefits as a share of gross domestic product (GDP) is more than twice that of the United States. Spending in Sweden is higher still. Finally, the Netherlands, a well-known "outlier" in disability expenditures, spends far more. Its figures include the equivalent of workers' compensation because Holland does not have a separate system for compensating workers injured on the job. The figures in Table 2 include only long-term disability cash benefits. They do not include spending on short-term sickness benefits, rehabilitation and return-to-work services, or wage subsidies for workers or employers (Aarts and de Jong 1996).

Summary

Based on its review of the strict eligibility criteria for DI and SSI benefits, the modest level of U.S. benefits, workers' attachment to their jobs after disability onset, and the comparatively low level of U.S. spending on long-term disability benefits, the panel found it hard to believe that cash benefits under DI or SSI are a strong deterrent to work.

At the same time, the panel found that gaps in access to health care can limit labor market options for disabled workers. Persons with disabilities have much higher medical expenses than the general population and are likely to have great difficulty being insured in private markets. Certainly, beneficiaries' fear of losing Medicare or Medicaid eligibility that is linked to DI or SSI is frequently cited as barrier to work. The panel concluded early in its deliberations that universal protection against health care costs would allay these fears and represent a breakthrough in disability income policy. The extent to which it would lead to reduced spending for disability benefits is an open question, given that countries with universal health insurance spend more on disability pensions. Nevertheless, the panel was convinced that beneficiaries who return to work despite their impairments should be assured of continued health care coverage. In the absence of comprehensive health care reform, the panel recommended specific incremental reforms to allay beneficiaries' fears about loss of health care coverage if they should return to work.

The short answer to the first question posed by the Congress is "no," DI and SSI cash benefits, in and of themselves, do not pose strong deterrents to remaining at work. The panel went on to consider the second and third questions posed by the Congress—that is, whether changes in cash support programs could be designed to better promote rehabilitation and work. It began by formulating its view of the nature of work disability, its causes and remedies.

Understanding Work Disability, Its Causes and Remedies

The Disability Policy Panel's approach to work disability tracks that followed by the Institute of Medicine and the World Health Organization (Pope and Tarlov 1991; World Health Organization 1980). The critical idea here is that "disability" is not solely a feature of persons. It is, instead, a relationship between persons and the environment in which they live and work. Work disability thus involves (1) a person's physical or mental impairment, (2) his or her other capacities or limitations, (3) the tasks of work, and (4) the broader environment in which he or she lives and works.

From this perspective the fact that a person has a physical or mental impairment may or may not translate into an incapacitating work disability. Physical incapacities may be offset by mental capacities that permit a different sort of work, and vice versa. Whether an impairment impedes work depends on the tasks of work and how work is organized—including the accessibility of and the availability of supports in the workplace. Whether people can function in a work environment is also dependent on the broader environment of family, social, and governmental supports that are available in the particular locality where they live.

Thinking about work disability in this way makes it clear that a broad range of potential remedies exist. Public policy can intervene at any of the four levels—impairment, capacities, tasks, or environment. Which level of intervention will be efficacious depends on the particular circumstances of each individual. As shown in the following table, these remedies involve health care, personal assistance services, education, training and vocational rehabilitation, on-the-job accommodations, and aspects of the broader environment—the demand for workers, public access, transportation, and civil rights, among others. All of these promising remedies lie outside the scope of disability cash benefits policy.

TABLE 3
Remedies to Address *Work Disability*

Element of Work Disability	Potential Remedies
Impairment	Health care may prevent or remedy the disabling consequences of an impairment.
	Personal assistance services or durable medical equipment can compensate for the consequences of some impairments.
Aptitude, skills, knowledge, abilities, and age	Education, training, vocational rehabilitation.
Tasks of work	Job accommodations, job restructuring, assistive equipment.
Broader environment	Safety, public access, transportation, telecommunications, nondiscrimination (Americans with Disabilities Act), availability of jobs.

In proposing changes in income support policies to promote work, the panel's analysis was tempered by two important findings. First, the most promising remedies for work disability lie in other policy arenas—in health care, education, training, and jobs. Second, many who receive DI or SSI benefits are not strong candidates for work. More than half of DI beneficiaries are over the age of 50. Their mortality rate is high—more than five times that of other working-age persons. They include persons who are very ill with life-threatening diseases, others who are in chronic pain that precludes physically demanding work, and others whose mental disorders significantly limit their ability to cope with the demands of work.

Consequently, changes that make income policies more "work friendly" are likely to be effective only for a subset of actual or potential beneficiaries. The panel's recommended changes are in two categories. The first set aims to maintain workers with disabilities in the workforce and thereby prevent or delay their entry to the disability rolls. The second set of proposals is designed to ease the exit from the benefit rolls for those who return to work.

Modifying Income Policy to Prevent Entry onto the Benefit Rolls

To support workers with disabilities to remain in the workforce, income policy must address two critical issues: (1) the progressive loss of family income as workers' impairments limit the kind or amount of work that they can do and (2) increased work expenses, particularly for those who require personal assistance in order to function.

Personal Assistance Tax Credit

In order to deal with the latter problem the panel recommended a personal assistance tax credit of 50% of expenditures for personal assistance services up to an annual limit of $15,000. This nonrefundable tax credit of up to $7,500 would be a substantial aid to a small proportion of persons with disabilities—that is, those who could be employed but who cannot now earn enough to pay for personal assistance services.

Disabled Worker Tax Credit

A much broader group of potential DI or SSI beneficiaries would be served by the panel's proposal for the creation of a disabled worker tax credit (DWTC). This tax credit is modeled after the existing earned income tax credit (EITC). It is a wage subsidy that targets low-income working people with disabilities. In particular, it is designed to (a) enable older workers who experience reduced earnings due to progressive impairments to remain at work with subsidized wages, (b) ease the transition from school to work for young people with developmental disabilities whose earnings are doubly limited by their youth and their disabilities, and (c) ease the transition off the DI and SSI benefit rolls for those who return to work. The first two groups are the main targets of the DWTC by making low-wage or part-time work yield an income equal to or greater than that available from disability cash benefits. The DWTC responds to the panel's finding that most beneficiaries desire to remain in the workforce and leave it only reluctantly as family income falls to unacceptable levels.

Because the primary utility of the proposal lies in preventing entry onto the benefit rolls in the first instance, eligibility for the proposed DWTC would be broader than eligibility for DI or SSI benefits. In the panel proposal, the DWTC would be available to persons who receive DI or SSI, certain denied applicants (those found unable to do their prior job but able to do other work), and persons found by their state vocational rehabilitation agency to be eligible for services because they have "a physical or mental impairment . . . that results in a substantial impediment to employment" (Section 7[8][A] of the Rehabilitation Act).

These criteria have two attractive features: First, they avoid self-reporting of disability on tax forms that would create an unacceptable "moral hazard" and a huge administrative burden of verification for the Treasury. In addition, by using criteria that are already being applied to applicants for DI and SSI benefits and vocational rehabilitation services, the proposal avoids creating new administrative machinery for making DWTC eligibility determinations.

Promoting Return to Work by Existing Beneficiaries

The panel expects that its proposed Disabled Worker and Personal Assistant Tax Credits would have some impact in promoting return to work by existing beneficiaries. In addition, the panel recommended a number of policy changes that it believes would assist existing and future DI and SSI beneficiaries return to work and leave the benefit rolls.

Return-to-Work Tickets (RTW)

The most innovative proposal in the panel's package of return-to-work initiatives is its proposal for return-to-work tickets. In general outline, the proposal is quite simple. DI beneficiaries would be given a voucher for return-to-work assistance. Beneficiaries could choose a service provider in the public or private sector to assist them in returning to work. If a provider were successful in returning a beneficiary to work, it would become entitled (for a period of five years) to one-half the value of the benefits that would have been paid to the beneficiary had that beneficiary remained on the rolls. If providers fail to help beneficiaries leave the rolls, they receive nothing. They are paid only for results and at a rate that saves money for the DI trust funds. After all, had the recipient not returned to work, the trust funds would have paid 100% of the benefits, not 50%. (The small group of persons who are expected to recover without further intervention would not be given vouchers.)

This proposal is premised on a number of factual understandings. First, the existing vocational rehabilitation program, alone, is having only very modest success. While about 400,000 to 600,000 new disabled-worker beneficiaries enter the rolls each year, only 4,000 DI beneficiaries are successfully rehabilitated by state vocational rehabilitation (VR) agencies.[6] The vast majority of those who leave the DI rolls do so because of death or transfer onto the retirement roll at age 65 (Mashaw and Reno 1996b). Hence, while this proposal is a major departure from past practice and to that degree completely untested, it is worth giving it a try. The proposal in no way excludes current public providers from participation. Beneficiaries may deposit their vouchers with existing VR agencies or other existing public providers as well as with private providers.

Second, because of the enormous heterogeneity of the beneficiary population, there is no agreement about what is an effective regimen for rehabilitation and return to work. The panel recognized that individual beneficiaries and providers are best able to decide on a case-by-case basis what plan of services, training, job location assistance, or other interventions is likely to succeed. The proposal is designed to attract new actors into the rehabilitation and return-to-work business. When one does not know what to do, it is often sensible to provide incentives for private innovation.

Third, this proposal increases the power and choices that beneficiaries have with respect to their own future. The RTW proposal empowers beneficiaries to negotiate a return-to-work plan with a willing service provider of their choice with the understanding that the trust funds will pay the provider only when the beneficiary successfully returns to work.

Fourth, the proposal gives providers a strong interest in their clients' ongoing success in the labor market. Because the provider is paid only while their client is successfully employed, they have a continuing interest in providing follow-up supports if needed. This contrasts with the traditional approach to VR, wherein a case is closed once a particular service plan is completed or a particular milestone is reached.

Fifth, the proposal may be administered by the Social Security Administration. In this respect, it is notable for what it does not do. It does not require the government to micro-manage a service plan to determine whether a particular service was "necessary" or the costs were "reasonable." Those arrangements would be negotiated directly between the beneficiary and the service provider. SSA would pay the provider based on information in its own records that indicate that the beneficiary is at work and benefits are no longer being paid.

The panel recognized that this proposal demands that private and public providers take risks that they are not currently bearing. For some providers this will not be attractive. Yet for others, and particularly for persons and organizations not now engaging in rehabilitation and return-to-work services for Social Security beneficiaries, this proposal may provide very attractive incentives. We cannot tell whether many will participate, and if they do, whether many persons will leave the disability rolls. SSA's actuaries estimate modest savings from the plan. As we suggested earlier, there is very little to lose here, and perhaps much to gain.

Some persons have been concerned that this proposal will encourage people to "cream" the disability rolls to assist first those who are most likely to succeed. The panel recognizes that this is the likely outcome. Some of the panel would have preferred but were unable to design a simple incentive program that would be of more assistance to people who are highly motivated to return to work but who have the greatest difficulties doing so. We do not believe, however, that this is a reason for not going forward with the return-to-work ticket proposal. The existing state VR program is required by law to serve first those with the most severe disabilities. And other state, local, and nonprofit social service agencies have as their mission to provide ongoing supports for very vulnerable populations. The panel's return-to-work ticket plan is in no way a substitute for existing public or nonprofit programs. They should remain available. The return-to-work proposal, if it has any positive effect, will make some people better off, no one worse off, and save scarce trust fund dollars. The Clinton administration's 1998 budget includes provisions to test a return-to-work plan based on the panel's proposal.

Continuity of Medical Care

As noted earlier, the panel heard repeatedly that beneficiaries' fears about losing Medicare or Medicaid that are linked to DI or SSI eligibility are significant barriers to work. In its analysis, the panel examined existing rules that allow former DI beneficiaries to purchase continued Medicare coverage if they return to work despite their impairments. It found that the complex rules for determining how much a former beneficiary would have to pay are beyond comprehension, even by policy experts. The panel, therefore, recommended a simplified Medicare buy-in that is understandable, predictable, and affordable. The buy-in premium would be related to the former beneficiary's earnings while working—that is, 7% of earnings in excess of $15,000 a year. It would be capped at the amount of the full premium charged under current law, which would be reached at annual earnings of about $68,000.

The panel also examined a number of state programs that allow disabled individuals to purchase Medicaid coverage when they are unable to get coverage in the private market, and it urged states to consider such innovations in their Medicaid programs.

The Clinton administration has endorsed proposals to extend health care to former disability beneficiaries. The 1998 fiscal year budget includes proposals to continue Medicare for DI beneficiaries who leave the rolls despite the continuation of their impairments, and it authorizes federal matching funds in the Medicaid program toward a means-tested Medicaid buy-in for former SSI beneficiaries who return to work. If adopted, these provisions would help to eliminate beneficiaries' fears about losing health care coverage when they return to work.

Work Incentives Administration

Disability cash benefits programs, particularly SSI, currently contain a substantial number of work incentive provisions. On paper, these are plausible means for easing the transition off the benefit rolls and into the workforce. In practice, however, they seem to have little effect. The reason for this disjunction seems to be poor understanding and administration of existing law. The panel concluded that because work incentive provisions are inherently complex, beneficiaries are likely to need help to understand and comply with them when they work. Some kinds of assistance could be offered by service providers who assist beneficiaries return to work, such as those who accept the return-to-work tickets the panel is recommending. Other tasks necessary to make work incentives work can be performed only by SSA or an entity employed by SSA. They include prompt processing of earnings reports from beneficiaries so that their benefits are adjusted promptly as their circumstances change. If return to work is to be a priority, investment in SSA's personnel and systems support for these functions is essential.

In the absence of such an investment, beneficiaries who return to work are at risk of being charged with large overpayments for past months in which their benefits should have been withheld or of going without benefits during months in which they need them and are entitled to them. This situation seems to have led to a widespread belief in the recipient community that it is simply too dangerous to return to work unless one's earnings are sufficient to end all benefits and avoid any further dealings with SSA. But immediate exit from benefits is not a very likely outcome for low-wage workers with uncertain work capacities. While some beneficiaries may be able to catapult off the benefit rolls, others find return to work to be an uncertain and gradual process.

To some degree, poor work incentives administration reflects actions of the Congress as well as the administering agency. Allocating too little in administrative funds and insisting that scarce resources be devoted to avoiding delays in initial determinations of claims means that other administrative actions are neglected. The panel's call for better administration of work incentive provision is, therefore, equally a call for the Congress to fund the administration of the statutes that it passes.

While many people seem to wish that work incentives could somehow be made simpler, the panel concluded that this was unlikely. To be sure, work incentive provisions can be simplified. However, virtually every simplification will decrease the target efficiency of the work incentive provisions involved and increase benefit payments (perhaps substantially) for small increases in workforce participation (Hoynes and Moffitt 1996). The panel concluded that while work incentive provisions are inherently complex, they can be made easier for beneficiaries to use with proper investment in personnel and systems to administer them. Without that investment, they are likely to fail in their intended purpose.

Continuing Disability Reviews (CDRs)

Lack of administrative resources, combined with the unhappy political history of benefits terminations in the early 1980s, had for some years virtually eliminated review of existing beneficiaries to determine whether they have recovered sufficiently to leave the benefit rolls. While the continuing disability reviews of the early 1980s were clearly too aggressive, the virtual abandonment of CDRs later in the 1980s went too far in the opposite direction. The panel therefore recommended that a program of fair and effective continuing disability reviews be reinstituted. The Congress and the administration are already moving in this direction.

Roads Not Taken

The panel considered a number of other approaches that have been suggested to promote return to work or to prevent the shift from work to disability benefits in the first place. Among proposals considered but not recommended are time-limited, long-term disability benefits; universal, short-term disability benefits; partial benefits for partial disability; and linking disability benefit determinations with enforcement of the Americans with Disabilities Act (ADA).

Time-limited, Long-Term Disability Benefits

Some have suggested that the way to promote return to work and to motivate SSA to conduct continuing disability reviews is to make most benefit allowances temporary or time-limited. The panel majority rejected this approach. Recovery rates are not high, and it is extremely difficult to predict at the time of award which beneficiaries will likely recover. A large-scale approach to time-limited benefits could, therefore, require the redetermination of a very large number of claims where the beneficiary did not in fact recover. A carefully targeted approach, in contrast, would be virtually indistinguishable from the CDR process that the panel recommended.

We emphasize that proposals to time-limit, long-term disability benefits—which are paid only after a five-month waiting period and only to those who meet a very strict test of long-term work disability—are very different from models for temporary disability benefits that are combined with early intervention services, as described below.

Short-Term Disability Insurance

It is conventional wisdom in the rehabilitation community that early intervention after an injury or illness is the key to maintaining work capacity. Other countries and some private employers in the United States combine early intervention techniques with temporary disability benefits. In Germany, for example, employers pay an ill or injured worker full salary for the first six weeks of absence from work, after which sickness funds pay for up to eighteen months of temporary disability, during which publicly financed rehabilitation services are provided before a determination of long-term disability is made[7] (Aarts and de Jong 1996; Social Security Administration 1995b). This approach is also used by some private employers and insurers in the United States, and some evidence suggests that coordinated disability case management and medical and vocational intervention, combined with short-term income support, is effective in limiting long-term work disability (Hunt et al. 1996; U.S. General Accounting Office 1996).

Many on the Disability Policy Panel were attracted to proposals to create a seamless web of coordinated early interventions with short-term disability insurance (SDI) as its core. The injunction from the House Ways and Means Committee to propose changes that would not substantially increase costs dissuaded the panel from proposing such a system.

Employers in the United States voluntarily offer short-term disability benefits and the coverage is very uneven. Among private sector workers, fully 30% have no formal sick leave or any form of short-term disability insurance. Another 26% have only sick leave, which typically provides wage replacement for a few days or weeks, far short of the five-month period that must elapse after disability onset before eligibility for DI

(Mashaw and Reno 1996a). Gaps in coverage are particularly likely among workers in small firms, part-time workers, and nonunionized blue-collar or clerical and service workers (U.S. Department of Labor 1994, 1996).

Despite its spotty coverage, private spending for short-term disability benefits was about $14.6 billion in 1992, and an additional $4.6 billion was paid through mandatory short-term disability programs in five states (Mashaw and Reno 1996b; Social Security Administration 1995). To fill the gaps in coverage would require either a new mandate for employers or employees to finance such benefits or a universal public program financed by tax revenues. When expenditures for medical intervention, vocational rehabilitation, work training, and other aspects are added, it becomes clear that implementing universal early intervention strategies in the United States would be very costly.

A brief review of the experience of the five states that have universal short-term disability insurance—California, New York, Rhode Island, New Jersey, and Hawaii—was instructive. They do not appear to have significantly lower incidence of DI benefit receipt. Furthermore, the vast majority of their SDI recipients have conditions that are, in fact, temporary. Consequently, careful screening of SDI caseloads would appear to be needed to target comprehensive interventions for the minority of SDI recipients who are in the early stages of what may become a long-term work disability.

The panel was also chastened by the realization that countries that pursue this strategy, like Germany and Sweden, still spend considerably more than does the United States on long-term disability benefits. And they are now seeking to reduce their spending on short-term disability benefits. Holland is privatizing its short-term disability benefits by shifting the cost from public budgets to employer mandates (de Jong 1997). And Germany is now lowering the 100% replacement rate provided by employer-financed sickness benefits (Andrews 1996).

Thus while many on the panel believed that overall social welfare would be improved by adopting the German model of SDI and early intervention services that are only selectively available to some American workers, none on the panel believed that the Congress was now willing to pay the bill. Such reforms thus await a change in our fiscal circumstances.

Partial Disability Benefits

It is well recognized that work disability is not a binary condition in which individuals are easily sorted into those able or unable to work.

Rather, work disability spans a broad continuum with many shades of gray. As such, a proposal to pay partial benefits to persons with partial work disabilities has some appeal.

Such proposals also have disadvantages. First, they tend to significantly increase spending for long-term disability benefits. Payment for partial disability is part of the explanation for the very high percentage of GDP allocated to disability benefits in the Netherlands. Partial disability benefits appear to be acceptable in the United States only in circumstances where the eligible population is constrained, such as in the veterans' compensation program and where payments are viewed as compensation in lieu of tort recoveries, as in workers' compensation programs, rather than as general income support. Partial disability can also be difficult to administer. Permanent partial disability determinations have proved to be one of the most contentious aspects of workers' compensation programs (Blue Ribbon Panel on Workers' Compensation 1992).

The panel's DWTC approach has much in common with the purpose of partial benefits. It provides income support to workers whose earning capacity is reduced but not eliminated by their impairments. But unlike partial disability benefits, the DWTC ties income supplements directly to work. This targeting of wage subsidies in the DWTC is more consistent with the panel's charge to recommend policies that promote work.

Linking Benefit Eligibility to the ADA

Finally, some people have suggested that the determination of eligibility for disability benefits should be coordinated with enforcement of the Americans with Disabilities Act in some way. The Disability Policy Panel, however, did not see how an appropriate relationship between these programs could be developed in the determination of benefit eligibility. The requirement that applicants exhaust their remedies under the ADA is unattractive from a number of perspectives. First, it would enormously protract an already lengthy determination process. Indeed, it could easily mean that eligible beneficiaries would be required to wait years instead of months in order to obtain income supports to which they were entitled. Second, it would put the risk of loss through noncompliance with the ADA on workers rather than employers. In short, it would punish the people the ADA is attempting to help while adding no new incentives for employers to comply with the nondiscrimination provisions of that statute.

This proposal also seriously misunderstands the logical relationships between the Americans with Disabilities Act and the DI and SSI cash benefits programs. First, the ADA covers a vastly larger universe of persons with disabilities and persons perceived to have disabilities. Second, the criteria and enforcement of the act are highly individualized. Workers must demonstrate that they remain capable of doing specific jobs for specific employers, and employers respond based upon the specific tasks of their particular place of business and the reasonableness of a particular accommodation given its costs and the economic health of the individual business involved.

These are quite different questions than the ones asked or answered by adjudication of DI and SSI disability claims. The question in these cash benefits programs is whether a worker having the characteristics of the applicant could normally do jobs available in the national economy that pay at the level of substantial gainful activity. The question is not whether there might be some job provided by some employer with some specific accommodation that the claimant could do. There is no inconsistency in workers being eligible for disability cash benefits based on the normal circumstances that would be expected, given their conditions, and those same workers ultimately leaving the rolls because of the discovery of some job with some particular accommodation at some particular job site that they can still perform.

Conclusion

The Disability Policy Panel's two-and-a-half years of deliberations, along with the research that it commissioned and attempted to digest, taught it many lessons concerning the relationship between disability cash benefits policy and work. Much of that learning is embodied in the proposals and recommendations that have been described in this chapter. We conclude, therefore, simply by stressing three major themes that emerged from our experience.

First, one should consider the proposals that were made by the Disability Policy Panel as modest down payments on the development of public policies that will prevent work disability and promote return to work among those with disabling impairments. This is true, in part, because resource constraints prevented the proposal of far-reaching reorganizations of American disability policy. Even more importantly, however, the major policies to promote work by those with impairments lie outside cash benefits programs. They are in areas like the provision of health care, basic and continuing education, and the creation and reorganization of jobs in the national economy.

Second, we were constantly reminded how often administrative resources attached to programs failed to match those programs' policy ambitions. For that reason, the panel attempted to design programs that were easy to administer. The important lesson is that if lawmakers and the American public generally want programs that work, we must match aspirations with resources. "Privatization" or "technical innovation," as in the case of our return-to-work tickets proposal, may sometimes substitute for increased administrative cost. But these opportunities are not ubiquitous. The widespread belief that government can always do more, of higher quality with less resources, is a triumph of hope over experience.

Finally, and most importantly, disability policy must retain a balanced approach between secure benefits for those who cannot work and effective programs to prevent loss of work income and promote return to work. Persons with work disabilities are highly heterogeneous. Their capacities and needs are extraordinarily diverse. We must continue to resist "one-size-fits-all" enthusiasms—whether those enthusiasms suggest that everyone with an impairment should be on a disability pension or that everyone with an impairment can return to self-supporting work in the competitive economy.

Endnotes

[1] For a more complete policy history of the program, see Mashaw and Reno 1996a, 1996b.

[2] Supplemental security income (SSI) provides a basic minimum income for Americans who are elderly, blind, or who have a severe work disability. Eligibility is based on a test of low income and limited assets, rather than on prior contributions to the social insurance trust funds. SSI is thus a "means-tested" program, but it uses the same definition of disability found in the DI statute.

[3] Other studies have found that the state of the economy, the availability of jobs, the availability of other public or private benefits, and the quality of program administration all influence the size of disability benefit rolls (Mashaw and Reno 1996a; Rupp and Stapleton 1998; Burkhauser 1994).

[4] These data on working-aged beneficiaries do not include children under age 18 or persons age 65 or older who receive SSI benefits on the basis of disability.

[5] These studies take account of the difference in tax treatment of various sources of income and the absence of work-related expenses. The studies generally presume that the beneficiary is a relatively healthy retiree. They do not take account of the additional costs of disabled workers, which include the need to support themselves without earnings during a five-month waiting period and other disability-related expenses, including health care during the first twenty-nine months after the onset of disability.

[6] State VR agencies are reimbursed by the Social Security Administration for the cost of services provided to beneficiaries who are successfully rehabilitated. The

measure of success is that the beneficiary completes nine months of earnings that constitute substantial gainful activity (SGA)—currently defined as $500 a month. If the beneficiary continues to earn in excess of the SGA level, benefits are ultimately terminated after a three-year period of extended eligibility. Some persons who are counted as rehabilitation successes by VR agencies do not ultimately leave the benefit rolls because they do not remain employed.

[7] Whether workers with disabilities have higher rates of employment in Germany than in the United States is an open question that merits further study. For Germany, available data relate to workers on the disability register, which means they count toward employers' hiring quotas. In contrast, U.S. data come from household surveys—the current population survey (CPS) and the survey of income and program participation (SIPP). If these data are at all comparable (and they may not be), then the employment experience of German and American workers with disabilities is not radically different.

In Germany, workers on the disability register accounted for about 4.5% of all employed persons in 1990. In the United States, persons with "limitations in the kind or amount of work they can do" accounted for 4.3% of employed persons in 1994, according to the CPS. [The more comprehensive measure of disability used in the 1991 SIPP found that 13.2% of American workers had either a work limitation or a limitation in performing tasks such as seeing, hearing, speaking, lifting, walking, climbing stairs, or performing housework or various activities of living.]

Disabled workers in the two countries appear to have similar rates of official unemployment—that is, being in the labor force without jobs and looking for work. In 1990, the German unemployment rate among workers with disabilities was about 13.3%, which was about two to three times higher than the overall unemployment rate of 4.8%. In the United States, the 1994 unemployment rate was 16.4% for persons with work limitations, according to the CPS. This, too, was about two to three times higher than the overall rate of 6.7%.

References

Aarts, L. J. M., and P. R. de Jong. 1996. "European Experiences with Disability Policy." In J. L. Mashaw et al., eds., *Disability, Work and Cash Benefits*. Kalamazoo, MI: W. E. Upjohn Institute for Employment Research.

Andrews, A. L. 1996. "New Hard Line by Big Companies Threatens German Work Benefits." *The New York Times*, October 1.

Berkowitz, M. et al. 1991. "Full Costs of Disability Final Report." Unpublished report for UNUM Corporation, Portland, ME.

Bound, J. 1989. "The Health and Earnings of Rejected Disability Insurance Applicants." *American Economic Review*, Vol. 79, no. 3 (June), pp. 482-503.

Blue Ribbon Panel on Workers Compensation. 1992. *Policy Statement on Permanent Partial Disability*. Denver, CO: National Conference of State Legislatures.

Burkhauser, R. V. 1994. *Employing People with Disabilities: What to Expect from the Americans with Disabilities Act*. CPR Paper no. 9, Maxwell School, Syracuse University.

Burkhauser, R. V. et al., 1993. "How People with Disabilities Fare When Public Policies Change." *Journal of Policy Analysis and Management*, Vol. 12, no. 2 (Spring).

Burkhauser, R. V., and M. Daly. 1996. "Employment and Economic Well-Being Following the Onset of a Disability." In J. L. Mashaw et al., eds., *Disability, Work and Cash Benefits.* Kalamazoo, MI: W. E. Upjohn Institute for Employment Research.

de Jong, P. R. 1997. U.S. Disability from a European Perspective." In V. P. Reno et al., eds., *Disability: Challenges for Social Insurance, Health Care Financing and Labor Market Policy.* Washington, DC: National Academy of Social Insurance.

Goldman, H., and A. Gattozzi. 1988. "Balance of Powers: Social Security and the Mentally Disabled." *Milbank Quarterly,* no. 66, pp. 531-51.

Haveman, R. J., B. Wolfe, and J. Warlick. 1984. "Disability Transfers, Early Retirement, and Retrenchment." In H. Aaron and G. Burtless, eds., *Retirement and Economic Behavior.* Washington, DC: Brookings Institution, pp. 65-93.

Hoynes, H. M., and R. Moffitt. 1996. "The Effectiveness of Financial Work Incentives in Social Security Disability Insurance and Supplemental Security Income: Lessons from Other Transfer Programs." In J. L. Mashaw et al., eds., *Disability, Work and Cash Benefits.* Kalamazoo, MI: W. E. Upjohn Institute for Employment Research.

Hunt, H. A., H. Habeck, P. Owens, and D. Vandergoot. 1996. "Disability and Work: Lessons from the Private Sector." In J. M. Mashaw et al., eds., *Disability, Work and Cash Benefits.* Kalamazoo, MI: W.E. Upjohn Institute for Employment Research.

Leonard, J. S. 1979. "The Social Security Disability Program and Labor Force Participation." National Bureau of Economic Research Working Paper No. 392. Cambridge, MA: NBER.

Mashaw, J. L. 1988. "Disability Insurance in an Age of Retrenchment: The Politics of Implementing Rights." In T. A. Marmor and J. L. Mashaw, eds., *Social Security: Beyond the Rhetoric of Crisis.* Princeton, NJ: Princeton University Press, pp. 151-76.

Mashaw, J. L., and V. P. Reno. 1996a. *The Environment of Disability Income Policy: Programs, People, History and Context.* Disability Policy Panel Interim Report. Washington, DC: National Academy of Social Insurance.

_____. 1996b. *Balancing Security and Opportunity: The Challenge of Disability Income Policy.* Disability Policy Panel Final Report. Washington, DC: National Academy of Social Insurance.

Mashaw, J. L., V. P. Reno, M. Berkowitz, and R. V. Burkhauser, eds. 1996. *Disability Work and Cash Benefits.* Kalamazoo, MI: W. E. Upjohn Institute for Employment Research.

Palmer, B. A. 1994. "Retirement Income Replacement Ratios: An Update." *Benefits Quarterly* (second quarter).

Parsons, D. O. 1980. "The Decline in Male Labor Force Participation." *Journal of Political Economy,* Vol. 88 (February), pp. 117-34.

Pope, A. M., and A. R. Tarlov. 1991. *Disability in America: Toward a National Agenda for Prevention.* Washington, DC: National Academy Press.

Reno, V. P., J. L. Mashaw, and B. Gradison, eds. 1997. *Disability: Challenges for Social Insurance, Health Care Financing and Labor Market Policy.* Washington, DC. National Academy of Social Insurance.

Rupp, K., and D. C. Stapleton, eds. 1998. *Growth in Disability Benefits: Explanations and Policy Implications.* Kalamazoo, MI: The Upjohn Institute.

Social Security Administration. 1995a. *Annual Statistical Supplement to the Social Security Bulletin.* Washington, DC: GPO.

_____. 1995b. *Social Security Programs throughout the World–1995*. SSA Publication no. 13-11805, Office of Research and Statistics, Research Report. Washington, DC: GPO.

_____. 1997. *Annual Statistical Supplement to the Social Security Bulletin*. Washington, DC: GPO.

_____. 1998. *Disabled Worker Beneficiary Statistics*. Office of the Chief Actuary. Washington, DC: GPO.

Smith, R. T., and A. M. Lilienfield. 1971. *The Social Security Disability Program: An Evaluation Study*. Research Report no. 39, Social Security Administration, Office of Research and Statistics. Washington, DC: GPO.

U.S. Bureau of the Census. 1993. *Americans with Disabilities: 1991-1992, Data from the Survey of Income and Program Participation* P70-33. Washington, DC: GPO.

_____. 1995. Current Population Survey, March 1994. Unpublished tabulations.

U.S. Department of Labor. 1994. *Employee Benefits in Medium and Large Private Establishments, 1993*. Bulletin 2456, May. Washington, DC: GPO.

_____. 1996. *Employee Benefits in Small Private Establishments, 1994*. Bulletin 2475, April. Washington, DC: GPO.

U.S. General Accounting Office. 1989. *Denied Applicants' Health and Financial Status Compared with Beneficiaries*. HRD-90-2. Washington, DC: GPO.

_____. 1996. *SSA Disability: Return-to-Work Strategies from Other Systems May Improve Federal Programs*. HEHS-96-133.Washington, DC: GPO.

World Health Organization 1980. *International Classification of Impairments, Disabilities and Handicaps: A Manual of Classification Relation to the Consequences of Disease*. Geneva, Switzerland: World Health Organization.

CHAPTER 10

Disputes and Dispute Resolution

TERRY THOMASON
McGill University

DOUGLAS E. HYATT
University of Toronto

KAREN ROBERTS
Michigan State University

A central problem for social insurance programs is the determination of benefit eligibility. For disability insurance, benefits are at least partially contingent on the existence and extent of work disability. Eligibility decisions are based on a complex set of medical questions and also—in most cases—the nature of the claimant's work and his or her vocational qualifications. The line dividing eligible and ineligible claimants is often indistinct. Although a majority of claims are resolved without difficulty, a significant number result in disputes, and those that do account for a large proportion of total administrative costs.

Disability insurance programs have administrative mechanisms and procedures outside the normal legal system to resolve disputes. In recent years, policymakers have become increasingly concerned about the effectiveness of these procedures. Program costs have risen precipitously, and there is a public perception that increasingly generous benefits are inducing workers to exaggerate the extent of their disabilities or even make fraudulent claims.

In addition, there is a perception that workers' compensation programs have become increasingly litigious, adding substantially to costs. In part, these perceptions have been fueled by an expansion of the definition of disability. The scope of compensable conditions has broadened to include soft tissue injuries, repetitive trauma syndromes, psychological disorders, and a variety of occupational diseases.[1] Accurate diagnosis of these conditions is problematic so that it is difficult to establish the extent of disability. For soft tissue injuries, repetitive trauma syndromes, and psychological ailments, diagnosis is primarily based on subjective symptoms. For all of these conditions, it is also difficult to determine whether or not and to what extent the condition is work-related. In addition, because workers are covered by a myriad of private and public disability insurance programs, litigation is also increasing as parties attempt to shift costs to other payers.

In this chapter we examine the role of disputes and dispute resolution in disability insurance programs. We are primarily interested in providing a framework that can be used to evaluate dispute resolution procedures within these programs. Our focus is on workers' compensation, since most existing research has examined dispute resolution in this program. However, the issues raised within the context of workers' compensation are issues applicable to disability insurance programs more broadly.

Two separate strands of literature investigate issues related to disputes and dispute resolution. The first is the work of economists who conceptualize disputes and dispute resolution as income maximization problems; actors make rational choices to initiate a dispute or appeal an adverse decision made at a lower level of the claims process based on the monetary costs and benefits of those choices.[2] The second strand has been pursued by psychologists examining the relationship between individual perceptions of fairness of dispute resolution procedures and behavior and attitudes. This chapter examines issues from both perspectives.

In the next section we examine institutional features of the dispute resolution process in the two principal disability insurance programs: workers' compensation and Social Security Disability Insurance (SSDI). We then consider the question of optimality in dispute resolution by examining two criteria: efficiency and equity. This is followed by an examination of the income maximization model and relevant empirical research. The literature on procedural fairness is discussed in the next section, followed by an analysis of three specific issues: compromise and release agreements, the role of the claimant's attorney, and the evaluation of permanent partial disability. Conclusions are presented in the final section.

The Institutional Framework

Workers' Compensation

Many features of workers' compensation programs are designed to avoid disputes. The strict liability standard, which makes employers responsible for benefits regardless of fault, limits issues regarding liability.[3] The determination of benefits is formulaic. Claimants who are totally disabled are paid weekly benefits equal to a given proportion of wages for the period of disability or until well-specified limits on duration or the total amount of benefits are reached. Most jurisdictions base permanent partial disability benefits on statutory schedules that prescribe maximum benefit duration by injury type. These rules are intended to provide objective criteria that limit disagreement over the amount of compensation due.

Unlike other social insurance programs, private insurers play a primary role in the determination of benefit amounts and benefit eligibility in workers' compensation. Insurers may deny liability for the claim, contending that it is not work-related. Moreover, if dissatisfied with the claimant's progress, the insurer may require that the claimant submit to a medical examination conducted by a physician chosen by the insurer; and on the basis of that examination, the insurer may discontinue benefits. Refusal to undergo examination is also grounds for benefit termination.

Disputes can arise when workers believe that they have unjustly been denied benefits. Although there is significant variation, these disputes are initially addressed in a two-stage procedure internal to the agency administering the compensation program. The first stage is an informal conference between the parties at which the issues are defined and possibilities for settlement are explored. If a negotiated agreement is not reached, the dispute will typically proceed to a hearing before an adjudicator employed by the compensation agency. Procedural rules are often relaxed: rules of evidence are not strictly enforced and proceedings are often administrative rather than adversarial. The decision at this initial stage may be appealed, usually to a higher level within the administrative agency. Depending on the jurisdiction, this internal appeal may consist of a trial *de novo* where evidence is presented, or it may be limited to the record developed at the earlier hearing. If dissatisfied with the final agency determination, either party may ask for judicial review. The review is usually on the basis of the record developed by the agency appellate bodies and is typically limited to questions of law, making the agency the final arbiter of facts.

Social Security Disability Insurance (SSDI)

Application for SSDI benefits is initially determined by the local office of the Social Security Administration (SSA) through a five-step process that begins with the simplest and easiest to observe criteria and moves to more complex tests requiring subjective judgment. Medical criteria are first satisfied; and if a presumption of inability to work cannot be established because the impairment is not on a prescribed "List of Impairments," the claimant's capacity for work is evaluated in two stages. Ability to work is first evaluated based on work that the claimant has done in the past. Failing that, the SSA determines whether the claimant is capable of doing other work. At this point, physical abilities, age, education, and work experience are taken into consideration. Actual availability of a job is not a criterion for determining benefits eligibility.

A three-stage appeals process internal to the SSA is available for claimants whose initial applications are denied. The local office that issued the initial decision first reconsiders claims. That decision may then be appealed to a hearing before an administrative law judge. Finally, claimants may take an adverse decision from the ALJ to the Appeals Council of the SSA. Claimants who are dissatisfied with the SSA's final decision may file suit in a federal district court.

SSDI differs from workers' compensation in several important ways. First, unlike workers' compensation, private insurers are not involved in the administration or financing of SSDI premiums. Second, while both programs are financed through payroll taxes, SSDI benefits are in no way linked to firm experience.[4] Third, SSDI provides benefits to long-term, totally disabled persons; it does not provide benefits to individuals suffering permanent partial disability. Fourth, benefits are solely conditioned on the existence of disability, so claimants do not have to demonstrate that their condition is work-related. Taken together, these factors suggest that SSDI claims administration is likely to be substantially less adversarial than that for workers' compensation programs and, consequently, less litigious.

Nevertheless, the number of disputes in the SSDI program has increased dramatically in recent years, as has the delay between the initial application and the final disposition of the claim. In part, this is due to increasing complexity of the medical evidence requirements, which cannot readily be provided by treating physicians and which are time consuming to evaluate.

Optimal Dispute Resolution: Criteria for Evaluation

Growing concern about the increasing cost and litigiousness of disability insurance programs has led to reform initiatives in several states.

These efforts raise public policy questions as to whether these reforms represent an improvement over the status quo. More generally, we can ask what an optimal dispute resolution procedure would look like.

Efficiency

One way to approach these questions is to ask which process(es) maximizes social welfare. Costs associated with dispute resolution are twofold: the direct costs of administration and the cost of judicial error (Posner 1973). The former includes the wages or opportunity costs of the parties, their representatives, witnesses, adjudicators and associated personnel (e.g., court stenographer, etc.), as well as the cost of office supplies, court rooms, etc., while the latter refers to costs incurred due to behavioral changes. As we shall see, both the income maximization and fairness strands of the dispute resolution literature address efficiency issues and, in particular, the potential impact of dispute resolution procedures on the behavior of the principal actors in workers' compensation programs.

Equity and Fairness

Efficiency is only one criterion by which to evaluate dispute procedures. Another is equity or the extent to which the procedure yields outcomes that may be considered fair or just (National Commission 1972). An inefficient procedure may be preferred to an efficient one, if the latter results in gross inequities.[5] While difficult to define precisely, equity requires that similarly situated claimants be treated similarly. In the context of a disability insurance program, "similarly situated" refers to degree of disability, so that in an equitable program, claimants who suffer identical losses as the result of their disability should receive similar benefits, while claimants with more severe disability should receive greater benefits. In this chapter we will attempt to address issues related to both criteria.

Income Maximization

As noted, two types of costs are associated with disputes and dispute resolution mechanisms: direct costs and indirect costs related to behavioral change. Judicial error may affect the firm's incentives to prevent accidents or it may affect either party's incentives to litigate claims. In this section we first discuss the theoretical impact of judicial error on the probability of workplace accidents, followed by an examination of the relationship between judicial error and litigation.[6]

Judicial Error and Accident Prevention

In general, the primary cost of judicial error stems from its undesirable impact on the deterrent effects of legal sanctions on behavior that the law seeks to control. Put simply, we assume there is an efficient penalty—which may, in fact, be zero or no penalty at all—that induces people to behave in a way that maximizes social welfare. Judicial error occurs when a judgment deviates from this penalty. For example, in the context of non-work-related accidents, efficiency implies that tortfeasors should be penalized when their costs of prevention are less than the expected costs of accident. Efficiency further implies that the penalty, in terms of damages, should exactly equal expected accident costs. If judges err either with respect to the application of the rule or the extent of damages, then people will either take too little care, if the expected penalty is too small, or too much care, if the expected penalty is too great.

However, the costs of judicial error are mitigated in the context of workers' compensation due to the contractual relationship between workers and employers. Specifically, wages are directly related to the workers' expected injury costs, since workers will demand higher wages for more hazardous jobs, and inversely related to the level of compensation benefits, since workers' injury costs decline when compensation benefits are paid. Judicial error that results in greater (less) workers' compensation benefits reduces (increases) the wage premium, so that the employer's accident costs, which include both the risk premium paid to workers in the form of higher wages as well as the costs of compensation benefits, will remain unchanged.

The fact that the impact of judicial error is mitigated in workers' compensation programs may explain the prevalence of informal hearing procedures and a relaxation of the rules of evidence relative to typical courtroom procedure. Formal hearing procedures and strict evidentiary rules increase the direct cost of dispute resolution by placing greater demands on the time of the participants. At the same time, these measures do not substantially reduce the cost of judicial error relative to tort suits where the tortfeasor is liable for the full cost of damages.

Judicial Error and Litigation Costs

Judicial error can also result in greater litigation costs. To examine this claim, we first develop a model of the dispute process. This model contemplates a series of stages that begin with some incident and potentially evolve into a full-blown formal dispute:[7]

1. The decision to file a claim: An injury occurs and the individual decides to either file or not file a claim.

2. Evaluating the claims experience: If a claim is filed, the employer commences claim administration.[8] The employer has a range of possible responses. He may accept the claim: make voluntary payments, provide requested medical care, and expedite a return to work. Alternatively, the employer may deny the claim and refuse to pay all benefits. Or the employer may initially pay benefits to the claimant and then at a later point cease benefit payments on the grounds that the claimant no longer suffers work-related disability.

3. Formal claim dispute and possible appeal: If the employee believes that the employer has wrongfully denied benefits, then he/she then formally disputes the claim by entering into the workers' compensation hearing process. The dispute resolution process may yield a settlement offer from either party. If the offer is accepted, the process ends. However, if no offer is forthcoming or if the offer is not accepted, then the claim is adjudicated. Either party may appeal the adjudicator's decision to an appellate tribunal.

Workers initiate claims when expected benefits exceed costs. Costs include the opportunity cost of the workers' time; the direct cost of resources invested in pursuit of claims, including the cost of legal representation; the risk of employer retribution in the form of disciplinary discharge or demotion; and the expected penalty that will be imposed if the claim is adjudged to be fraudulent. In other words, the claimant will initiate a claim when the claimant's expected award (R_p) is greater than the cost of litigation, (C_p) or $R_p - C_p > 0$.

Once a claim is initiated, the employer will oppose it on the basis of a similar cost-benefit calculus. Alternatively, employers will be prepared to offer settlements (S) to claimants that are less than or equal to their expected costs of adjudicating the claim, including both the costs of the award (R_d) and the costs of litigation (C_d). If the expected costs of adjudicating the claim are less than or equal to zero, no settlement offer will be forthcoming.

Claimants will accept an employer's settlement offer where the adjudicated award net of the costs of adjudication is less than the settlement $(R_p - C_p \leq S)$. If we assume there are no problems due to strategic behavior, this implies that claims will be litigated if the claimant's expected award from litigation is greater than the employer's expected costs, i.e., if $R_d + C_d < R_p - C_p \Rightarrow$ litigation.

It is important to note that both parties are uncertain of the actual award the claimant will receive if the claim is litigated, so that both parties may estimate the actual award with error. If we designate the "actual" award as R and the size of the parties' errors as r_d and r_p, we can represent the parties' expectations as follows: $R_d = R + r_d$ and $R_p = R + r_p$, where r_p and r_d are random variables. Substituting and rearranging, the conditions for litigation may be restated as $C_p + C_d < r_p - r_d \Rightarrow$ litigation. This implies that the parties will litigate disputes when total costs are less than the difference between the claimant's and employer's prediction errors.

The parties form expectations about the probability of success based on prior decisions involving cases with similar fact situations. Judicial error makes it more difficult for the parties to accurately predict the size of the award, increasing the variability of the parties' error terms, which, in turn, increases the variability of the difference between the claimant and the insurer's prediction error. It can be shown that as the variability of the error differential increases, so does the probability of litigation and, consequently, litigation costs (Thomason 1991).

Empirical Evidence

There is virtually no research that directly measures the impact of judicial error on accident prevention or litigation probability or costs. However, a few studies examine implications of the income maximization model, which suggests that adjudication decisions are determined through a cost-benefit calculus made by the parties to a dispute.

The model suggests that the probability of a dispute is negatively related to the cost of litigation and positively related to the expectation differential (the difference between the claimant's and the insurer's estimates of the expected outcome of litigation). This latter result implies that the probability of a dispute is positively related to the variability of the expected award. If we assume, as seems likely, that award variability is positively related to the size of the expected award, then we would also expect to find that dispute probability is positively related to award size. In most jurisdictions, award size is a function of two variables, the weekly benefit and the duration of benefits. Weekly benefits are equal to a proportion of the claimant's wage, subject to a minimum and a maximum, while benefit duration is a function of the extent of the claimant's disability.

Several studies have investigated the impact of award size on dispute probability using a variety of proxies, including the extent of medical care received by claimants, a physician's rating of the claimant's disability, and the number of weeks of temporary disability. In general, this research has confirmed the hypothesized relationship between award size and dispute probability. Specifically, a positive relationship has been found between the likelihood of a dispute and the size of the weekly benefit (Hunt 1982); the claimant's loss of functional capacity (Borba and Appel 1987); the duration of temporary total disability (Roberts 1992); claim costs (Hyatt and Kralj 1995); and a dummy variable indicating that the claim was permanently, as opposed to temporarily, disabled (Fournier and Morgan 1996). In addition, Thomason (1991) and Thomason and Burton (1993), using samples of PPD claims from New York, both found that settlement probability was negatively related to weekly benefit payments and proxies for injury severity.

Fewer studies have examined the relationship between dispute costs and litigation probability since administrative data sets typically lack such information.[9] An exception is Borba and Appel's (1987) analysis of permanent disability claims in California. They found that factors related to lowering the opportunity cost of a dispute—such as the receipt of disability income from sources other than workers' compensation, the number of other employed individuals in the worker's household, and the presence of another household member who became employed subsequent to the injury—increase the probability of hiring an attorney and therefore the probability of litigation.

Thomason (1991), Roberts (1992), and Thomason and Burton (1993) all find that uncertainty with respect to the outcome of the dispute resolution process has the expected impact on litigation probability. Using a sample of Michigan claims, Roberts estimates dispute probability using, among other variables, a proxy for financial uncertainty: the delay between the injury and the first payment of benefits. As expected, this variable is positively related to litigation probability.[10] Similarly, Thomason (1991) and Thomason and Burton (1993) found that award variability was positively related to settlement probability and negatively related to settlement size as predicted.[11] These results suggest that judicial error increases litigation costs by increasing uncertainty. Importantly, Roberts' result also indicates that workers' compensation agencies could decrease litigation costs by reducing the time between the injury and first payment of benefits.

Finally, using Delaware claims data, Falaris, Link, and Staten (1995) estimated regression equations to predict award size and settlement probability. In Delaware, compensation claims may be resolved through a negotiated settlement or through formal adjudication by the compensation agency, the Industrial Accident Board (IAB). These equations were used to predict claimant awards under two assumptions: (1) the claimant settled or (2) the award was adjudicated by the IAB. Comparing the predicted awards of claimants who did or did not appeal their claim to the IAB, they find an efficient sorting by claimants. Specifically, they find that predicted adjudicated awards of claimants who appealed decisions to the IAB were greater than those of claimants who did not. Likewise, the predicted settlements of claimants who settled were higher than the settlements of those who did not.

Taken together, these studies indicate that the parties respond to the private incentives presented by the dispute process. To the extent that private incentives are at odds with social objectives, social welfare is suboptimal. This implies that the design of dispute resolution procedures should consider their impact on claimant and employer incentives. In addition, results from the Thomason (1991), Roberts (1992), and Thomason and Burton (1993) studies indicate that the probability of litigation is positively related to uncertainty. This suggests that judicial error can increase litigation costs by increasing dispute frequency so that attempts to reduce litigation costs by decreasing the quantum of due process available to claimants can perversely lead to the opposite result.

Claimant and Employer Heterogeneity

Thus far, our income maximization model assumes relative equality both between employers and claimants and among the members of each group separately. However, significant differences between employers and claimants—and among the members of each group—are likely to affect both the probability and outcome of a dispute. First, it is reasonable to believe that relative to employers, compensation claimants are risk-averse; the benefits at stake in a dispute are typically a substantial portion of the workers' income. Injured workers are likely to be reluctant to risk losing benefits through an uncertain adjudicatory process. Second, employers are typically repeat players in the dispute resolution process, while compensation claimants are not. As such, employers have developed expertise that the typical claimant lacks and will therefore make more effective use of legal resources. Claimants are less likely to understand their rights and duties, including their right to compensation. To gain equivalent expertise, claimants must engage legal counsel, which can result in principal-agent problems as described below.

Concerns over power inequality between employer and workers have inspired the development of several institutional features of dispute resolution processes in workers' compensation. These include statutory language and case law that establishes a presumption of compensability where an injury has occurred in the course of employment or that otherwise provides that doubts should be resolved in favor of the claimant. Similarly, a perceived power imbalance has led legislators in most states to prohibit discrimination against workers who have initiated workers' compensation claims and, in three Canadian provinces, to obligate employers to reemploy workers who have suffered a disability as the result of a workplace accident.[12]

As there are significant differences between employers and claimants, so there are differences among individuals within these groups. Workers vary with respect to their employment alternatives, their financial resources, and their access to (and ability to process) information about the dispute resolution process. Claimants with greater financial resources or better employment alternatives are likely to be less risk averse than are other claimants. In terms of the cost-benefit model described in the previous section, their reservation price for settlement is likely to be higher, so that they can expect to receive higher benefits than more risk-averse claimants. More highly educated claimants will better understand the dispute resolution process and so will be better able to predict the outcome of a dispute and to effectively use legal resources. These claimants will also receive greater benefits.

Several studies find that differences among claimants are important determinants of their experience in the dispute resolution process. For example, using data from permanent partial disability claims from New York, Thomason (1994) examined employer claims management activity. Specifically, he estimated both the probability that employers deny liability for the claim (also known as claim "controversion") and the probability of employer-initiated benefit reductions. He found that employers were less likely to adjust claims of English-speaking claimants or claimants represented by an attorney. Similarly, Hyatt and Kralj (1996) report that Ontario claimants who lacked facility with English or French were more likely to have their claims granted or partially granted than claimants who cannot speak either official language.

Employers are also heterogeneous in some important respects. Large employers are more likely to effectively use legal resources than smaller employers for two reasons. First, large employers have more experience with the dispute process, ceteris paribus, and will therefore develop greater in-house expertise. Among other things, this expertise will allow them to avoid some of the principal-agent problems discussed below. Second, large employers have greater incentive to oppose a claim due to the way insurers establish loss reserves and calculate experience-rating modifications to compensation costs.

Large employers are more likely to be self-insured, and self-insured employers only pay for disputed compensation costs when they lose. On the other hand, employers who purchase insurance through a carrier are experience-rated on the basis of their loss histories, which include both current and reserved losses. Loss reserves are created for contested as well as noncontested claims, which means that the employer's experience rating—and, therefore, his or her compensation costs—are partially based on the contested losses. Since it can take several years for the dispute to be resolved and since experience rating in most U.S. jurisdictions is based on a moving three-year average of past losses, the employer's costs are partially based on losses that ultimately may never be realized. Finally, if losses are over-reserved, that is, if the insurer creates a larger reserve for a claim than is actually paid out, the surplus will not be refunded to the employer. Thus the smaller employer has less incentive than large, self-insured employers to oppose compensation claims.[13] We would expect that, ceteris paribus, claimants employed by smaller firms will receive greater benefits than similarly situated claimants employed by larger firms.

Hyatt and Kralj (1995) examined the impact of workers' compensation insurance premium experience rating on the probability of an employer's appeal of an unfavorable decision by the agency administering the workers' compensation program. They hypothesized that since experience rating creates a financial incentive for employers to reduce workers' compensation costs, experience-rated employers will receive greater benefits from successfully appealing a claim than employers who are not experience-rated. Using a sample of almost 162,000 lost-time claims arising in 1986 in Ontario, the authors found that experience-rated employers are significantly more likely to appeal claims than non-experience-rated employers.

Research reviewed in this section offers preliminary evidence that current dispute resolution processes used by disability insurance programs can produce inequitable outcomes. Claimants with greater access to legal resources—as proxied by language abilities—obtain greater awards than claimants with less access. In this regard, it is important to note that compensation from a disability insurance program is typically the only source of income for the severely disabled claimant. Erroneous decisions about eligibility or the extent of compensation can have far-reaching consequences for an especially vulnerable group, so that even if inequities were few and far between, they should be a matter of concern for public policy.

Procedural Justice and Perceptions of Fairness

While equity is an important concern in and of itself, the equity of dispute resolution processes also has efficiency implications. Claimant perceptions of fairness influence a variety of behaviors affecting social welfare, and anecdotal evidence suggests that it is important to consider fairness perceptions in the design and operation of disability insurance programs. An example from Canada illustrates the point.

Unlike the United States, private insurers play no role in Canadian workers' compensation programs, so that historically provincial workers' compensation agencies acted as both the initial adjudicator of the claim and the sole avenue for appeal.[14] In the 1970s, injured workers in several Canadian jurisdictions began to express considerable dissatisfaction with provincial compensation agencies, which they considered to be "huge, autocratic bureaucrac[ies], which exercise [their] mandate in a paternalistic and defensive fashion" (McCombie 1984). By 1980 Weiler (1980) found that injured workers were "most aggrieved by the administration of workers compensation" and that "[t]here is a growing feeling that the Workers' Compensation Board has become a faceless, impersonal, even dehumanizing organization, one which puts injured workers through a mail-order assembly line." These and similar sentiments, which are expressions of a perception of a lack of fundamental fairness in the administrative process, led to the creation of independent appeals tribunals in several provinces in the latter half of the 1980s and early 1990s.

What Is Fairness and Why Is It Valued?

Evidence suggests that people distinguish between two types of fairness: distributive fairness (or justice), or the fairness of outcomes, and procedural fairness (or justice), or the fairness of the process that generates those outcomes (Barrett-Howard and Tyler 1986). The literature further indicates that while people evaluate these two types of fairness separately, distributive fairness perceptions influence the evaluation of procedural justice; people pay more attention to procedural fairness when they are unhappy about the distribution resulting from the process. For example, Greenberg (1987) and Wazeter (1991) found that workers are more concerned about the fairness of wage determination processes if they believe that their wages are unfairly low. This does not mean that procedural justice evaluations depend on perceptions of distributive outcomes.

Rather it suggests that when people believe that the distribution is unfair, they more carefully evaluate procedures used to distribute outcomes than when they think that the distribution is unfair.

Research investigating claimant perceptions of the claims process suggests that the breakdown of the employment relationship, the lack of information and/or assistance navigating the claims process, and humiliating treatment by professionals during the claims process are at the core of claimant dissatisfaction (Sum 1996; Ray 1986). In other words, compensation claimants are apparently less dissatisfied with distributive than procedural issues. As indicated, not only do people distinguish between the two types of fairness, but also they appear to accept or reject an outcome based on their perceptions of the process. That is, evidence suggests that people are more likely to accept and abide by a decision when they feel/believe a fair process generated it.[15] For these reasons, the remainder of this discussion will focus on procedural fairness.

Procedural fairness is not a unitary concept. At least three dimensions have been identified: (1) the degree of opportunity to influence outcomes (or voice), which is valued for its potential material effect on decisions—the more opportunity for voice, the fairer the process; (2) structural characteristics, which refer to aspects of procedural rules associated with the decision-making process, such as the consistency of administration and the completeness of decision-maker information; and (3) the quality of interpersonal interactions, which refers to the degree to which participants are treated with dignity, neutrality, and as though they are valued.

In addition, it is hypothesized that procedural fairness is valued for two reasons (Korsgaard and Roberson 1995; Tyler 1989). First, since people believe that fair processes are more likely to generate fair outcomes, fairness is valued for the economic benefits it may generate. Compensation claimants may perceive a fair process as providing higher benefits or better return-to-work offers. Second, fairness is valued because it tells participants that they are intrinsically valued. This quality is significant for the compensation claims process, since claimants may draw inferences about their status in the organization based on the perceived fairness of this process. An injured employee who is treated with a lack of respect or who is not given full information about benefit entitlements or details of the process may interpret these events as indicating that their status has changed from "valued employee" to that of someone who is seen as abusing the system (Roberts and Gleason 1994; Sum 1996).

While causality is not clear, there is evidence indicating that contested claims coincide with the destruction of the employment relationship. Understanding claimant perceptions of procedural fairness may help identify aspects of the claims process that could be altered to reduce the probability and cost of disputes as well as the indirect costs of ruptured work relationships. Fairness perceptions may influence claimants' propensity to file compensation claims, their willingness to return to work and subsequent behavior on the job, and the probability that they will utilize the appeals process.

Procedural Justice and the Employment Relationship

Organizational citizenship is a concept that provides a good analogue to the workers' compensation claims process. Organizational citizenship is typically defined in terms of behaviors or "actions taken by employees that benefit the organization" (Eskew 1993:186). These beneficial actions are outside formal job descriptions, often not recognized or explicitly rewarded through performance evaluation, and are taken at the employee's discretion. In the compensation context, ambiguity surrounding disability (how seriously injured an employee really is, the extent of recovery and ability to return to work, and so on) permits employers to interpret an individual's claim subjectively. While not articulated in these terms, employers appear to want injured workers to be good "citizens" of the organization—make the extra effort, cooperate, and exhibit other positive extra-role behaviors (Moorman, Niehoff, and Organ 1993). Injured workers employed in workplaces they view as following procedurally fair rules may be less likely to make unnecessary workers' compensation claims and more likely to return to work promptly and make every effort to be fully productive—in other words, be good organizational citizens.

Recalling the stages of dispute presented earlier, there is a period when an injured worker participates in and evaluates the claims process. There are many different behaviors an employer would like to see the employee exhibit during this period (other than a simple decision not to contest the claim) that would define the employee as a good organizational citizen. These include no unnecessary lost time, a return to work as soon as it is medically feasible, cooperation over medical treatment decisions, adherence to prescribed medical regimens, and/or providing information requested by the organization and/or insurance company on a timely basis.

Although there is no research linking fairness and citizenship in the workers' compensation context, we may extrapolate from research in other contexts. In a study of employees in a multisite firm, Tansky (1993) examined the relationship between organizational citizenship and assessments of the overall fairness of the firm's policies, procedures, and implementation.[16] She found that overall fairness perceptions were positively and significantly related to two of her five organizational citizenship behaviors: altruism and conscientiousness at the workplace. There is also evidence that fairness perceptions affect organizational citizenship even during periods when outcomes are negative. One study found individuals who had been laid off by what they viewed as a fair process were more likely to remain productive and cooperative workers after being notified that they were to be terminated than were laid-off workers who felt that the process was unfair (Bies, Martin, and Brockner 1993). A second study found that procedural justice perceptions mitigate the strength of individual reactions to income loss resulting from lay-off (Brockner et al. 1994).

Procedural Fairness and the Emergence of a Dispute

Workers may dispute claims out of a sense of injustice due to a perception of unfair treatment by their employers as a result of their becoming injured and basically seek "their day in court" to get a fair hearing (Youngblood, Trevino, and Favia 1992). Similarly, if employees perceive the hearings process as fair, they may be less likely to appeal outcomes, even if unfavorable (Lind et al. 1993).

Using a sample of 182 Michigan claimants, Roberts (1996) examined the impact of different dimensions of procedural justice on dispute probability, controlling for several variables related to award size. She found that while the relationship between dispute probability and the claimants' overall fairness perception was not statistically significant, dispute probability was significantly and negatively related to one dimension of procedural fairness, claimant perceptions of information accuracy. That is, injured workers who believed that employers, treating physicians, and claims examiners had sufficient information to make accurate decisions were less likely to dispute a claim than workers who did not have this belief. Similar results were obtained by Borba and Appel (1987) who found that permanently disabled workers who were satisfied with the information received from their insurance company were less likely to hire lawyers, as were long service workers who were satisfied with their employer's dissemination of information regarding benefits. These results are particularly interesting since they are consistent with predictions of income maximization, i.e., award uncertainty increases dispute probability.

Research has also found that other fairness dimensions are related to dispute probability. Although unable to find a direct link between procedural justice and the decision to dispute a claim, Roberts and Young (1997) found that fairness perceptions affected the claimant's return-to-work decision, which, in turn, influenced the dispute decision. Specifically, they found that interactional fairness—that is, the quality of interactions that the claimant had with professionals in the course of the claims process—had the greatest impact on the return-to-work decision. More generally, Mitchell, Zhu, and Lee (1995) found that the likelihood that claimants would hire an attorney was negatively related to both the helpfulness of the employer and the claimant's satisfaction with the carrier.

Procedural Justice and Formal Appeals

When a claim is contested, it is likely that claimants will shift their attention to the formal adjudication process and will evaluate its fairness to determine whether or not to appeal the hearing or trial outcome. A process perceived as fair confers legitimacy on its outcomes, which, in turn, induces compliance (Tyler 1990).[17] Thus a procedurally fair process should reduce utilization of the appeals process. Lind and his associates (Lind and Tyler 1988; Lind et al. 1993) examined litigants' reactions to corporate arbitration awards and subsequent decisions to challenge those awards in court. Their results suggest that the decision to accept or reject the arbitrator's judgment was related to the evaluation of procedural justice and that procedural justice concerns mediated the litigant's perception of the outcome.

Studies examining fairness perceptions for various dispute mechanisms typically distinguish between process control and outcome control (Lind and Tyler 1988). For example, mediation may offer participants outcome control since they do not have to accept the neutral's recommendations, but not process control. In contrast, arbitration offers some process control but little outcome control since participants select the information they wish to present, but the arbitrator's decision is binding. In a study of miners' grievances that had been resolved either through mediation or arbitration, Shapiro and Brett (1993) found that mediation was seen as a procedurally fairer process than arbitration. They also found that mediation was perceived to offer both more process and more outcome control. Actual opportunity to influence the outcome affected the miners' fairness perceptions for both processes, but only when they lost the dispute or reached a settlement after a significant compromise.

A common complaint by injured workers is that it is difficult to collect information about the process, giving rise to a feeling of helplessness (Roberts and Gleason 1994). For those dissatisfied with their treatment during the claims process or who lose at the mediation or hearing level, this lack of clarity may prompt them to formally dispute or appeal a claim decision. Shapiro and Brett's results also suggest that mediation may increase the participants' overall sense of the fairness of the compensation program's adjudicative processes.

Specific Issues

Thus far we have explored two different approaches to the topic of disputes and dispute resolution in the context of disability insurance. We now turn our attention to some specific issues of particular concern to policymakers: (1) the extent of attorney involvement in the claim process, (2) methods for evaluating the extent of permanent partial disability, and (3) the use of negotiated settlements as a means for resolving compensation disputes.

Role of Attorneys in the Appeal Process

While procedures utilized by compensation programs are designed to limit the need for representation, legal counsel is typically considered essential in contested cases. Legal fees can substantially reduce claimant benefits since they generally are paid by the claimant; however, as previously indicated, without representation, claimants are at a substantial disadvantage. Compensation programs use a variety of mechanisms to provide adequate representation without significantly reducing benefits. Most state programs limit attorney fees; however, there is a danger that these limitations will reduce the supply of competent attorneys willing to represent injured workers. Some jurisdictions subsidize representation by offering free legal services to injured workers, while others require the employer or insurer to pay claimant legal fees. However, policymakers have become increasingly alarmed about growing litigiousness in compensation programs, which some believe is directly related to more extensive involvement by claimant attorneys.[18]

From an income maximization perspective, attorneys increase transaction costs but potentially improve the accuracy of decision making (and consequently reduce the costs of judicial error) by ensuring that adjudicators are aware of information that otherwise would have been ignored. Extrapolating from the procedural justice literature, attorney involvement should increase worker perception that the claims process is fair by providing information about and guiding the claimant through that process.

Conventional wisdom assumes that the primary effect of legal representation is to raise claimant benefits and, therefore, compensation costs. However, attorneys are unlikely to have interests identical to those of their clients, and the relationship is subject to principal-agent problems of hidden information and hidden action. Among other things, claimants are likely to rely on lawyers for information concerning the value of the claim as well as the probability of prevailing in court. In addition, claimants are typically unaware of the attorney's actions on his or her behalf. While contingent fees are designed to align attorney and claimant interests, Thomason (1991) has shown that this fee arrangement is not effective where, as seems likely, there are fixed costs associated with adjudication. Principal-agent problems are exacerbated where the state limits attorney fees.

Several studies have found a positive relationship between legal representation and various measures of benefit utilization. Butler and Worrall (1985) found that claimants represented by attorneys experienced longer spells of temporary total disability benefits, while Worrall et al. (1993) found that the legal representation was positively associated with the probability of permanent disability. Using a sample of Wisconsin claims, Boden (1988) found that the probability that an injured worker would receive permanent disability benefits based on lost-wage-earning capacity (as opposed to less generous benefits based on functional impairment) is greater for claimants represented by legal counsel than otherwise. However, due to endogeneity problems between injury severity and the demand for or supply of representation, it is difficult to draw conclusions concerning the impact of legal representation on the basis of any of these studies.

Using a large sample of permanent partial disability claims from New York, Thomason (1991) found that injured workers who retained legal representation were more likely to accept a lump-sum settlement in exchange for an agreement to release the claimant from further liability.[19] In addition, the size of the lump-sum settlement was less for those represented by an attorney, although formally adjudicated awards were higher. He found that the expected value to a worker of legal counsel is -$5,847. This was due to the increased probability of receiving a lump-sum settlement if a lawyer is retained and the smaller lump-sum settlement received, on average, by those who are represented by a lawyer.

Durbin and Helvacian (1996) hypothesize that attorneys perform two functions for claimants: (1) they provide information and navigational services designed to guide claimants through the claims process and (2) they provide negotiating skills to influence the value of settlement. To examine this hypothesis, they estimate equations predicting total benefits paid to claimants and total costs, defined as the sum of claimant benefits and legal fees, using three samples of "high cost" PPD claims from fifteen states: a sample of sprains and strains claims, a sample of fractures, and a combined sample. They employed a two-stage estimation procedure in which equations predicting the probability of attorney involvement and the probability of a lump-sum settlement were estimated in the first stage.[20] Predicted probabilities were then included in the second stage estimation of costs and benefits.

They found that after controlling for the probability of a lump-sum settlement, attorney representation was positively and significantly related to total costs for all three samples; however, the relationship between representation and benefits was only significant for the total and the sprains/strains sample. They interpreted this relationship as indicating that attorneys provide both navigational and negotiating services for soft-tissue injuries but only provide navigational services for fractures.

Permanent Partial Disability Evaluation

Most compensation disputes involve conflict over the extent or existence of permanent disability. These questions call upon a medical judgment and are difficult—perhaps impossible—questions to answer definitively. There is substantial variation among workers' compensation programs with respect to methods used to evaluate PPD. In a few states, functional impairment is the sole basis for PPD compensation—a simple formula is used to translate the claimant's physical impairment rating into a specific award—while others use additional factors, such as the claimant's age, education, and occupation, to modify the functional impairment rating.[21] In still others, the PPD award is based on the claimant's actual wage loss—the difference between pre- and post-injury wages, although functional impairment is used to determine the award in those instances where the claimant is unemployed at the time that the award is determined.[22]

Evidence suggests that factors other than those contemplated by the statutory language influence the PPD award. For example, Durbin and Kish (1998) found that the impairment rating was only one of several variables that systematically influence final disability ratings and that there was less than a one-to-one relationship between impairment and final ratings. Among other things, weekly benefits were negatively related to the final rating, a result that the authors interpret as evidence that adjudicators "redistribute" income to "poorer" workers.[23] In addition, claimants represented by attorneys received higher ratings than claimants who were not, after controlling for the treating physician's impairment rating.

Many jurisdictions use an adversarial process: the PPD rating is based on evidence adduced by the parties. This typically results in a phenomenon known as "dueling doctors": each party solicits expert medical testimony from a sympathetic physician who supports that party's position vis-à-vis the extent of worker's disability. Some question this approach, arguing that medical testimony from "hired guns" does not significantly improve the quality of decisions, while incurring significant costs. For this reason, several jurisdictions employ independent medical examiners who are responsible for the determination of the extent of disability.

The "dueling doctor" phenomenon raises questions concerning the impact of physician ratings on adjudicator decisions. Boden (1992) used a sample of PPD claims from Maryland to investigate whether adjudicators "split-the-difference" when evaluating disability on the basis of ratings supplied by claimant and insurer/employer physicians. He estimated regression equations predicting final disability ratings as a function of the claimant and employer physician ratings as well as a number of control variables, including measures of injury severity.

Boden finds evidence consistent with "split-the-difference" behavior. Only claimant and employer physician ratings influenced the final rating. In addition, as judged by the coefficient estimates for these two variables—which were approximately equal to 0.5—adjudicators gave equal weight to both. Boden draws two conclusions. First, "splitting-the-difference" provides claimants with incentives to seek legal representation, as attorneys can identify physicians who will provide the claimant with a generous disability rating. Second, "splitting-the-difference" discourages voluntary resolution of disputes through a negotiated settlement.

Comparing outcomes of dispute resolution processes in states with high and low rates of litigation, Boden and Victor (1994) found certain institutional features distinguished litigious and nonlitigious systems.[24] Specifically, in nonlitigious systems (1) written guidelines were used for the evaluation of PPD that allow the parties to know with reasonable certainty the size of the award; (2) the use of nonpartisan experts was encouraged (as opposed to "dueling doctors") in the evaluation process; (3) adjudicators were not allowed to split the difference between adversarial positions and encouraged the voluntary resolution of disputes;[25]

and (4) the workers' compensation agency ensured that benefits were paid by insurers in a timely manner by monitoring insurer behavior and penalizing noncompliance and that workers understood what they could expect.

These results are consistent with both the procedural justice and income maximization perspectives. The procedural fairness literature suggests that a process whereby individual decision makers set their own biases aside and objectively assess the information will be perceived as fairer than a partisan exchange where agents present information consistent with the positions of the parties they represent. And where decisions are seen as generated by a fair process, the parties are more likely to abide by those decisions and less likely to appeal. Similarly, since some of these procedural mechanisms (written guidelines and nonpartisan experts) reduce uncertainty with respect to the eventual award, the income maximization model predicts that the parties are more likely to settle and less likely to adjudicate a dispute.

Compromise and Release Agreements

One method used to determine PPD awards is the "compromise and release" (C&R) agreement. C&Rs are negotiated agreements between claimants and insurers whereby claimants accept a lump sum and, in exchange, release the employer from further liability with respect to the claim. The National Commission on State Workmen's Compensation Laws cited C&Rs as "one of the most controversial aspects of the workmen's compensation program in many states" (National Commission 1972). Proponents argue that C&Rs offer a procedure to resolve disputes when there are legitimate doubts regarding the compensability of the claim and eliminate the costs of resolving the dispute through an adversarial process. In addition, a lump-sum payment avoids the administrative costs associated with indefinite future payments. Opponents fear that C&Rs will seriously undercompensate injured workers who lack bargaining power and who are otherwise financially vulnerable to insurer manipulation. Further, workers have no recourse for additional compensation if their physical condition deteriorates in the future as a direct result of the injury. For the latter reasons, a few jurisdictions either prohibit or limit the use of compromise and release agreements.

Using a sample of New York PPDs, Thomason and Burton (1993) estimated the probability of settlement as well as the size of the award for both negotiated and adjudicated claims. They found that claimants who accept compromise and release agreements receive substantially less than the amount they would have received through adjudication. They estimated an implicit discount rate of approximately 25% is required to equate the value of the future stream of benefits from an adjudicated claim with a lump-sum C&R. While there is no good standard to measure whether such a discount rate is "unjust," these results suggest that insurers who are likely to have lower discount rates than claimants can save substantial costs by pursuing C&Rs.

Thomason and Burton attributed these results to the behavior of two other actors in the claims process: claimant attorneys and insurers. As noted, attorneys have an interest in settling rather than adjudicating claims, and in fact, the evidence suggests that claimants represented by attorneys are more likely to settle and for a lesser amount than claimants without representation. Insurers also have an incentive to settle claims as C&Rs transform an uncertain benefit stream into a certain lump-sum payment. In fact, they find evidence that settlement probability is positively related to the extent of claims management activity by the insurer.

These results suggest that public policy initiatives to encourage the voluntary resolution of disputes, as recommended by Boden and Victor, be approached with caution. In a final offer selection procedure, risk-averse claimants are likely to substantially discount proposed settlements. Among other things, this will result in inequitable awards. For example, Thomason and Burton (1993) found that female claimants and claimants with less seniority were more likely to settle claims and for lesser amounts than male or more senior employees.

Conclusions

Disputes are an unavoidable byproduct of disability insurance programs. Significantly more than other social insurance programs, benefit eligibility is based on criteria that are often vague and equivocal. There are reasons to believe that the design of dispute resolution procedures has significant social welfare implications. Despite its centrality to the effective functioning of disability insurance programs, the issue of disputes and dispute resolution procedures in disability insurance remains a relatively underresearched topic. Very little is known about the optimal design of dispute procedures.

In this chapter we have examined two approaches to the problem of disputes and dispute resolution. The first suggests that parties will respond to economic incentives presented by the institutional framework of dispute resolution. To the extent that those incentives are at odds with social objectives, utilization of dispute resolution procedures will result in suboptimal social welfare. This approach also suggests that the design of dispute resolution procedures can also have important equity implications. The second recognizes that the parties—and, in particular, claimants—are concerned with and therefore affected by the process as well as the outcomes of dispute resolution. Importantly, this research implies that perceptions of equity and fairness have important implications for systemic efficiency. In other words, inequities are not only a matter of concern in and of themselves but also for their effects on social welfare.

Both approaches shed some light on the public policy debate surrounding the appropriate design of dispute resolution processes. In the current climate of fiscal stringency, policymakers have become increasingly concerned with the costs of extensive litigation in disability insurance programs. Recent reform proposals have sought to lower transaction costs by eliminating adversarial processes—such as the substitution of independent medical examiners for "dueling doctors—or by eliminating or streamlining appeal procedures, including alternative dispute resolution procedures like final offer selection arbitration. However, theory and research reviewed in this chapter suggest that a reduction in the quantum of due process could result in a greater probability of judicial error. Consequently, these reforms could have the perverse effect of increasing systemic costs and reducing social welfare.

The equity implications of these proposals are also an important consideration. Research indicates that within the context of the workers' compensation program, a power imbalance between claimants and employers can result in awards that are substantially less than the compensation intended by legislation. (In this context, it must be remembered that this legislation is itself the product of a compromise in which injured workers accepted limited benefits in return for a guaranteed right to compensation.) Other research implies that claimants are differentially treated based on their access to legal resources. Reforms that limit claimant litigation may also exacerbate inequities, adversely affecting more vulnerable claimants. For example, a final offer selection procedure could lead lower-income claimants (who may be more risk averse) to propose final offers that are substantially less than the expected adjudicated award. And, as indicated, the perception of fairness (or a lack thereof) can itself have an impact on efficiency.

Many important questions remain unanswered. While the procedural justice literature indicates that fairness perceptions can affect dispute behavior in important ways, there is little research examining the perceptions of compensation claimants. With few exceptions, there is little research on the efficacy of specific institutional features: Should rules of evidence be strictly enforced? Should there be one, two, or three steps in the appeals process? Should disability programs subsidize legal representation for claims? The answers to these and other questions await further research.

Endnotes

[1] As Speiler and Burton (this volume) point out, in recent years many states have begun to limit eligibility or compensation for these conditions.

[2] See Cooter and Rubinfield (1989) for an overview.

[3] There are legal tests for determining which injuries and diseases are work-related. These are examined by Speiler and Burton in this volume.

[4] Indeed, employers frequently assist workers who are applying for DI benefits.

[5] This is analogous to the distinction between myopic and panoramic efficiency made by Berkowitz and Burton (1987:27).

[6] More rigorous (and more general) discussion of these issues may be found in Kaplow (1994) and Kaplow and Shavell (1995; 1996).

[7] In the following discussion, the "event" is a workplace injury. However, the model would apply equally well where the "event" is the diagnosis of a disease condition that is potentially occupationally related or the onset of permanent and total disability whose origin was personal rather than work-related.

[8] Although workers' compensation claims are typically administered by insurance adjusters, injured workers tend to interpret how well or badly they have been treated as emanating from their employer's concern or lack of concern for their well-being (Roberts and Gleason 1994).

[9] Wages may be used as a proxy for the claimant's opportunity cost, but this variable is confounded with award size since it is directly related to the weekly benefit payment. Since weekly benefits and wages are highly correlated, it is often not feasible to include both in regression equations due to problems with multicollinearity.

[10] Her regression equation also included a dummy indicating whether the claimant was hospitalized. The hospitalization coefficient, although not significantly different from zero in an equation including the delay measure, was positive and significant when the delay variable was excluded. She interprets this pattern as suggesting that "it is the uncertainty about future benefits, rather than future health resulting from a severe injury, that increases the probability of contesting a claim" (Roberts 1992:259).

[11] In both studies, award variability was measured by first categorizing injuries by type of injury—defined by the body part injured and the nature of the injury (e.g., fracture, burn, etc.)—and then estimating the variability of PPD awards given to injuries of the same type.

[12] Policymakers in these three provinces (Quebec, Ontario, and Nova Scotia) also hoped to facilitate the claimant's rehabilitation and return to productive employment.

[13] However, smaller firms are more likely to be covered by non-experience-rated workers' compensation insurance policies, and the carriers will have an incentive to dispute workers' claims. This will mitigate the hypothesized large firm effect on dispute likelihood.

[14] "Privative clauses" contained in Canadian statutory language authorizing compensation programs severely limit the right of appeal of adverse decisions to the courts. Typically, courts are only permitted to review a compensation claim if there is evidence of a violation of natural justice, bias or fraud, or a lack of jurisdiction by the workers' compensation board.

[15] For a full review of the literature on fairness and compliance, see Tyler (1990).

[16] She used five categories of organizational citizenship: altruism, courtesy, sportsmanship, conscientiousness, and civic virtue. Fairness perception data were collected from employees, while data on organizational citizenship were collected from their supervisors.

[17] In a lab study, Mondak (1993) examined this and a competing hypothesis that institutional legitimacy precedes procedural justice and induces compliance independently of procedural justice perceptions and was unable to support the Tyler hypothesis.

[18] Durbin and Helvacian (1996) estimate that attorney involvement adds approximately $11 billion per year to workers' compensation costs in the U.S., approximately 15% of the total.

[19] His estimating equations included various controls for injury severity.

[20] This two-stage estimation procedure controls for endogeneity problems between injury severity and demand for (or supply of) legal representation.

[21] In some states, these other factors are also quantified and incorporated into a formula determining the PPD award by statute.

[22] The procedural justice literature suggests that consistency is an important structural characteristic of fairness. To the extent that PPD evaluation varies significantly across jurisdictions, workers may perceive the evaluation process as unfair.

[23] Alternatively, higher weekly benefits may lead claimants to pursue marginal claims.

[24] These states were Wisconsin, Maryland, New Jersey, and Oregon.

[25] For example, Wisconsin uses final offer selection to determine the PPD award.

References

Barrett-Howard, E., and T. Tyler. 1986. "Procedural Justice as a Criterion in Allocation Decisions." *Journal of Personality and Social Psychology*, Vol. 50, pp. 296-304.

Berkowitz, Monroe, and John F. Burton, Jr. 1987. *Permanent Disability Benefits in Workers' Compensation*. Kalamazoo, MI: W. E. Upjohn Institute for Employment Research.

Bies, Robert, Christopher Martin, and Joel Brockner. 1993. "Just Laid Off, but Still a 'Good Citizen?' Only If the Process Is Fair." *Employee Responsibilities and Rights Journal*, Vol. 6, no. 3, pp. 227-38.

Boden, Leslie I. 1988. *Reducing Litigation. Evidence from Wisconsin.* Cambridge, MA: Workers' Compensation Research Institute.

_____. 1992. "Dispute Resolution in Workers' Compensation." *Review of Economics and Statistics*, Vol. 43, no. 3, pp. 493-502.

Boden, Leslie I., and Richard Victor. 1994. "Models for Reducing Workers' Compensation Litigation." *Journal of Risk and Insurance*, Vol. 61, no. 3, pp. 458-75.

Borba, Philip S., and David Appel. 1987. "The Propensity of Permanently Disabled Workers to Hire Lawyers." *Industrial and Labor Relations Review*, Vol. 40, no. 3 (April), pp. 418-29.

Brockner, Joel, Mary Konovsky, Rochelle Cooper-Schneider, Robert Folger, Christopher Martin, and Robert Bies. 1994. "Interactive Effects of Procedural Justice and Outcome Negativity on Victims and Survivors of Job Loss." *Academy of Management Journal*, Vol. 37, no. 2 (April), pp. 397-409.

Butler, Richard J., and John D. Worrall. 1985. "Work Injury Compensation and the Duration of Nonwork Spells." *Economic Journal*, Vol. 95, pp. 714-24.

Cooter, Robert, and Daniel Rubinfeld. 1989. "Economic Analysis of Legal Disputes and their Resolution." *Journal of Economic Literature*, Vol. 27, no. 3 (September), pp. 1067-97.

Durbin, David L., and Nurhan M. Helvacian. 1996. "Attorney Involvement in High-Cost Workers' Compensation Claims." Mimeo, NCCI.

Durbin, David L., and Jennifer Kish. 1998. "Factors Affecting Permanent Partial Disability Ratings." *Journal of Risk and Insurance*, Vol. 65, no. 1, pp. 81-99.

Eskew, Don E. 1993. "The Role of Organizational Justice in Organizational Citizenship Behavior." *Employee Responsibilities and Rights Journal*, Vol. 6, no. 3, pp. 185-94.

Falaris, Evangelos M., Charles R. Link, and Michael E. Staten. 1995. *Causes of Litigation in Workers' Compensation Programs.* Kalamazoo, MI: W. E. Upjohn Institute for Employment Research.

Founier, Gary M., and Barbara A. Morgan. 1996. "Litigation in the Florida Workers' Compensation System." Mimeo, Florida State University.

Greenberg, Jerald. 1987. "A Taxonomy of Organizational Justice Theories." *Academy of Management Review*, Vol. 12, no. 1, pp. 9-22.

Hunt, H. Allan. 1982. *Workers' Compensation in Michigan: A Closed Case Survey.* Kalamazoo, MI: W. E. Upjohn Institute for Employment Research.

Hyatt, Douglas E., and Boris Kralj. 1995. "The Impact of Workers' Compensation Experience Rating on Employer Appeals Activity." *Industrial Relations*, Vol. 34, no. 1 (January), pp. 95-106.

_____. 1996. "The Impact of Representation (and Other Factors) on the Outcomes of Employee-initiated Workers' Compensation Appeals." Mimeo, Center for Industrial Relations, University of Toronto.

Kaplow, Louis. 1994. "The Value of Accuracy in Adjudication: An Economic Analysis." *Journal of Legal Studies*, Vol. 23, pp. 307-401.

Kaplow, Louis, and Steven Shavell. 1995. "Accuracy in the Determination of Liability." *Journal of Law and Economics*, Vol. 37, pp. 1-15.

_____. 1996. "Accuracy in the Assessment of Damages." *Journal of Law and Economics*, Vol. 39, pp. 191-210.

Korsgaard, M. Audrey, and Loriann Roberson. 1995. "Procedural Justice in Performance Evaluation." *Journal of Management*, Vol. 21, no. 4, pp. 657-69.

Lind, E. Allen, Carol Kulik, Maureen Ambrose, and Maria De Vera Park. 1993. "Individual and Corporate Dispute Resolution: Using Procedural Fairness as a Decision Heuristic." *Administrative Science Quarterly*, Vol. 38, no. 2 (June), pp. 224-51.

Lind, E. Allen, and Tom Tyler. 1988. *The Social Psychology of Procedural Justice*. New York: Plenum.

McCombie, Nick. 1984. "Justice for Injured Workers: A Community Responds to Government Reform." *Canadian Community Law Journal*, Vol. 7, pp. 136-73.

Mondak, Jeffery. 1993. "Institutional Legitimacy and Procedural Justice." *Law and Society Review*, Vol. 27, no. 3, pp. 599-608.

Moorman, Robert, B. Niehoff, and Dennis Organ. 1993. "Treating Employees Fairly and Organizational Citizenship Behavior." *Employee Responsibilities and Rights Journal*, Vol. 6, no. 3, pp. 209-25.

National Commission on State Workmen's Compensation Laws. 1972. *The Report of the National Commission on State Workmen's Compensation Laws*. Washington, DC: U.S. Government Printing Office.

Posner, Richard A. 1973. "An Economic Approach to Legal Procedure and Judicial Administration." *Journal of Legal Studies*, Vol. 2, pp. 399-459.

Ray, M. 1986. *Work-related Injury: Workers' Assessments of its Consequences for Work, Family, Mental, and Physical Health*. Pullman, WA: Injured Worker Project, Washington State University.

Roberts, Karen. 1992. "Predicting Disputes in Workers' Compensation." *Journal of Risk and Insurance*, Vol. 59, pp. 252-61.

_____. 1996. "Perceptions of Fairness and the Decision to Dispute in Workers' Compensation." *John Burton's Workers' Compensation Monitor*, Vol. 8, no. 2 (March/April), pp. 4-16.

Roberts, Karen, and Sandra Gleason. 1994. "Procedural Justice in the Workers' Compensation Claims Process." In J. Rojot and H. Wheeler, eds., *Employee Rights and Industrial Justice*. Deventer, The Netherlands: Kluwer, pp. 77-88.

Roberts, Karen, and Willard Young. 1997. "Procedural Fairness, Return to Work, and the Decision to Dispute in Workers' Compensation." *Employee Responsibilities and Rights Journal*, Vol. 10, no. 3 (September), pp. 193-213.

Shapiro, D., and Jeanne Brett. 1993. "Comparing Three Processes Underlying Judgments of Procedural Justice: A Field Study of Mediation and Arbitration." *Journal of Personality and Social Psychology*, Vol. 65, pp. 1167-77.

Sum, Juliann. 1996. "Navigating the California Workers' Compensation System: The Injured Worker's Experience." Prepared for the Commission on Health and Safety and Workers' Compensation. Labor Occupational Health Program, University of California at Berkeley.

Thomason, Terry. 1991. "Are Attorneys Paid What They're Worth: Contingent Fees and the Settlement Process." *Journal of Legal Studies*, Vol. 20, pp. 187-223.

_____. 1994. "Correlates of Workers' Compensation Claims Adjustment." *Journal of Risk and Insurance*, Vol. 61 (March), pp. 59-77.

Thomason, Terry, and John F. Burton, Jr. 1993. "The Economics of Workers' Compensation in the United States: Private Insurance and the Administration of Compensation Claims." *Journal of Labor Economics*, Vol. 11, pp. S1-S37.

Tyler, Tom. 1989. "The Psychology of Procedural Justice: A Test of the Group-Value Model." *Journal of Personality and Social Psychology*, Vol. 57, no. 5, pp. 830-38.

_____. 1990. *Why People Obey the Law*. New Haven, CT: Yale University Press.

Wazeter, David. 1991. *The Determinants and Consequences of Teacher Salary Schedules*. Unpublished doctoral dissertation, Cornell University.

Weiler, Paul C. 1980. *Reshaping Workers' Compensation for Ontario*. Toronto, ON: Ontario Ministry of Labor.

Worrall, John D., David Durbin, David Appel, and Richard J. Butler. 1993. "The Transition from Temporary Total to Permanent Partial Disability: A Longitudinal Analysis." In David Durbin and Phillip S. Borba, eds., *Workers' Compensation Insurance: Claim Costs, Prices and Regulation*. Boston: Kluwer Academic Publishers.

Youngblood, S., L. Trevino, and M. Favia. 1992. "Reactions to Unjust Dismissal and Third-Party Dispute Resolution: A Justice Framework." *Employee Responsibilities and Rights Journal*, Vol. 5, pp. 283-307.

CHAPTER 11

Convergence: A Comparison of European and United States Disability Policy

LEO J.M. AARTS
Leiden University

RICHARD V. BURKHAUSER
Syracuse University

PHILIP R. DE JONG
Leiden University

> Far too many people rely on social benefits, while too few citizens are at work contributing to economic growth and the financing of social welfare expenditures. The benefit rules and the high levels of taxation required to finance the system affect human motivation in a negative direction and may increase the propensity to work unofficially in the "black economy." (Ministry of Finance 1994:7)

Few people who listened to the debate surrounding the passage of the 1996 welfare reforms in the United States, which were intended to "end welfare as we know it," will be surprised by the language in the preceding quote. What may be more surprising is that it comes from a blue ribbon report to the Swedish Ministry of Finance entitled "Social Security in Sweden—How to Reform the System." Sweden, like most other Western European nations in the 1990s, elected legislative majorities pledged to fundamentally reevaluate their traditional social welfare policies. The loss of productivity and the growing tax burden that are by-products of large social welfare systems are gradually eroding their popular support in European countries. While social equity is still a major goal of public policy in these countries, the real social costs of achieving this goal are now so high that even traditional supporters of the welfare state have begun to call for reform.

Countries like Sweden and the Netherlands, which were once looked upon as models of the modern democratic welfare state, now acknowledge that more of the same is no longer possible. Germany, struggling to economically integrate its eastern states which were politically integrated in 1990, has also joined the countries of Europe that are restructuring their social welfare systems. All three countries have experienced unprecedented postwar levels of transfer dependency and slow growth in the 1990s. In addition, all three are attempting to come to terms with the competitive pressures of a single European market and the budget deficit restrictions that European Union members must meet to satisfy the requirements for entry into the Single Currency Union in 1999.

One of the requirements of the Maastricht Treaty of 1992 is especially important to social welfare policy: to qualify for entry into the Single Currency Union a country must have a public deficit of less than 3% of its GDP, and the accounting frame includes social insurance funds. In Germany, large deficits in their health care and sick pay schemes have been difficult to reduce. Post-World War II high unemployment rates make the government hesitant to increase payroll taxes, and government efforts to cut entitlements have been blocked by nationwide strikes. Decisions on major reforms in Germany must therefore wait until the next round of national elections in 1998. In Sweden, there are no deficits but there are calls for tax reduction and benefit cuts as a mechanism for reducing the post-World War II high unemployment rates that Sweden has experienced over the 1990s. As is the case in Germany, political stalemate has prevented major reforms to date and is threatening to delay Sweden's entry into the Single Currency Union. In contrast, the Netherlands, once considered the most generous welfare state in Europe, has after several false starts initiated major welfare reforms, including a major overhaul of its disability system. Hence its actions since 1992 may well make the Netherlands the harbinger of future European policy changes.

To the social, economic, and fiscal pressures that are common to Sweden, the Netherlands, Germany, and the U.S. must be added the less immediate but very real pressure of aging populations. The aging baby boomers in each of these countries add a major long-term dimension to the growing public debate on the need to make existing social welfare systems more sustainable. In each country, changes in disability policy and the programs that it encompasses have been at the center of this debate.

In this chapter we put the disability program in the broader context of social policy reform. We first provide measures of the relative importance of disability policy in the Netherlands, Sweden, and Germany compared to the U.S., and of each country's reliance on transfer programs to support people with disabilities who do not work relative to work-based programs aimed at keeping people with disabilities employed. We then compare policies and experiences in the U.S. with those in these three European countries to show how different disability insurance systems operate and accommodate external economic pressures. In particular, we propose a broader context from which to view disability policy and the current wave of reforms that appear to be leading to a convergence of disability policies between the U.S. and the Netherlands—two countries that have traditionally been at the opposite extremes across the distribution of welfare state intervention and generosity levels.

A Cross-National Comparison of Disability Transfer Populations

Table 1, derived from Aarts, Burkhauser, and De Jong (1996), suggests that economic and political forces play an important role in determining the relative size of the disability transfer population and how it changes over time. This table shows the ratio of disability transfer recipients per thousand workers by age over the past quarter century in the U.S., the Netherlands, Sweden, and Germany.[1] All four countries have experienced growth in this ratio since 1970, but the initial starting points and the patterns of growth are different, and these cross-national differences cannot be explained by differences in underlying health conditions in the four countries.[2]

In the U.S., the 52% increase in the relative disability transfer rolls in the 1970s was the result of both substantial increases in real social security benefits and the easing of eligibility standards for older workers. It was among those aged 45 and over that the ratio grew most rapidly (see Burkhauser and Haveman [1982] for a discussion of this period of disability policy history). Growth in the U.S. was only exceeded by that in the Netherlands, which experienced explosive growth—151%—in its overall transfer ratio during the decade.

In the U.S., the political responses to rapid program growth were both the introduction of a stricter set of eligibility criteria and more vigorous enforcement of program rules. The political backlash caused by the heavy-handed enforcement of these new rules led to a substantial relaxation in program rules in the mid-1980s. A strong economy over

TABLE 1

Disability Transfer Recipients Per Thousand Workers by Age, in Four OECD Countries, 1970 to 1995

Age	1970	1975	1980	Growth Change 1970-1980 (percent)	1985	1990	Growth Change 1980-1990 (percent)	1995	Growth Change 1990-1995 (percent)
Aged 15 to 64 Years									
United States	27	42	41	52	41	43	5	64	49
The Netherlands	55	84	138	151	142	152	10	142	-7
Sweden	49	67	68	39	74	78	15	106	36
Germany[a]	51	54	59	16	72	55	-7	47	-15
Aged 15 to 44									
United States	11	17	16	45	20	23	44	39	70
The Netherlands	17	32	57	235	58	62	9	57	-8
Sweden	18	20	19	6	20	21	11	32	52
Germany[a]	7	6	7	0	8	5	-29	6	20
Aged 45 to 59									
United States	33	68	83	151	71	72	-13	103	43
The Netherlands	113	179	294	160	305	339	15	271	-20
Sweden	66	95	99	50	108	116	17	151	30
Germany[a]	75	64	84	12	103	75	-11	87	16
Aged 60 to 64									
United States	154	265	285	85	254	250	-12	314	26
The Netherlands	299	437	1,033	245	1,283	1,987	92	1,872	-6
Sweden	229	382	382	67	512	577	51	716	24
Germany[a]	419	688	1,348	222	1,291	1,109	-18	890	-20

[a] German data refer to the population in the western states of the Federal Republic of Germany.

Source: Derived and updated from Aarts, Burkhauser, and De Jong (1996), Table 1.1.

the rest of the decade postponed the inevitable growth in the rolls due to these changes, so that by 1990 the relative disability transfer population was only slightly greater than it had been at the start of the decade. However, the pattern of program growth in the U.S. over the 1980s was much different than in the 1970s and signaled an important change in the characteristics of the new disability transfer population.

In the 1970s the U.S. joined the Netherlands, Sweden, and Germany in using its disability transfer system to provide early retirement benefits for older workers with health conditions that affected their ability to work but who were not yet old enough to be eligible for benefits through the traditional social security retirement system. The growth in the disability transfer rolls in Germany and Sweden during the 1970s was almost completely confined to workers aged 45 and over. Only in the Netherlands were workers under the age of 45 a significant component of the disability transfer population. The use of disability transfers as a bridge to early retirement in the U.S. is consistent with the creation of Social Security Disability Insurance (SSDI) in the 1950s as a program limited to older workers.

Retrenchment in U.S. disability policy in the early part of the 1980s together with a strong economy in the remainder of the 1980s led to a mere 5% increase in the relative disability transfer population during the decade. Only Germany, which experienced a decline in its disability transfer ratio, had smaller growth among the four countries shown in Table 1. But this small increase in overall growth in the U.S. conceals a 44% increase in the relative disability population aged 15 through 44, an increase that far exceeded that of younger workers in the other countries. This increase put the U.S. ahead of Sweden and Germany in the use of disability transfer recipients per worker over this younger age range, even though the U.S. was well below these two countries in overall disability transfer prevalence rates.

Propelled by the economic recession of the early 1990s in the U.S., the relative disability transfer population aged 15 to 44 rose by 70% between 1990 and 1995, and the overall relative disability transfer ratio rose by 49%. This is in sharp contrast to what was happening in the Netherlands and Germany. Both countries experienced declines in their ratio of transfer recipients per worker. Only in Sweden did the ratio rise, but at a lower rate than in the U.S. Hence by 1995, not only did the overall ratio of transfer recipients per worker in the U.S. exceed that of Germany, but for persons aged 15 to 44 the use of disability transfers in the U.S. was now higher than in either Sweden or Germany. Only the

Netherlands had a higher ratio of disability transfer recipients per worker among the younger population, but unlike the U.S., this ratio fell in the Netherlands over the first five years of the 1990s. Table 1 suggests that the 1990s will be seen as a period of convergence in the prevalence of disability transfers as the two prototype welfare states—Sweden and the Netherlands—struggle to reduce their disability transfer populations and the U.S. substantially adds to its disability transfer population. Only Germany appears to have continued to follow disability policies that make its overall disability transfer recipient to worker ratio invariant to cyclical and secular influences over the past twenty-five years.

Three changes in disability policy rules prior to the 1990s recession contributed to the upsurge in the disability transfer population in the U.S. First, the definition of mental impairment necessary to receive benefits was loosened. Second the requirement that the federal government show proof of medical improvements in a beneficiary's condition before benefits could be terminated were put into place in the mid-1980s. Finally, Supplementary Security Income (SSI)—a means-tested welfare program for the aged or those with disabilities—eligibility criteria for children were loosened as a result of the 1990 Supreme Court decision in *Sullivan v. Zebley*.

These administrative and court-enforced changes in U.S. Social Security regulations have dramatically altered the disability transfer system's population and its traditional role as a bridge to early retirement benefits for older workers. The massive increase in the numbers of SSI-children program beneficiaries and the sharp increase in the number of younger beneficiaries on both SSI and SSDI have increasingly moved the U.S. toward the forefront of countries using disability transfers to provide income support to younger people. In 1996 Congress initiated reforms in disability policy that attempted to reduce the number of children who would be eligible for SSI under *Zebley*. In 1997 the Social Security Administration developed a set of guidelines for eligibility based on these reforms, but it is too soon to tell what impact these reforms will have on future program growth.

Table 2 provides an alternative aggregate measure of the importance of government disability policy. It shows the share of Gross Domestic Product (GDP) directly spent on pay-as-you-go disability transfer and work-based programs by governments in the U.S., the Netherlands, Sweden, and Germany. In 1991 the share of GDP spent on people with disabilities through the public sector in the U.S. was small compared to Sweden, Germany, or the Netherlands. In Sweden and the Netherlands public expenditures on work-related and cash transfer programs for people with disabilities were 4.08% and 5.24% of GDP, respectively. In Germany, 2.22% of GDP was spent on such programs, while in the U.S. it was less than 1%.

TABLE 2

Public Expenditures on Work-related Programs and Cash Transfers for People with Disabilities, as a Percentage of GDP, 1991[a]

	Total	Vocational Rehabili- tation	Direct Job Subsidies	Transfer Benefits	Work-related Expenditures as a Share of Total Disability Expenditures
United States	0.75	0.05	(c)	0.7	6.7
The Netherlands	5.24	(c)	0.64	4.6	12.2
Sweden	4.08	0.10	0.68	3.3	19.1
Germany[b]	2.22	0.13	0.09	2.0	9.9

[a] Expenditures on public or private health care-related expenses, private insurance disability payments or rehabilitation. The efficiency costs of government intervention into the labor market in the form of quotas or mandated accommodation are not included in these figures.
[b] German data refer to the western states of Germany.
[c] Less than 0.01 percent.
Source: OECD (1992); OECD (1993), Tweede Kamer der Staten-Generaal (1994), authors' calculations.

But while a greater share of GDP was spent on both work and transfer programs in these European countries than in the U.S., the U.S. spent the largest share of its total program budget on transfers and, hence, the smallest share on vocational rehabilitation or direct job subsidies. The increasing upsurge in disability transfer spending in the U.S. since 1991 is likely to make this emphasis on transfers even more pronounced in the remainder of the 1990s.

Placing Disability Programs within the Broader Social Welfare System

To understand how disability policy varies across the countries we have been describing, it is useful to look at these policies in a broader context. Disability programs are only one part of a social welfare system that attempts to ameliorate the consequences of a separation from the labor market over a worker's lifetime for economic as well as health reasons. When such a separation is imminent, these programs can influence the response of both employers and workers.

Figure 1 illustrates various government policies to ameliorate job loss caused by economic or health factors as a series of paths that workers may take as they move from full-time work to normal retirement. For workers who remain on the job over their work life, the path to retirement is straightforward. Not until they reach early retirement age do they have to choose between retirement and continued work. But for a significant number of workers, job separation before retirement is a reality which social welfare policy must anticipate.

To put Figure 1 into focus, it is useful to recognize that the typical working-age person with a disability was able-bodied during most of his or her lifetime. For instance, for the U.S., Burkhauser and Daly (1996) find that in 1992, 70% of men and women who reported having a health-related work impairment said it started during their work life. Hence the social welfare policy of the country may influence whether such workers remain in the labor force or shift to some form of transfer program. Figure 1 illustrates five paths that workers may take following the onset of a health-related impairment.

The *early retirement path* (a) encompasses public and private provisions that allow workers to retire before traditional retirement ages. Since the end of the 1970s these provisions have become immensely popular and, together with disability insurance, account for a substantial part of the decrease in male labor force participation at older ages reported in Table 3. In 1970 the male labor force participation rates in all four countries were approximately the same, with four out of five men aged 55 to 64 in the labor force. By 1995 men in all four countries had experienced dramatic drops in work at these ages. While the Netherlands and Germany experienced the greatest declines—only around one-half of men aged 55 to 64 were in the labor force in 1995 in these two countries—both Sweden and the U.S. also experienced substantial declines. When early retirement schemes are actuarially fair, they are neutral with respect to the financial inducement to retire. However, in general such schemes are not neutral and instead encourage workers to retire early. They allow workers with some health conditions to exit from the labor market without going along the formal health path.

The *work path* (b) encompasses public programs that provide or encourage rehabilitation (either publicly or privately provided) to overcome the work limitations caused by a disability. It also includes more direct labor market intervention through the creation of specific government jobs for people with disabilities, subsidies to those who employ such workers or to the workers themselves, job quotas, and job protection

FIGURE 1

Alternative Life Paths Following the Onset of a Health-related Work Limitation

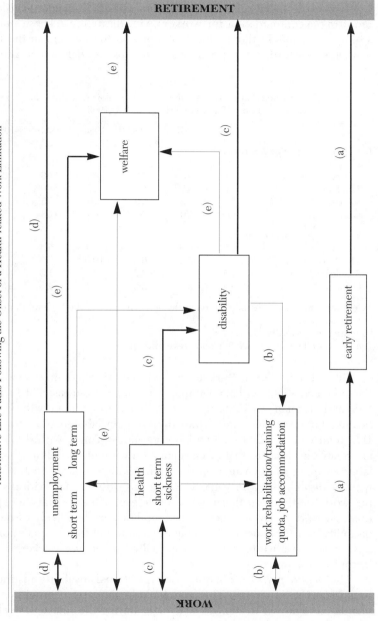

legislation—dismissal rules, etc., or general antidiscrimination legislation requiring accommodation for workers with disabilities. These policies attempt to maintain those with disabilities on the job and in the labor market, either through the carrot of subsidies or the stick of mandates.

TABLE 3

Labor Force Participation Rates and Unemployment Rates in Four OECD Countries, 1970 to 1995

	1970	1975	1980	1985	1990	1995
Labor Force Participation Rates,						
Aged 55 to 64						
United States	81	76	72	68	68	66
The Netherlands	81	72	63	47	46	42
Sweden	85	82	79	76	75	70
Germany[a]	80	70	67	60	58	53[b]
Overall Unemployment Rate						
United States	4.8	8.3	7.0	7.1	5.4	5.6
The Netherlands	1.0	5.2	6.0	10.6	7.5	7.0
Sweden	1.5	1.6	2.0	2.8	1.5	7.6
Germany[a]	0.6	3.6	2.9	7.1	4.8	8.4[b]

[a] German data refer to the population in the western states of the Federal Republic of Germany.
[b] Figure refers to 1994.
Source: OECD Labor Force Statistics, several years.

Table 4, taken from Burkhauser and Daly (forthcoming), compares the labor activity of working-age men with and without disabilities in the U.S. and Germany in 1988. It suggests that German men with disabilities are far better integrated into the German labor market than are U.S. men with disabilities. The labor earnings of men with disabilities are relatively closer to that of German men without disabilities than are labor earnings of such men in the U.S. when compared to U.S. men without disabilities. Unlike the U.S., the majority of men with disabilities work full-time. Furthermore, at each level of work—full-time, part-time, no work—German men with disabilities are less likely to receive disability transfer benefits. The major commitment to work path policies in Germany relative to the U.S., especially for younger workers, is one factor in these outcomes.

The *health path* (c) encompasses traditional disability insurance-based transfer programs. This may include short-term programs that mandate employers to replace lost wages during the first few weeks of

TABLE 4

Labor Force Participation of Working-Age Men with and without
Disabilities in the United States and Germany in 1988[a]

	United States Male Population		German Male Population[b]	
	With Disability	Without Disability	With Disability	Without Disability
Total population				
(thousands)	4,438,294	45,345,115	1,386,739	12,131,683
Percent of population	8.9	91.1	10.3	89.7
Median labor earnings	$13,816	$32,438	36,715 DM	47,424 DM
Labor Force Activity[c]				
Full-Time work	45.6	84.2	58.4	81.4
Receive disability transfers[d]	16.3	2.5	0.7	0.7
Part-Time Work	25.9	13.6	9.5	13.6
Receive disability transfers[d]	31.1	4.4	13.5	1.2
No Work	28.5	2.2	32.1	5.0
Receive disability transfers[d]	73.8	5.8	62.6	8.2
Total	100.0	100.0	100.0	100.0
Receive disability transfers[d]	36.5	2.8	21.8	1.1
N	319	3,431	193	2,023

[a] Population is limited to men aged 25 to 59 who were either household heads or spouses in 1988 and 1989.
[b] German data refer to the population in the western states of the Federal Republic of Germany.
[c] Full-time men work at least 1,820 hours (35 hours per week). Part-time men work between 1 and 1,820 hours.
[d] Men who received disability-related transfers.
Source: 1989 Response-Nonresponse File of the Panel Study of Income Dynamics and the 1993 Syracuse University Public Use File of the German Socio-Economic Panel; and Burkhauser and Daly (forthcoming).

sickness or to directly provide such replacement through short-term social insurance. In all European countries, this would include providing health care at no marginal expense to the worker. After some point, workers are then eligible to move to a long-term disability insurance program, which often requires meeting both health and employment criteria. This path eventually merges with the social security retirement program. As we saw in Table 1, the population on this path varies substantially across countries and over time.

The *unemployment path* (d) encompasses short-term unemployment benefits to replace lost wage earnings due to cyclical economic downturns.

At some point longer-term unemployment insurance is made available, often at a lower replacement rate. Eventually, this also merges with the social security retirement system. As can be seen in Table 3, business cycles influence unemployment rates in all four countries. However, there has been a long-term increase in official unemployment rates in all three European countries relative to the U.S. over the last twenty-five years, with Germany and Sweden experiencing the greatest increases over the last five years. Disentangling exits from a job because of a health condition and exits from a job because of economic forces is in practice a difficult and often controversial task, especially as these exits are influenced by the rules established by a country's social welfare system. Because the unemployment rate is often seen as a marker of a country's economic success, there is also the added problem that government policymakers will use the disability path to reduce the long-term unemployment rolls. (See Aarts, Burkhauser, and de Jong [1992], for evidence of this in the Netherlands relative to other countries.)

The *welfare path* (e) encompasses the set of means-tested programs that serve as a safety net for those workers without jobs who are not eligible for health- or unemployment-based social insurance programs. Welfare programs can be universal, subject only to a means test and/or linked to an inability to work either because of poor health, poor job skills, or child-rearing responsibilities. This track can continue past retirement age for those few individuals who are not eligible for social security retirement benefits. In the U.S., which has no universal means-tested programs, Supplemental Security Income (SSI) provides such a floor for those aged 65 and over and for disabled adults and the families of disabled children. Much of the growth in disability transfers for the U.S. population aged 15-41 (shown in Table 1) comes from this program. In the Netherlands, Sweden, and Germany more universal welfare programs offer alternative sources of income for both adults and children unrelated to their health status.

Choosing among Life Paths

When a health condition begins to affect one's ability to work, both the worker and his or her employer must make important job-related decisions. These decisions may be influenced by the social policies of the country. The worker will consider the relative rewards of continued movement along the work path versus entry onto an alternative path. In like manner, an employer's willingness to accommodate workers will also be influenced by the social policies within which the firm must operate.

In countries where welfare benefits are low or difficult to obtain compared to disability transfers, unemployment benefits are of short duration, and little is available in terms of rehabilitation and job protection, it is likely that the supply of applicants for the health path will be relatively large. This supply of applicants will increase as the replacement rate increases and as the period over which benefits can be received lengthens. In such a country, e.g., the Netherlands and the U.S., increases in applications for benefits put tremendous pressure on the disability system in times of serious economic downturns. Alternatively, when the protection offered by the unemployment path is similar to that offered by the health path, and minimum non-health-related social welfare is available as a universal benefit, as in Germany, much less application pressure is put on the disability gatekeepers during economic downturns. And in Sweden, where health benefits are even more generous than in the Netherlands, application pressure is less severe because all persons suffering a health impairment are required to receive rehabilitation. Following rehabilitation, it is government policy to provide jobs in the public sector if private sector jobs are unavailable. In Germany, not only are the disability benefits lower than in Sweden and the Netherlands, but a combination of mandatory rehabilitation and a quota system also deflect much of the economic-based pressure on the disability system.

We have used Figure 1 as a framework for discussing how the incentive structure inherent in a country's social welfare system influences the supply of disability candidates. But we can also use Figure 1 to describe the "demand" for such candidates. To enter any of the five paths described in Figure 1, it is necessary to satisfy entry requirements. The entry rules for early social security retirement insurance program benefits are usually straightforward. A worker must have worked in covered employment for a given time or have performed other easily measured activities (e.g., attended school, raised children) and must be a given age. Such eligibility criteria are easy to administer, which makes the task of the front-line gatekeepers routine. They simply follow relatively objective criteria with little room for individual interpretation.

Of course, the overall size of the population on the retirement rolls will change if a higher benefit is paid or the age of eligibility is lowered, but gatekeeper discretion will not enter into this change. Gatekeepers will simply follow new criteria. Determining eligibility for the various paths open to those who have a health condition that begins to affect their work but who are below early retirement age is not as clear-cut.

Unlike age, disability is a complex concept that has both health- and work-related components. In a search for easily measured screens for benefits, most long-term disability benefit systems require a waiting period of around one year between the onset of the condition and eligibility. They also require a check of how much the person is actually working. Evidence from either a private physician or a physician employed by the system is then used to determine the seriousness of the health condition with respect to the person's ability to work. While the first two pieces of evidence are easily observable, the third is less so. Doctors can evaluate health conditions as they relate to a norm, but there is no unambiguous way to relate a health condition to ability to work. Hence much of the problem with administrating a disability system is in establishing criteria for eligibility and developing procedures that will ensure consistency in its use. Here, gatekeeper discretion in carrying out established criteria is much greater than it is for retirement.

Access to the work path and the health path may be closely coordinated, as in Germany and Sweden, where a centralized group of gatekeepers determines who is provided with rehabilitation services and who goes directly onto the disability transfer rolls. However, these paths may also be administered in quite independent ways. In the U.S., rehabilitation services are administered by a gatekeeper with little or no connection to those who administer the disability transfer system. And in the Netherlands the emphasis on income protection and the use of the disability insurance program as an exit route from the labor market has discouraged the use of rehabilitation services.

All of these factors affect the way in which front-line disability gatekeepers respond to changes in supply and to the voices of those at higher levels of administrative responsibility who are attempting to control the overall flow of people into the system. In periods of economic downturn, the number of workers who leave their job rises and applications to transfer programs increase. In the U.S. and the Netherlands, two countries with generous disability benefits relative to other alternatives, tremendous pressure has been put on their disability system over the last twenty-five years to provide income for those unemployed workers and their families. That same pressure has been seen in Sweden since 1990. Such pressure may lead to a specific easing of the rules or simply a change in the interpretation of the rules. In this way "demand" may shift to accommodate supply. In Germany such pressures have also led to special disability-related entitlements, but they have been confined to workers aged 60 and above.

A Comparison of Work and Transfer[3]

The disability systems of the U.S., the Netherlands, Sweden, and Germany share common features. Each provides some form of wage replacement for those with short-term or longer-term disabilities that result in lost wage earnings. Each provides a social minimum floor of benefits for persons with disabilities regardless of past earnings. Each has some commitment to integrating people with disabilities into the labor market. But the level of benefits, the eligibility criteria for the programs, the relative share of resources used in these programs, and their administration varies greatly across countries. In Table 5 we summarize the major features of each country's disability system.

Temporary Disability Transfer Programs

With the exception of the U.S., which leaves it to employers to provide "sick pay" to replace lost earnings due to short-term sickness or disability, temporary disability benefits are a standard part of each country's disability transfer system shown in Table 5.[4] While the National Academy of Social Insurance (1996) estimates that about 44% of private sector employees in the U.S. are covered by some type of short-term disability insurance, all workers in the Netherlands, Sweden, and Germany are covered against the risk of wage loss due to temporary sickness through agencies either directly or indirectly under government supervision. These programs typically last up to one year and, for those who require it, are seen as bridges to the longer-term disability insurance program. Sick pay usually covers all health contingencies. The degree of risk sharing varies. In recent years both the Netherlands and Sweden have attempted to reduce program costs by requiring individual firms to bear more of the costs of these programs through experience rating contributions. This has moved them closer to the U.S. system in which private firms bear direct responsibility for such costs.

Work-related Disability Transfer Programs

If a disability is work-related, there is a transition from temporary disability benefits to a work injury program in each country shown in Table 5, with the exception of the Netherlands. Work injury programs were the first form of social insurance in all four countries, but the distinction between work-related and other causes of disability were abolished in the Netherlands disability insurance program in 1967.

Workers' compensation schemes in the U.S. are difficult to summarize since they originated at the state level and continue to vary by state.

TABLE 5

Disability Policies in Four Western Industrial Countries in 1997

	United States	The Netherlands	Sweden	Germany
I. Temporary Disability Transfer Programs				
Benefit level	No government-based program but is part of the fringe benefit package of about 44% of private sector employees	70% of earnings[a]	Day 2-3: 75% of earnings Day 4-14: 90% Day 15-365: 80% Day 366 on: 70%	80% of earnings[a]
Qualifying conditions		Inability to perform current job	Inability to perform current job (short-term), other suitable job (longer term)	Inability to perform current job
Maximum duration		52 weeks	Unlimited	78 weeks
Funding:				
Contributions		Employer	Employer, employee, government	Employer, employee
Risk sharing		Firm[b]	National[c]	Region, industry, or firm
Administration		Private sector (firms and private agencies) under supervision of the National Institute of Social Insurance	National agency under direct government supervision	Nongovernmental agencies run by employees' and employers' representatives under direct government supervision
II. Longer-Term Disability Transfer Programs				
Work Related Programs:				
Benefit level	Varies by state, most commonly 66.7% of last earnings with dollar maximums	No specific program for work-related injuries	70% of last earnings	66.7% of last earnings
Partial benefits	Varies by state, percentage of full pension, corresponding to loss of earnings capacity		Percentage of full pension, corresponding to loss of earning capacity	Percentage of full pension, corresponding to loss of earning capacity

TABLE 5 (*Continued*)

Disability Policies in Four Western Industrial Countries in 1997

	United States	The Netherlands	Sweden	Germany
II. Longer-Term Disability Transfer Programs, cont.				
Waiting period	Varies by state		Flexible	Flexible
Qualifying conditions	Loss of earnings capacity due to work injury or occupational disease		Loss of earning capacity due to work injury or occupational disease of at least 6.7%	Loss of earning capacity due to work injury or occupational disease of at least 20%
Maximum duration	Varies by state and type of impairment		Age 65	Age 65
Funding:				
Contributors	Varies by state, most commonly fully paid by employer		Employer	Employer
Risk sharing	Risk group		National	Risk group
Administration	Varies by state; combinations of state funds, private insurers, and self-insured employers, supervised by state agencies		National agency under direct government supervision	State agencies under direct government supervision
Non-work-related Programs:				
Benefit level	90% of first $437 of average yearly earnings, plus 32% of the next $2,198 of average yearly earnings, plus 15% of each additional dollar of average yearly covered earnings. Benefits increase if worker has dependent children[d]	70% of last earnings during 6 to 72 months depending on age at onset- if older than 33; thereafter, or if younger than 33, 70% of minimum wage plus 1.4% of (earnings-minimum wage) for each year older than 15 (maximum benefit is $27,000 per year)	65% of assessed earnings	General disability: 60% (plus 1.5% times max [55, age]) of assessed earnings

TABLE 5 (*Continued*)

Disability Policies in Four Western Industrial Countries in 1997

	United States	The Netherlands	Sweden	Germany
II. *Longer-Term Disability Transfer Programs (cont.)*				
Partial benefits	None	Percentage of full pension, corresponding to loss of earning capacity (minimum of 15 percent)	75%, 50%, or 25% of full pension corresponding to loss of earning capacity	Occupational disability: 40% (plus 1% times max [55, age]) of assessed earnings
Waiting period	5 months	12 months	Flexible	Flexible
Qualifying conditions	Inability to perform any substantial gainful activity	Incapacity for gainful activity	Inability to work in commensurate employment (above age 60; in previous work)	General: incapacity for gainful activity. Occupational: 50% reduction of capacity in usual occupation
Maximum duration	Age 65	Age 65	Age 65	Age 65
Funding:				
Contributors	Employer, employee	Employer, employee	Employer, employee, government	Employer, employee, government
Risk Sharing	National	National; in 1998 funding of new awards will be experienced-rated at the level of the firm	National	National
Administration	State agencies under direct federal government supervision	Privately competing administrative offices under supervision/coordination of the National Institute of Social Insurance	National agency under direct government supervision	State agencies under federal government supervision

TABLE 5 (*Continued*)
Disability Policies in Four Western Industrial Countries in 1997

	United States	The Netherlands	Sweden	Germany
III. Work-enhancing Disability Programs				
Rehabilitation/redeployment Programs Incentives for:				
Disabled employee	Trial work benefits[f]	Trial work benefits[f]	Increased benefits[g]	Trial work benefits
Employers	Anti-Discrimination Laws	Wage subsidies, subsidies for workplace accommodation	Wage subsidies	"Disabled worker" protection, enforced quota regulation
DI administration	None	None	None	Some
Institutional links with disability insurance programs	Limited significance	Potentially strong, weak in practice	Strong	Strong
Training/workplace adjustment	Programs available, limited significance	Programs available, limited significance	Programs available, very significant	Programs available, very significant
Sheltered workshops	Available, limited significance	Available, substantial significance	Available, substantial significance	Available, limited significance
Public/private employment for disabled	Both of limited significance	Both of limited significance	Mainly public sector, significant	Mainly private sector, significant

[a] Benefits are capped at some level.
[b] Except for pregnancy leave and coverage of temporary employees, which are funded by government.
[c] First six weeks experienced-rated by firm.
[d] A means-based minimum benefit is paid to those ineligible for disability insurance or whose benefits are below the social minimum. Bend points are for 1996. They automatically increase each year based on increases in average covered earnings.
[e] Means-tested benefits payable to disabled people with a job.
[f] Continued benefit entitlement while at work on probation or participating in a rehabilitation program.
[g] Rehabilitation program participants receive 90% of lost earnings.
Source: Updated version of data published in Aarts, Burkhauser, and De Jong (1996) and U.S. Department of Health and Human Services, SSA (1996).

However, in such programs, benefits most commonly replace about two-thirds of earnings up to some maximum. This is similar to replacement rates in Sweden and Germany. All three countries use a loss of earning capacity model which allows for partial benefit payments. Experience rating is used in the U.S. and Germany and is under the supervision of state agencies in these countries. Employers are responsible for funding the system in all three countries.

Non-work-related Disability Transfer Programs

The primary source of disability transfer benefits in all four countries is their non-work-related disability transfer schemes. These programs cover social risks—i.e., non-work-related contingencies—and usually consist of an employment-related social insurance scheme and a separate arrangement for disabled persons with little or no earnings history.

Benefit levels. In the Netherlands and Sweden, a two-tier disability insurance program provides compensation for loss of earnings capacity due to long-term impairments. The first tier is available to all citizens with disabilities. These national disability insurance programs typically offer flat-rate benefits that are earnings-tested. They target those disabled at birth or in early childhood and provide benefits after age 18. In the Netherlands, these basic benefits also cover self-employed people with disabilities. In Germany, employees who become disabled before age 55 enjoy entitlements as if they had worked and contributed to the national pension system until age 55. In the U.S., the means-tested disability program—Supplemental Security Income—provides transfers to those ineligible for Social Security Disability Insurance benefits or whose insurance benefits are below the social minimum.

Eligibility for the primary tier of benefits is restricted to labor force participants in all four countries. These primary benefits are based on age or employment history and wage earnings. In Germany, Sweden, and the U.S., an earnings-related disability insurance program is part of the legal pension system. Coverage depends on contribution years. More specifically, at least three years (Sweden), three out of the last five years (Germany), or twenty out of the last forty quarters (U.S.) preceding a disability must be spent in paid employment. In Germany and Sweden wage earners are required to participate, and the self-employed may participate voluntarily or are covered by universally flat-rate social insurance benefit programs. In the U.S. both wage earners and the self-employed are required to participate. The Netherlands has no contribution requirement for earnings-related benefits in terms of years of covered employment, but in 1993 it introduced a system of age-dependent supplemental benefit levels that simulate a contribution years requirement.

Qualifying conditions. By definition, eligibility for disability pensions is based on some measure of (residual) capacity or productivity. The U.S. has the strictest disability standard: inability to perform any substantial gainful activity with regard to any job in the economy. Full benefits are based on a formula that provide higher replacement rates for low-wage earners. Germany has a dual system: full benefits for those who lose two-thirds or more of their earning capacity with regard to any job available in the economy, and partial benefits equal to two-thirds of a full benefit for those who are more than 50% disabled with regard to their usual occupation. Under the Handicapped Act of 1974, workers having a permanent reduction in their labor capacity of at least 50% are entitled to the status of "severely disabled" (*Schwerbehinderte*). Workers are entitled to extra vacation and enjoy protection against dismissal. Although being recognized as a severely disabled worker does not give access to cash benefits, it allows one to retire at age 60 with a full pension, given sufficient (15) contribution years.

Sweden has a more lenient eligibility standard. Capacity to work is measured with regard to commensurate employment instead of the more stringent standards in Germany and the U.S. and in the Netherlands since 1994. Moreover, the Swedish program has four disability categories, depending on the size of residual capacity, with corresponding full and partial pensions.

The Dutch disability program is unique in that it distinguishes seven disability categories ranging from less than 15% disabled to 80% to 100% disabled. The minimum degree of disability yielding entitlement to benefits is 15%. The degree of disablement is assessed by consideration of the worker's residual earning capacity. Since 1994, capacity is defined by the earnings flow from any job commensurate with one's residual capabilities as a percentage of pre-disability usual earnings. The degree of disablement, then, is the complement of the residual earning capacity and defines the benefit level. Prior to 1994, only jobs that were compatible with one's training and work history could be taken into consideration. Since then, in an effort to reduce the flow of new entrants onto the disability rolls, not only has the definition of suitable work been broadened, but the medical definition of disability has been tightened too. Under the new ruling, the causal relationship between impairment and disablement has to be objectively assessable.

Replacement rates. Table 6, based on Blöndal and Pearson (1995), provides gross replacement rates in 1993 for the four countries in our study. Because in each country benefits are related to past earnings and the degree of disability, no simple summary value can capture the full distribution of such benefit possibilities. Table 6 values are based on a "typical" worker who gains entitlement at age 40, who has worked since age 18, and has either an "average" age-earnings profile or a two-thirds of average profile. Benefits are shown for a male who is single or married without children. An average replacement rate is then calculated for all the cases considered. Sweden and the Netherlands are most generous, with overall replacement rates of 74% and 63%, respectively. This is followed by Germany at 46% and the U.S. at 30%. The gap in replacement rates for the U.S. is somewhat exaggerated by this comparison since the rates are importantly influenced by the presence of dependent children. In the U.S., children of disabled workers are eligible to receive benefits equal to 50% of the worker's benefit, as is a spouse under the age of 55 who is caring for at least one child under the age of 16. Hence for a married disabled worker with one child in Table 6, replacement rates would double to 48% for the average earner and 72% for the worker with two-thirds of average earnings. While such replacement rates would still place the U.S. below the Netherlands and Sweden in replacement rate generosity, they are in a range similar to those of Germany.

Administration. Lower replacement rates and stricter standards for eligibility in the U.S. and Germany (seen in Tables 5 and 6) partially explain the lower prevalence of disability transfer recipients per worker in these two countries relative to Sweden and the Netherlands. However, it is the administration of their programs prior to the recent reforms in the Dutch system that distinguishes the Netherlands from Sweden.

Prior to its recent reforms, Dutch disability policy differed from other nations in its lack of a separate work injury scheme and in its more elaborate system of partial benefits. More importantly, its social insurance programs (disability and unemployment insurance, as well as sickness benefits) were run by autonomous organizations—industrial associations—that lacked direct governmental (political) control. Representatives of employers' organizations and trade unions managed these organizations. Until March 1997, membership in a legally specified Industrial Association was obligatory for every employer. The industrial associations had discretion

TABLE 6

Gross Replacement Ratios for Long-Term Disability Benefits, 1993

| Country | Average Earner | | | | Two-Thirds Average Earner | | | | Average |
| | Two-Thirds Disability | | Full Disability | | Two-Thirds Disability | | Full Disability | | |
	Single	Couple	Single	Couple	Single	Couple	Single	Couple	
United States	0[a]	0[a]	24	24	0[a]	0[a]	36	36	30
The Netherlands	51	51	76	76	58	58	80	80	63
Sweden	53	57	79	90	57	63	88	100	74
Germany	37	37	56	56	37	37	56	56	46

[a] Partial disability benefits are available to workers injured on the job via the Workers' Compensation system but no partial benefits are available via the primary nonwork-related insurance system.

Definitions: The individual is assumed to gain entitlement at 40 years of age with a full contribution record from age 18. Earnings are assumed to increase monotonically by 5% nominal and 2% real each year, reaching the ratio of average earnings the year before entitlement. Each figure is the average of the case of a single person and a married person with a dependent (but not disabled) spouse. (If the latter gives rise to an additional allowance, this is included.) The individual has no children. No "constant care" allowances are included. The final column gives a simple average of all cases considered.

Source: Based on Blöndal and Pearson (1995).

to develop benefit award and rehabilitation policies without having to bear the fiscal consequences, as disability program expenditures were funded by a uniform contribution rate. Thus administrative autonomy was not balanced by financial responsibility.

In Germany and Sweden, disability insurance is part of the national pension program run by an independent national board that is closely supervised by those who are politically responsible for the operation of the social security system and therefore subject to parliamentary control. These boards monitor disability plans and safeguard uniformity in award policy by issuing rules and guidelines to local agencies. The difference between these countries and the Netherlands, prior to the recent reforms, was that their disability systems were under some form of government budgetary control.

In the Netherlands, disability assessments were made by teams of insurance doctors and vocational experts employed by the administrative offices of the industrial associations. These teams also had to determine the rehabilitation potential of disability claimants and to rehabilitate those with sufficient residual capacities. A further potentially important difference from other European countries, then, was that the Dutch disability assessment teams were legally obliged to examine every benefit claimant personally, not just administratively. This may have spurred a liberal, conflict-avoiding attitude, especially since neither the gatekeepers themselves nor their managers were confronted with the financial consequences of award decisions.

Sweden administratively checks disability claims by means of written, medical, and other reports to prevent the program gatekeepers from being influenced by self-reports and the physical presence of claimants. In Germany, too, award decisions are made using medical reports and applying uniform decision rules developed by specialists' panels, each covering a diagnostic group. In the U.S., individual states administer disability determinations. While there is some variation in the acceptance rates across states, a monitoring process is in place that links these state agencies to those—Congress and the federal executive branch—who are politically responsible for the program.

Like other fringe workers, persons with disabilities have a higher than average sensitivity to cyclical downswings. Even in the absence of a disability transfer program, it is likely they would have a greater risk of job loss during a recession. However, when gatekeepers are allowed to use their discretion to determine eligibility, unemployed workers may swell the disability roles. A recent illustration of this sensitivity can be found in Sweden. During the early 1990s the Swedish welfare state was no longer willing to cushion cyclical unemployment by providing public sector jobs. As a consequence, both unemployment and disability transfer program beneficiaries soared (see Tables 1 and 3).

European workers who lose their jobs are usually covered by unemployment insurance. Entitlement to earnings-related unemployment insurance benefits is of limited duration and is followed by flat-rate, means-tested social assistance. In the Netherlands, Germany, and Sweden, entitlement duration depends on age; workers older than 58 or 60 may stay on unemployment insurance until they reach pensionable age (65) or qualify for disability insurance benefits on nonmedical, labor market grounds. The use of disability benefits as a more generous, less stigmatizing alternative to unemployment benefits was quite common in these countries between 1975 and 1990. It provided employers with a flexible instrument to reduce the labor force at will and kept official unemployment rates low. This approach was used without question in Sweden until 1992 when, in reaction to rising costs, the law was changed and disability pensions based solely on unemployment could no longer be awarded. Note in Table 3 that official unemployment rates in Sweden in 1995 were 7.6%, four times higher than in previous years, in part because the use of the disability and early retirement transfer rolls to "hide" unemployment in this manner has been reduced.

The Netherlands had similar experiences. Until 1987, the law explicitly recognized the difficulties that impaired workers might have in finding commensurate employment by prescribing that the benefit adjudicators should take account of poor labor market opportunities. The administrative interpretation of this so-called labor market consideration was so generous that it led to a full disability benefit to almost anyone who passed the low threshold of a 15% reduction in earnings capacity. The share of unemployed or "socially disabled" among disability insurance beneficiaries, applying the pre-1994 eligibility standards, is estimated to be 40% (see Aarts and De Jong 1992). The fact that the abolition of this legal provision could not halt the growth in the incidence of disability transfer payment recipients, as can be seen in Table 1, induced further amendments between 1992 and 1994.

Even in Germany, labor market considerations influence disability determinations to some degree. In 1976 the German Federal Court ruled that if insured persons have limited residual capacities and the Public Employment Service is unable to find them a commensurate job within one year, they can be awarded a full disability pension retroactively.

Because partial disability benefits are based on the availability of commensurate work, certified skilled workers may refuse any job that is not at least semiskilled in nature. A semiskilled worker is required to accept only unskilled jobs that are prominent in pay and prestige. Unskilled workers who are not eligible for a full disability pension must accept any job or turn to unemployment or welfare. These regulations, in combination with a slack labor market, have reduced the proportion of partial disability pensioners from 30% in 1970 to less than 5% in the early 1990s. In the U.S., vocational criteria are also used to determine disability eligibility. Their use is sensitive to economic conditions. It is argued that the increase in disability rolls in the early 1990s was, in part, caused by the recession of 1991 (see Rupp and Stapleton forthcoming).

Work-enhancing Disability Programs

While in all four countries public spending on work-related programs is a small share of total public spending on disability programs, such programs are important aspects of any attempt to integrate people with disabilities into the workforce.

Rehabilitation Services

Assessment of rehabilitative potential is the other side of disability assessment. To reduce the flow of workers onto longer-term disability transfer programs, impairments should be reversed, or their limiting consequences corrected, as soon as possible. The ultimate goal of a vocational rehabilitation plan is return to work. This involves more than treatment, training, and the provision of corrective devices. It also involves job mediators and employers. Swift rehabilitation and redeployment depend on the willingness of all these different actors to invest money, time, and/or effort to boost the employment possibilities of impaired workers. The job of some of these participants (doctors, ergonomists, and job mediators) is to help people overcome their handicaps. For others—the impaired workers and their employers—it is to some degree a matter of choice, and hence of incentives, as to whether they engage in rehabilitative efforts.

As Table 2 shows, policies differ with respect to public spending on rehabilitative services and on employment programs for disabled workers. Rehabilitative services consist of providing corrective devices such as wheelchairs, workplace accommodations, or seeing eye dogs, and services such as training, therapy, counseling, or job mediation. Given the broad accessibility of health care in European welfare states, there are no serious financial impediments to obtaining medical rehabilitation. However, over the past years, as part of the changes in their welfare programs, Sweden and the Netherlands have introduced patient fees for an increasing number of health and rehabilitation services.

National policies also differ to the degree that they require rehabilitation efforts. Mandatory rehabilitation is a possible outcome of the disability determination process in both Germany and Sweden. Moreover, Germany has hiring quotas, which stipulate that firms should employ a certain percentage of workers who are registered as handicapped. Dutch and Swedish civil law does not require quotas but does mandate firms to provide commensurate work to employees who have become disabled on their current jobs. These mandates in principle are more far-reaching than the more modest mandates imposed on firms by the Americans with Disabilities Act in the U.S.

In addition to cash compensation, Dutch disability insurance offers in-kind provision of job accommodation and training costs to promote the employment of impaired workers. But public rhetoric with regard to these types of subsidies far exceeds reality. As we indicated in Table 2, spending in this area was minimal in 1991. In 1993, spending on general accommodations at home as well as at work under the Dutch disability insurance program amounted to 800 million guilders. Only 20 million guilders (2.5% of such general accommodation expenditures and about 0.1% of total disability expenditures) was used for vocational rehabilitation and workplace adjustment. The amount was low because few claims were filed. The rest was spent on provision for general daily activities (mobility, dwelling, etc.). On a per capita basis, Germany spends over 40 times more than the Netherlands on vocational rehabilitation.

Various aspects of the disability pension system reflect the German commitment to work. First, a relatively large amount of money is spent on vocational rehabilitation (see Table 2). Impaired workers are referred to rehabilitation by the adjudicators of either the sickness insurance or the disability pension systems or by the local employment agencies. Furthermore, to encourage employment of disabled workers, the Handicapped Act subsidizes employer expenses related to job accommodations.

The Swedish Social Security Administration and its regional and local offices do not have their own rehabilitation personnel or facilities. Instead, they enlist the services of various medical, vocational, and other professionals in this field. Each county has its own labor market board and special centers for vocational rehabilitation and guidance. The centers are operated by the National Labor Market Board through the county labor market boards. Some of them specialize in groups with specific disabilities. The labor market boards oversee more detailed examinations than are given at the employment offices to determine the work capacity of people with disabilities and to provide general help in developing the capacities necessary to work. However, in most cases, specific occupational training for the disabled is provided under the same programs that train people without disabilities. The labor market boards also oversee training for the nondisabled. The share of nondisabled receiving training has gradually increased over time and is now about 50% of all those being trained.

Recently, emphasis in Sweden has been put on early intervention for those receiving sickness benefits and on the coordination of all the parties involved in rehabilitation (i.e., medical professionals, unions, employers, company doctors, vocational professionals, and employment service administrators) as necessary. New legislation gives the social insurance offices the responsibility for initiating and coordinating rehabilitation. This has enabled social insurance administrators to act more like private insurers with a responsibility to contain costs. The government has established cost reduction goals for all the regional offices regarding sickness and disability payments. In sum, the trend of recent years has been to make more resources available for rehabilitation at lower costs. Yet rehabilitation success is importantly influenced by more general labor market conditions. High unemployment in Sweden in the 1990s has made it extremely difficult to place "rehabilitated" workers in private sector jobs.

Employment Policies

Provision of jobs for workers with disabilities can take several forms. One is job creation in the public sector, either as part of an employment policy targeted at the broader unemployed population or via a targeted approach of sheltered workshops for those with disabilities. Another is to provide wage subsidies to private business. Finally, employers may be forced to make room for disabled workers by regulations such as requirements involving accommodation for recognized workers with disabilities, job protection, and employment quotas.

Sheltered Work

The Netherlands and Sweden have sheltered work programs. The Netherlands has a national network of sheltered workshops, employing 88,000 people with disabilities (1.5% of total employment). Sweden has 35,000 handicapped workers (0.83% of total employment) in sheltered jobs. In both countries, the operating costs of these workshops are almost fully funded by government. On average, wages are higher than disability benefits, and part-time earnings may be combined with partial benefits. Work is not mandatory in either country.

Wage Subsidies and Partial Benefits

Apart from being an insurance device to compensate for lost earning capacity, partial benefits also were intended to encourage work by permitting those capable of some work but at reduced earnings levels to do so and still receive partial benefits. In fact, the introduction of the fine grid of seven disability categories under Dutch disability insurance was created to further rehabilitative aims by encouraging part-time work experiences when the program was enacted in 1967. Hence partial benefits were intended to help workers with disabilities find commensurate employment. However, through the liberal application of "labor market considerations," it became routine to award full benefits to the partially disabled under the presumption of a shortage of employment opportunities. This lenient approach was supposed to have been changed by the 1987 amendments, which banned labor considerations when assessing residual capacities. However, the old routines proved difficult to change and the amendments did not produce the expected results. At the end of 1995, 75% of current disability beneficiaries still had an award based on full disability. Hence new cuts and changes were introduced in 1993 and 1994.

Sweden and Germany have also seen a growing share of full disability beneficiaries. In 1995, 85% of Swedish and 95% of German beneficiaries (up from a 1965 low of 67%) were labeled as fully disabled. In addition to its partial benefit option, Sweden also encourages work through a separate wage subsidy program. The compensation rate paid to the employer varies depending on the disability, the duration of employment (compensation is generally higher in the first years after a person is hired, and subsidies are not available for already employed persons), the sector in which the person is employed, and the person's age (compensation is highest for disabled youth). On average, the compensation rate was 73% in July 1992 for those in their first year of support and 61% for those assisted for longer periods. These wage subsidies are used by about 1% of all workers.

Quotas

The German Handicapped Act requires that public and private employers with more than 15 employees hire one severely disabled person for every 16 job slots or pay a monthly compensation of 200 deutsche marks for each unfilled quota position. In 1990 approximately 900,000 severely disabled persons were employed, while 120,000 were unemployed. Despite the carrot of subsidies for workplace adjustments and the stick of monthly fines, in 1990 disabled persons made up only 4.5% of the targeted workforce, well below the 6% quota. In 1990, only 19% of the 122,807 public and private employers subject to the quota managed to fill it; 44% of all firms employed some severely disabled persons, fewer than were required to do so by the Handicapped Act. The remaining 37% employ no disabled persons.

Compliance with the German quota rules has declined steadily since 1983; the share of severely disabled workers in private sector employment fell from 5.4% in 1983 to 3.6% in 1994, while in the public sector it dropped from 6.5% in 1983 to 5.2% in 1994. Likewise, the unemployment rate among the severely disabled increased from 11.7% in 1983 to 15.8% in 1995. Or, in relative terms, the discrepancy between that and the total unemployment rate increased from 2.6 to 6.4 percentage points over the same 12-year period (Winkler 1996). Such evidence shows that Handicapped Act compliance is far from complete and the gap is growing. Nonetheless, the employment rate of disabled workers outside of sheltered workshops is high by international standards, even by comparison with Sweden, and as Table 4 showed, German men with disabilities are far more integrated into the labor force than are U.S. men with disabilities.

Job Protection

Dutch legal regulations oblige employers to provide commensurate work to employees who have become disabled in their current jobs. After the onset of impairment, individuals can only be dismissed if continued employment in one's usual, or alternative, work would put an unreasonable strain upon the employer. An absolute dismissal ban is in force during the first two years of disability. After these two years the employer is usually granted permission to dismiss. Similarly, German workers who are designated as severely disabled have the right to demand workplace adjustments and enjoy protection against dismissal.

New Directions in Dutch Disability Policy

The disparity between the Dutch disability program experience since 1970 and that of the other countries may be largely explained by differences in incentive structures. Some of these incentives are intended and reflect national preferences. For instance, a strong preference for rehabilitation in Germany and Sweden has induced legislators to mandate rehabilitation for workers under the age of 60 with functional limitations unless they are "severely" disabled. This policy is supported by a quota system in Germany and by wage subsidies and employment programs in Sweden. Such a policy gives a clear signal to the insured population that eligibility for disability transfer benefits is based on complete and irreparable loss of earning capacity. Likewise, the U.S.' requirement of a minimum period of five months without any substantial gainful activity resulting from severe disablement, during which time benefits from other sources are often unavailable as well, is meant to deter applications for a disability benefit. Until the reforms of 1993 and 1994, such clear signals were missing in the Netherlands.

In Germany, Sweden, and the U.S., disability insurance is part of a national pension system that includes old age and survivors' benefits, for which entitlement is related to contributions paid. This pension system is administered by civil servants or local agencies under direct government control. In the Netherlands, disability insurance until recently was part of the system of employment-based (wage-related) insurances, including sickness benefits and unemployment insurance, managed by the social partners. These sickness and disability benefits became tools of labor and management to achieve outcomes that were not always in the national interest. Trade unions used the disability program to guarantee generous and easily accessible transfer benefits to its members who no longer wanted to work or were unable to find work. Firms used these programs to silently shed redundant workers. It was not until the end of the 1980s that the political process, which had relied upon consensus among the partners, began to unravel under the strain of the growing tax burden. International comparisons of labor market and social security data, an increasing stream of private research, and several highly visible parliamentary investigations finally convinced the public and its legislators that using the disability insurance system as a pseudo-unemployment program was fiscally and socially harmful.

In 1987, after prolonged public debate, the Dutch parliament enacted legislation to reform the system. Benefit levels were cut and a legal basis for disentangling the risks of disability and unemployment was introduced. However, the 1987 social welfare reforms ultimately failed because they did not affect the incentive structure of employers and gatekeepers, and further adjustments were required. After a difficult political process, in which Social Democrats and Christian Democrats—the traditional defenders of the autonomy of the social partners—suffered great losses, some of the residual weaknesses in the system were repaired in 1993 and 1994, at the risk of abandoning the decades-old requirement of consensus among the social partners. These reforms provided both administrative and financial incentives to workers and firms to refrain from overuse of the disability transfer programs by making eligibility standards more stringent and by more directly linking program use to program costs.

The Disability Insurance Changes of 1993

Since August 1993, eligibility standards and the process for continued eligibility have been dramatically tightened. Previously, benefit awards were considered to be permanent. No process existed for reevaluation. In 1993, periodic review of those on the disability rolls was made a structural part of the system. As previously mentioned, the new eligibility standards require that the medical cause of disablement be objectively assessable. In 1993, one-third of current beneficiary awards were based on psychological complaints such as stress. Another third were based on musculoskeletal system complaints, many of which included pain that was difficult to substantiate. The prevalence of conditions that are difficult to assess led system reformers to suspect substantial moral hazard problems which more objectivity-based rulings are intended to reduce. Furthermore, since 1993 the extent of disablement is assessed with respect to all jobs in the economy, whereas formerly adjudications were made with respect to a relatively strict notion of suitable employment—as is still done in Sweden and Germany.

The disability status of all beneficiaries who in 1993 were younger than 45 was reviewed based on these new standards. These reviews, which affected almost half of 1993 beneficiaries, are scheduled to be completed by 1998. In 1994 and 1995, 91,500 beneficiaries aged 40 and younger were reviewed; 29% had their benefits terminated, and 16% were reclassified into a lower disability category with lower benefits (Ctsv 1996a:51). In 1994 alone, 52% faced a termination (37%) or reduction (15%) of their benefits as a result of the reviews. A sample taken at the end of 1995 shows that one year after the reviews, nearly one-quarter of those 52% who had suffered a loss of benefit income had increased their work effort. More specifically, among those who were not gainfully employed at the time of the review, 30% held a job one year later. Most of the others were still dependent on some form of transfer income (Ctsv 1996b:49-62). The reviews were successful in reducing the beneficiary population but less so in increasing the work effort of those who had a full award before they were reexamined using the stricter rules.

Under the new benefit calculation process enacted in August 1993 with the stricter eligibility standards, the disability benefit period is divided into two parts: a short-term wage-related benefit, with the previously existing 70% replacement ratio, followed by a benefit with a potentially lower replacement ratio. Both the duration of the wage-related benefit period and the replacement ratio thereafter depend on one's age at the onset of disablement.

Wage-related benefits range from none for those up to 32 years of age to six years for those aged 58 and over. All of these periods are preceded by the existing 12-month waiting time covered by wage-related sickness benefits. During the follow-up period, a fully disabled beneficiary receives a base amount of 70% of the minimum wage plus a supplement depending on age at onset according to the formula: [(age - 15) x 1.4 percent] ° [wage - minimum wage]. For beneficiaries with residual earning capacities, these replacement rates are adjusted in accordance with their degree of disability.

Forms of Privatization

These new benefit rules are a sharp break from a quarter century of disability entitlement to permanent wage-related benefits. Age now serves as a proxy for work history, or "insurance years," introducing a quasi-pension element into the disability system. These new benefit rules will substantially lower the government-provided replacement rates for the average Dutch worker reported in Table 5 and bring them closer to the German level. However, the reduction in government-provided disability insurance has also spurred a lively market in which private insurers are competing with corporate and industry pension funds to cover the gap between the old and new systems. These supplements are financed by premiums that differ by the firm's level of risk. Specific firms and even complete branches of industry signed collective bargaining agreements that readjust the gap between the old and new replacement rate so that by 1994, 85% of all employees were covered by such gap insurance.

Employers have shown a surprisingly strong willingness to purchase gap coverage. Apparently, their stated interest in reducing labor cost was outweighed by their desire to maintain a generous exit option for their redundant workers. The eagerness of private insurers to offer supplemental coverage is less surprising. After all, the new benefit calculation formula implies that younger and better-paid workers face a lower replacement rate. In other words, workers with a low disability risk experienced the greatest cuts in their replacement rate. Under such favorable self-selection conditions, coverage of these cuts up to the original 70% replacement, or even higher, is an attractive proposition for private insurers.

An additional form of privatization was introduced in 1994, when employers were mandated to cover the first weeks of sick pay themselves and to contract with a private provider of occupational health services to monitor sick spells, advise firms on the nature and extent of the health risks to which their manpower is exposed, and suggest ways to reduce these risks.

In March 1996, the Sickness Benefit Act was abolished and employer responsibility for coverage of sick pay was extended to a maximum of 12 months, after which disability insurance takes over. Apart from the obligation of firms to replace 70% of earnings lost to sickness laid down in tort law, sick pay insurance is now completely privatized and firms may choose freely whether they want to bear their sick pay risk themselves or have it covered by a private insurer.

Beginning in 1998, experience rating of firms will be phased into the disability insurance scheme. Current benefits are still funded by the existing uniform pay-as-you-go contribution rates, but new beneficiaries will be paid out of premiums that are levied according to the "polluter pays principle." If an employee is awarded a disability benefit, the firm will face a higher contribution rate, and vice versa if a firm employs a disability beneficiary. Moreover, firms are allowed to opt out of the public insurance system, but only with respect to the coverage of the first five years of benefit recipiency. The Dutch also began in 1997 to consider introducing elements of experience rating into their unemployment insurance system. All these changes are moving Dutch disability policy in the direction of assigning the program costs to individual firms and workers more directly and away from the socialization of risks that dominated past policies.

Changing the Administration

In the debate over disability policy the focus gradually shifted toward the program administrators. In 1992 the Dutch State Auditor issued a report on the Social Security Insurance Council's supervision of Social Insurance administration during 1988 and 1989, the years following the 1987 Social Welfare Reforms. It concluded that the Social Insurance Council's supervisory performance had not been in conformity with the intentions of the legislature, and furthermore, that the Deputy Minister of Social Affairs and Employment had failed to recognize this and to take proper corrective action.

In 1993 a multiparty parliamentary committee investigated the administration of the wage-replacing social insurance programs, with special attention to the operation of the disability insurance scheme for private sector workers. A vast number of current and former administrators, civil servants, and those politically accountable were publicly interrogated by the committee. The picture that emerged from the nightly televised summaries was devastating to the image of the Insurance Associations and the Social Insurance Council. What most suspected, and what had previously been shown by research, was now publicly confirmed. The committee's report created broad political support for drastic changes regarding, in particular, the dominant and autonomous position of the "social partners" in management social insurance.

Political pressure stirred up by public disclosure of the traditionally lax policy of the administrators challenged gatekeepers to change their way of doing business. Ministerial directives to apply the new, more stringent eligibility standards appear to have taken hold.

In March 1997, the legally protected monopoly of the social insurance (industrial) associations over the administration and coverage of sickness and disability risks was broken. The associations were abolished and replaced by a new coordinating body—the National Institute of Social Insurance. This institute has a tripartite board (social partners plus public servants) and an independent president. Its main task is to set up and manage a market in which private firms that administer the public social insurance (unemployment and disability insurance) and that once were completely controlled by the insurance associations have to bid against each other for contracts with firms or branches. As of 2000, these newly created markets for social insurance administration will be open to all competitors not just the privatized administrations of the former insurance associations.

Preliminary evidence that the new rules have been effective in changing the disability culture in the Netherlands is that benefit terminations due to recovery (i.e., being found fit for generally accepted work) increased by about 40% during 1994. Among the total population at risk, the incidence of new disability awards decreased by about 15% in 1994, but among private sector employees new disability awards dropped by 25%. At the same time, days lost to sickness dropped by 15%. While the disability benefit cuts have been offset to some degree by collective bargaining, supplements above the 70% level have mostly been abolished. Therefore, the decrease in awards may well be the combined result of increased stringency of the gatekeeper and lower application rates.

A reduced number of awards and a sharp increase of benefit terminations resulted in a 2% decrease of the private employee disability
insurance beneficiary population in 1994. This was the first year in the
history of Dutch disability policy in which the beneficiary population
actually fell from the previous year. In 1995 the drop in the number of
beneficiaries was even steeper—6%. As Table 1 shows, after twenty
years of growth in the ratio of disability transfer receipts to workers,
between 1990 and 1995 this ratio fell by 7%.

Conclusions

Our cross-national study confirms that incentives matter. Differences
in institutional settings, and the incentive structure such settings imply,
are a plausible explanation of the diverging trends in the relative disability
transfer populations described in Table 1. These populations will be
unnecessarily large unless the adverse incentives for employers and
employees to use the disability transfer system as an alternative for rehabilitation or unemployment insurance are counterbalanced by administrative regulations or routines that either reduce the discretionary powers of
individual employers and employees or provide contrary incentives. This
is the lesson of the Netherlands. It is a lesson that the U.S. and Sweden
should carefully consider as they ponder how to stem the rising tide of
younger persons onto their disability transfer rolls.

Administrative organizations need standardized assessment and
review protocols, the authority to enforce compliance with quotas or
other labor market regulations where they exist, and the ability to prescribe and mandate rehabilitation. But the administration also needs the
motivation to apply the available instruments adequately.

While a competitive market environment motivates private insurance carriers, public services require either bureaucratic control mechanisms or budget containment of some sort. In the four countries discussed here, disability insurance is publicly administrated, but there are
significant differences in administrative design. In the U.S., government
bears direct responsibility for the administration. Allocation of benefits
is safeguarded by combining bureaucratic control with budget containment. In the Netherlands, on the other hand, until 1995 government
had only indirect administrative responsibilities. Both the actual administration and its supervision and control were delegated to semipublic
organizations run by the social partners. Bureaucratic controls were
weak and budget containment mechanisms virtually nonexistent. German and Swedish administrations are somewhere in between, Germany

being closer to the Netherlands in allowing some influence from labor and management but under much stricter government control. Sweden is closer to the U.S., with benefits administered by government agencies and the social partners having a direct connection only to the provision of employment services. In both Germany and Sweden the administrative system is closely monitored by government to ensure that disability insurance is administered according to the public interest.

What seems clear from the experiences of Germany, Sweden, and the Netherlands is that regardless of the administrative structure in which disability transfer programs operate, the option to award partial benefits has had limited impact on such determinations. It is unclear to what extent factors such as labor market consideration or assessment problems make gatekeepers reluctant to award partial benefits, but in all three countries disability applicants are either declared fully disabled or rejected from the program.

Currently, the Dutch administrative structure of wage-related public disability insurance is being dismantled. The reforms discussed in the preceding section have increasingly sought to privatize the system. These proposals have provoked a more fundamental discussion of the appropriate public-private mix in covering social risks. To strike a better balance between equity and efficiency, some form of "managed competition" seems appropriate. The issue, however, of whether and under what conditions private carriers would be willing to provide coverage of the disability risk has not yet been spelled out. While it is early to tell if the Dutch disability system has finally been brought under control, it is clear that many of the processes and policies that were responsible for its growth have been changed.

Social, economic, fiscal, and demographic pressures are all forcing changes in European social welfare systems that are moving them in the direction of a more actuarially fair but potentially more adversarial U.S.-style social insurance system. The main order of business for European welfare states today is to cut social expenditures and benefit dependency and to increase financial support by promoting private employment. To the extent that this change in social policy is successful, it will also lead to convergence in social welfare spending between countries like Sweden, Germany, and the Netherlands, on the one hand, and poorer countries like Greece and Portugal, which are still developing their social welfare programs.[5] While social spending in all European Community member states (except Luxembourg) increased from 22.5% of GDP in 1980 to 26.2% in 1993, the drastic changes in policies of comprehensive welfare states, like the Netherlands, may lead to an actual reduction of this GDP share, thus spurring further convergence. Because disability policy in the Netherlands has been a primary mechanism for increased social spending, it has been the main target of reform by those who are attempting to bring social spending into compliance with the Single Currency Union guidelines.

Over the last two decades, Dutch disability policy has been used as an example of what not to do in cross-national comparisons. Ironically, it may now be seen as the trendsetter among European countries in terms of introducing the privatization of disability risks in order to achieve these Single Currency Union goals.

Acknowledgment

This study was in part funded by the National Institute on Aging, Program Project #1-PO1-AG09743-01, "The Well-Being of the Elderly in a Comparative Context."

Endnotes

[1] The ratio of transfer population recipients to workers in the Netherlands is somewhat exaggerated relative to the other countries in this table since, except in the Netherlands which does not distinguish program eligibility based on the cause of disability, beneficiaries covered by work-related injuries or diseases are excluded. For instance, the U.S. data include only those persons receiving Social Security Disability Insurance or Supplemental Security Income benefits based on their own disability. Those who receive only workers' compensation benefits are not included. In addition, the table does not distinguish between full and partial beneficiaries.

[2] Using data from the U.S. Health and Retirement Survey and the Dutch CERRA Retirement Survey, Burkhauser, Dwyer, Lindeboom, Theeuwes, and Woittiez (forthcoming) show that men aged 51 to 61 in the U.S. and the Netherlands report similar patterns of problems with activities of daily living despite dramatic differences in their labor force participation and disability transfer receipt.

[3] The summary of disability program details in the remainder of this paper is based on Aarts and De Jong (1996a) for the Netherlands, Frick and Sadowski (1996) for Germany, Wadensjö and Palmer (1996) for Sweden, and Berkowitz and Burkhauser for the U.S. (1996). Table 5 is updated and extended from Aarts and De Jong (1996b).

[4] Short-term disability benefits are mandated in five states in the U.S. However, for the great majority of workers short-term sickness benefits are provided on a firm-by-firm basis without such mandates.

[5] Among the 12 countries that were members of the European Community in 1980, the coefficient of variation in social expenditures as a percentage of GDP decreased from 0.28 in 1980 to 0.20 in 1993—almost 30% (Goudswaard and Vording 1996).

References

Aarts, Leo J.M., and Philip R. de Jong. 1992. *Economic Aspects of Disability Behavior.* Amsterdam: North-Holland Publishing.

_____. 1996a. "The Dutch Disability Program and How It Grew." In L.J.M. Aarts, R.V. Burkhauser, and Ph.R. de Jong, eds., *Curing the Dutch Disease: An International Perspective on Disability Policy Reform.* Aldershot, UK: Avebury, pp. 21-46.

_____. 1996b. "Evaluating the 1987 and 1993 Social Welfare Reforms: From Disappointment to Potential Success." In L.J.M. Aarts, R.V. Burkhauser, and Ph.R. de Jong, eds., *Curing the Dutch Disease: An International Perspective on Disability Policy Reform.* Aldershot, UK: Avebury, pp. 47-70.

Aarts, Leo J.M., Richard V. Burkhauser, and Philip R. de Jong. 1992. "The Dutch Disease: Lessons for U.S. Disability Policy," *Regulation,* Vol. 15, no. 2 (Spring), pp. 75-86.

_____, eds. 1996. *Curing the Dutch Disease: An International Perspective on Disability Policy Reform.* Aldershot, UK: Avebury.

Berkowitz, Edward D., and Richard V. Burkhauser. 1996. "A United States Perspective on Disability Programs." In L.J.M. Aarts, R.V. Burkhauser, and Ph.R. de Jong, eds., *Curing the Dutch Disease: An International Perspective on Disability Policy Reform.* Aldershot, UK: Avebury, pp. 71-92.

Blöndal, Sveinbjörn, and Mark Pearson. 1995. "Unemployment and Other Non-Employment Benefits," *Oxford Review of Economic Policy,* Vol. 11, no. 1, pp. 136-69.

Burkhauser, Richard V., and Mary C. Daly. 1996. "The Potential Impact on the Employment of People with Disabilities." In Jane West, ed., *The Americans with Disabilities Act: Early Implementation.* Cambridge, MA: Blackwell Publishers, pp. 153-92.

_____. Forthcoming. "The Importance of Labor Earnings for Working Age Males with Disabilities: A Dynamic Cross-National View." Federal Reserve Bank of San Francisco, Economic Review.

Burkhauser, Richard V., and Robert H. Haveman. 1982. *Disability and Work: The Economics of American Policy.* Baltimore: Johns Hopkins University Press.

Burkhauser, Richard V., Debra Dwyer, Maarten Lindeboom, Jules Theeuwes, and Isolde Woittiez. Forthcoming. "Health, Work, and Economic Well-Being of Older Workers, Aged 51 to 61: A Cross-National Comparison Using the United States HRS and the Netherlands CERRA Data Sets." In James Smith and Robert Willis, eds., *Wealth, Work, and Health: Innovations in Measurement in the Social Sciences,* Ann Arbor, MI: University of Michigan Press.

Ctsv (College van Toezicht Sociale Verzekeringen). 1996a. Augustus-rapportage. Zoetermeer.

_____. 1996b. In en uit de WAO. Zoetermeer.

Frick, Bernd, and Dieter Sadowski. 1996. "A German Perspective on Disability Policy." In L.J.M. Aarts, R.V. Burkhauser. and Ph.R. de Jong, eds., *Curing the Dutch Disease: An International Perspective on Disability Policy Reform.* Aldershot, UK: Avebury, pp. 117-32.

Goudswaard, K.P., and H. Vording. 1996. "Is Harmonization of Income Transfer Policies in the European Union Feasible?" Paper presented at the 52nd Congress of the International Institute of Public Finance. Tel-Aviv.

Ministry of Finance. 1994. "Social Security in Sweden—How to Reform the System." Report to the Expert Group on Public Finance. Stockholm.

National Academy of Social Insurance. 1996. "Balancing Security and Opportunity: The Challenge of Disability Income Policy." Report of the Disability Policy Panel. Washington, DC.

Organization of Economic Cooperation and Development. Various years. Labor Force Statistics. Paris: OECD.

Rupp, Kalman, and David Stapleton, eds. Forthcoming. *Growth in Income Entitlement Benefits for Disability: Explanations and Policy Implications*. Kalamazoo, MI: W.E. Upjohn Institute for Employment Research.

Tweede Kamer der Staten-Generaal. 1994. Sociale Nota 1994. The Hague.

Winkler, A. 1996. "Integration of Persons with Disabilities into the Labor Market and State Intervention." Center for Labor and Social Policy Working Paper. Germany: University of Trier.

Wadensjö, Eskil, and Edward E. Palmer. 1996. "Curing the Dutch Disease from a Swedish Perspective." In L.J.M. Aarts, R.V. Burkhauser, and Ph. R. de Jong, eds., *Curing the Dutch Disease: An International Perspective on Disability Policy Reform*. Aldershot, UK: Avebury, pp. 133-56.